您 翻 开 的 将 是 一 本 值 得 世 代 阅 读 的 好 书

人一生要读的经典英文名著大全集

ENGLISH CLASSICS COLLECTION

江 涛◎主编

石油工业出版社

图书在版编目（CIP）数据

人一生要读的经典英文名著大全集：汉英对照/江涛主编.
北京：石油工业出版社，2012.2
(江涛英语)
ISBN 978-7-5021-8905-1

Ⅰ.人…
Ⅱ.江…
Ⅲ.① 英语-汉语-对照读物 ② 世界文学-作品综合集
Ⅳ.① H319.4 ② I

中国版本图书馆CIP数据核字（2012）第003134号

人一生要读的经典英文名著大全集
主编 江 涛

出版发行：石油工业出版社
（北京安定门外安华西里3区18号 100011）
网址：www.petropub.com.cn
编辑部：(010) 64253667 发行部：(010) 64252978
经 销：全国新华书店
印 刷：北京晨旭印刷厂

2012年2月第1版 2012年2月第1次印刷
787 × 1092 毫米 开本：1/16 印张：28.25
字数：597 千字

定 价：49.80元
（如出现印装质量问题，我社发行部负责调换）

《江涛英语》系列丛书编委会

《人一生要读的经典英文名著大全集》编委会

丛书序

“读书使人充实，讨论使人机智，笔记使人准确。读史使人明智，读诗使人灵秀，数学使人周密，科学使人深刻，伦理学使人庄重，逻辑修辞之学使人善辩：凡有所学，皆成性格。”

这是散文大家培根《论读书》中的经典名句。还记得初中时在语文课本里读到这些句子，只觉得字字珠玑，反复诵读，有满口留香之感。甚至在多年以后想起，回味那时那刻，仍能从神经末梢感觉到一阵悸动。这就是经典文字的魅力所在吧。如同好的音乐，余音绕梁，三日不绝。

中学时期，豆蔻年华，正是一个人从被迫学习阶段向主动学习阶段过渡的时期。面对家长的殷殷期盼、老师的不断鞭策，学习似乎只是一种负担，被迫地接受知识，这乃是低级学习阶段；迈入大学，风华正茂，渐渐能体会到学习的乐趣和益处，愿意去主动学习自己必须掌握的知识，这乃是中级学习阶段；初涉职场，雄心万丈，若能在业余时间主动去汲取对自己有益的养分，去充实自己的精神世界，提高自身的文化修养，这乃是高级阶段。能达到高级阶段的人是智者。

智者，会采取最有效率的方式来充实自己——即选择经典的东西来学习。究竟何为经典？经典往往出自大家，是经久不衰的传世之作，是经过历史选择出来的最有价值的、最能体现时代精髓的、最具代表性的、最完美的作品。经典之作能开阔心胸，使自己拥有快乐的精神力量。

这套《人一生要读的经典英文》系列就是我们为您精心打造的，它跨越了年龄和阅历的界限，只为助君一臂之力，成为生活的智者。

《人一生要读的经典英文大全集》精选了最经典的散文、名人故事、童话寓言、诗歌，等等，全方位囊括了各种体裁的不朽之作。

《人一生要读的经典双语哈佛家训大全集》甄选了能集中教导人生哲理的英语文章。该书与哈佛大学传授人生哲理的理念相同，既是一部育才读本，又是可改变命运的智慧锦囊。

《人一生要读的经典双语哈佛情商大全集》精选了能集中教导人修身养性的英语文章，可提高情商、陶冶性情，亦可增长生活的智慧。

《人一生要读的经典英文名著大全集》筛选出了几百年来近百位名家的传世之作，让读者领略各个时代诸位大家的文学风采。

《人一生要读的经典英文演讲大全集》遴选了史上最睿智激昂、最有魅力的名人演讲，涉及内容广泛，所挑选的演讲人更是声名远扬。

我们迫不及待地要把这一套《人一生要读的经典英文系列》丛书奉献给读者，希望它们能给读者们带来快乐的精神力量、积极的心态和强大的自信心。有了这些，人生又何患不幸福呢?

经典，值得用一生去品读，去拥有。

前言
PREFACE

名著是世界文化的精髓，是思想的沉淀，是血与泪的铭记，是生命存在的见证，是历史走过的痕迹。

名著是本厚重的书，要囊括全面是一项浩大的工程。编者不敢说海纳百川但尽力把世界各大名著尽收其中，以此作为一份厚重的礼物奉献给您。

带着这份崇敬、这份欣喜，请翻开这本书。

在您细细品读之前，请允许我们为您稍微介绍一下这本书吧。

首先，我们来看看这本书跟其他的名著类书籍相比有哪些明显的特点和优势。

● **全面收录名家之作**。一本在手，熟读世界精品。本书包括5个单元（注，本书中名家之作并没有特别排序，均是随机排列）。

1．第1、2、3单元分别列出**英国、美国、法国**三国的名家名作，每单元10位名家，每位名家3部名著，共90部；

2．第4单元列出了**中东欧（俄国、德国、捷克等国）**一些国家的名家名作，共10位名家，每位名家3部作品，共30部；

3．第5单元较前四个单元有些不同，本单元列出了30位名家，不分国籍，每位名家1部名著，共30部。

全书共150部名著，涵盖了几百年来70位名家的经典之作，其中既有像《神曲》这样古老的作品，也有像《生命中不能承受之轻》这样较新的作品；既有描写生动的小说，也有情感丰富的诗歌、散文、戏剧等。部部沉淀出思想的智慧，供您品鉴。

● **有详有略，内容含量丰富，设置贴心**。除了对名著内容的简要介绍外，本书还包含了对名家的中英文简介、名著经典段落的中英文节选、名著相关赏析等内容，其包罗万象足以让读者了解名著的各个方面。以下用图例说明：

1 最伟大的戏剧天才——莎士比亚

William Shakespeare (April 26, 1564—April 23, 1616) was an English poet and playwright, widely regarded as the greatest writer in the English language and the world's pre-eminent dramatist. His surviving works, including some collaborations, consist of about 38 plays, 154 sonnets, two long narrative poems, and several other poems. His early plays were mainly comedies and histories, genres he raised to the peak of sophistication and artistry by the end of the 16th century. He then wrote mainly tragedies until about 1608, including Hamlet, King Lear, and Macbeth, considered some of the finest works in the English language.

威廉·莎士比亚（1564年4月26日—1616年4月23日）是一名英国诗人兼剧作家，他被公认为是英语语言界最伟大的作家，也是全世界最杰出的剧作家。包括一些和别人共同创作的作品，他现存的著作包括38部戏剧、154首十四行诗、2首长篇叙事诗和其他诗作。他的早期作品主要以喜剧和历史剧为主，在16世纪末期他将这些艺术体裁的艺术性和深度推向了顶峰。之后，他才开始以悲剧的创作为主直到1608年，其中包括一些被誉为最优秀的英语作品，如《哈姆雷特》、《李尔王》和《麦克白》等。

不是简单的名字罗列。每位名家都有一个属于自己的经典名称，为世人公认。这一称呼与名字的匹配更突显这位名家之所以被称之为“名”的原因。

中英文名家简介，包括作者的出生年月、作品风格、主要作品等内容。这部分让您既了解名家，又了解一些著作的外文名称与一些文学流派的英文表达方法。

名家图片，让名家在您脑海中更加形象化。

《哈姆雷特》完成于1601年，一共10幕，是莎士比亚留下的篇幅最长的一部戏剧。目前国内最著名的《哈姆雷特》的译本是卞之琳采用诗体翻译译出的《莎士比亚哈姆雷特》和梁实秋采用散文体翻译形式译著的《莎士比亚全集》。

作品的中文介绍，内容包括，作品写作/出版的年代，作品的详细内部结构、写作背景以及目前国内较好的版本等。目的在于让您在最短时间内对名著有个基本了解，并在选择中文译本的时候心中有数。请您注意：此处著作名后面批注的内容就是国内或国外名家对本部名著的评价。然而由于资料有限，并不是每一部名著都配有名家评价。

Hamlet
哈姆雷特

To be, or not to be—that is the question.
生存还是毁灭，这是一个问题。

——Hamlet《哈姆雷特》

同时这里也突出了名著之精髓所在。

名著导读

King Claudius, who now rules Denmark, has married Queen Gertrude, the late King's wife. Hamlet, the late King's son, meets the Ghost of his father, who reveals he was poisoned by King Claudius and who tells him to avenge his death. At last, Queen Gertrude drinks a poisoned cup meant for her son. Hamlet fences against Laertes but is cut by Laertes' sword. Now dying, Hamlet stabs King Claudius with this same sword, killing him.

现如今统治丹麦的克劳迪斯国王，娶了先王遗孀格特鲁德皇后。先王的儿子哈姆雷特遇见了父亲的鬼魂，鬼魂告诉哈姆雷特自己是被克劳迪斯国王毒死的，他要儿子为他报仇。最后，格特鲁德皇后喝掉了本是为她儿子准备的毒酒。哈姆雷特接受了雷欧提斯的挑战，却不幸被雷欧提斯的毒剑刺中。哈姆雷特临死前，又将毒剑插进了克劳迪斯国王的胸膛，杀死了这个凶手。

名著导读。对本部名著背景、梗概的介绍。引导读者充分地了解其作品，与作者产生共鸣，融入他的时代、他的思想，了解其传达的信息。

名段选读

To be, or not to be—that is the question:
Whether 'tis nobler in the mind to suffer
The slings and arrows of outrageous fortune
Or to take arms against a sea of troubles
And by opposing end them.
To die—to sleep—
No more; and by a sleep to say we end
The heartache and the thousand natural shocks
That flesh is heir to. 'Tis a consummation
Devoutly to be wish'd. To die—to sleep.
To sleep! perchance to dream: ay, there's the rub !
For in that sleep of death what dreams may come
When we have shuffled off this mortal coil ,
Must give us pause. There's the respect
That makes calamity of so long life.

生存还是毁灭，这是一个问题。
是默默承受暴戾命运的枪林弹雨，
还是挺身还击世间无边的苦难，
通过反抗来将所有的一切结束，
这两种行为，究竟哪种更高尚?
死了，睡了，什么都结束了。
如果这样一觉能够让我们摆脱
心里的痛楚和肉体所遭受的无数打击，
那它正是我们衷心企盼的圆满结局。
死了，睡了；
睡着了也许就会做梦：对，问题就在这儿!
在这种死亡的睡眠中我们会梦到什么?
即使我们摆脱了尘世的牵绊，
顾及于此也未免心生踌躇。
这种考虑，让我们在漫长的人生中饱受煎熬。

——选自《哈姆雷特》第3幕第1场

名段选读。中英文名著选段。众所周知，并不是所有的名著都是用英文写成的，因此对于德国、俄国、捷克等非英语国家名家的作品，我们选择了它们较好的英文译本，然后再由专人将它翻译成中文。之所以这么做，是为了让读者在感受名著的同时也能够学习到英文。在每段选段之后我们以“——选自《》第X章/节/幕……”的形式清楚地表明了选段的出处，在出处这一部分用双引号引起来的标题是该章节的名称；而在小说集中，出处部分除了小说集的名称外用书名号括起来的标题是小说集中选出该选段的小说的名称。

我们迫不及待地把本书奉献给您，希望您在品味名家原汁原味的经典英文（其中包括非英语国家的名家之作所翻译出的不俗之作）的同时，能感受到快乐的精神力量、积极的心态和强大的自信心。

目录
CONTENTS

Chapter 1 英国名家名著榜

Chapter 2 美国名家名著榜

Chapter 3 法国名家名著榜

Chapter 4 中东欧国家名家名著榜

Chapter 5 其他名家名著榜

Chapter 1

英国名家名著榜

1 最伟大的戏剧天才——莎士比亚

William Shakespeare (April 26, 1564—April 23, 1616) was an English poet and playwright, widely regarded as the greatest writer in the English language and the world's pre-eminent dramatist. His surviving works, including some collaborations, consist of about 38 plays, 154 sonnets, two long narrative poems, and several other poems. His early plays were mainly comedies and histories, genres he raised to the peak of sophistication and artistry by the end of the 16th century. He then wrote mainly tragedies until about 1608, including *Hamlet*, *King Lear*, and *Macbeth*, considered some of the finest works in the English language.

威廉·莎士比亚（1564年4月26日—1616年4月23日）是一名英国诗人兼剧作家，他被公认为是英语语言界最伟大的作家，也是全世界最杰出的剧作家。包括一些和别人共同创作的作品，他现存的著作包括38部戏剧、154首十四行诗、2首长篇叙事诗和其他诗作。他的早期作品主要以喜剧和历史剧为主，在16世纪末期他将这些艺术体裁的艺术性和深度推向了顶峰。之后，他才开始以悲剧的创作为主直到1608年，其中包括一些被誉为最优秀的英语作品，如《哈姆雷特》、《李尔王》和《麦克白》等。

★《哈姆雷特》完成于1601年，共10幕，是莎士比亚留下的篇幅最长的一部戏剧。目前国内最著名的《哈姆雷特》的译本是卞之琳采用诗体翻译出的《莎士比亚哈姆雷特》和梁实秋采用散文体翻译形式译著的《莎士比亚全集》。

Hamlet
哈姆雷特

To be, or not to be—that is the question.

生存还是毁灭，这是一个问题。

——*Hamlet*《哈姆雷特》

名著导读

King Claudius, who now rules Denmark, has married Queen Gertrude, the late King's wife. Hamlet, the late King's son, meets the Ghost of his father, who reveals he was poisoned by King Claudius and who tells him to avenge his death. At last, Queen Gertrude drinks a poisoned cup meant for her son. Hamlet fences against Laertes but is cut by Laertes sword. Now dying, Hamlet stabs King Claudius with this same sword, killing him.

现如今统治丹麦的克劳迪斯国王，娶了先王遗孀格特鲁德皇后。先王的儿子哈姆雷特遇见了父亲的鬼魂，鬼魂告诉哈姆雷特自己是被克劳迪斯国王毒死的，他要儿子为他报仇。最后，格特鲁德皇后喝掉了本是为她儿子准备的毒酒。哈姆雷特接受了雷欧提斯的挑战，却不幸被雷欧提斯的毒剑刺中。哈姆雷特临死前，用同一把毒剑插进了克劳迪斯国王的胸膛，杀死了这个凶手。

名段选读

To be, or not to be—that is the question:
Whether 'tis nobler in the mind to suffer
The slings and arrows of **outrageous**① fortune
Or to take arms against a sea of troubles
And by opposing end them.
To die—to sleep—
No more; and by a sleep to say we end
The heartache and the thousand natural shocks
That flesh is heir to. 'Tis a **consummation**②
Devoutly to be wish'd. To die—to sleep.
To sleep! **perchance**③ to dream: ay, there's the **rub**④ !
For in that sleep of death what dreams may come
When we have **shuffled off**⑤ this mortal coil⑥,
Must give us pause. There's the respect
That makes **calamity**⑦ of so long life.

生存还是毁灭，这是一个问题。
是默默承受暴戾命运的枪林弹雨，
还是挺身还击世间无边的苦难，
通过反抗来将所有的一切结束，

这两种行为，究竟哪种更高尚?
死了，睡了，什么都结束了。
如果这样一觉能够让我们摆脱
心里的痛楚和肉体所遭受的无数打击，
那它正是我们衷心企盼的圆满结局。
死了，睡了;
睡着了也许就会做梦：对，问题就在这儿!
在这种死亡的睡眠中我们会梦到什么?
即使我们摆脱了尘世的牵绊，
顾及于此也未免心生踌躇。
这种考虑，让我们在漫长的人生中饱受煎熬。

——选自《哈姆雷特》第3幕第1场

注释

★“哈姆莱特！……您懂得这个字眼的意义吗？——它伟大而又深刻：这是人生，这是人，这是您，这是我，这是我们每一个人，或多或少，在那崇高的或是可笑的、但总是可悯的悲伤的意义上……”

——俄国文学评论家　别林斯基

① outrageous [aut'reidʒəs] *adj.* 极无礼的，令人惊讶的
② consummation [ˌkɔnsə'meiʃən] *n.* 完成，圆满成功
③ perchance [pə'tʃɑːns] *adv.* 【古英语】偶然，可能
④ rub [rʌb] *n.* 困难，障碍
⑤ shuffle off【词组】摆脱，推卸
⑥ mortal coil【词组】人世间的苦难
⑦ calamity [kə'læmətɪ] *n.* 灾难，灾祸

《罗密欧与朱丽叶》写于1579年，共5幕，是莎士比亚著名正剧，其主人公已成为世界文学作品中最出名、最深受读者和观众喜爱的一对情侣。国内最著名的译本是朱生豪先生的译本。

Romeo and Juliet
罗密欧与朱丽叶

My only love sprung from my only hate! Too early seen unknown, and known too late!
唯一的真爱竟绽放于我唯一的仇恨中。未知真相就已相识，而当相识，一切已经太晚。

——*Romeo and Juliet*《罗密欧与朱丽叶》

名著导读

The Montagues and the Capulets of Verona, Italy, are in the midst of a long-standing feud when Romeo Montague drops in on a masquerade party at the Capulets'. While there he meets and woos the daughter of the house, Juliet. She likewise returns his passion, and their secret meeting later that night on her bedroom balcony begins a series of tragic events that no one could have foretold.

意大利维罗纳的蒙太古和凯普莱特两大家族存有世仇，一天，蒙太古家族的罗密欧溜进了凯普莱特家举办的化妆舞会，在那儿他邂逅了主人的女儿朱丽叶并爱上了她。朱丽叶回应了罗密欧的热情，当天深夜他们在朱丽叶卧房的阳台秘密幽会，然而谁也不曾料到，他们的爱情拉开了一连串悲剧的序幕。

名段选读

Romeo: What is her mother?

Nurse: Marry, bachelor, her mother is the lady of the house. And a good lady, and a wise and **virtuous**[①]. I nursed her daughter that you talked withal; I tell you, he that can lay hold of her shall have the chinks.

Romeo: Is she a Capulet? Odear account! My life is my foe's debt.

Benvolio: Away, be gone; the sport is at the best.

Romeo: Ay, so I fear; the more is my unrest.

Capulet: Nay, gentlemen, prepare not to be gone; We have a **trifling**[②] foolish **banquet**[③] towards.—Is it even so? Why then, I thank you all; I thank you, honest gentlemen; good-night.—More torches here!—Come on then, let's to bed. Ah, sirrah (to 2 Capulet), by my fay, it waxes late; I'll to my rest.

(**Exeunt**[④] all but Juliet and Nurse.)

Juliet: Come hither, nurse. What is yond gentleman?

Nurse: The son and heir of old Tiberio.

Juliet: What's he that now is going out of door?

Nurse: Marry, that, I think, be young Petruchio.

Juliet: What's he that follows there, that would not dance?

Nurse: I know not.

Juliet: Go ask his name: if he be married, My grave is like to be my wedding-bed.

Nurse: His name is Romeo, and a Montague; The only son of your great enemy.

Juliet: My only love sprung from my only hate! Too early seen unknown, and known too late! **Prodigious**⑤ birth of love it is to me, That I must love a **loathed**⑥ enemy.

Nurse: What's this? What's this?

Juliet: A **rhyme**⑦ I learned even now Of one I danced withal.

罗密欧： 她母亲是谁？

奶妈： 小伙子，她母亲就是这栋房子的女主人，她真是一位不错的夫人，又聪明又善良，刚才与您说话的那个女孩就是夫人的女儿，我是她的保姆。我告诉你，要是哪个男人打动了她的芳心，那可是口袋里叮当作响，发大财啰。

罗密欧： 她是凯普莱特家族的人？哦，天哪！我的生命就握在仇人的手里啦。

班伏里奥： 走吧，走吧。舞会要结束了。

罗密欧： 唉，我正担心这个呢，我的心再也不能平静下来了。

凯普莱特： 不，先生们，不要走啊，等下我们还有一场小小的酒宴呢——你们还是要走吗？为什么呢？那么我感谢所有来宾，感谢你们，正直的绅士们，晚安吧。再点些蜡烛，拿过来，我们要休息了。哎呀，（对两个凯普莱特家族的年轻人说道），年轻人，现在太晚了，我要去睡觉了。

（所有人都退场，只留下朱丽叶和奶妈。）

朱丽叶： 奶妈，过来。那边的那位先生是谁？

奶妈： 是老蒂贝里奥的儿子和继承人。

朱丽叶： 那个正走出大门的人又是谁？

奶妈： 上帝，我想是年轻的彼特鲁乔。

朱丽叶： 那个跟在后面没有跳舞的先生又是谁？

奶妈： 我不清楚。

朱丽叶： 过去问问他叫什么。如果他已经结婚了，那么我的坟墓就会成为我的婚床。

奶妈： 他叫罗密欧，是蒙塔古家族的人，你的头号仇人的独生子。

朱丽叶： 唯一的真爱竟绽放于我唯一的仇恨中。未知真相就已相识，而当相识，一切已经太晚。爱情已经在我心底生根蔓延，我注定要去爱一个众人憎恶的敌人。

奶妈： 你在说什么？你在说什么？

朱丽叶： 是我从一个舞伴那里学来的几句诗。

——选自《罗密欧与朱丽叶》第1幕第5场

注释

① virtuous ['vɜːtʃuəs] *adj.* 品行端正的；善良的

② trifling ['traɪflɪŋ] *adj.* 不重要的，微不足道的

③ banquet ['bæŋkwɪt] *n.* 宴会

④ exeunt ['eksɪʌnt] *vi.* 退场

⑤ prodigious [prə'dɪdʒəs] *adj.* 惊人的，异常的
⑥ loathe [ləʊð] *vi.* 讨厌，厌恶
⑦ rhyme [raɪm] *n.* 押韵诗，韵文

《威尼斯商人》大约创作于1596年至1597年，是莎士比亚早期的重要作品，同时也是一部具有极大讽刺性的喜剧。该作品歌颂仁爱、友谊和爱情，同时也反映了资本主义早期商业资产阶级与高利贷者之间的矛盾，表现了作者对资产阶级社会中金钱、法律和宗教等问题所持有的人文主义思想。国内最著名的译本是朱生豪先生的译本。

The Merchant of Venice
威尼斯商人

The quality of mercy is not strained,
It droppeth as the gentle rain from heaven
Upon the place beneath: it is twice blest;
It blesseth him that gives and him that takes:
仁慈不是强迫出来的，
它就好比细雨从天上落下，
温柔地滋润大地：仁慈会受到双倍的庇佑，
不仅庇佑施予者，也庇佑受惠者。

——*The Merchant of Venice*《威尼斯商人》

名著导读

A young Venetian, Bassanio, needs a loan of three thousand ducats so that he can woo Portia, a wealthy Venetian heiress. He approaches his friend Antonio, a merchant. Antonio is short of money because all his wealth is invested in his fleet, which is currently at sea. He goes to a Jewish moneylender, Shylock. Shylock agrees to make the short-term loan but the loan must be repaid in three months or Shylock will exact a pound of flesh from Antonio. Meanwhile, two of Antonio's ships have been wrecked and Antonio's creditors are pressurising him for repayment. Bassanio hurries back to Venice. Portia arrives in her disguise to defend Antonio.

年轻的威尼斯人巴萨尼奥需要借三千块去向鲍西亚求婚，鲍西亚是一个富有的威尼斯女继承人，于是他向朋友安东尼奥求助。安东尼奥是个商人，但他也正缺钱，因为他把所有积蓄都投资到了他的船队上，而船队还未返航。于是安东尼奥去找犹太高利贷者夏洛克，夏洛克同意放一笔短期贷款，但是要求必须在三个月内还清，否则就要从安东尼奥身上割下一磅肉。在此期间，安东尼奥的两艘船失事，于是债主夏洛克过来逼债。巴萨尼奥匆忙赶回来，鲍西亚也乔装打扮，来到威尼斯为安东尼奥辩护。

名段选读

Portia: Do you **confess**[①] the bond?

Antonio: I do.

Portia: Then must the Jew be merciful.

Shylock: On what **compulsion**[②] must I? tell me that.

Portia:

The quality of mercy is not strained,
It droppeth as the gentle rain from heaven
Upon the place beneath: it is twice blest;
It blesseth him that gives and him that takes:
'Tis mightiest in the mightiest: it becomes
The throned monarch better than his crown;
His **sceptre**[③] shows the force of **temporal**[④] power,
The attribute to awe and majesty,
Wherein doth sit the dread and fear of kings;
But mercy is above this sceptred sway;
It is **enthroned**[⑤] in the hearts of kings,
It is an attribute to God himself;
And earthly power doth then show likest God's
When mercy seasons justice. Therefore, Jew,
Though justice be thy **plea**[⑥], consider this,
That, in the course of justice, none of us
Should see **salvation**[⑦] : we do pray for mercy;
And that same prayer doth teach us all to render
The deeds of mercy.
I have spoke thus much
To **mitigate**[⑧] the justice of thy plea,
Which if thou follow, this strict court of Venice
Must needs give sentence 'gainst the merchant there.

鲍西亚：你承认这张契约吗？

安东尼奥：我承认。

鲍西亚：这样的话，就要指望犹太人仁慈一点了。

夏洛克：我有什么义务要仁慈？你说说看。

鲍西亚：

仁慈不是强迫出来的，
它就好比细雨从天上落下，
温柔地滋润大地：仁慈会受到双倍的庇佑，
不仅庇佑施予者，也庇佑受惠者。
仁慈有着至高无上的力量，
它胜过君王头上的王冠。
君王的权杖象征着世俗的权力，
世人的敬畏与它的无上威严，
只是源自人们对国王的恐惧和害怕；
但是仁慈凌驾于国王的统治之上，
它受到国王们的衷心推崇，
仁慈的力量来源于上帝，
如果在律法中增添仁慈，
尘世的力量便可与上帝比拟。
因此，犹太人，你想想，尽管你要求公正，
但在这场公正的审判里，
没有人看到丝毫救赎：我们祈求仁慈，
但是同样的祷告也告诉我们要以仁慈的举动回报。
我已经说了很多，
希望你可以不再坚持要求这严苛的公正，
但如果你主意没变，
那么公正的威尼斯法庭必须对这个商人进行判决。

——选自《威尼斯商人》第4幕第1场

注释

① confess [kən'fes] *vt.* 供认，承认

② compulsion [kəm'pʌlʃən] *n.* 强迫

③ sceptre ['septə] *n.* 王权，权杖

④ temporal ['tempərəl] *adj.* 现世的，暂时的

⑤ enthrone [ɪn'θrəʊn] *vt.* 使占最高地位，推崇
⑥ plea [pli:] *n.* 恳求，申诉
⑦ salvation [sæl'veiʃən] *n.* 拯救，救助
⑧ mitigate ['mɪtɪgeit] *vt.* 减轻，缓和

2 "浪漫主义"诗人的重要代表——珀西·比希·雪莱

Percy Bysshe Shelley (August 4, 1792—July 8, 1822) was one of the major English Romantic poets and is critically regarded among the finest lyric poets in the English language. He is most famous for such classic anthology verse works as Ozymandias, Ode to the West Wind, To a Skylark, and The Masque of Anarchy, which are among the most popular and critically acclaimed poems in the English language. His major works, however, are long visionary poems which included Queen Mab, Alastor, The Revolt of Islam, Adonaïs, and the unfinished work The Triumph of Life.

珀西·比希·雪莱（1792年8月4日—1822年7月8日）是英国浪漫主义诗人的重要代表之一。同时，他也被认为是英国文学史上最优秀的抒情诗人之一。雪莱因其古典诗作《奥西曼迭斯》、《西风颂》、《致云雀》、《虐政的假面游行》等而闻名于世，这些是英语文学作品中最受欢迎和赞赏的诗歌。他的主要作品还包括富于想象的长诗，如《麦布女王》、《阿拉斯特》、《伊斯兰的反叛》、《阿多尼斯》，以及未完成的作品《生命的胜利》。

雪莱的《西风颂》写于1918年一个秋日的午后。当时他正旅居意大利，处于创作的高峰期。这首诗一共有5节，每节14行。该诗有多个翻译版本，一些比较出名的译者，如郭沫若、王佐良、江枫、施颖洲等均对此诗进行过翻译。

Ode to the West Wind
西风颂

If Winter comes, can Spring be far behind?

如果冬天来了，春天还会远吗？

——*Ode to the West Wind*《西风颂》

名著导读

The poem expresses the hope that its words will inspire and influence those who read or hear it. It begins with three cantos describing the wind's effects upon earth, air, and ocean. The last two cantos are Shelley speaking directly to the wind, asking for its power, to lift him like a leaf, a cloud or a wave and make him its companion in its wanderings. He asks the wind to take his thoughts and spread them all over the world so that the youth are awoken with his ideas. The poem ends with an optimistic note which is that if winter days are here then spring is not very far.

本诗表达了诗人希望其文字能鼓舞和影响读到或听到该诗的人们的愿望。诗歌前三节描写了西风对大地、天空和海洋的影响。最后两节里，雪莱直接对西风诉说，请求西风发挥威力，将自己像树叶、浮云或者海浪一样托起，并让自己成为它的伴侣，一同遨游天际。他请求西风把自己的思想传遍整个世界来唤醒年轻人。全诗以一种乐观向上的基调结尾：冬天来了，春天还会远吗？

名段选读

Make me thy **lyre**[①], even as the forest is:
What if my leaves are falling like its own!
The **tumult**[②] of thy **mighty**[③] harmonies
Will take from both a deep, autumnal tone,
Sweet though in sadness. Be thou, Spirit fierce,
My spirit! Be thou me, **impetuous**[④] one!
Drive my dead thoughts over the universe
Like withered leaves to quicken a new birth!
And, by the **incantation**[⑤] of this verse,
Scatter, as from an unextinguished hearth
Ashes and sparks, my words among mankind!
Be through my lips to unawakened earth
The trumpet of a **prophecy**[⑥]! O Wind,
If Winter comes, can Spring be far behind?

让我像森林一样做你的七弦琴，
哪怕我的叶子像森林的叶凋落！
你强劲的和弦乐所发出的呼号，
将会染有树林和我深邃的秋意，

虽忧伤而甜蜜。但愿你给予我
狂热的精神！但愿你我合成勇猛的一体！
请把我枯死的思想向世界吹落，
就像你为了促新生将落叶扫除，
请听，通过这篇符咒似的诗歌，
我的话语传遍了人间各个角落，
像未灭炉中吹出的灰烬和火花！
但愿我能够吹响这预言的号角，
用我的唇唤醒这个沉睡的世界！噢，西风！
如果冬天来了，春天还会远吗？

——选自《西风颂》第5节

注释

① lyre ['laiə(r)] *n.* 里拉（古希腊一种七弦琴）
② tumult ['tjuːmʌlt] *n.* 喧哗，吵闹
③ mighty ['maitɪ] *adj.* 强有力的，巨大的
④ impetuous [ɪm'petjuəs] *adj.* 猛烈的，莽撞的
⑤ incantation [ˌɪnkæn'teiʃən] *n.* 咒语
⑥ prophecy ['prɔfəsɪ] *n.* 预言，先兆

《致云雀》写于1820年，诗人当时处于创作的高峰期。《致云雀》可被看作一首交响乐，共有21节，每节四短一长的设计，模拟云雀的鸣叫。该诗有多个翻译版本，一些比较出名的译家，如江枫、吕志鲁等均对此诗进行过翻译。

To a Skylark
致云雀

Hail to thee, blithe Spirit!
你好啊！快乐的精灵！

——*To a Skylark*《致云雀》

名著导读

In this poem, a skylark soars into the sky singing happily. As it flies upward, the clouds make it invisible, but its song enables the poet to follow its flight. All the earth and air is filled with its song. The unseen but still singing skylark is compared to a maiden in love, a glowworm throwing out its beams of light, a rose in bloom diffusing its scent, and the sound of rain on twinkling grass by the poet. Shelly desires that the skylark will share at least half of the secret of its happiness. His mouth will not stop speaking praise of the skylark and wishes that the world will see and hear it the way he does.

在本诗中，一只云雀欢唱着冲向了天空。随着它越飞越高，云彩遮住了它的身影，但是它的歌声让诗人能够和它一起飞翔。它的歌声响彻了整个大地和天空。这只看不见却依旧歌唱的云雀被诗人比作了恋爱中的少女、闪烁着荧光的萤火虫、一朵芳香四溢的盛开着的玫瑰和雨滴洒落在青草上的声响。雪莱希望云雀至少能够与自己分享一半它快乐的秘诀。他会一直赞美云雀并希望全世界和他一样，看见云雀，并听到它的歌唱。

名段选读

Hail to thee, **blithe**① Spirit!
Bird thou never **wert**②,
That from Heaven, or near it,
Pourest thy full heart
In **profuse**③ strains of **unpremeditated**④ art.

Higher still and higher
From the earth thou springest
Like a cloud of fire;
The blue deep thou wingest,
And singing still dost **soar**⑤, and soaring ever singest.

In the golden lightning
Of the **sunken**⑥ sun,
O'er which clouds are brightening,
Thou dost float and run;
Like an **unbodied**⑦ joy whose race is just begun.

你好啊！快乐的精灵！
不，你从不是鸟儿，
你来自天堂或是天堂的不远处，
以自然的艺术，
在源源不断的乐音中倾吐你全部的心声。

更高，向更高处，

你从地面飞跃而上，
像一团火云，
翱翔于蔚蓝深邃的天空，
一边歌唱，一边飞翔。

黄昏的落日，
散发着金色的光芒，
在那明亮的云间，
你纵情盘旋、驰骋，
仿佛无形的欢乐刚开始它的远征。

——选自《致云雀》第1–3节

注释

① blithe [blaɪð] *adj.* 愉快的
② wert [wɜːt] *v.* be动词的第二人称的过去式(古)
③ profuse [prə'fjuːs] *adj.* 很多的，丰富的
④ unpremeditated [ˌʌpriː'medɪteitɪd] *adj.* 无预谋的，偶然的
⑤ soar [sɔː(r)] *vi.* 往上飞舞
⑥ sunken ['sʌŋkən] *adj.* 沉没的
⑦ unbodied [ˌʌn'bɔdid] *adj.* 无实体的，无形的

《解放了的普罗米修斯》是雪莱的代表诗歌之一，全诗共分4幕，是他移居罗马时创作的，完成于1819年。当时，欧洲神圣同盟和英国贵族资产阶级的黑暗统治以及它们对人民的残酷镇压，激起了诗人极大的愤慨。于是他利用古希腊神话的素材，创作了这一诗剧，表达了自己反抗暴政的思想。该诗有多个翻译版本，一些比较出名的译者，如邵洵美、查良铮等均对此诗进行过翻译。

Prometheus Unbound
解放了的普罗米修斯

This is alone Life, Joy, Empire, and Victory.
这才是生命、欢乐、王权和胜利。

——*Prometheus Unbound*《解放了的普罗米修斯》

名著导读

In thiPrometheus Unbound is a four-act play concerned with the torments of the Greek mythological figure Prometheus and his suffering at the hands of Zeus. It is inspired by Aeschylus's Prometheus Bound and concerns Prometheus' release from captivity. Unlike Aeschylus' version, however, there is no reconciliation between Prometheus and Zeus. Instead, Zeus is overthrown, which allows Prometheus to be released.

《解放了的普罗米修斯》是一部四幕诗剧，讲述了希腊神话人物普罗米修斯在宙斯手下所遭受的苦难和折磨。本诗剧的创作受到了埃斯库罗斯（希腊悲剧诗人）的《被缚的普罗米修斯》的启发，并注重了普罗米修斯的解放。然而，和埃斯库罗斯的版本不同的是，该诗剧中普罗米修斯和宙斯并没有和解。宙斯被推翻才使普罗米修斯获得解放。

名段选读

This is the day, which down the **void**[①] **abysm**[②]
At the Earth-born's spell yawns for Heaven's **despotism**[③],
And Conquest is dragged captive through the deep:
Love, from its awful throne of patient power
In the wise heart, from the last **giddy**[④] hour
Of dead endurance, from the slippery, steep,
And narrow verge of crag-like agony, springs
And folds over the world its healing wings.

Gentleness, Virtue, Wisdom, and Endurance,
These are the seals of that most firm assurance
Which bars the pit over Destruction's strength;
And if, with infirm hand, Eternity,
Mother of many acts and hours, should free
The **serpent**[⑤] that would clasp her with his length;
These are the spells by which to reassume
An empire o'er the **disentangled**[⑥] doom.

To suffer woes which Hope thinks infinite;
To forgive wrongs darker than death or night;
To defy Power, which seems **omnipotent**[⑦];
To love, and bear; to hope till Hope creates
From its own **wreck**[⑧] the thing it contemplates;
Neither to change, nor **falter**[⑨], nor **repent**[⑩];
This, like thy glory, Titan, is to be

Good, great and joyous, beautiful and free;
This is alone Life, Joy, Empire, and Victory.

就是在这天，世界陷入无底的深渊，
它用人世间的符咒去反抗天上的暴君，
征服者被拖进了幽深的囚笼：
爱，从它令人敬畏且拥有无限权力的宝座上，
从它的智慧里，从它受尽煎熬的最后时间里，
从它那似悬崖般光滑、陡峭、狭窄的痛苦边缘
一跃而起，
用它那能愈合伤口的羽翼庇护了整个世界。

和善、美德、智慧和忍耐，
都是最坚固的封印，
可以阻拦一切毁灭的力量；
如果“永恒”，一切行为和时间的母亲，
放松警惕，让那条毒蛇逃出了囚笼，
被它细长的身体缠住手脚；
这些法宝能消除一切厄运，
重振帝国王权之雄风。

承受一切“希望”认为是无尽的痛苦；
原谅一切比死亡和黑夜更加黑暗的罪行；
藐视一切似乎是无所不能的“权威”；
去爱，去宽容，不放弃希望，
希望会从苦难的残骸中重塑；
不要改变，不要动摇，也不要后悔；
泰坦，这些如同你的荣耀，
善良、伟大、快乐、美丽和自由；
这才是生命、欢乐、王权和胜利。

——选自《解放了的普罗米修斯》第4幕

注释

① void [vɔɪd] *adj.* 无底的
② abysm [ə'bɪzəm] *n.* 深渊
③ despotism ['despətɪzəm] *n.* 独裁
④ giddy ['gɪdi] *adj.* 眼花的，头晕的

⑤ serpent ['sɜːpənt] *n.* 蛇；大蛇，毒蛇

⑥ disentangle [ˌdɪsɪn'tæŋgl] *vt.* 解开，松开

⑦ omnipotent [ɔm'nɪpətənt] *adj.* 全能的

⑧ wreck [rek] *n.* 残骸

⑨ falter ['fɔːltə(r)] *vi.* 支吾

⑩ repent [rɪ'pent] *vi.* 懊悔

3 欧洲浪漫主义运动的杰出代表——约翰·济慈

John Keats (October 31, 1795—February 23, 1821), an English Romantic poet, was regarded as the "poet of poets". Along with Lord Byron and Percy Bysshe Shelley, he was one of the key figures in the second generation of the Romantic Movement. During his life, his poems were not generally well received by critics; however, his reputation grew and he held significant posthumous influence on many later poets, including Alfred Tennyson and Wilfred Owen. The poetry of Keats is characterized by sensual imagery, most notably in the series of odes, including *Ode to a Nightingale*, *Ode on a Grecian Urn, and To Autumn*. Today his poems and letters are considered as among the most popular and analysed in English literature.

约翰·济慈（1795年10月31日—1821年2月23日），英国浪漫主义诗人，被誉为"诗人中的诗人"。与拜伦以及珀西·比希·雪莱一起，被认为是第二次浪漫主义运动的关键人物之一。济慈在世时，他的诗大多未受到评论家们的好评；然而，在他死后，他的声誉与日俱增，并且对后来的一些诗人产生了巨大的影响，包括阿尔弗烈德·坦尼森和威尔弗雷德·欧文。济慈的诗歌以感性意象为特点，最显著地体现在一系列的诗颂中，包括《夜莺颂》、《希腊古瓮颂》和《秋颂》。如今他的诗篇和信件被认为是英国文学史上最受欢迎和最值得研究的作品之一。

《夜莺颂》完成于1818年，共8节80多行。诗人用美丽的比喻和一泻千里的流利语言表达了对生命的渴望和对自由世界的深深向往。这首诗的译本目前在国内最常见的有徐志摩、闻一多和查良铮等三人翻译的。

Ode to a Nightingale
夜莺颂

Was is a vision, or a waking dream?

是幻想，还是一个醒着的梦？

——*Ode to a Nightingale*《夜莺颂》

名著导读

Ode to a Nightingale is a personal poem that describes Keats's journey into the state of Negative Capability. The tone of the poem rejects the optimistic pursuit of pleasure found within Keats's earlier poems, and it explores the themes of nature, transience and mortality. The nightingale described within the poem experiences a type of death but it does not actually die. Instead, the songbird is capable of living through its song, which is a fate that humans cannot expect. The poem ends with an acceptance that pleasure cannot last and that death is an inevitable part of life.

《夜莺颂》是一首描写诗人陷入消极情绪的诗歌。该诗的语调一改济慈早期诗歌中对快乐的积极向上的追求，转而探索自然、生命的无常和死亡等主题。诗中的夜莺虽然经历了某种形式的死亡，但事实上并未死去，反而在自己的歌声中得以继续生存，而这是人类不能奢求的命运。在诗的结尾，作者承认快乐不会永久，死亡是生命中不可避免的一部分。

名段选读

Thou wast not born for death, **immortal**① Bird!
No hungry generations tread thee down;
The voice I hear this passing night was heard
In ancient days by emperor and **clown**②:
Perhaps the self-same song that found a path
Through the sad heart of Ruth, when, sick for home,
She stood in tears amid the alien corn;
The same that oft-times hath
Charmed magic **casements**③, opening on the foam
Of perilous seas, in faery lands **forlorn**④.

Forlorn! the very word is like a bell
To toll me back from thee to my sole self!

Adieu[⑤]! the fancy cannot cheat so well
As she is famed to do, deceiving elf.
Adieu! adieu! Thy **plaintive**[⑥] anthem fades
Past the near meadows, over the still stream,
Up the hill-side; and now 'tis buried deep
In the next valley-glades:
Was is a vision, or a waking dream?
Fled[⑦] is that music—Do I wake or sleep?

永生的鸟儿，你不会死去！
饥饿的世代无法将你摧垮；
今夜，我偶然听到的歌声
曾是古代的君主和农夫听到过的：
也许这相同的歌声
也曾激荡着露丝悲伤的心，
使她站在陌生的谷田里流着泪思念家；
这歌声还常常
牵动着仙女的心扉，她打开窗户
在凄凉的仙境中，凝视着波涛汹涌的大海上翻滚的浮沫。

凄凉！正是这个像钟声一样的词语
把我从你那里拉回到孤独的自我！
再见啊！不能总是被幻想欺骗
正如她一贯的做法，这骗人的小精灵。
再见啊！再见！你哀伤的圣歌消失了
穿过附近的草地，淌过平静的溪流。
爬上山丘；此时它已被深深地
埋葬在附近的山谷沼泽地：
是幻想，还是一个醒着的梦？
那歌声消失了——我是醒着？还是在睡梦里？

——选自《夜莺颂》第7–8节

注释

① immortal [ɪ'mɔːtl] *adj.* 不朽的

② clown [klaʊn] *n.* 乡下人

③ casement ['keismənt] *n.* 窗户

④ forlorn [fə'lɔːn] *adj.* 孤独的，凄凉的

⑤ adieu [ə'dju:] *int.* 再见；再会
⑥ plaintive ['pleintɪv] *adj.* 悲哀的，哀伤的
⑦ flee [fli:] *vt.* 逃走

《希腊古瓮颂》完成于1819年5月，共5节50行。该诗布局精美、形象美、韵律美、语言美，表明了诗人对永恒美的向往和追求，阐明了“真”、“美”学说。这首诗目前在国内最常见的有卞之琳、朱维基、朱湘和查良铮的四个翻译版本。

Ode on a Grecian Urn
希腊古瓮颂

"Beauty is truth, truth beauty,"—that is all
ye know on earth, and all ye need to know.
“美就是真，真就是美”
那就是所有你知道的，和所有你应该知道的。

——*Ode on a Grecian Urn*《希腊古瓮颂》

名著导读

Divided into five stanzas of ten lines each, the ode contains a narrator's discourse on a series of designs on a Grecian urn. The poem focuses on two scenes: one in which a lover eternally pursues a beloved without fulfillment and another of villagers about to perform a sacrifice. The final lines of the poem declare that "'beauty is truth, truth beauty,'—that is all/Ye know on earth, and all ye need to know", and literary critics have debated whether they increase or diminish the overall beauty of the poem. Critics have focused on other aspects of the poem, including the role of the narrator, the inspirational qualities of real-world objects, and the paradoxical relationship between the poem's world and reality.

该颂歌分为5节，每节10行，包括了叙述者对一个希腊古瓮上一系列的图案做出的描述。本诗聚焦于两个场景：一个是情人长久地追求爱人而不得，另一个是村民们准备祭祀。诗的最后几行写到：“‘美就是真，真就是美’那就是所有你知道的，和所有你应该知道的。”文学批评家们就这几句是提升还是降低了这首诗的整体美感而争论不已。批评家们同样关注这首诗的其他部分，包括叙述者的角色、现实世界中物质鼓舞人心的特质以及诗中的世界和现实世界之间矛盾的关系。

名段选读

Who are these coming to the sacrifice?
To what green altar, O mysterious priest,
Lead'st thou that **heifer**[①] lowing at the skies,
And all her silken **flanks**[②] with garlands drest?
What little town by river or sea shore,
Or mountain-built with peaceful citadel,
Is emptied of this folk, this **pious**[③] morn?
And, little town, thy streets for evermore
Will silent be; and not a soul to tell
Why thou art **desolate**[④], can ever return.

O Attic shape! Fair attitude! with **brede**[⑤]
Of marble men and maidens **overwrought**[⑥],
With forest branches and the **trodden**[⑦] weed;
Thou, silent form, dost tease us out of thought
As doth eternity: Cold pastoral!
When old age shall this generation waste,
Thou shalt remain, in midst of other woe
Than ours, a friend to man, to whom thou sayst,
"Beauty is truth, truth beauty,"—that is all
Ye know on earth, and all ye need to know.

这些去祭祀的人是谁?
作为祭祀的小母牛，对天哀嚎，
啊，神秘的祭祀，你要带她去哪里?
她柔软的身躯点缀着花环
是去往哪个河边或海岸旁的小镇，
或者建在山上的宁静城堡，
来了这些人，在这个虔诚的黎明?
小镇，你的街道会永远寂静；
没有一个灵魂能够回来
告诉你为什么会变得如此荒凉。

啊，雅典的外形！美好的写照！
妆点着大理石雕的盛装男女，

还有林木枝叶和被踩踏的野草;
你,沉默的形体,如同永恒,
使我们超越了思想:冰冷的牧歌!
当这一代人晚年迟暮
在我们未曾承受过的忧伤中,
你将继续作为人类的朋友并对他们说,
"美就是真,真就是美"
那就是所有你知道的,和所有你应该知道的。

——选自《希腊古瓮颂》第4-5节

注释

① heifer ['hefə(r)] *n.* 小母牛
② flank [flæŋk] *n.* 侧面,侧腹
③ pious ['paiəs] *adj.* 虔诚的
④ desolate ['desələt] *adj.* 荒凉的
⑤ brede [bri:d] *n.* 编制,刺绣
⑥ overwrought [ˌəuvə'rɔ:t] *adj.* (文)过度考究的
⑦ tread [tred] *vt.* 践踏

《秋颂》*完成于1819年9月,共3节33行。在《秋颂》这首诗里,济慈向世人铺陈了秋天的迷人风光,热情地歌颂了秋天之美。这首诗有很多优秀的翻译版本,目前国内最著名的也最常见的是查良铮的译本。

Ode to Autumn
秋颂

Where are the songs of Spring? Ay, where are they?
Think not of them, thou hast thy music too.
春天的颂歌在哪里?是啊,它们在哪里?
不用细数它们,你自有自己的乐章。

——*Ode to Autumn*《秋颂》

名著导读

Ode to Autumn is known as the subtlest and most beautiful of all Keats odes. It seems generally agreed that *Ode to Autumn* is a rich and vivid description of nature. The first stanza describes the natural process and the remaining two stanzas are sensuous observations of the consequences of that process: first sights of the harvest in its final stages; then, post-harvest sounds, heralding the coming of winter. These three stanzas represent the seasonal sequence of events: pre-harvest ripeness, late-harvest repletion and post-harvest natural music.

《秋颂》被公认是济慈所有颂歌中最细腻最优美的一首。人们普遍认为《秋颂》用华丽的语言生动描写了大自然。诗的第一节描写了秋的自然进程，后两节是对这些进程所带来的结果——首先是秋末的丰收，然后是收获后的余响，这余响预示着冬天的到来——感性观察。这三个诗节描绘出了秋季事件发生的顺序：收获前万物成熟，收获晚期的物资丰盈，收获后大自然的乐章。

名段选读

Season of mists and **mellow**①fruitfulness,
Close bosom-friend of the maturing sun;
Conspiring with him how to load and bless
With fruit the vines that round the thatch-**eaves**② run;
To bend with apples the **mossed**③ cottage-trees,
And fill all fruit with ripeness to the core;
To swell the **gourd**④, and plump the **hazel**⑤ shells
With a sweet **kernel**⑥; to set budding more,
And still more, later flowers for the bees,
Until they think warm days will never cease,
For Summer has o'er-brimmed their clammy cell.

Who hath not seen thee oft amid thy store?
Sometimes whoever seeks abroad may find
Thee sitting careless on a granary floor,
Thy hair soft-lifted by the winnowing wind;
Or on a half-reaped **furrow**⑦ sound asleep,
Drowsed⑧ with the fume of poppies, while thy hook
Spares the next swath and all its twined flowers;
And sometimes like a **gleaner**⑨ thou dost keep
Steady thy laden head across a **brook**⑩;
Or by a cider-press, with patient look,

Thou watchest the last oozings, hours by hours.

Where are the songs of Spring? Ay, where are they?
Think not of them, thou hast thy music too,
While barred clouds bloom the soft-dying day
And touch the stubble-plains with rosy hue;
Then in a **wailful**⑪ choir the small **gnats**⑫ mourn
Among the river sallows, borne aloft
Or sinking as the light wind lives or dies;
And full-grown lambs loud bleat from hilly **bourn**⑬;
Hedge-crickets sing, and now with treble soft
The redbreast whistles from a garden-croft;
And gathering swallows **twitter**⑭ in the skies.

薄雾弥漫，成熟丰收的季节，
和炙热的太阳是亲密的知心朋友；
与他共同努力与祝愿
让果实累累的藤蔓环绕屋檐；
让沉甸甸的苹果压弯屋前长满苔藓的果树，
让所有的果实熟透；
让葫芦胀大，用甜蜜的核仁让榛子壳变丰满；
让更多的种子发芽，
让更多的花朵为蜜蜂延长花期，
直到他们觉得温暖的日子再也不会结束，
因为夏天早已溢满了他们湿冷的蜂巢。

有谁没发现你常常徘徊在谷仓？
无论是谁在田野上都可发现你的踪迹——
有时你无忧无虑地坐在打麦场上，
发丝随着扬谷器吹出的风儿飞扬；
间或在收割了一半的犁田上熟睡，
在罂粟的花香中打着瞌睡，而你的镰刀
也不再理会下一畦花田和繁茂开放的花朵；
有时你像一个拾穗人，
稳健地背负自己的收获，跨过一条小溪；
间或连续数小时坐在苹果压榨机旁，
耐心看着缓缓渗出的果浆。

春天的颂歌在哪里？是啊，它们在哪里？
不用细数它们，你自有自己的乐章，
当波纹状的乌云把即将结束的一天映照，
以胭红抹上残梗散碎的田野；
一群小小的昆虫合唱着悲伤的曲调，
穿梭在河边的柳条间，
随着微风高高地飞起或者落下；
山那边长大的小羊咩咩地呼喊着；
树篱下的蟋蟀唱着歌，非常柔和动听；
花园里的知更鸟在高声吟唱；
天空中成群结队的燕子喧闹着划过天际。

——《秋颂》

注释

★“跟随着济慈，我们走进一间温室：一种柔和湿润的温暖遇到了我们；我们的眼睛为颜色鲜明的花与多汁的果实所吸引……”

——丹麦文学批评家　勃兰克斯

① mellow ['meləʊ] *adj.* 成熟的，圆润的

② eave [iːv] *n.* 屋檐

③ moss [mɔs] *vt.* 使长满苔藓

④ gourd [gɔːd] *n.* 葫芦

⑤ hazel ['heizl] *n.* 榛子

⑥ kernel ['kɜːnəl] *n.* 仁，核

⑦ furrow ['fɜːrəʊ] *n.* 犁沟

⑧ drowse [drauz] *vi.* 打瞌睡

⑨ gleaner ['gliːnə] *n.* 拾穗人

⑩ brook [bruk] *n.* 小溪

⑪ wailful ['weilful] *adj.* 悲叹的，哀悼的

⑫ gnat [næt] *n.* 蚊

⑬ bourn [buən] *n.* 目的地，界限

⑭ twitter ['twɪtə] *vt.*（鸟）叽叽喳喳地叫

4 “意识流小说”的主要代表——詹姆斯·乔伊斯

James Augustine Aloysius Joyce (February 2, 1882—January 13, 1941) was an Irish novelist and poet, considered to be one of the most influential writers in the modernist avant-garde of the early 20th century. Joyce is best known for *Ulysses*, a landmark novel which perfected his stream of consciousness technique and combined nearly every literary device available in a modern re-telling of *The Odyssey*. Other major works are the short-story collection *Dubliners*, and the novels *A Portrait of the Artist as a Young Man* and *Finnegans Wake*, and his complete oeuvre includes three books of poetry, a play, occasional journalism, and his published letters.

詹姆斯·奥古斯丁·阿洛伊修斯·乔伊斯（1882年2月2日—1941年1月13日）是爱尔兰小说家、诗人，他被誉为是20世纪早期现代主义前卫派最有影响力的作家之一。乔伊斯的代表作是《尤利西斯》，这是一部具有划时代意义的作品。这部小说完美地体现了他高超的意识流技巧，并且还将当时所有可用的文学手法都结合在了一起，是希腊史诗《奥德赛》的现代再叙。其他的主要作品有短篇小说集《都柏林人》、小说《青年艺术家的画像》、《芬尼根守夜人》。他全部的作品还包括3本诗集、1部戏剧、一些报刊文章和多封发表的信件。

《尤利西斯》写于1914年至1921年间，出版于1922年。全书共分为3部18章，每一章节都有其独特的写作技巧，并对应一个《奥德赛》的故事主题。目前国内较著名的译本是萧乾、文洁若夫妇合译的版本和金堤翻译的版本。

Ulysses
尤利西斯

Longest way round is the shortest way home.

最绕的道路就是抵达目的地最快的捷径。

——*Ulysses*《尤利西斯》

名著导读

At its most basic level, *Ulysses* is a book about Stephen's search for a symbolic father and Bloom's search for a son. In this respect, the plot of *Ulysses* parallels Telemachus's search for Odysseus, and vice versa, in *The Odyssey*. Bloom's search for a son stems at least in part from his need to reinforce his identity and heritage through progeny. Stephen's search involves finding a symbolic father who will, in turn, allow Stephen himself to be a father. Both men, in truth, are searching for paternity as a way to reinforce their own identities.

从最基本的层面来说，《尤利西斯》这部小说讲述的是斯蒂芬寻找象征性父亲和布卢姆寻找儿子的故事。就这方面来说，《尤利西斯》的故事情节与《奥德赛》中忒勒玛科斯寻找奥德赛的故事相对照，反之亦然。布卢姆想寻找一个儿子，至少有一部分原因是他需要通过子嗣来巩固自己的地位和继承权。斯蒂芬寻找一个象征性的父亲是希望这个人反过来也可以让他成为父亲。实际上，这两个人都是通过寻求一种父子关系来巩固各自的地位。

名段选读

Tired I feel now. Will I get up? O wait. Drained all the manhood out of me, little **wretch**[①] She kissed me. My youth. Never again. Only once it comes. Or hers. Take the train there tomorrow. No. Returning not the same. Like kids your second visit to a house. The new I want. Nothing new under the sun. Care of P. O. Dolphin's barn. Are you not happy in your? Naughty darling. At Dolphin's barn charades in Luke Doyle's house. Mat Dillon and his **bevy**[②] of daughters: Tiny, Atty, Floey, Maimy, Louy, Hetty. Molly too. Eightyseven that was. Year before we. And the old major partial to his drop of spirits. Curious she an only child, I an only child. So it returns. Think you're escaping and run into yourself. Longest way round is the shortest way home. And just when he and she. Circus horse walking in a ring. Rip van Winkle we played. Rip: tear in Henny Doyle's overcoat. Van: breadvan delivering. Winkle: **cockles**[③] and **periwinkles**[④]. Then I did Rip van Winkle coming back. She leaned on the sideboard watching. Moorish eyes. Twenty years asleep in Sleepy Hollow. All changed. Forgotten. The young are old. His gun **rusty**[⑤] from the dew. What is that flying about? Swallow? Bat probably. Thinks I'm a tree, so blind. Have birds no smell? **Metempsychosis**[⑥]. They believed you could be changed into a tree from grief. Weeping willow. Ba. There he goes. Funny little beggar. Wonder where he lives. Belfry up there. Very likely. Hanging by his heels in the odour of **sanctity**[⑦]. Bell scared him out, I suppose. Mass seems to be over. Could hear them all at it. Pray for us. And pray for us. And pray for us. Good idea the repetition. Same thing with ads. Buy from us. And buy from us. Yes, there's the light in the priest's house. Their frugal meal.

我现在累了，要起来吗？哦，等一下。那个小坏蛋把我的元气都吸光了！她吻了我，我的青春，一去不复返了。我只有一次青春，她也如此。明天坐火车去那里吧。不，回去的时候就不一样了。就像孩子再次回到同一所房子里会感到厌倦，我想要的是新的。但是在阳光下没有什么是新的。照管海豚仓邮局。难道你在属于自己的地方不幸福吗？亲爱的小淘气。在海豚仓邮局的卢克•柯南道尔家里玩猜字谜游戏。有马特•狄龙和他的一大群女儿：蒂尼、阿蒂、弗洛伊、梅米、卢伊、海蒂，还有莫利。那是七八年前，是我们结婚的前一年。还有那个老陆军少校，喜欢一点一点喝着酒的那个。奇怪的是，她是家里的独生女，我也是家里唯一的孩子。所以就这样循环下去了。想着可以逃脱，却和自己撞了个满怀。最绕的道路就是抵达目的地最快的捷径。就在这时候，他和她。马戏团的马绕着圈儿走。我们在玩"瑞普•凡•温克尔"，瑞普（英文中"rip"有"裂缝"的意思）：亨尼•柯南道尔的大衣裂了一道缝。凡（英文中"van"有"面包车"的意思）：面包车运货。温克尔（英文中"winkle"有"食用螺"的意思）：鸟蛤和滨螺。接下来，我扮演瑞普•凡•温克尔回来的场景。她倚着餐具柜，看着我。摩尔人的眼睛。在睡谷沉睡了20年，一切都变了，都被遗忘了。当时年轻的现在也老了。他的枪由于沾了露水也生锈了。这是什么在飞来飞去？是燕子？可能是蝙蝠。也许它认为我是一棵树，真是瞎了。难道鸟没有嗅觉的吗？轮回转世。它们相信人因为悲伤会变成树。哭泣的柳树。它又飞走了，滑稽的小乞丐。我在想它住在哪里，很可能在钟楼那边。很可能它会在一片虔诚的气息中用脚后跟倒挂着。我猜是钟声把它们吓出来了。弥撒似乎已经结束。还可以听见会众的声音。为我们祈祷。为我们祈祷。为我们祈祷。这样重复很不错。就像广告一样。来我们这里买。来我们这里买。来我们这里买。是的，牧师的房子里有灯光，他们正在吃简单的晚餐。

——选自《尤利西斯》第2部第13章

注释

① wretch [retʃ] *n.* 恶棍，坏蛋

② bevy ['bevɪ] *n.* 一批，一团

③ cockle ['kɔkl] *n.* 鸟蛤

④ periwinkle ['perɪwɪŋkl] *n.* 滨螺

⑤ rusty ['rʌstɪ] *adj.* 生锈的，腐蚀的

⑥ metempsychosis [ˌme'tempsɪ'kəʊsɪs] *n.* 轮回

⑦ sanctity ['sæŋktəti:] *n.* 圣洁，神圣

《青年艺术家的画像》写于1904年至1914年间，完稿于意大利的里雅斯特。这部半自传体小说共分5章，是乔伊斯第一次运用意识流手法写就的长篇小说。目前国内较著名的译本是黄雨石的版本和李靖民的版本。

A Portrait of the Artist as a Young Man
青年艺术家的画像

It was very big to think about everything and everywhere. Only God could do that.

要全方位地考虑到每一件事和每一个地方是一项艰巨的任务，只有上帝才可以做到。

——*A Portrait of the Artist as a Young Man*《青年艺术家的画像》

名著导读

Joyce's novel traces the intellectual and religio-philosophical awakening of young Stephen Dedalus as he begins to question and rebel against the Catholic and Irish conventions in which he has been raised. He becomes more and more determined to free himself from all limiting pressures, and eventually decides to leave Ireland to escape them. Like his namesake, the mythical Daedalus, Stephen hopes to build himself wings on which he can fly above all obstacles and achieve a life as an artist.

乔伊斯的这部小说讲述的是年轻人史蒂芬•泰达路斯在开始质疑和反抗自小以来信仰的天主教和爱尔兰旧习之后，在智慧和宗教哲学上的觉醒历程。他越来越坚定地想摆脱所有压迫和束缚，寻求自我的解放，最后他决定离开爱尔兰，逃离束缚他的一切。史蒂芬希望像神话中那个同样叫泰达路斯的人一样，为自己做一对翅膀，这样他就可以飞越一切障碍，过一名艺术家的生活。

名段选读

That was in his writing: and Fleming one night for a **cod**① had written on the opposite page:

Stephen Dedalus is my name,

Ireland is my nation.

Clongowes is my dwellingplace

And heaven my expectation.

He read the verses backwards but then they were not poetry. Then he read the **flyleaf**② from the bottom to the top till he came to his own name. That was he: and he read down the page again. What was after the universe?

Nothing. But was there anything round the universe to show where it stopped before the nothing place began?

It could not be a wall; but there could be a thin thin line there all round everything. It was very big to think about everything and everywhere. Only God could do that. He tried to think what a big thought that must be; but he could only think of God. God was God's name just as his name was Stephen. DIEU was the French for God and that was God's name too; and when anyone prayed to God and said DIEU then God knew at once that it was a French person that was praying. But, though there were different names for God in all the different languages in the world and God understood what all the people who prayed said in their different languages, still God **remained**③ always the same God and God's real name was God.

那是他的笔迹：有一天晚上佛莱明开玩笑地在这页纸的背面写下了这些话：

史蒂芬·泰达路斯是我名姓，

爱尔兰是我祖国。

克朗戈伍斯是我居住地

天堂是我梦想。

他把这行诗倒过来读，却不像是诗了。然后他从下往上念着扉页上的字，一直到自己的名字。那就是他。接着他又顺着将这诗读了一遍。宇宙的尽头是什么呢?

什么都没有。那么在宇宙周围是否存在某些东西以在那一切虚无开始之前表明宇宙结束的位置呢?

它不可能是一堵墙，但有可能是普遍存在于事物周围的一根极细的线。要全方位地考虑到每一件事和每一个地方是一项艰巨的任务，只有上帝才可以做到。他试着想象那种高难度的思维会是什么样子的，但他只能想到上帝。上帝就是上帝的名字，就像史蒂芬是他的名字一样。“迪厄”是法语里对上帝的称呼，那也是上帝的名字。当有人向上帝祈祷，喊了一声“迪厄”时，上帝马上就会知道这是一个法国人在祈祷。尽管在世界上各种不同的语言里对上帝有不同的称呼，而且上帝能听懂所有人用他们自己的语言所作的祈祷。但上帝还是那个上帝，上帝真正的名字就是上帝。

——选自《青年艺术家的画像》第1章

注释

① cod [kɔd] *n.* 玩笑，愚弄

② flyleaf ['flaili:f] *n.* 章节后的空白

③ remain [rɪ'mein] *vt.* 依然，保持

《都柏林人》从1904年开始创作，于1914年出版。这部短篇小说集置景于20世纪二三十年代的都柏林，截取中下层人民生活的横断面，15个故事汇集起来，宛若一幅印象主义的绘画。目前国内较著名的译本是李靖民的版本、张冰梅的版本和王逢振的版本。

Dubliners
都柏林人

His soul swooned slowly as he heard the snow falling faintly through the universe and faintly falling, like the descent of their last end, upon all the living and the dead.

他听见雪花穿过宇宙微弱地飘了下来，落在所有的生者和死者身上——就好像这是它最后的归宿，而他的灵魂也慢慢沉醉其中了。

——*Dubliners*《都柏林人》

名著导读

Dubliners is a collection of 15 short stories by James Joyce. The fifteen stories were meant to be a naturalistic depiction of the Irish middle class life in and around Dublin in the early years of the 20th century. The initial stories in the collection are narrated by children as protagonists, and as the stories continue, they deal with the lives and concerns of progressively older people. This is in line with Joyce's tripartite division of the collection into childhood, adolescence and maturity.

《都柏林人》是詹姆斯•乔伊斯15个小故事的合集。这15个故事是对20世纪初生活在都柏林及其周围的爱尔兰中产阶级生活的真实写照。小说集的前几篇故事是以小孩为主角并由他们进行叙述的，随后的故事则着眼于逐渐年长的人们，描述了他们的生活与关注点。这与乔伊斯把这本小说集划分为孩童时期、青少年时期和成年时期三个部分是一致的。

名段选读

Generous tears filled Gabriel's eyes. He had never felt like that himself towards any woman, but he knew that such a feeling must be love. The tears gathered more thickly in his eyes and in the partial darkness he imagined he saw the form of a young man standing under a dripping tree. Other forms were near. His soul had approached that region where dwell the vast hosts of the dead. He was conscious of, but could not apprehend, their **wayward**① and **flickering**② existence. His own identity was fading out into a grey **impalpable**③ world: the solid world itself, which these dead had one time reared and lived in, was dissolving and dwindling.

A few light taps upon the pane made him turn to the window. It had begun to snow again.

He watched sleepily the flakes, silver and dark, falling obliquely against the lamplight. The time had come for him to set out on his journey westward. Yes, the newspapers were right: snow was general all over Ireland. It was falling on every part of the dark central plain, on the treeless hills, falling softly upon the Bog of Allen and, farther westward, softly falling into the dark mutinous Shannon waves. It was falling, too, upon every part of the lonely churchyard on the hill where Michael Furey lay buried. It lay thickly drifted on the crooked crosses and headstones, on the spears of the little gate, on the barren thorns. His soul **swooned**④ slowly as he heard the snow falling **faintly**⑤ through the universe and faintly falling, like the descent of their last end, upon all the living and the dead.

加布里埃尔的眼眶里饱含着泪水。他之前从不曾对任何女人有过如此强烈的感觉，但是他知道这种感觉就是爱。眼泪在他眼中越积越多，在不完全的黑暗中，他想象着自己看到了一个年轻男人的轮廓，这个男人正站在一棵滴着水的树下。附近其他事物的轮廓也清晰可见。他的灵魂靠近了那个住着很多死人的地方。他意识到了，但是不能理解他们飘忽不定和忽隐忽现的存在方式。他自己的身份已经慢慢模糊，融进了那个阴沉、难解的世界：这些死人曾经成长和生活过的固态世界，也正在逐渐融化和缩小。

窗玻璃上轻轻的敲击声吸引了他，他转向窗户。又开始下雪了。他睡眼朦胧地看着这些晶莹却又阴郁的雪花，缓缓地在灯火中斜斜飘落下来。时间到了，他该踏上前往西方世界的旅程了。是的，报纸上说得没错：整个爱尔兰都下起了雪。雪花飘落在中部平原的每一处，飘落在光秃秃的山丘，轻柔地降落在艾伦沼泽上，再往西一点，轻轻地落进香农河灰暗汹涌的波涛里。雪花也飘落在山上孤寂墓地的各个角落，麦可·费瑞就葬在那里。雪落在弯曲的十字架和墓石上、小栅栏和荒芜的荆棘上，厚厚地积了一层。他听见雪花穿过宇宙微弱地飘了下来，落在所有的生者和死者身上——就好像这是它最后的归宿，而他的灵魂也慢慢沉醉其中了。

——选自《都柏林人》：《往生者》

注释

① wayward ['weiwəd] *adj.* 不定的，任性的

② flickering ['flɪkərɪŋ] *adj.* 忽隐忽现的

③ impalpable [ɪm'pælpəbl] *adj.* 难解的，不能感知的

④ swoon [swu:n] *vi.* 着迷，惊讶

⑤ faintly ['feintlɪ] *adv.* 微弱地，模糊地

5 十九世纪英国批判现实主义文学代表人物——查尔斯·狄更斯

Charles John Huffam Dickens (February 7, 1812—June 9, 1870) was the most popular English novelist of the Victorian era and he remains popular, responsible for some of English literature's most iconic characters. Among his best-known works are *Oliver Twist* (1838), *David Copperfield* (1850), *Bleak House* (1852), *Little Dorrit* (1855), *A Tale of Two Cities* (1859), *Great Expectations* (1861). He was a prolific writer. His best known book, *A Christmas Carol*, is about a cruel miser who becomes kind and generous. His finest novel, arguably considered his masterpiece, is *Bleak House*, which attacks long, drawn-out lawsuits and other injustices. *Little Dorrit* is a work of satire on the shortcomings of the government and society of the period.

查尔斯·狄更斯（1812年2月7日—1870年6月9日）是维多利亚时期最著名的英国小说家，因塑造了许多英国文学上栩栩如生的人物而闻名于世。他著名的作品有《雾都孤儿》（1838）、《大卫·科波菲尔》（1850）、《荒凉山庄》（1852）、《小杜丽》（1855）、《双城记》（1859）、《远大前程》（1861）。他一生著作颇丰。最有名的作品《圣诞颂歌》是关于一个野蛮的吝啬鬼变得慷慨善良的故事。他最出色的小说《荒凉山庄》毋庸置疑也是他最杰出的作品，抨击了一些冗长的、旷日持久的诉讼案和其他的不公正现象。《小杜丽》则讽刺那个时期政府的腐败和社会的弊端。

《雾都孤儿》，共53章，是1838年出版的写实小说。小说以雾都伦敦为背景，讲述了一个孤儿悲惨的身世及遭遇。最佳译本由荣如德于1984年翻译，上海译文出版社出版。世界知名导演大卫·里恩，罗曼·波兰斯基也都曾将此书拍成电影。

Oliver Twist
雾都孤儿

Now, if, during this brief period, Oliver had been surrounded by careful grandmothers, anxious aunts, experienced nurses, and doctors of profound wisdom, he would most inevitably and indubitably have been killed in no time.

现在看来，如果在那段短暂的时间里，奥利弗是被细心的祖母、焦虑热心的姑妈、经验丰富的护士和知识渊博的医生所包围着，照顾着，那么毋庸置疑，他必然会立即死掉。

——*Oliver Twist*《雾都孤儿》

名著导读

The story is about an orphan Oliver Twist, who is born into a life of poverty and misfortune in a workhouse in an unnamed town and escapes from a workhouse and travels to London where he meets the Artful Dodger, leader of a gang of juvenile pickpockets. Oliver is led to the lair of their elderly criminal trainer Fagin, naively unaware of their unlawful activities. Finally, convinced of Oliver's innocence, Rose Maylie takes the boy in and nurses him back to health.

故事讲述的是一个叫奥利弗•特维斯特的孤儿，他出生在某个不知名小镇的济贫院里，命运不济，生活贫困。后来，他逃离了济贫院来到伦敦，在那儿他遇到了“机灵鬼”——青少年窃贼团伙的首领。天真的奥利弗对他们的违法行为一无所知，他被带到了年长的扒手训练者费金的贼窟。最后，露西•梅丽相信奥利弗的清白并收养了他，在她的悉心照顾下，奥利弗恢复了健康。

名段选读

Although I am not disposed to maintain that the being born in a workhouse, is in itself the most fortunate and **enviable**① circumstance that can possibly befall a human being, I do mean to say that in this particular instance, it was the best thing for Oliver Twist that could by possibility have occurred. The fact is, that there was considerable difficulty in inducing Oliver to take upon himself the office of **respiration**②,—a troublesome practice, but one which custom has **rendered**③ necessary to our easy existence; and for some time he lay gasping on a little flock mattress, rather unequally **poised**④ between this world and the next: the balance being decidedly in favor of the latter. Now, if, during this brief period, Oliver had been surrounded by careful grandmothers, anxious aunts, experienced nurses, and doctors of profound wisdom, he would most inevitably and indubitably have been killed in no time. There being nobody by, however, but a pauper old woman, who was rendered rather **misty**⑤ by an unwonted allowance of beer; and a parish surgeon who did such matters by contract; Oliver and Nature fought out the point between them. The result was, that, after a few struggles, Oliver breathed, **sneezed**⑥, and proceeded to advertise to the inmates of the workhouse the fact of a new burden having been imposed upon the parish, by setting up as loud a cry as could reasonably have been expected from a male infant who had not been possessed of that very useful appendage, a voice, for a much longer space of time than three minutes and a quarter.

尽管我并不想说出生在济贫院本身是发生在一个人身上最幸运、最令人羡慕的事情，但是对奥利弗·特维斯特这个特例而言，这的确是件再好不过的事了。事实上，让小奥利弗自己呼吸都是件相当困难的事情——呼吸是一件很麻烦的事情，却恰恰是我们生存所必需的。有那么一会，他躺在小小的羊毛垫上喘着气，在这个世界和另一个世界之间徘徊，艰难地保持平衡：而毫无疑问，这个平衡更倾向于后者。现在看来，如果在那段短暂的时间里，奥利弗是被细心的祖母、焦虑热心的姑妈、经验丰富的护士和知识渊博的医生所包围着，照顾着，那么毋庸置疑，他必然会立即死掉。然而，他周围没有任何人，只有一个靠救济维持生计的老太婆，她因为破例被允许喝点啤酒而喝得迷迷糊糊的，还有个教区的外科医生，他只是因为合同不得不留在这里。奥利弗和自然的较量有了一个结果。在几次挣扎后，结果是奥利弗开始呼吸了，打喷嚏，并且大声哭了起来，作为一个在比三分十五秒还要长的时间之前还没有拥有声音这一相当有用的附属物的男性婴儿来说，这哭声如此响亮是合情合理的。他响亮的哭声向所有住在济贫院的人宣布：这个教区又增加了新的负担。

——选自《雾都孤儿》第1章

注释

① enviable ['enviəbl] *adj.* 令人羡慕的，可羡慕的

② respiration [ˌrespə'reiʃən] *n.* 呼吸

③ render ['rendə(r)] *vt.* 致使，提出

④ poised ['pɔizd] *adj.* 蓄势待发的，平衡

⑤ misty ['mɪstɪ] *adj.* 含糊的

⑥ sneeze [sni:z] *vi.* 打喷嚏

《双城记》*，有3部，共45章，完成于1859年。它是一部描述法国大革命时代的长篇历史小说，“双城”指的是巴黎与伦敦。早期的罗稷南译本是比较经典的版本。

A Tale of Two Cities
双城记

It was the best of times, it was the worst of times, it was the age of wisdom, it was the age of foolishness, it was the epoch of belief, it was the epoch of incredulity, it was the season of Light, it was the season of Darkness, it was the spring of hope, it was the winter of despair, we had everything before us, we had nothing before us, we were all going direct to Heaven, we were all going direct the other way...

那是最好的时代，那是最糟的时代；那是智慧的年代，那是愚蠢的年代；那是充满信仰的时期，那是充满怀疑的时期；那是光明的季节，那是黑暗的季节；那是希望的春天，那是绝望的冬天；我们拥有了一

切，但也一无所有；我们都直接奔向天堂，但也直接投身地狱……

——*A Tale of Two Cities*《双城记》

名著导读

The novel depicts the plight of the French peasantry demoralized by the French aristocracy in the years leading up to the revolution, the corresponding brutality demonstrated by the revolutionaries toward the former aristocrats in the early years of the revolution. It follows the lives of several protagonists through these events. The most notable are Charles Darnay and Sydney Carton. Darnay is a French once-aristocrat who falls victim to the indiscriminate wrath of the revolution despite his virtuous nature, and Carton is a dissipated British barrister who endeavours to redeem his ill-spent life out of his unrequited love for Darnay's wife, Lucie Manette.

这篇小说描述的是法国大革命前夕，法国贵族使农民陷入水深火热之中，以及革命者在革命早期对以前的贵族报复性的残忍行为的揭露。通过这些事件，小说描述了几个主要人物的生活。最主要的是查理·代尔纳和西德尼·卡尔顿。代尔纳曾经是一名法国贵族，尽管他本性善良，但因革命的怒火不分善恶，最终还是沦为革命的牺牲品。卡尔顿是一名闲散浪荡的英国律师。他对代尔纳妻子露西的爱虽是一厢情愿，但出于这种爱，他努力想挽回虚度的生命。

名段选读

It was the best of times, it was the worst of times, it was the age of wisdom, it was the age of foolishness, it was the epoch of belief, it was the epoch of incredulity, it was the season of Light, it was the season of Darkness, it was the spring of hope, it was the winter of despair, we had everything before us, we had nothing before us, we were all going direct to Heaven, we were all going direct the other way—in short, the period was so far like the present period, that some of its noisiest authorities insisted on its being received, for good or for evil, in the **superlative**[①] degree of comparison only.

There were a king with a large jaw and a queen with a plain face, on the throne of England; there were a king with a large jaw and a queen with a fair face, on the throne of France. In both countries it was clearer than crystal to the lords of the State preserves of loaves and fishes, that things in general were settled for ever.

It was the year of Our Lord one thousand seven hundred and seventy-five. Spiritual revelations were conceded to England at that favoured period, as at this. Mrs. Southcott had recently attained her five-and-twentieth blessed birthday, of whom a **prophetic**[②] private in the Life Guards had **heralded**[③] the sublime appearance by announcing that arrangements were made for the swallowing up of London and Westminster. Even the Cock-lane ghost had been laid only a round dozen of years, after rapping out its messages, as the spirits of this very year last past (supernaturally **deficient**④ in originality) rapped out theirs. Mere messages in the earthly order of events had lately come to the English Crown and People, from a congress of British subjects in America: which, strange to relate, have proved more important to the human race than any communications yet received through any of the chickens of the Cock-lane brood.

那是最好的时代，那是最糟的时代；那是智慧的年代，那是愚蠢的年代；那是充满信仰的时期，那是充满怀疑的时期；那是光明的季节，那是黑暗的季节；那是希望的春天，那是绝望的冬天；我们拥有了一切，但也一无所有；我们都直接奔向天堂，但也直接投身地狱——总之，那个时期和现在是如此相像，无论它是好的或是坏，一些最喧闹的权威专家们坚持只用最高级的词来评价它。

英国的王位上坐着一个大下巴的国王和一个相貌平庸的王后；而法国的王位上则是一个大下巴的国王和一个美貌的王后。在这两个国家，对于那些拥有国家财富的贵族们来说，这个大局是永远不会变的，这一点比水晶还要清晰明了。

那是在公元1775年。在那个受人喜爱的时期，神灵感应在英国得到普遍认可，就像现在这样。索思科特夫人刚刚度过了她第二十五个充满祝福的生日。皇家近卫骑兵团一个有预知能力的士兵预言了这位夫人光辉的形象，宣布她已经做好安排，准备占领伦敦和威斯敏斯特。雄鸡巷的幽灵在做出预言之后沉寂了十二年之久，而去年的幽灵们（超自然地缺乏原创性）甚至也做出了类似的预言。英国的王室和百姓最近才从在美洲的英国属民议会那里听到世间上的一点消息。令人惊奇的是，事实证明这些消息对人类来说比那些雄鸡巷的后代通过通灵得来的预言更为重要。

——选自《双城记》第1部第1章

注释

★“狄更斯读了卡赖尔的《法国大革命》，大受感动，决心再试写一部历史的罗曼斯。卡赖尔送来两车书供他参考，可是狄更斯大部分未加使用，因为他不想写革命史，已有卡赖尔的架构在前，无再写之必要，他只要捕捉那一时代的气氛，用一个故事来说明流血只能造成更多的流血，仇仇相报无有已时，只有仁爱的心才能挽救浩劫。”

——中国著名散文家、学者、文学批评家　梁实秋

① superlative [su'pɜːlətɪv] *adj.* 最上的，无比的

② prophetic [prə'fetɪk] *adj.* 预言的，先知的

③ herald ['herəld] *vt.* 预言，宣布

④ deficient [dɪ'fɪʃənt] *adj.* 不足的，缺乏的

《大卫·科波菲尔》*，共64章，发表于1850年，带有自传性质，狄更斯借“大卫自身的历史和经验”，回顾和总结自己的生活道路，表现出他的人生态度、道德理想。目前，张谷若和董秋斯的译本是最好的版本。

David Copperfield
大卫·科波菲尔

“I went away, dear Agnes, loving you. I stayed away, loving you. I returned home, loving you!”

“我离开了，亲爱的爱格妮思，因为爱着你。我留在外面，因为我爱你。我回家，因为我爱你！”

——*David Copperfield*《大卫·科波菲尔》

名著导读

The story deals with the life of David Copperfield from childhood to maturity. The story follows David as he grows to adulthood, and is enlivened by the many well-known characters who enter, leave and re-enter his life. These include Peggotty, his faithful former housekeeper for his mother, her family, and their orphaned niece Little Emily who lives with them and charms the young David as well as David's romantic but self-serving school friend, Steerforth and Agnes Wickfield.

这篇小说讲述了大卫·科波菲尔从儿时到成年的生活。随着大卫的逐渐长大，许多著名的人物走进他的生活，然后离开而又再次进入他的生命。这些人中有辟果提——他母亲以前忠诚的管家、她的家人，还有和他们住在一起的侄女小爱弥丽，她是个孤儿，她吸引了年轻的大卫和他的校友——充满浪漫情怀却自私自利的斯提福兹和阿格尼斯·威克菲尔。

名段选读

“Agnes! Ever my guide, and best support! If you had been more mindful of yourself, and less of me, when we grew up here together, I think my **heedless**[①] fancy never would have wandered from you. But you were so much better than I, so necessary to me in every boyish hope and disappointment, that to have you to confide in, and rely upon in everything, became a second nature, **supplanting**[②] for the time the first and greater one of loving you as I do!” Still weeping, but not sadly—joyfully! And **clasped**[③] in my arms as she had never been, as I had thought she never was to be!

“When I loved Dora—fondly, Agnes, as you know—”

“Yes!” she cried, **earnestly**[④]. “I am glad to know it!” “When I loved her—even then, my love would have been incomplete, without your sympathy. I had it, and it was perfected. And when I lost her, Agnes, what should I have been without you, still!"

Closer in my arms, nearer to my heart, her trembling hand upon my shoulder, her sweet eyes shining through her tears, on mine!

"I went away, dear Agnes, loving you. I stayed away, loving you. I returned home, loving you!"

And now, I tried to tell her of the struggle I had had, and the conclusion I had come to. I tried to lay my mind before her, truly, and entirely. I tried to show her how I had hoped I had come into the better knowledge of myself and of her; how I had resigned myself to what that better knowledge brought; and how I had come there, even that day, in my **fidelity**[⑤] to this. If she did so love me (I said) that she could take me for her husband, she could do so, on no deserving of mine, except upon the truth of my love for her, and the trouble in which it had ripened to be what it was; and hence it was that I revealed it. And O, Agnes, even out of thy true eyes, in that same time, the spirit of my child-wife looked upon me, saying it was well; and winning me, through thee, to tenderest recollections of the Blossom that had withered in its bloom!

"爱格妮思！我永远的向导，最好的支持者！当我们一起在这里长大的时候，如果你更多地关心自己，而更少地关心我的话，我想我对你默默的爱恋是不会变的。但是你比我优秀得多，在我儿时每一次充满希望和失望的时候，都会依赖你，向你吐露心事，这已经代替了我本来的天性，那是对我来说更重要的，一直这样爱着你的天性！"她依然在哭泣，但不是伤心地——而是欣喜地哭泣着！她就在我的怀里，她以前从未这样过，我也从没想过她会这样！

"当我过去爱着多拉的时候——深爱着她，爱格妮思，正如你所知——"

"是的！"她真心地喊道。"我听说之后很开心！""当我爱着她的时候——甚至在那个时候，如果没有你的赞同，我的爱情就不会完整。拥有了你的支持，我的爱情就完美了。当我失去她的时候，爱格妮思，要是没有你，我不知道自己会是什么样子！"

她朝我依偎得更近了，更靠近我的心，她颤抖的手放在我的肩上，她那迷人的双眼透过泪光凝视着我！

"亲爱的爱格妮思，我离开，因为我爱你。我留在外面，因为我爱你。我回来了，因为我爱你！"现在，我努力告诉她我曾经有过的挣扎，以及我最后得出的结论。我努力将自己的心真诚地、完全地袒露在她面前。我尽力让她知道我曾经多么希望更加了解她，更加了解我自己；我是如何让自己接受那种了解带来的结果；甚至包括在那天，我是怎样怀着一颗忠实的心去了那里。如果她过去真的那么爱我（我说过），她可以让我成为她的丈夫，她可以这么做并不是想从我这里得到什么，而是因为我对她真挚的爱情，以及在爱情成熟的过程中所遇到的困难，因此，我向她吐露了我的爱情。噢，爱格妮思，在那个时候，透过你那真诚的目光，我青梅竹马的妻子在看着我，对我表示赞同。因为你，我又忆起那在繁盛时凋落的爱情之花！

——选自《大卫·科波菲尔》第62章

注释

★“《大卫·科波菲尔》使他重温他的过去，这就是为什么他在临终前不久这样说道：在我所有的著作中，我最喜欢这一部……正如许多溺爱的父母一样，我在内心的最深处有一个宠爱的孩子，他的名字就是《大卫·科波菲尔》。”

——英国作家　赫·皮尔逊《狄更斯传》

① heedless ['hi:dləs] *adj.* 不注意的，不谨慎的

② supplant [sə'plɑ:nt] *vt.* 替换

③ clasp [klɑ:sp] *vt.* 紧抱；扣紧

④ earnestly ['ɜ:nɪstlɪ] *adv.* 认真地，诚挚地

⑤ fidelity [fɪ'delətɪ] *n.* 忠诚，尽责

6 "自然主义"的重要代表人——托马斯·哈代

Thomas Hardy (June 2, 1840—January 11, 1928) was an English novelist, poet. While his works typically belong to the naturalist movement, several poems display elements of the previous romantic and enlightenment periods of literature, and his fascination with the supernatural. During his lifetime he was much better known for his novels, such as *Tess of the d' Urbervilles* and *Far from the Madding Crowd*, which earned him a reputation as a great novelist. Hardy's poetry has come to be as well-regarded as his novels and has had a significant influence over modern English poetry.

托马斯·哈代（1840年6月2日—1928年1月11日）是英国小说家、诗人。尽管他的作品属于典型的自然主义，但也有几首诗作表现出先前文学史上浪漫主义时期和启蒙运动时期的元素特征，也表现出他对超自然的痴迷之情。他一生主要以小说闻名，比如《德伯家的苔丝》和《远离尘嚣》为他成为一位伟大的小说家赢得了巨大声誉。哈代的诗歌和他的小说一样受到人们欢迎，对英国现代诗歌有着深远的影响。

《远离尘嚣》发表于1874年，共57章，是哈代第一部成功的长篇小说，也是他此后一系列以威塞克斯乡村为背景的优秀长篇小说的第一部。这一系列作品反映了资本主义发展在英国农村城镇的社会、经济、道德、人伦、风俗等方面所引起的深刻而剧烈的变化。译林出版的张冲译本是较好的翻译版本。

Far from the Madding Crowd
远离尘嚣

It appears that ordinary men take wives because possession is not possible without marriage, and that ordinary women accept husbands because marriage is not possible without possession.

似乎一般男人娶妻是因为没有婚姻就无法占有，而一般女人嫁人是因为无法占有就没有婚姻。

——*Far from the Madding Crowd*《远离尘嚣》

名著导读

It's about the love and hatred between one woman and three men with different personalities. The whole story is set in the country. However, the peacefulness of country life can not wear down the desire to love and be loved in human's initial nature. The title thus is ironic: the four main characters—Bathsheba, Troy, Boldwood Oak, and Fanny Robin—are all passionate beings who find the "value of life" neither quiet nor cool.

这是关于一个女人与三个性格迥异的男人之间的爱恨情仇。整个故事的背景是在乡村。然而，宁静的乡村生活并不能磨灭人类天性中对爱与被爱的渴望。书名也因此而颇具讽刺意味；文中的四个主人公——芭丝谢芭、特洛伊、伯德伍德·奥克、范妮·罗宾——都是充满热情的人，他们发现人生的价值既不是平静也不是冷漠。

名段选读

Yet Farmer Boldwood, whether by nature kind or the reverse to kind, did not exercise kindness, here. The rarest offerings of the purest loves are but a self-indulgence[①], and no generosity at all. Bathsheba, not being the least in love with him, was eventually able to look calmly at his offer. It was one which many women of her own station in the neighborhood, and not a few of higher rank, would have been wild to accept and proud to publish. In every point of view, ranging from politic to passionate, it was desirable that she, a lonely girl, should marry, and marry this earnest, well-to-do, and respected man. He was close to her doors: his standing was sufficient: his qualities were even supererogatory[②]. Had she felt, which she did not, any wish whatever for the married state in the abstract, she could not reasonably have rejected him, being a woman who frequently appealed to her understanding for deliverance[③] from her whims. Boldwood as a means to marriage was unexceptionable: she esteemed and liked him, yet she did not want him. It appears that ordinary men take wives because possession is not possible without marriage, and that ordinary women accept husbands because marriage is not possible without possession; with totally differing aims the method is the same on both sides. But the understood incentive on the woman's part was wanting here. Besides, Bathsheba's position as absolute mistress of a farm and house was a novel one, and the novelty[④] had not yet begun to wear off.

然而不管农场主伯德伍德的本性是仁慈还是冷漠，反正在这里他并没有表现出仁慈。即使是最纯洁的爱侣所提出的最罕有的求婚，也不过是一种自我放纵，毫无慷慨性可言。

芭丝谢芭根本不爱他，因此最终能冷静地看待他的求婚。但附近许多和她社会地位相当，甚至有的地位更高，却一定会欣喜若狂地接受这样的求婚，然后骄傲地四处炫耀。从任何角度来说，是慎重也好，热情也罢，她这样一个单身女孩本就是要嫁人的，而嫁给这个诚挚、富足、受人尊敬的男人对她而言应该很有吸引力才对。他住在她家附近，有一定的社会名望，并且拥有过硬的品质和才能。要是当时她能幻想一下婚后的大致状态，她就不会这么理智地拒绝他了，但她是一个总是依靠自身一时兴致而行事的女人。作为结婚对象而言，伯德伍德是无可挑剔的，她尊敬他，也喜欢他，但并不想嫁给他。似乎一般男人娶妻是因为没有婚姻就无法占有，而一般女人嫁人是因为无法占有就没有婚姻。尽管双方的目的完全不同，但方法却是一样的。但是，女人的内在动机却是令人费解的。而且，作为一个农场和房子的绝对女主人，这对芭丝谢芭来说是新奇的，而且这种新奇感还没有开始消退。

——选自《远离尘嚣》第20章

注释

① self-indulgence [ˈselfɪnˈdʌldʒəns] *n.* 放纵，任性

② supererogatory [ˌsuːpəreˈrɑɡətərɪ] *adj.* 额外的，多余的

③ deliverance [dɪˈlɪvərəns] *n.* 释放，解救

④ novelty [ˈnɔvltɪ] *n.* 新奇

《德伯家的苔丝》*于1891年正式出版，分7个阶段，共59章。它也属于威塞克斯乡村背景系列的优秀长篇小说之一，作者对维多利亚时代的社会现实、宗教、婚姻观念进行了深刻而猛烈的批判。张谷若1957年的译本是比较好的版本。

Tess of the d'Urbervilles
德伯家的苔丝

For since her eyes last fell upon it she had learnt that the serpent hisses where the sweet birds sing.

因为自从上次看见它以后，她便明白，凡是有甜美的鸟儿歌唱的地方，都会有毒蛇嘘嘘地叫。

——*Tess of the d'Urbervilles*《德伯家的苔丝》

名著导读

It tells of Tess Durbeyfield, the daughter of a poor and **dissipated**① villager, when learning that she may be descended from the ancient family of d'Urberville, Tess leaves her house to find her rich relatives, only to be raped and have a child. Throughout the rest of this fascinating novel, Tess is tormented by guilt at the thought of her impurity and vows to never marry. She is tested when she meets Angel, the clever son of a priest, and falls in love with him. After days of pleading, Tess gives in to Angel and consents to marry him. However, Angel deserts Tess when he finds the innocent country girl he fell in love with is not so pure.

小说讲述的是苔丝·德北菲尔德——一个贫穷、游手好闲的村民女儿的故事。当得知自己可能是古老的德伯家族的后代后，苔丝离家去寻找富贵的亲戚，结果却遭强奸，并生了一个孩子。这本引人入胜的小说的后半部分，苔丝始终被内心的罪恶感所折磨，她认为自己失去了贞操，便发誓不再结婚。但当她遇到牧师聪明的儿子安吉尔，便深深地爱上了他，于是她的誓言受到了考验。在安吉尔数日的恳求下，苔丝妥协了，同意嫁给他。然而，当安吉尔发现自己所爱的那个天真的乡村少女并不是那么纯洁时，就抛弃了苔丝。

名段选读

It was a Sunday morning in late October, about four months after Tess Durbeyfield's arrival at Trantridge, and some few weeks **subsequent**[②] to the night ride in The Chase. The time was not long past daybreak, and the yellow **luminosity**[③] upon the horizon behind her back lighted the ridge towards which her face was set—the barrier of the vale wherein she had of late been a stranger—which she would have to climb over to reach her birthplace. The ascent was gradual on this side, and the soil and scenery differed much from those within Blakemore Vale. Even the character and accent of the two peoples had shades of difference, despite the **amalgamating**[④] effects of a roundabout railway; so that, though less than twenty miles from the place of her **sojourn**[⑤] at Trantridge, her native village had seemed a far-away spot. The field-folk shut in there traded northward and westward, travelled, courted, and married northward and westward, thought northward and westward; those on this side mainly directed their energies and attention to the east and south.

The incline was the same down which d'Urberville had driven her so wildly on that day in June. Tess went up the remainder of its length without stopping, and on reaching the edge of the **escarpment**[⑥] gazed over the familiar green world beyond, now half-veiled in mist. It was always beautiful from here; it was terribly beautiful to Tess today, for since her eyes last fell upon it she had learnt that the serpent hisses where the sweet birds sing, and her views of life had been totally changed for her by the lesson. Verily another girl than the simple one she had been at home was she who, bowed by thought, stood still here, and

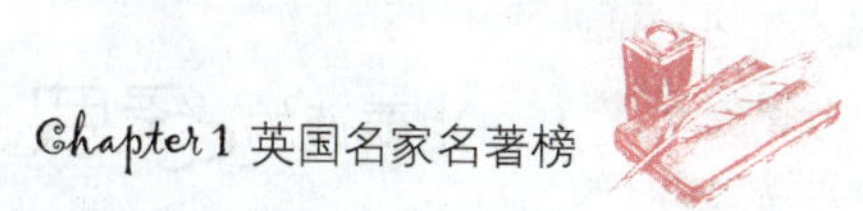

turned to look behind her. She could not bear to look forward into the Vale.

那是在十月末一个星期天的早上，苔丝·德北菲尔德来到特兰里奇大约四个月，距他们骑马在猎苑走夜路已有几个礼拜了。天亮后不久，背后地平线上金红色的光芒照亮了她面向的那道山脊，这道山脊是山谷的屏障，最近她变成了这个山谷里的一个陌生人，她必须翻越这道山脊，才能回到她的出生地。这边的山坡是逐渐上升的，这里的土壤和风景与布莱克莫尔谷里的大不一样。尽管有一条蜿蜒的铁路起着连接两地的作用，但这两个地方的人在性格和口音方面都有着很大的差异；因此，尽管离她在特兰里奇的寄居之处还不到二十英里，但她出生的乡村看起来似乎仍然是一个遥远的地方。被封闭在那里的人们一般到北边和西边去做生意、旅行、求婚、结婚，想着西边和北边；而这边的人则主要把他们的精力和心思集中于东边和南边。

这就是六月里的那天德贝维尔载着她疯狂驱车下去的那道斜坡。苔丝一刻不停地走完了剩下的路程，来到断崖的边缘，她望着远处那个熟悉的绿色世界，现在它在雾中若隐若现。从这儿望去，它一直都是那么美丽；而今天，在苔丝眼中，它更是出奇的美丽，因为自从上次看见它以后，她便明白，凡是有甜美的鸟儿歌唱的地方，都会有毒蛇咝咝地叫，经历过这次教训，她的人生观已经完全发生改变。现在的她已经真正变成了另一个姑娘，已不再是家乡那个天真的女孩子。她心事重重，呆呆地站在这儿，又转过身去看着身后。她不忍再看前面的山谷。

——选自《德伯家的苔丝》第12章

注释

★“苔丝招致毁灭的真正原因是属于现实的性质，女主人公的贫苦和无依无靠，社会上盛行的社会风习——这些情况都决定了这个女子的悲惨命运。”

——苏联文学批评家　阿尼克斯特

① dissipated ['dɪsəˌpeitɪd] *adj.* 闲游浪荡的

② subsequent ['sʌbsɪkwənt] *adj.* 随后的

③ luminosity [ˌluːmɪ'nɔsəlɪ] *n.* 光明，光辉

④ amalgamate [ə'mælgəmeɪt] *vt.* 合并

⑤ sojourn ['sɔdʒən] *n.* 逗留，旅居

⑥ escarpment [ɪ'skɑːpmənt] *n.* 悬崖

《无名的裘德》发表于1895年，共6部，小说以悲怆的笔调叙述了英国维多利亚时代一位对事业以及理想有追求的乡村青年裘德一生的悲剧。目前国内最著名的是张谷若的译本。

Jude the Obscure
无名的裘德

Do not do an immoral thing for moral reasons!

不要用道德的理由去做不道德的事情！

——*Jude the Obscure*《无名的裘德》

名著导读

Jude, poor and working-class, longs to study at the University, but his ambitions to go to university are **thwarted**[1] by class prejudice and his **entrapment**[2] in a loveless marriage. He falls in love with his unconventional cousin, Sue, and their refusal to marry when free to do so confirms their rejection of and by the world around them. The shocking fate that overtakes them is an indictment of a rigid and uncaring society.

出身贫寒的裘德一心希望进入大学学习，但因阶层成见以及无爱婚姻的束缚，他求学的梦想受到了阻碍。他爱上了性格叛逆的表妹苏，但当他们可以自由结婚时，他们却拒绝结婚，这让周围的人们更加排斥他们。吞噬他们的可怕命运是对僵化而无情的社会的控诉。

名段选读

"At first I did not love you, Jude; that I own. When I first knew you I merely wanted you to love me. I did not exactly **flirt**[3] with you; but that inborn craving which undermines some women's morals almost more than unbridled passion—the craving to attract and captivate, regardless of the injury it may do the man—was in me; and when I found I had caught you, I was frightened. And then—I don't know how it was—I couldn't bear to let you go—possibly to Arabella again—and so I got to love you, Jude. But you see, however fondly it ended, it began in the selfish and cruel wish to make your heart ache for me without letting mine ache for you."

"And now you add to your cruelty by leaving me!"

"Ah—yes! The further I **flounder**[4], the more harm I do!"

"O Sue!" said he with a sudden sense of his own danger. "Do not do an immoral thing for moral reasons! You have been my social salvation. Stay with me for humanity's sake! You know what a weak fellow I am. My two arch-enemies you know—my weakness for womankind and my impulse to strong liquor. Don't abandon me to them, Sue, to save your own soul only! They have been kept entirely at a distance since you became my guardian-angel! Since I have had you I have been able to go into any temptations of the sort, without risk. Isn't my safety worth a little sacrifice of **dogmatic**⑤ principle? I am in terror lest, if you leave me, it will be with me another case of the pig that was washed turning back to his **wallowing**⑥ in the mire!"

Sue burst out weeping. "Oh, but you must not, Jude! You won't! I'll pray for you night and day! "

"Well—never mind; don't grieve," said Jude generously. "I did suffer, God knows, about you at that time; and now I suffer again. But perhaps not so much as you. The woman mostly gets the worst of it in the long run!"

"She does." "Unless she is absolutely worthless and **contemptible**⑦. And this one is not that, anyhow!"

"一开始我并不爱你，裘德，这一点我承认。当我刚认识你的时候，我只是想让你爱上我。确切地说，我并不是在跟你调情，而只是出于内心天生的一种渴望——吸引、迷惑男人的渴望，不管会对这个男人造成什么伤害，这种渴望甚至比放纵的激情更加腐蚀女人的道德；但当我发现我俘获了你，却又害怕了。然后——我也不知道是怎么回事——我不能忍受你离开——你很可能会回到阿拉贝拉身边——于是我开始爱上你了，裘德。但是你看，不管我最后是多么深爱你，这段感情一开始就是因为我自私和残忍的念头，我想要你为我心痛，而我却不用为你心痛。"

"现在你要离开，这对我更加残忍！"

"啊，是呀！我心里越挣扎，对你的伤害就越大！"

"哦，苏！"他说，突然意识到了自己的危险。"不要用道德的理由去做不道德的事情！你一直是我的救世主。出于人道，你留在我身边吧。你知道我是一个多么脆弱的人。你知道我有两个头号大敌——对女人的软弱和对烈酒的冲动。不要光顾着拯救你自己的灵魂而将我丢弃给这两个敌人，苏！自从你成为我的守护天使后，我就已经完全远离它们了。自从有了你，我已经能应付类似的诱惑，并且不会有任何风险。难道我的安全问题就不值得你稍微去牺牲一下那些教条原则吗？如果你离开我，我恐怕我会像一只洗过却又再回到泥里打滚的猪一样！"

苏突然哭了起来。"哦，但是你不可以这样，裘德！你不会的！我会日夜为你祈祷！"

"好啦——没关系；别伤心。"裘德大方地说。"上帝知道的，那时我确实为你而感到痛苦，现在我又要再承受一次。但我的痛苦也许不如你多，终究通常都是女人受到的伤害最大！"

"确实如此。""除非她这个人毫无价值，令人鄙夷。但不管怎么说，你都不是那种人！”

——选自《无名的裘德》第6部第4章

注释

① thwart [θwɔ:t] *vt.* 挫败

② entrapment [ɪn'træpmənt] *n.* 诱捕，圈套

③ flirt [flɜ:t] *vi.* 调情

④ flounder ['flaʊndə(r)] *vi.* 挣扎

⑤ dogmatic [dɔg'mætɪk] *adj.* 教条的，武断的

⑥ wallow ['wɔləʊ] *vi.* 打滚

⑦ contemptible [kən'temptəbl] *adj.* 可鄙的，卑劣的

7 "现代主义"的重要代表人——戴维·赫伯特·劳伦斯

David Herbert Lawrence (11 September 1885—2 March 1930) was an English novelist, poet, playwright, essayist and literary critic. His collected works represent an extended reflection upon the dehumanizing effects of modernity and industrialization. Lawrence is now valued by many as a visionary thinker and significant representative of modernism in English literature. Lawrence is perhaps best known for his novels *Sons and Lovers, The Rainbow, Women in Love and Lady Chatterley's Lover.*

戴维·赫伯特·劳伦斯(1885年9月11日—1930年3月2日)是英国小说家、诗人、戏剧家、散文家和文学评论家。他的作品集深层次地反映了对人们在现代化和工业化影响下丧失人性的深入思考。如今劳伦斯被公认为是一位具有洞察力的思想家和英国文学史上现代主义的重要代表。劳伦斯因为他的经典巨作《儿子与情人》、《虹》、《恋爱中的女人》和《查特莱夫人的情人》而闻名于世。

《儿子与情人》发表于1913年，分2卷，共15章。劳伦斯通过现实主义和心理分析的写作方法，描写了19世纪末英国工业社会中下层人民的生活和特定环境下母子间和两性间的复杂、变态的心理。目前比较完整的译本出自上海译文出版社。

Sons and Lovers
儿子与情人

There was something divine in it; then she would submit, religiously, to the sacrifice.

这其中有一些圣洁的东西，那么她就会虔诚地屈服，做出牺牲。

——*Sons and Lovers*《儿子与情人》

名著导读

The book aimed at depicting this woman's grasp, Mrs. Morel. As her sons grow up, she selects them as lovers—first the eldest, then the second. These sons are urged into life by their **reciprocal**① love of their mother—urged on and on. But when they come to manhood, they can't love, because their mother is the strongest power in their lives. The result of all this is that her son, Paul, throws Miriam over for a married suffragette, Clara Dawes, who fulfills the sexual component of his ascent to manhood but leaves him, as ever, without a complete relationship to challenge his love for his mother.

这部小说以描写莫瑞尔夫人为主线。随着儿子的长大成人，莫瑞尔夫人选择把儿子当作自己的情人——首先是大儿子，然后又是小儿子。两个儿子也把母亲当成自己的爱人，并在这种爱中逐渐长大。但是成年后，他们没办法去爱人，因为母亲一直是他们生活中最有影响力的人。这样所导致的结果是：保罗因为一位已婚妇女克拉拉·道斯而抛弃了米丽安，因为克拉拉满足了保罗成年时期的性需求，但是她后来也离开了保罗。最后保罗依然没有一段完整的爱情来对抗他对母亲的爱。

名段选读

Miriam **plunged**② home over the meadows. She was not afraid of people, what they might say; but she dreaded the issue with him. Yes, she would let him have her if he insisted; and then, when she thought of it afterwards, her heart went down. He would be disappointed, he would find no satisfaction, and then he would go away. Yet he was so insistent; and over this, which did not seem so all-important to her, was their love to break down. After all, he was only like other men, seeking his satisfaction. Oh, but there was something more in him, something deeper! She could trust to it, in spite of all desires. He said that possession was a great moment in life. All strong emotions concentrated there. Perhaps it was so. There was something divine in it; then she would submit, religiously, to the sacrifice. He should have her. And at the thought her whole body **clenched**③ itself involuntarily, hard, as if against something; but Life forced her through this gate of suffering, too, and she would submit. At any rate, it would give him what he wanted, which was her deepest wish. She **brooded**④ and brooded and brooded herself towards accepting him.

He courted her now like a lover. Often, when he grew hot, she put his face from her, held it between her hands, and looked in his eyes. He could not meet her gaze. Her dark eyes, full of love, earnest and searching, made him turn away. Not for an instant would she let him forget. Back again he had to torture himself into a sense of his responsibility and hers. Never any relaxing, never any leaving himself to the great hunger and **impersonality**⑤ of passion; he must be brought back to a deliberate, **reflective**⑥ creature. As if from a swoon of passion she caged him back to the littleness, the personal relationship. He could not bear it. “Leave me alone—leave me alone!” he wanted to cry; but she wanted him to look at her with eyes full of love. His eyes, full of the dark, impersonal fire of desire, did not belong to her.

米丽安从沼泽地跌跌撞撞回了家。她并不害怕别人说什么，她担心的是与他之间所发生的事情。是的，如果他坚持的话，她会把自己奉献给他的。然而当时她一想到这件事的后果，心就沉下去了。他会很失望，会得不到满足，然后就会离开她。他迫切想要得到的，对她来说并不是那么重要，她只是害怕他们的爱情关系会因此而破裂。说到底，他和其他男人一样，只是要寻求自身欲望的满足。但是，在他内心深处应该不止于此，应该还有一些更深层次的东西。那是抛开所有欲望，值得她相信的真情。他说过，占有是人生中的一个重大时刻，所有的强烈感情都会凝聚于这一瞬间。也许确实是这样的，这其中有一些圣洁的东西，那么她就会虔诚地屈服，做出牺牲。他应该拥有她。一想到这，她整个身体便不由自主地缩紧了起来，变得僵硬，似乎在反抗些什么，但是生活迫使她必须去经历这道苦难之门，她会屈服的。不论如何，她最大的愿望就是让他得到想要的一切。她再三考虑着去接受他。

现在他像情人一样对她大献殷勤。常常当他很热情的时候，她会将他的脸转过来，把它捧在手里，凝视着他的眼睛。每次他都会躲开她凝视的目光，因为她深邃的眼睛里充满了爱意、真诚和探寻，这让他不得不转过脸去。他一刻也没忘记过她的那种眼神。他又必须再次陷入责任感的折磨当中，他从不松懈，也从不放任他强烈的饥渴和毫无人情味的激情，他必须重新成为一个深思熟虑和慎重的人。就好像她禁锢着他，把他从令他心醉神迷的激情中带到现实世界。他不能忍受，“别烦我，别烦我！”他想大吼，但是她希望他用充满爱意的眼神看着自己。他的眼睛，满是黑暗和非理智的欲火，但并不属于她。

——选自《儿子与情人》第2卷第11章

注释

① reciprocal [rɪ'sɪprəkl] *adj.* 相互的，相互给予的

② plunge [plʌndʒ] *vi.* 颠簸，（马等）猛烈前冲

③ clench [klentʃ] *vt.* 抓紧

④ brood [bru:d] *vi.* 沉思，担忧

⑤ impersonality [ɪmˌpɜ:sə'nælətɪ] *n.* 无人情味，冷静

⑥ reflective [rɪ'flektɪv] *adj.* 熟虑的

《查特莱夫人的情人》是劳伦斯的最后一部长篇小说，同时也是西方十大情爱经典小说之一。1928年由劳伦斯私人出版。当时的劳伦斯对人物及情节的刻画已经炉火纯青，对他所探索的两性关系也有了更深思熟虑的答案。目前国内的正规版本是赵苏苏翻译的版本。

Lady Chatterley's Lover
查特莱夫人的情人

Ours is essentially a tragic age, so we refuse to take it tragically.

实际上，这是一个悲剧的时代，所以我们不能用悲剧的态度对待生活。

——*Lady Chatterley's Lover*《查特莱夫人的情人》

名著导读

It is the story of Connie, Constance Reid, who marries Sir Clifford Chatterley in 1917 only to have him wounded in the war such that he must be confined to a wheelchair permanently soon afterwards. Lady Chatterley enjoys an extremely passionate relationship with Oliver Mellors, the gamekeeper on their estate. The later stages of the novel move onto the issue of her pregnancy by Mellors and her trip to Venice to disguise the true parentage of the child. The truth is eventually uncovered and the novel ends with a sense of fulfillment for both Lady Chatterley and Mellors although the situation is never fully resolved.

故事讲述的是1917年康妮（康斯坦斯·里德）嫁给了贵族克利福德·查特莱为妻，但是查特莱在战争中负伤，从此必须永远坐在轮椅上生活。查特莱夫人便尽情享受着与庄园守林人奥利弗·梅勒斯充满激情的关系。小说的后半部分康妮怀了梅勒斯的孩子，为了避人耳目，康妮去威尼斯度假。但真相最终还是暴露了。最后尽管事情并没有完全解决，但是查特莱夫人和梅勒斯都有了一种满足感。

名段选读

Ours is essentially a tragic age, so we refuse to take it tragically. The **cataclysm**① has happened, we are among the ruins, and we start to build up new little habitats, to have new little hopes. It is rather hard work: there is now no smooth road into the future: but we go round, or **scramble**② over the obstacles. We've got to live, no matter how many skies have fallen.

This was more or less Constance Chatterley's position. The war had brought the roof down over her head. And she had realized that one must live and learn. She married Clifford Chatterley in 1917, when he was home for a month on leave. They had a month's honeymoon. Then he went back to Flanders: to be shipped over to England again six months later, more or less in bits. Constance, his wife, was then twenty-three years old, and he was twenty-nine.

His hold on life was **marvellous**③. He didn't die, and the bits seemed to grow together again.

For two years he remained in the doctor's hands. Then he was **pronounced**[4] a cure, and could return to life again, with the lower half of his body, from the hips down, paralyzed for ever.

This was in 1920. They returned, Clifford and Constance, to his home, Wragby Hall, the family "seat". His father had died, Clifford was now a **baronet**[5], Sir Clifford, and Constance was Lady Chatterley. They came to start housekeeping and married life in the rather forlorn home of the Chatterleys on a rather inadequate income. Clifford had a sister, but she had departed. Otherwise there were no near relatives. The elder brother was dead in the war. Crippled for ever, knowing he could never have any children, Clifford came home to the smoky Midlands to keep the Chatterley name alive while he could.

事实上，这是一个悲剧的时代，所以我们不能用悲剧的态度对待生活。灾难已经发生，我们站在一片废墟上。但是我们开始建立新的、小小的栖身之地，开始拥有一些新的、微小的希望。这是相当艰难的，通向未来的路不会一帆风顺，但我们可以绕道而行，或攀越障碍。不管发生什么事，就算天塌下来我们也得活下去。

这在一定程度上可以说是康斯坦斯·查特莱处境的写照。战争让她头顶的那片天塌下来了。而她也意识到人必须活下去，而且要不断学习。1917年，她嫁给了克利福德·查泰莱，他请假在家待了一个月。他们度了一个月的蜜月，然后他就回到佛兰德斯：六个月后他被运回英格兰，一身伤残。他的妻子，康斯坦斯，那时23岁，他29岁。

他对生活的坚韧让人惊奇。他并没有死，那些伤口似乎也重新愈合起来。整整两年他一直在接受医生的治疗。然后医生宣称他痊愈了，但是他的腰部以下却永久瘫痪了。

那是在1920年，康斯坦斯和克利福德回到了他们的家——祖传宅邸拉格比庄园。克利福德的父亲已经去世了，而这时克利福德已经是一位准男爵，康斯坦斯是查特莱夫人。他们在查特莱冷清的家中开始了居家婚姻生活，学着在手头拮据的情况下如何持家。克利福德有一个妹妹，但是已经离开了，哥哥也在战争中牺牲，这样他们就没有近亲了。知道自己再也不可能有孩子了，克利福德还是回到烟雾弥漫的米德兰，为的是尽可能地不让查特莱这个姓氏没落。

——选自《查特莱夫人的情人》第1章

注释

① cataclysm ['kætəklɪzəm] *n.* 大变动，大灾难
② scramble ['skræmbl] *vi.* 攀爬，争夺
③ marvellous ['mɑːvələs] *adj.* 不可思议的，非凡的
④ pronounce [prærnauns] *vt.* 宣称，发表意见
⑤ baronet ['bærənɪt] *n.* 准男爵

《恋爱中的女人》发表于1920年，共31章。是劳伦斯最伟大、最有代表性、最脍炙人口的两部长篇小说之一（另一部是《虹》），最好的译本出自译林出版社。

Women in Love
恋爱中的女人

"You think, don't you," she said slowly, "that I only want physical things? It isn't true. I want you to serve my spirit."

"你认为，"她慢慢地说："我只想要肉体方面的慰藉，不是吗？这不是真的，我也需要你精神上的安慰。"

——*Women in Love*《恋爱中的女人》

名著导读

It is a **sequel**① to his earlier novel *The Rainbow* (1915), and follows the continuing loves and lives of the Brangwen sisters, Gudrun and Ursula. The story opens with sisters Ursula and Gudrun Brangwen, characters who also appeared in *The Rainbow*, discussing marriage, then walking through a haunting landscape ruined by coal mines, smoking factories, and sooty dwellings. Soon Gudrun will choose Gerald, the icily handsome mining industrialist, as her lover; Ursula will become involved with Birkin, a school inspector—and an erotic interweaving of souls and bodies begins.

《恋爱中的女人》是劳伦斯早期作品《虹》(1915)的续篇，继续讲述布兰温姐妹——古德兰和厄休拉的爱情和生活。故事开头，小说《虹》中的主人公厄休拉和古德兰两姐妹谈论着婚姻，然后走过一片被煤矿、冒着黑烟的工厂和熏黑的住房破坏了的风景，这画面令人难以忘怀。不久以后，古德兰选择冷漠帅气的矿主杰拉尔德作为自己的情人。而厄休拉与督学伯基相爱——于是一段灵与肉的交织就此开始了。

名段选读

They went and sat down on the roots of the trees, in the shadow. And being silent, he remembered the beauty of her eyes, which were sometimes filled with light, like spring, **suffused**② with wonderful promise. So he said to her, slowly, with difficulty:

"There is a golden light in you, which I wish you would give me." It was as if he had been thinking of this for some time.

She was **startled**③; she seemed to leap clear of him. Yet also she was pleased.

"What kind of a light," she asked.

But he was shy, and did not say any more. So the moment passed for this time. And gradually a feeling of sorrow came over her.

"My life is unfulfilled," she said.

"Yes," he answered briefly, not wanting to hear this.

"And I feel as if nobody could ever really love me," she said.

But he did not answer.

"You think, don't you," she said slowly, "that I only want physical things? It isn't true. I want you to serve my spirit."

"I know you do. I know you don't want physical things by themselves. But, I want you to give me—to give your spirit to me—that golden light which you—which you don't know—is, give it me—"

After a moment's silence she replied:

"But how can I, you don't love me! You only want your own ends. You don't want to serve me, and yet you want me to serve you. It is so one-sided!"

It was a great effort to him to maintain this conversation, and to press for the thing he wanted from her, the **surrender**④ of her spirit.

"It is different," he said. "The two kinds of service are so different. I serve you in another way—not through yourself—somewhere else. But I want us to be together without bothering about ourselves—to be really together because we are together, as if it were a phenomenon, not a thing we have to maintain by our own effort."

"No," she said, **pondering**⑤. "You are just **egocentric**⑥. You never have any enthusiasm; you never come out with any spark towards me. You want yourself, really, and your own affairs. And you want me just to be there, to serve you."

But this only made him shut off from her.

他们来到树下并坐了下来。沉默中，他想起了她迷人的眼睛，她的眼睛如泉水般明亮，充满了美好的希望。因此他慢慢地，艰难地对她说：

"在你身上有一种金色的光芒，我希望你可以把它给我。"他说这话的时候好像已经思考了很久一样。

她很吃惊，似乎想跳离开他身边。然而，她也很高兴。

"什么样的光？"她问。

但是他很腼腆，并没有继续往下说。所以那个时刻就这样过去了。渐渐地，一股悲伤向她袭来。

"我的生活很不圆满。"她说。

"是吗？"他的回答很简短，并不是很想听到这些话。

"我觉得好像没有人会真正地爱我。"她说。

但是他没有回答。

“你认为，”她慢慢地说，“我只想要肉体方面的慰藉，不是吗？这不是真的，我也需要你精神上的安慰。”

“我知道你需要。我知道你寻求的不只是肉体上的东西。但是，我希望你给我——给我一些精神上的慰藉——你不知道自己所拥有的那种金色的光芒——我希望你能给我。”

在片刻的沉默后，她回答：

“但是你根本不爱我，我怎么可以给你！你所想的都是你自己。你根本不想属于我，你只是想我臣服于你。这太不公平了！”

他绞尽脑汁让谈话继续下去。因为他想从她那里得到他想要的，那就是她精神上的屈服。

“这是不同的，”他说：“这两种臣服完全是不同的。我是通过另外一种方式臣服于你——不是通过你自己——而是其他某个方面。但是我希望我们在一起不会给彼此增添烦恼——我们是真正地在一起。就好像我们在一起是一种自然而然的现象，而不是靠彼此的努力去维持。

“不，”她思索着说：“你只是以自我为中心。你从来没有热情，你对我也从来不会激起任何火花。你关心的只是你自己，真的，只是你自己的事情。你只是想要我全心全意地围着你转，为你牺牲。”

但是这只是让他对她关上了心扉。

——选自《恋爱中的女人》第19章

注释

① sequel ['si:kwəl] *n.* 续集，继续

② suffused [sə'fju:zd] *adj.* 弥漫的，充满了的

③ startled ['stɑ:tld] *adj.* 大吃一惊的，惊吓的

④ surrender [sə'rendə(r)] *n.* 投降，屈服

⑤ ponder ['pɒndə(r)] *vi.* 默想，沉思

⑥ egocentric [ˌegəʊ'sentrɪk] *adj.* 自我中心的，自私自利的

8 二十世纪现代主义和女性主义的先锋——弗吉尼亚·伍尔芙

Adeline Virginia Woolf (January 25, 1882—March 28, 1941) was an English author, essayist, publisher, and writer of short stories, regarded as one of the foremost modernist literary figures of the twentieth century. During the interwar period, Woolf was a significant figure in London literary society and a member of the Bloomsbury Group. Her most famous works include the novels *Mrs. Dalloway* (1925), *To the Lighthouse* (1927) *and Orlando* (1928), and the book-length essay *A Room of One's Own* (1929).

弗吉尼亚·伍尔芙（1882年1月25日—1941年3月28日），英国女作家、散文家、出版人、短篇小说家，她被认为是二十世纪现代主义文学的先锋之一。第一次世界大战结束和第二次世界大战开始之前的这段时间里，伍尔芙是伦敦文学界的重要人物，同时也是布鲁姆斯伯里文化圈的成员之一。她最知名的小说包括《达洛威夫人》（1925）、《到灯塔去》（1927）、《奥兰多》（1928）和长篇随笔《自己的房间》（1929）。

《墙上的斑点》*写于1917年,发表于1919年，为伍尔夫的第一部意识流小说。小说打破传统既定俗套，通过人物头脑中的瞬间印象和冥想、内心活动和情绪变化，思接千载，视通万里，反映生活本质，揭示永恒真理。目前国内较著名的译本是李乃坤的版本和文美惠的版本。

The Mark on the Wall
墙上的斑点

Why, if one wants to compare life to anything, one must liken it to being blown through the Tube at fifty miles an hour—landing at the other end without a single hairpin in one's hair!

如果要把生活比作什么的话，它就像一个人被风卷着以每小时五十英里的速度穿过地铁通道——降落在另一端，然后头上的发夹一个也不剩！

——*The Mark on the Wall*《墙上的斑点》

名著导读

The only character in ***The Mark on the Wall*** is a person engaged in an act of contemplation. As (presumably) she looks at the mark, the range of her mind expands outward from this initial observation, reaching back into the past when she first noticed it, and then in many directions as association leads to association, thought to further thought, and onward to reflection on these thoughts and on the process of thought itself.

《墙上的斑点》中的唯一的主人公是一个陷入遐想的人。当她看见墙上的斑点，思绪便从起初的观察点向外发散开，一开始她想到自己第一次注意到这个斑点的时候，接着思绪向多角度发散、联想和思索层层相连，不断深入，然后她又开始反思这些思绪以及思考的过程本身。

名段选读

But as for that mark, I'm not sure about it; I don't believe it was made by a nail after all; it's too big, too round, for that. I might get up, but if I got up and looked at it, ten to one I shouldn't be able to say for certain; because once a thing's done, no one ever knows how it happened. Oh! dear me, the mystery of life; The inaccuracy of thought! The ignorance of humanity! To show how very little control of our possessions we have—what an accidental affair this living is after all our civilization—let me just count over a few of the things lost in one lifetime, beginning, for that seems always the most mysterious of losses—what cat would gnaw, what rat would nibble—three pale blue canisters of book-binding tools? Then there were the bird cages, the iron hoops, the steel skates, the Queen Anne coal **scuttle**①, the **bagatelle**② board, the hand organ—all gone, and jewels, too. **Opals**③ and **emeralds**④, they lie about the roots of **turnips**⑤. What a scraping paring affair it is to be sure! The wonder is that I've any clothes on my back, that I sit surrounded by solid furniture at this moment. Why, if one wants to compare life to anything, one must liken it to being blown through the Tube at fifty miles an hour—landing at the other end without a single hairpin in one's hair! Shot out at the feet of God entirely naked! Tumbling head over heels in the **asphodel**⑥ meadows like brown paper parcels pitched down a shoot in the post office! With one's hair flying back like the tail of a race-horse. Yes, that seems to express the rapidity of life, the **perpetual**⑦ waste and repair; all so casual, all so **haphazard**⑧...

但是说到那个斑点，我不确定它到底是什么，我不认为它是钉子留下的痕迹，因为它太大、太圆了。我是可以站起来去看看，但是即使我站起来仔细瞧它，我十有八九也说不准它到底是什么。因为当一件事情一旦发生了，人们从来都不会知道它是怎么发生的。哦，我的天啊！生活是多么神秘！思维是多么不准确！人类是多么无知！为了表明我们对

自己私有物品的掌控是多么的无力——在人类全部文明发展到今天之后，这样的生活显得是多么具有偶然性啊——就让我来列举一些在人的一生中我们所遗失的东西吧，首先要说的是看起来在所有遗失物中丢失得最神秘的物品——装着订书机的那三个浅蓝色罐子——有哪只猫会咬它们，哪只老鼠会啃它们？然后鸟笼、铁箍、钢滑冰鞋、安妮皇后时期的煤篓、弹子戏球台、手风琴，都不见了，还有珠宝也是。猫眼石和绿宝石等珠宝也被丢在了芜菁的根旁边。那些肯定都是节衣缩食攒下来的！我现在身上还能穿着衣服，周围还能有结实的家具，还真是一个奇迹！如果要把生活比作什么的话，它就像一个人被风卷着以每小时五十英里的速度穿过地铁通道——降落在另一端，然后头上的发夹一个也不剩！光着身子落在上帝脚下，以头着地的方式落在开满水仙花的草地上，就像邮局中嗖的一声扔过来的棕色纸质包裹，头发统统向后飞扬，像赛马的尾巴一样。是啊，这些比喻似乎可以描述生活的速度以及无休止的浪费和修理；一切都那么随意，那么偶然……

——选自《墙上的斑点》

注释

★“《墙上的斑点》作为一篇纯正的意识流代表作享誉中外文坛。它以一种全新的面貌出现，随即就以其全新的面貌征服了读者，征服了世界。”

——首都师范大学中文系副教授　易晓明

① scuttle ['skʌtl] n. 煤筐
② bagatelle [ˌbægə'tel] *n.* 弹子球戏
③ opal ['əupl] *n.* 猫眼石
④ emerald ['emərəld] *n.* 绿宝石
⑤ turnip ['tɜːnɪp] *n.* 芜菁
⑥ asphodel ['æsfədel] *n.* 水仙
⑦ perpetual [pə'petʃuəl] *adj.* 永久的
⑧ haphazard [hæp'hæzəd] *adj.* 偶然的，无计划的

《达洛威夫人》★是由弗吉尼亚·伍尔芙在1925年发表的一部长篇意识流小说。小说描述了主人公克莱丽莎·达洛威一战后在英国一天的生活细节。该小说作为伍尔芙的代表作之一，被时代杂志TIME评为1923-2005百部最佳英文小说之一。目前国内较著名的译本是孙梁和苏美的合译版本以及瞿世镜的版本。

Mrs. Dalloway
达洛威夫人

The young man had killed himself; but she did not pity him; with the clock striking the hour, one, two, three, she did not pity him, with all this going on.

那个年轻人自杀了，但是她却一点也不可怜他。时钟敲响了一声、两声、三声，在这样的情况下，她不可怜他。

——*Mrs. Dalloway*《达洛威夫人》

名著导读

Clarissa Dalloway goes around London in the morning, getting ready to host a party that evening. The nice day reminds her of her youth at Bourton and makes her wonder about her choice of husband. Clarissa's party in the evening is a slow success. It is attended by most of the characters she has met in the book, including people from her past. She hears about Septimus' suicide at the party and gradually comes to admire the act of this stranger, which she considers an effort to preserve the purity of his happiness.

清晨，克莱丽莎•达洛威就在伦敦四处奔走，为当天晚上的聚会做准备。这个美好的一天让她想起了自己年轻时在柏顿的时光，并让她怀疑自己是否选对了丈夫。克莱丽莎的聚会办得马马虎虎，她遇过到的大部分人包括她的旧交都参加了聚会。在晚会上，她听说了塞普蒂默斯自杀的消息，并开始渐渐佩服这个陌生人的勇敢行为，她认为这是他为维护自己纯洁的幸福而做出的努力。

名段选读

It held, foolish as the idea was, something of her own in it, this country sky, this sky above Westminster. She parted the curtains; she looked. Oh, but how surprising!—in the room opposite the old lady stared straight at her! She was going to bed. And the sky. It will be a solemn sky, she had thought, it will be a dusky sky, turning away its cheek in beauty. But there it was—**ashen**① pale, raced over quickly by **tapering**② vast clouds. It was new to her. The wind must have risen. She was going to bed, in the room opposite. It was fascinating to watch her, moving about, that old lady, crossing the room, coming to the window. Could she see her? It was fascinating, with people still laughing and shouting in the drawing room, to watch that old woman, quite quietly, going to bed. She pulled the **blind**③ now. The clock began striking. The young man had killed himself; but she did not pity him; with the clock striking the hour, one, two, three, she did not pity him, with all this going on. There! the old lady had put out her light! the whole house was dark now with this going on, she repeated, and the words came to her, Fear no more the heat of the sun. She must go back to them. But what an extraordinary night! She felt somehow very like him—the young man who had killed himself. She felt glad that he had done it; thrown it away. The clock was striking. The **leaden**④ circles dissolved in the air. He made her feel the beauty; made her feel the fun. But she must go back. She must assemble. She must find Sally and Peter.

And she came in from the little room.

这片乡村的天空，这片笼罩着威斯敏斯特的天空包含着某种属于她自己的东西，当然这个想法非常愚蠢。她拉开窗帘，凝视窗外，天哪，多么奇怪啊！——对面房间的老妇人正直直地看着她！这个老妇人正准备睡觉。还有那天空，她原以为不再晴朗美丽的天空会变得肃穆阴郁。但是眼前这片天空——灰灰白白的，不断有慢慢变小的巨大云团飘过。这对她来说可是一件新鲜事！一定是起风了。对面房间的老妇人正准备睡觉。她兴致勃勃地看着老妇人在房间里走来走去，穿过房间，来到窗边。老妇人能看到自己吗？客厅的人们还在大声谈笑，而她却在静静地看着那位老太太准备睡觉，这真的太有趣了。她拉下百叶窗，这时时钟开始敲响。那个年轻人自杀了，但是她却一点也不可怜他。时钟敲响了一声、两声、三声，这一切过后，她还是不可怜他。看！老妇人熄灯了！整幢楼被黑暗笼罩，这时，她开始重复一句突然想到的话：不再害怕太阳的炙热。她必须得回到客人中间去了。但是这是多么特别的一个夜晚！不知怎的，她觉得自己很喜欢他——那个自杀的年轻人。她很高兴他那样做了(自杀了)，抛开了一切烦恼。时钟仍在响。沉闷的声音消散在空气中。他让她感受到了美好和乐趣。但是她必须回去了，必须与众人待在一起。她必须找到萨莉和彼得。于是，她从小房间出来，进了客厅。

——选自《达洛威夫人》

注释

★“伍尔芙对统治阶层和对他们持批评态度的人都有着一定的同情，表现在对达洛威夫人晚会上的权贵既讽刺又羡慕的描述上。”

——英国诗人、著名文学批评家　威廉·燕朴逊

① ashen [ˈæʃən] *adj.* 灰白的

② taper [ˈteipə(r)] *vt.* 逐渐变细

③ blind [blaind] *n.* 百叶窗

④ leaden [ˈledən] *adj.* 沉闷的

《到灯塔去》★是1927年发表的一部长篇意识流小说，全书并无起伏跌宕的情节，内容分3个部分，依次为：窗、时光流逝、灯塔。目前国内较著名的译本是瞿世镜的版本和林之鹤的版本。

To the Lighthouse
到灯塔去

Who will blame him if he does homage to the beauty of the world?

他向心中的美好表示敬意，有什么好责备的呢？

——*To the Lighthouse*《到灯塔去》

名著导读

The story takes place on the Isle of Skye just before the First World War. The Ramsay family have a holiday home overlooking the sea and the distant lighthouse. During the summer the family, which consists of Mr and Mrs Ramsay and their eight children, invite numerous friends and colleagues to stay. The book contains three sections or "movements": the first part takes place during an afternoon and an evening in the house, the second portion—which may be considered the night—is a ten year interlude during which time Mrs Ramsay dies and two of her children die. The house remains empty throughout this time. The third section is a return visit to the restored house, by some of the family their guests, and the time element is the duration of one morning.

故事发生在第一次世界大战前的斯凯岛上。拉姆齐家有一栋度假屋，在那里能够远眺大海和海中的灯塔。时夏，拉姆齐全家，包括拉姆齐夫妇和他们的8个孩子，邀请了很多朋友和同事来这里度假。全书包括了三个部分或者可以说是三个“乐章”：第一部分的故事发生在度假屋中的某个下午和傍晚；第二部分——可以被认为发生在晚上——是一段历时10年的插曲，在这期间，拉姆齐太太和2个孩子相继去世。这段时间，度假屋一直是空着的。第三部分是拉姆齐家的一些成员和他们的客人再次拜访经过修葺之后的度假屋，此时的时间是某个清晨。

名段选读

He stood stock-still, by the **urn**①, with the **geranium**② flowing over it. How many men in a thousand million, he asked himself, reach Z after all? Surely the leader of a forlorn hope may ask himself that, and answer, without **treachery**③ to the expedition behind him, "One perhaps." One in a generation. Is he to be blamed then if he is not that one? Provided he has toiled honestly, given to the best of his power, and till he has no more left to give? And his fame lasts how long? It is permissible even for a dying hero to think before he dies how men will speak of him hereafter. His fame lasts perhaps two thousand years. And what are two thousand years? (asked Mr Ramsay ironically, staring at the hedge.) What, indeed, if you look from a mountain top down the long wastes of the ages? The very stone one kicks with one's boot will **outlast**④ Shakespeare. His own little light would shine, not very brightly, for a year or two, and would then be merged in some bigger light, and that in a bigger still. (He looked into the hedge, into the intricacy of the twigs.) Who then could blame the leader of that forlorn party which after all has climbed high enough to see the waste of the years and the perishing of the stars, if before death **stiffens**⑤ his limbs beyond the power of movement he does a little consciously raise his numbed fingers to his brow, and square his shoulders, so that when the search party comes they will find him dead at his post, the fine figure of a soldier? Mr Ramsay squared his shoulders and stood very upright by the urn.

Who shall blame him, if, so standing for a moment he dwells upon fame, upon search parties, upon cairns raised by grateful followers over his bones? Finally, who shall blame the leader of the doomed expedition, if, having adventured to the uttermost, and used his strength wholly to the last ounce and fallen asleep not much caring if he wakes or not, he now perceives by some pricking in his toes that he lives, and does not on the whole object to live, but requires sympathy, and whisky, and some one to tell the story of his suffering to at once? Who shall blame him? Who will not secretly **rejoice**[⑥] when the hero puts his **armour**[⑦] off, and halts by the window and gazes at his wife and son, who, very distant at first, gradually come closer and closer, till lips and book and head are clearly before him, though still lovely and unfamiliar from the intensity of his isolation and the waste of ages and the perishing of the stars, and finally putting his pipe in his pocket and bending his magnificent head before her——who will blame him if he does homage to the beauty of the world?

他静静地站在开满了天竺葵的瓮旁。他问自己，在十亿人中有多少人能到达Z呢？敢死队的队长也肯定会这么问自己，然后他会怀着对身后敢死队员的忠诚，自己回答说：“可能只有一个吧。”一代人中只有一个。如果他不是那个人，会受到责备吗？假设他已经恪尽职守，竭尽全力直到付出所有呢？他的盛名能持续多久？即使一个垂死的英雄也允许在死前思考身后人们会怎么评价他。他的名声可能持续两千年。两千年又算得了什么呢？(拉姆齐嘲讽地自问，眼睛盯着树篱。)若你站在山顶俯视那些曾虚度的年华，这些的确又算得了什么呢？你的靴子踢到的石子比莎士比亚的年纪都要大。一个人的光辉总是微弱地闪耀个一两年，接着就会融入到一些更明亮的光辉中去，然后再融入到更大的光辉中。(他看着树篱，看着错综纷乱的嫩枝。)谁有资格指责那个敢死队长呢？最起码他已经攀登得足够高，足以看到岁月的流逝和星体的消亡，如果在死亡把他的四肢变得僵硬麻木，无法动弹之前，他有意识地将失去知觉的手指举到额头并挺直了肩膀，那么搜寻队伍发现他时，看到的便是一个士兵的英姿。拉姆齐先生挺了挺肩膀，笔直地站在瓮旁。

如果他站着沉思片刻，想着自己的名声、搜寻队以及后世敬仰者为自己建造的墓碑，谁会责备他呢？最后，当敢死队的首领已经拼死冒险，精疲力竭，然后沉睡过去不去考虑自己能否醒来的时候，脚趾的刺痛让他感觉到自己还活着，他并不抗拒活下来，但是他需要同情、威士忌以及立刻有人听他诉说自己的遭遇，谁又会因此而责备他呢？当英雄脱下盔甲，停在窗边，凝视着妻子和儿子——起初他们离得很远，之后越走越近，直到嘴唇、书和脑袋都清晰可见——尽管他感到强烈的孤独，尽管时光流逝，斗转星移，他们依旧那么可爱而陌生，最后他还是把烟斗放进口袋，向妻子低下了高贵的头——有谁不为他暗暗感到高兴呢？他向心中的美人表示敬意，有什么好责备的呢？

——选自《到灯塔去》“窗”

注释

★“阅读了《灯塔》之后再来阅读任何一本普通的小说，会使你觉得自己是离开了白天的光芒而投身到木偶和纸板做成的世界中去。”

——南非著名学者　林德尔·戈登

① urn [ɜːn] *n.* 瓮，缸

② geranium [dʒə'reiniəm] *n.* 天竺葵

③ treachery ['tretʃərɪ] *n.* 背叛

④ outlast [ˌaut'lɑːst] *vt.* 比……长久

⑤ stiffen ['stɪfən] *vt.* 使僵硬，使生硬

⑥ rejoice [rɪ'dʒɔɪs] *vi.* 高兴，庆祝

⑦ armour ['ɑːmə(r)] *n.* 盔甲

9 英国本土最受欢迎的作家——简·奥斯汀

Jane Austen (December 16, 1775—July 18, 1817) was an English novelist whose works of romantic fiction set among the gentry earned her a place as one of the most widely read writers in English literature, her realism and biting social commentary cementing her historical importance among scholars and critics. From 1811 until 1816, with the release of *Sense and Sensibility* (1811), *Pride and Prejudice* (1813), *Mansfield Park* (1814) and *Emma* (1816), she achieved success as a published writer. The second half of the twentieth century saw a proliferation of Austen scholarship and the emergence of a Janeite fan culture.

简·奥斯汀(1775年12月16日—1817年7月18日)，英国著名小说家，她描写乡绅名流的浪漫主义小说作品使她成为英国文学史上读者最多的作家之一，她的现实主义和尖锐的社会评论巩固了她在学者和评论家中历史性的重要地位。1811年到1816年间，随着《理智与情感》(1811)、《傲慢与偏见》(1813)、《曼斯菲尔德庄园》(1814)以及《爱玛》(1816)的发表，作为一名出版作家，她取得了成功。二十世纪后半叶见证了简·奥斯汀学术成就的蓬勃发展和简迷文化的兴起。

《傲慢与偏见》*是简·奥斯汀最早完成的作品，全文共3卷，合61章。她在1797年8月完成，1813年1月发表。这部作品以日常生活为素材，生动地反映了18世纪末到19世纪初的英国乡镇生活和世态人情。目前国内最流行的译本有译林出版社孙致礼的译本和上海译文出版社王科一的译本。

Pride and Prejudice
傲慢与偏见

It is a truth universally acknowledged, that a single man in possession of a good fortune, must be in want of a wife.

一个富有的单身汉必然需要一位妻子，这是一个普遍公认的真理。

——*Pride and Prejudice*《傲慢与偏见》

名著导读

In Georgian England, Mrs. Bennet raises her five daughters—Jane, Elizabeth, Mary, Kitty and Lydia with the purpose of getting married with a rich husband that can support the family. They are not from the upper class, and their house in Hertfordshire will be inherited by a distant cousin if Mr. Bennet dies. When the wealthy bachelor Mr. Bingley and his best friend Mr. Darcy arrive in town to spend the summer in a mansion nearby their property, the shy and beautiful Jane falls in love for Mr. Bingley, and Elizabeth finds Mr. Darcy a snobbish and proud man, and she swears to loathe him forever. At last, Elizabeth remove all her prejudice to him and became the deeply love.

在乔治王时代的英格兰，班纳特太太有五个千金——简、伊丽莎白、玛丽、凯蒂和莉迪亚，她一心想让女儿们嫁给能够供养他们的家庭的有钱人。她们不是贵族，而且如果班纳特先生去世，她们的房产将会由一个远房表兄继承。富有的单身汉宾利和他最好的朋友达西来到这个镇子过夏天，住在她们家附近的一个大宅里，腼腆而又美丽迷人的简爱上了宾利，而伊丽莎白发现达西是一个势利且傲慢的人，她发誓永远讨厌他。最后，伊丽莎白消除了对达西所有的偏见，并深深地爱上了他。

名段选读

It is a truth universally acknowledged, that a single man in possession of a good fortune, must be in want of a wife.

However little known the feelings or views of such a man may be on his first entering a neighbourhood, this truth is so well fixed in the minds of the surrounding families, that he is considered the **rightful**[①] property of some one or other of their daughters.

"My dear Mr. Bennet," said his lady to him one day, "have you heard that Netherfield Park is let at last?" Mr. Bennet replied that he had not.

"But it is," returned she; "for Mrs. Long has just been here, and she told me all about it."

Mr. Bennet made no answer.

"Do you not want to know who has taken it?" cried his wife impatiently.

"You want to tell me, and I have no **objection**[②] to hearing it." This was invitation enough.

"Why, my dear, you must know, Mrs. Long says that Netherfield is taken by a young man of large fortune from the north of England; that he came down on Monday in a chaise and four to see the place, and was so much delighted with it that he agreed with Mr. Morris immediately; that he is to take possession before Michaelmas, and some of his servants are to be in the house by the end of next week."

"What is his name?"

"Bingley."

"Is he married or single?"

"Oh! single, my dear, to be sure! A single man of large fortune; four or five thousand a year. What a fine thing for our girls!"

"How so? how can it affect them?"

"My dear Mr. Bennet," replied his wife, "how can you be so **tiresome**[③]! You must know that I am thinking of his marrying one of them."

一个富有的单身汉必然需要一位妻子，这是一个普遍公认的真理。

这样一个男子搬进社区的时候，虽然人们并不了解他的感受、见解如何，但这个真理在周围家庭的观念中是如此的根深蒂固，以至于认为他是他们其中某个人的女儿的正当财产。

"亲爱的班纳特，"一天他夫人对他说："你听说了尼斯菲尔德庄园终于租出去了吗？"班纳特先生回答说他还不知道。

"但确实是的，"她回答道："朗太太刚刚来这里了，她什么都告诉我了。"

班纳特先生没有回应。

"你不想知道是租给谁了吗？"他的妻子不耐烦地大声叫嚷道。

"你想告诉我，我就听着呗。"这话算得上是个邀请了。

"为什么，亲爱的，你必须知道，朗太太说尼斯菲尔德庄园是被一个来自英格兰北部的阔少爷租走的；星期一他坐着一辆四匹马的大车来这里看房子，他非常喜欢那儿，所以就直接和莫里斯先生达成了协议；他在米迦勒节之前就能住进去，并且下周之前他的一些仆人会先搬进这个房子里。"

"他叫什么名字？"

"宾利。"

"结婚了还是单身？"

"哎呀，亲爱的，是单身！确确实实的单身汉！一个拥有大笔财产的单身男子，一年有四五千英镑的收入。对我们的女儿来说是多好的事儿啊！"

"为什么？这跟她们有什么关系呢？"

"亲爱的班纳特，"他的妻子回答说："你怎么这么烦人，你要知道我正在考虑他和我们某个女儿结婚的事呢。"

——选自《傲慢与偏见》第1卷第1章

注释

★"使一部作品成为经典名著的，不是评论家们的交口赞誉、教授们的阐述研究、用作学校里的教科书，而是使一代又一代的众多读者在阅读这部作品中得到的愉悦，受到启迪，深受教益。我个人认为，《傲慢与偏见》总体来说，是所有小说中最令人满意的一部作品。”

——英国当代著名小说家及创作家　毛姆

① rightful ['raitfl] *adj.* 正当的，合法的

② objection [əb'dʒekʃən] *n.* 反对，异议

③ tiresome ['taiəsəm] *adj.* 无聊的，烦人的

《爱玛》*创作于1815年，共3部，55章。是奥斯汀生前最后出版的小说，也是奥斯汀作品中艺术上思想上最成熟的一部长篇小说。或许没有哪部小说在喜剧效果方面，能使奥斯汀的《爱玛》相形见绌。国内最流行的译本有译林出版社孙致礼的译本和上海译文出版社祝庆英的译本。

Emma
爱玛

A man would always wish to give a woman a better home than the one he takes her from; and he who can do it, where there is no doubt of her regard, must, I think, be the happiest of mortals.

一个男人总是希望给女人一个比她娘家更好的家；并且如果他做到了，而她对他的爱也是毋庸置疑的，我认为他一定就是世上最幸福的人了。

——*Emma*《爱玛》

名著导读

Emma is the story of Miss Emma Woodhouse, a well-to-do young woman in a small English town. After her governess, Miss Taylor, marries and becomes Mrs. Weston, Emma is left with her hypochondriac, hyper-concerned father as her sole companion. She therefore takes the poor, unconnected, yet gentle Harriet under her wing. Emma's love of matchmaking leads her to **meddle**① in Harriet's love life, and to set up some romantic misadventures of her own.

《爱玛》讲述的是爱玛·伍德豪斯小姐的故事，她是一个住在英国小镇的家境富裕的年轻女子。她的女家庭教师泰勒小姐结婚成为维斯顿夫人之后，就只剩下她那患有忧郁症并且忧虑过度的父亲陪伴着她。因此爱玛把出身贫苦、无依无靠且性格温和的哈丽特置于她的保护之下。爱玛做媒的爱好让她干涉了哈丽特的爱情生活，并且造成了她自己爱情上的一些困扰。

名段选读

"He is a most fortunate man!" returned Mr. Knightley, with energy. "So early in life—at three-and-twenty—a period when, if a man chuses a wife, he generally chuses ill. At three-and-twenty to have drawn such a prize! What years of **felicity**[②] that man, in all human **calculation**[③], has before him!—Assured of the love of such a woman—the disinterested love, for Jane Fairfax's character vouches for her disinterestedness; every thing in his favour,—equality of situation—I mean, as far as regards society, and all the habits and manners that are important; equality in every point but one—and that one, since the purity of her heart is not to be doubted, such as must increase his felicity, for it will be his to bestow the only advantages she wants.—A man would always wish to give a woman a better home than the one he takes her from; and he who can do it, where there is no doubt of her regard, must, I think, be the happiest of mortals.—Frank Churchill is, indeed, the favourite of fortune. Every thing turns out for his good.—He meets with a young woman at a watering-place, gains her affection, cannot even **weary**[④] her by **negligent**[⑤] treatment—and had he and all his family sought round the world for a perfect wife for him, they could not have found her superior.—His aunt is in the way.—His aunt dies.—He has only to speak.—His friends are eager to promote his happiness.—He had used every body ill—and they are all delighted to forgive him.—He is a fortunate man indeed!"

"他是最幸运的男人。"奈特利先生激动地回答说。"在很年轻的时候——二十三岁——在这个时期如果一个男人有了妻子，通常他的选择是很糟糕的。而他在二十三岁时就能有这么好的妻子！不管从什么角度来说，都有那么多年的幸福在等着他呢！确定拥有这样一个女人的爱——无私的爱，因为简·费尔法克斯的人品保证了她的爱是无私的；所有的事情都对他有利，——门当户对——我的意思是考虑到社会地位、各种重要的习惯和风俗；各方面都是相配的，除了一点——她心灵的纯洁是毋庸置疑的，这就会给他的幸福添彩，因为给她想要的幸福会让他也觉得幸福。一个男人总是希望给女人一个比她娘家更好的家；并且如果他做到了，而她对他的爱也是毋庸置疑的，我认为他一定就是世上最幸福的人了。——的确，费兰克·邱吉尔特别幸运。事实证明所有的事情都有利于他。——他在温泉遇到了一位年轻女子，得到了她的芳心，甚至疏忽了她的时候她也没有厌烦——并且哪怕他和所有的家人寻遍世间所有地方来给他找一个完美的妻子，可能也找不到比她更优秀的。——他的姨母阻挠他。——他的姨母去世了。——他只要开口就行了。——他的朋友都乐于促成他的幸福。——他曾经亏欠了大家——而他们都很乐意原谅他。——他确实是一个幸运的人！"

——选自《爱玛》第3部第13章

注释

★"作者对人世的了解，以及读者一定会认识到的她那种表现人物的特殊的老练手法，使我们想起了佛兰德斯画派的某些优点。"

——历史小说家　瓦尔特·司各特

① meddle ['medl] *vi.* 干涉，干预

② felicity [fə'lɪsətɪ] *n.* 快乐，幸福

③ calculation [ˌkælkju'leiʃən] *n.* 计算

④ weary ['wɪrɪ] *vt.* 使疲乏，使厌烦

⑤ negligent ['neglɪdʒənt] *adj.* 疏忽的，不在意的

《理智与情感》★发表于1811年，共50章。是简·奥斯汀富于幽默情趣的处女作。本书和作者的《傲慢与偏见》堪称姐妹篇，同样以细腻的笔触和生动的对白叙述没有富裕嫁妆的少女恋爱结婚的故事。译林出版社孙致礼的译本被公认为是该小说优秀的译本。

Sense and Sensibility
理智与情感

Her imagination was busy, her reflections were pleasant, and the pain of a sprained ankle was disregarded.

她沉浸在想象中，心中满是喜悦，扭伤的脚踝还在疼，她也顾不得去理会了。

——*Sense and Sensibility*《理智与情感》

名著导读

The story is about Elinor and Marianne, two daughters of Mr Dashwood by his second wife. They have a younger sister, Margaret, and an older half-brother named John. When their father dies, the family estate passes to John, and the Dashwood women are left in reduced circumstances. The novel follows the Dashwood sisters to their new home, a cottage on a distant relative's property, where they experience both romance and heartbreak. The contrast between the sisters' characters is eventually resolved as they each find love and lasting happiness. Through the events in the novel, Elinor and Marianne encounter the sense and sensibility of life and love.

这是关于达什伍德和他第二任妻子的两个女儿，埃莉诺和玛丽安的故事。她们有个妹妹名叫玛格利特和一个同父异母的哥哥约翰。他们的父亲去世后，家产传给了约翰，而家

里的女人却陷入生活困窘。于是达什伍德姐妹去了她们的新家，一个远房亲戚的农舍，在那里她们经历了浪漫和心碎。随着她们找到各自的真爱和永恒的幸福，姐妹俩个性差异的冲突也最终解决。通过小说中发生的事件，埃莉诺和玛丽安遭遇了生活和爱情中的理智和情感。

名段选读

She thanked him again and again; and, with a sweetness of address which always attended her, invited him to be seated. But this he declined, as he was dirty and wet. Mrs. Dashwood then begged to know to whom she was obliged. His name, he replied, was Willoughby, and his present home was at Allenham, from whence he hoped she would allow him the honour of calling tomorrow to enquire after Miss Dashwood. The honour was readily granted, and he then departed, to make himself still more interesting, in the midst of an heavy rain.

His manly beauty and more than common gracefulness were instantly the theme of general admiration, and the laugh which his **gallantry**① raised against Marianne received particular spirit from his exterior attractions.—Marianne herself had seen less of his person that the rest, for the confusion which **crimsoned**② over her face, on his lifting her up, had robbed her of the power of regarding him after their entering the house. But she had seen enough of him to join in all the admiration of the others, and with an energy which always adorned her praise. His person and air were equal to what her fancy had ever drawn for the hero of a favourite story; and in his carrying her into the house with so little previous **formality**③, there was a rapidity of thought which particularly recommended the action to her. Every circumstance belonging to him was interesting. His name was good, his residence was in their favourite village, and she soon found out that of all manly dresses a shooting-jacket was the most becoming. Her imagination was busy, her reflections were pleasant, and the pain of a **sprained**④ ankle was disregarded.

她再三地感谢他；并且用她惯有的亲切话语招待他坐下来。但他拒绝了，因为他身上又脏又湿。然后达什伍德夫人恳求知道她该感谢的这个人是谁。他回答说，他叫威洛比，现在家在艾伦镇，他希望达什伍德夫人能允许他有幸拜访和问候达什伍德小姐。这请求很快得到了同意。随后更让人觉得更有趣的是，他在大雨中告辞离开了。

他的英俊和超乎寻常的优雅得体立刻赢得了大家的普遍赞赏，他对玛丽安的殷勤引起了众人对玛丽安的调笑，而他迷人的外表更让大家有了调侃的兴致。——玛丽安自己没有怎么看清楚他的容貌以及其他的行为，因为他抱着她，慌乱中她的脸颊变得绯红，也让她在他们进屋之后不敢仔细看他。但是她看到的一切已经足以让她参与到其他人对他的赞美中来，这种参与带着一种随之而生的活力。他的仪表和风度正好符合她曾经幻想的最美好的故事里男主角的形象；而且他思维敏捷，能够立刻做出决定，不拘礼节地抱她走进屋子。关于他的每一件事都是有趣的。他的名字很不错，他住在他们最喜爱的村子里，而且她很快发现在所有男装里面，射击夹克是最好看的。她沉浸在想象中，心中满是喜悦，扭伤的脚踝还在疼，她也顾不得去理会了。

——选自《理智与情感》第9章

注释

★“这个世界，凭理智来领悟是个喜剧，凭情感来体会是个悲剧。”

——英国著名学者　沃尔波尔

① gallantry ['gæləntrɪ] *n.* 勇气

② crimson ['krɪmzən] *vi.* 使绯红，变得绯红

③ formality [fɔː'mælətɪ] *n.* 礼节，程序

④ sprain [sprein] *vt.* 扭伤

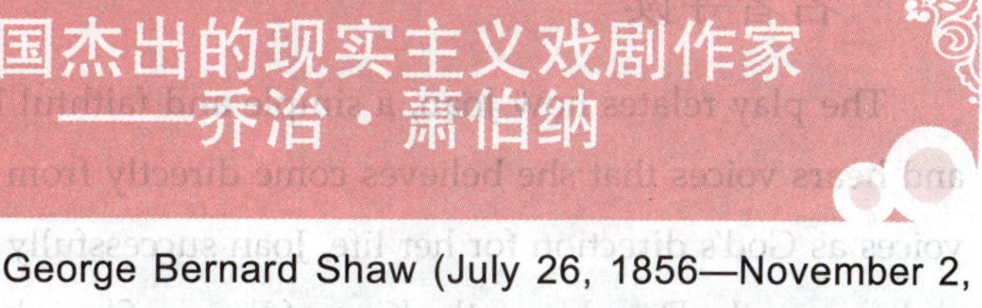

10 英国杰出的现实主义戏剧作家——乔治·萧伯纳

George Bernard Shaw (July 26, 1856—November 2, 1950) was an Irish playwright and a co-founder of the London School of Economics. Although his first profitable writing was music and literary criticism, in which capacity he wrote many highly articulate pieces of journalism, his main talent was for drama, and he wrote more than 60 plays. Among these, *Widower's Houses and Mrs. Warren's Profession* savagely attack social hypocrisy, while in plays such as *Arms* and the *Man and The Man of Destiny* the criticism is less fierce. Nearly all his writings deal sternly with prevailing social problems, but have a vein of comedy to make their stark themes more palatable.

乔治·萧伯纳(1865年7月26日—1950年11月2日)是爱尔兰剧作家，也是伦敦经济学院的创始者之一。虽然萧伯纳最初赚钱的作品是关于音乐和文学的评论文章，并且他在这一领域创作了很多广为流传的新闻作品，但是他的大部分才能都倾注在了戏剧上，他一生创作了60多部剧本。在这些剧作中，《鳏夫的房产》和《华伦夫人的职业》猛烈抨击了社会的伪善，而《武器与人》和《风云人物》的笔触就不是那么锋利了。萧伯纳几乎所有的作品都犀利地揭示了主要的社会弊端，但是幽默风趣的写作风格使这些枯燥的主题生动起来。

《圣女贞德》是萧伯纳代表剧作之一，写于1923年。全剧分6幕，作者以满腔同情描写了这位在法国遭受侵略之际起于乡野之间，献身于救国事业的巾帼英雄。目前国内较著名的译本是向洪全、胡仁源和刘炳善的版本。

Saint Joan
圣女贞德

O God that madest this beautiful earth, when will it be ready to receive Thy saints? How long, O Lord, how long?

创造了这个美好世界的上帝，你准备什么时候接受你的圣徒呢？要多久，上帝啊，还要多久？

——*Saint Joan*《圣女贞德》

名著导读

The play relates how Joan, a simple and faithful French country girl, sees visions and hears voices that she believes come directly from God. Accepting the visions and voices as God's direction for her life, Joan successfully drives the English from Orleans and crowns the Dauphin as the King of France. She is burned at the stake for her efforts.

淳朴善良、充满信仰的法国农村女孩贞德看到了某些幻象，并听到了某些声音，她相信这些是上帝直接给她的启示。贞德以这些幻象和声音作为上帝的指引，成功地把英国入侵者赶出了奥尔良，并帮助法国王储加冕。然而最后贞德却因此被判处火刑。

名段选读

Charles: Poor old Joan! They have all run away from you except this **blackguard**① who has to go back to hell at twelve o'clock. And what can I do but follow Jack Dunois' example, and go back to bed too? *(He does so.)*

Joan: *(sadly)* Goodnight, Charlie.

Charles: *(mumbling in his pillows)* Goo ni. *(He sleeps. The darkness envelops the bed.)*

Joan: *(to the soldier)* And you, my one faithful? What comfort have you for Saint Joan?

The Soldier: Well, what do they all amount to, these kings and captains and **bishops**② and lawyers and such like? They just leave you in the ditch to bleed to death; and the next thing is, you meet them down there, for all the airs they give themselves. What I say is, you have as good a right to your notions as they have to theirs, and perhaps better. *(Settling himself for a lecture on the subject)* You see, it's like this. If—*(the first stroke of midnight is heard softly from a distant bell.)* Excuse me: a pressing appointment—*(He goes on tiptoe.)*

The last remaining rays of light gather into a white **radiance**③ descending on Joan. The hour, continues to strike.

Joan: O God that madest this beautiful earth, when will it be ready to receive Thy saints? How long, O Lord, how long?

查尔斯：可怜的贞德！所有的人都离你而去，只剩下这个十二点必须下地狱的混蛋。我呢,除了跟杰克·迪努瓦一样去睡觉，还能做些什么呢？*（他去睡觉了。）*

贞德：*（伤心地）*晚安，查理。

查尔斯：*（在枕头上咕哝）*晚安。*（他睡觉了。黑暗笼罩着整张床。）*

贞德：*（对士兵说）*你是我忠诚的朋友吗？你对圣女贞德有什么要说的？

士兵：这些国王、首领、主教、律师加起来算得了什么？他们只会任由你流血而死，别看他们总是一副高傲的神情，但是你会在地狱看到他们的。要我说，你有权利坚守自己的信仰，就像他们坚守自己的一样，或许你的信仰更高尚。*（士兵就此事发表着他的长篇大论）*你看，就是这样的。如果——*（凌晨的第一声钟响缓缓地自远方传来）*抱歉，我还有事得先走了——*（士兵蹑手蹑脚地离开了。）*

最后的光线聚集成一团白光照在贞德身上。时间一如既往地流逝。

贞德：创造了这个美好世界的上帝，你准备什么时候接受你的圣徒呢？要多久，上帝啊，还要多久？

——选自《圣女贞德》第6幕

注释

① blackguard ['blægɑːd] *n.* 无赖，流氓

② bishop ['bɪʃəp] *n.* 主教

③ radiance ['reidiəns] *n.* 光辉

《华伦夫人的职业》写于1893到1894年间，1894年首演。这是一部4幕剧，作品批判不讲道德、贪婪、腐朽的资产阶级生活，揭发了披着华贵外衣者的堕落。目前国内较著名的译本是贺哈定和吴晓园的合译本。

Mrs. Warren's Profession
华伦夫人的职业

If people arrange the world that way for women, there's no good pretending it's arranged the other way.

如果女人的世界已经被安排好了是这样，那么我们假装它是另外一个样子也没有任何意义。

——*Mrs. Warren's Profession*《华伦夫人的职业》

名著导读

The story centers on the relationship between Mrs Kitty Warren, a **brothel**[1] owner, and her daughter, Vivie. Mrs Warren is a middle-aged woman whose Cambridge-educated daughter, Vivie, is horrified to discover that her mother's fortune was made managing high-class brothels. The two women make a brief reconciliation when Mrs Warren explains her impoverished youth, which originally led her into prostitution. The reconciliation ends when Vivie learns that the highly profitable business remains in operation. Vivie walks out of her mother's life, apparently for good.

故事主要讲述了妓院老板凯蒂·华伦夫人和女儿薇薇的关系。华伦夫已经是个中年

人，女儿毕业于剑桥大学。一天，薇薇发现母亲的财产都是靠经营高级妓院得来的，她很反感。但是当华伦夫人告诉薇薇因为贫穷导致她卖淫之后，母女俩的关系在短期内得以缓和。后来薇薇得知母亲还在继续经营妓院后，母女俩又闹僵了。于是薇薇永远地走出了母亲的生活。

名段选读

Vivie: *(fascinated, gazing at her)* My dear mother: you are a wonderful woman: you are stronger than all England. And are you really and truly not one wee bit doubtful…or…or…ashamed?

Mrs Warren: Well, of course, dearie, it's only good manners to be ashamed of it: it's expected from a woman. Women have to pretend to feel a great deal that they don't feel. Liz used to be angry with me for **plumping** ② out the truth about it. She used to say that when every woman could learn enough from what was going on in the world before her eyes, there was no need to talk about it to her. But then Liz was such a perfect lady! She had the true instinct of it; while I was always a bit of a **vulgarian** ③. I used to be so pleased when you sent me your photos to see that you were growing up like Liz: you've just her ladylike, determined way. But I can't stand saying one thing when everyone knows I mean another. What's the use in such **hypocrisy** ④? If people arrange the world that way for women, there's no good pretending it's arranged the other way. No! I never was a bit ashamed really. I consider I had a right to be proud of how we managed everything so respectably, and never had a word against us, and how the girls were so well taken care of. Some of them did very well: one of them married an ambassador. But of course now I daren't talk about such things: whatever would they think of us! (She yawns). Oh dear! I do believe I'm getting sleepy after all. (She stretches herself lazily, thoroughly relieved by her explosion, and **placidly** ⑤ ready for her night's rest).

薇薇：（入神地凝视着她）亲爱的妈妈，你是一个了不起的女人：你比整个英格兰的人都强大。你难道真的一点都没犹豫过……或者……或者……觉得难为情？

华伦夫人：当然，亲爱的。不过难为情只是出于礼貌，或者是出于世人对一个女人的要求。女人不得不假装有很多感受，但实际上她们并没有感受到。莉斯曾因为我说出事实而生气。她过去常常说当每一个女人都可以从眼前的世界中学到足够多的时候，就没有必要跟她谈论这些了。但是莉斯那时是如此的完美，她对这种事的直觉很准，而我就是庸人一个。过去每次看到你寄来的照片中你像莉斯一样在长大，变成熟，我就特别高兴：你像她一样高雅、果断。但是我不能忍受自己言不由衷。这样的虚伪有什么意思？如果女人的世界已经被安排好了是这样，那么我们假装它是另外一个样子也没有任何意义。不！实际上我一点也不觉得难为情。我们把所有的事都安排得如此体面，没有人对我们说三道四，我们把姑娘们照顾地很好——我想我有权利为这些感到自豪。有些姑娘过得很好：其中一个嫁给了一位大使。但是当然了，我现在不敢谈论这样的事：不管他们怎么看待我们！（她打了一个哈欠）亲爱的，我想我很困了。（她伸了个懒腰，彻底平息了自己的怒火，平静地准备去休息）

——选自《华伦夫人的职业》第2幕

注释

① brothel ['brɔθl] *n.* 妓院
② plump [plʌmp] *vi.* 冲口说出
③ vulgarian [vʌl'geəriən] *n.* 俗人
④ hypocrisy [hɪ'pɔkrəsɪ] *n.* 伪善
⑤ placidly ['plæsɪdlɪ] *adv.* 平静地

《卖花女》创作于1912年，根据皮格马利翁的神话故事编写而成。全剧共有5幕，嘲讽了资产阶级上流社会中绅士淑女们的种种丑恶嘴脸。目前国内较著名的译本是杨宪益的版本。

Pygmalion
卖花女

If you're going to be a lady, you'll have to give up feeling neglected if the men you know don't spend half their time snivelling over you and the other half giving you black eyes.

如果你想成为一名淑女，你就不能因为你认识的男人没有在他一半的时间里为你哭鼻子然后在另外一半的时间把你打得鼻青脸肿而感到自己被忽视了。

——*Pygmalion*《卖花女》

名著导读

Professor of phonetics Henry Higgins makes a bet that he can train a bedraggled Cockney flower girl, Eliza Doolittle, to pass for a duchess at an ambassador's garden party by teaching her to assume a **veneer**① of gentility, the most important element of which, he believes, is **impeccable**② speech. The play is a sharp **lampoon**③ of the rigid British class system of the day and a comment on women's independence, packaged as a romantic comedy.

语言学教授亨利·希金斯与友人打赌，他能够将一个浑身脏兮兮、满口乡音的卖花女伊丽莎·杜利特尔训练成别人眼中公爵夫人的模样，去出席一个大使的游园会。希金斯教伊丽莎如何保持优雅和高贵，最重要的一点是拥有无懈可击的谈吐。这部浪漫喜剧尖锐地讽刺了英国当时苛刻的等级制度，同时也探讨了女性的独立。

名段选读

Higgins: It's all you'll get until you stop being a common idiot. If you're going to be a lady, you'll have to give up feeling neglected if the men you know don't spend half their time **snivelling**[4] over you and the other half giving you black eyes. If you can't stand the coldness of my sort of life, and the strain of it, go back to the **gutter**[5]. Work til you are more a brute than a human being; and then **cuddle**[6] and **squabble**[7] and drink til you fall asleep. Oh, it's a fine life, the life of the gutter. It's real; it's warm; it's violent; you can feel it through the thickest skin: you can taste it and smell it without any training or any work. Not like Science and Literature and Classical Music and Philosophy and Art. You find me cold, unfeeling, selfish, don't you? Very well: be off with you to the sort of people you like. Marry some sentimental hog or other with lots of money, and a thick pair of lips to kiss you with and a thick pair of boots to kick you with. If you can't appreciate what **you've got, you'd better get what you can appreciate.**

Liza: *(desperate)* Oh, you are a cruel **tyrant**[8]. I can't talk to you: you turn everything against me: I'm always in the wrong. But you know very well all the time that you're nothing but a **bully**[9]. You know I can't go back to the gutter, as you call it, and that I have no real friends in the world but you and the Colonel. You know well I couldn't bear to live with a low common man after you two; and it's wicked and cruel of you to insult me by pretending I could. You think I must go back to Wimpole Street because I have nowhere else to go but father's. But don't you be too sure that you have me under your feet to be trampled on and talked down. I'll marry Freddy, I will, as soon as he's able to support me.

希金斯：如果你不停止这些白痴行为，你得到的就只有这些。如果你想成为一名淑女，你就不能因为你认识的男人没有在他一半的时间里为你哭鼻子然后在另外一半的时间把你打得鼻青脸肿而感到自己被忽视了。如果你不能忍受我的生活的冷酷和压力，那就回你的贫民窟去吧。工作到粗鲁得不像人，然后亲热、争吵、酗酒，每天醉生梦死。哦，这也是不错的生活，典型的下等人的生活——真实、温暖、暴力——再厚的脸皮都可以感受得到；不用训练或做准备就能感受到它。它不像科学、文学、古典音乐、哲学和艺术。你认为我冷酷、麻木、自私，不是吗？很好：去你喜欢的人那里去吧。嫁给某个感情脆弱或有钱的蠢猪，让他用肥厚的嘴唇亲你，用大靴子踢你。如果你不能欣赏你已经得到的，那就去找你能欣赏的吧。

伊丽莎：*（绝望地）*哦，你这个残酷专横的人。我没法和你交谈：你处处和我作对，不管怎样我总是错的。但是你一直很清楚自己是个恃强欺弱的人。你知道我不可能回到你

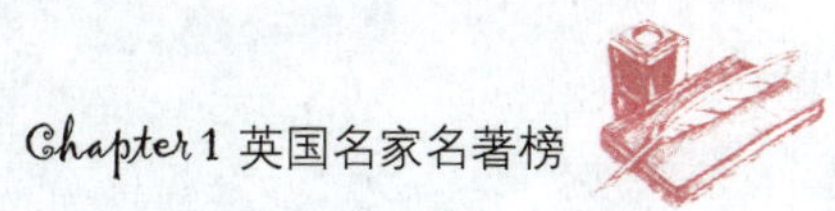

所说的贫民窟里去，除了你和上校，我没有真正的朋友。认识你们俩后，你知道我不可能和一个低俗平庸的人生活，但是你却声称我愿意这么做，用这种方式侮辱我，你太邪恶、太残忍了。你认为我只能回到温波街，因为除了父亲家我没有其他的地方可以去。你就那么肯定我会任你践踏蹂躏吗？我会嫁给弗雷迪，只要他一有能力养我，我就嫁给他。

——选自《卖花女》第5幕

注释

① veneer [və'niə] *n.* 外表，虚饰

② impeccable [ɪm'pekəbl] *adj.* 无瑕疵的，没有缺点的

③ lampoon [læm'puːn] *n.* 讽刺文章

④ snivel ['snɪvl] *vi.* 流鼻涕，哭泣

⑤ gutter ['gʌtə] *n.* 贫民区

⑥ cuddle ['kʌdl] *vi.* 拥抱

⑦ squabble ['skwɔbl] *vi.* 发生口角，大声争吵

⑧ tyrant ['tairənt] *n.* 暴君似的人，专横的人

⑨ bully ['bulɪ] *n.* 恃强凌弱者

Chapter 2

美国名家名著榜

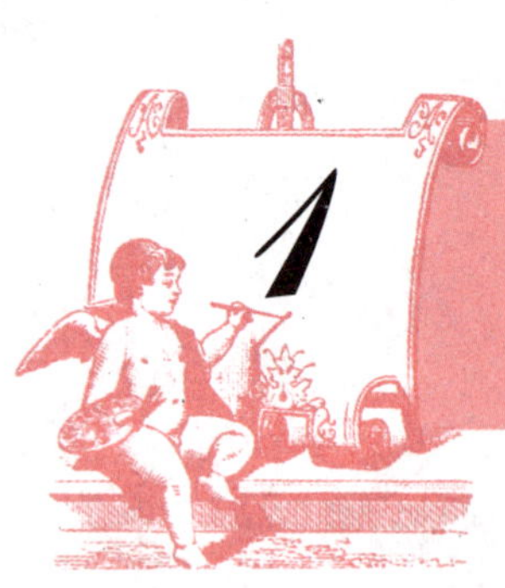

1 美国现代小说的先驱——西奥多·德莱塞

Theodore Dreiser (August 27, 1871—December 28, 1945), American author, outstanding representative of naturalism, whose novels depict real-life subjects in a harsh light. Dreiser's novels were held to be **amoral**①, and he battled throughout his career against **censorship**② and popular taste. This started with Sister Carrie (1900). Dreiser's principal concern was with the conflict between human needs and the demands of society for material success. While he wrote about "raw" experiences of life in his earlier works, in his later writing he considered the impact of economic society on the lives of people in the remarkable trilogy—*The Financier*, *The Titan*, and *The Stoic*. His best known work is *An American Tragedy* which shows a young man trying to succeed in a materialistic society.

西奥多·德莱塞(1871年8月27日—1945年12月28日)是美国作家、杰出的自然主义代表，他的小说尖锐地描述了现实生活主题。德莱塞的小说无关于道德，他的整个创作生涯都在与审查制度和世俗品味做斗争。这种斗争开始于《嘉莉妹妹》(1900)。德莱塞主要关注的是人类需要和社会对物质成功的需求之间的矛盾。他的早期作品主要描写“原始的”生活经历，而在后期作品中，他在著名的三部曲——《金融家》、《巨人》、《斯多葛》中思考了经济社会对人们生活的影响。他最著名的作品是《美国的悲剧》，描述了一个努力想在物欲横流的社会获得成功的年轻男子。

《美国的悲剧》发表于1925年，这部小说共分3卷，是西奥多·德莱塞最为重要的作品。目前国内最著名的译本是许汝祉的《美国的悲剧》和潘庆·的《美国的悲剧》。

An American Tragedy
美国的悲剧

He could not and would not let her do this to him. His life would be ruined!

他不能也不会让她得逞。不然，他的生活就毁了！

—*An American Tragedy*《美国的悲剧》

名著导读

An American Tragedy tells the story of a **bellboy**[3], Clyde Griffiths, who sets out to gain success and fame. After an automobile accident, Clyde is employed by a distant relative, owner of a collar factory. He **seduces**[4] Roberta Alden, an employee at the factory, but falls in love with Sondra Finchley, a girl of the local **aristocracy**[5]. Roberta, pregnant, demands that Clyde marry her. He takes Roberta rowing on an isolated lake and accidentally murders her. Clyde's trial, conviction, and execution occupy the remainder of the book.

《美国的悲剧》讲述的是一个名叫克莱德·格里菲思的服务生追求功成名就的故事。在一次交通事故后，克莱德受雇于一个拥有衣领工厂的远房亲戚。他勾引了工厂员工罗伯塔·奥尔登，却与当地一名贵族的女儿桑德拉·芬赤利相爱。怀孕的罗伯塔要求克莱德和她结婚。他带着罗伯塔去远郊的一个湖上划船，并且意外地杀了她。小说的剩余部分描写了克莱德被审讯、定罪、处决的情节。

名段选读

The thought was like some sweet, **disarranging**[6] poison to Clyde. It fevered and all but betrayed him mentally. If only—if only—it were not for Roberta now. That terrifying and all but insoluble problem. But for that, and the opposition of Sondra's parents which she was thinking she would be able to overcome, did not heaven itself await him? Sondra, Twelfth Lake, society, wealth, her love and beauty. He grew not a little wild in thinking of it all. Once he and she were married, what could Sondra's relatives do? What, but **acquiesce**[7] and take them into the glorious bosom of their **resplendent**[8] home at Lycurgus or provide for them in some other way—he to no doubt eventually take some place in connection with the Finchley Electric Sweeper Company. And then would he not be the equal, if not the superior, of Gilbert Griffiths himself and all those others who originally had ignored him here—joint heir with Stuart to all the Finchley means. And with Sondra as the central or crowning jewel to so much sudden and such Aladdin-like **splendor**[9].

No thought as to how he was to overcome the time between now and October. No serious consideration of the fact that Roberta then and there was demanding that he marry her. He could put her off, he thought. And yet, at the same time, he was painfully and nervously conscious of the fact that at no period in his life before had he been so treacherously poised at the very **brink**[10] of disaster. It might be his duty as the world would see it—his mother would say so—to at least extricate Roberta. But in the case of Esta, who had come to her rescue? Her lover? He had walked off from her without a qualm and she had not died. And why, when Roberta was no worse off than his sister had been, why should she seek to destroy him in this way? Force him to do something which would be little less than social, artistic, passional or emotional **assassination**[11]? And when later, if she would but spare him for this, he could do so much more for her—with Sondra's money of course. He could not and would not let her do this to him. His life would be ruined!

这种想法对于克莱德来说就像是某种甜蜜却又扰乱心绪的毒药。它让他发狂了，差一点就背叛了自己的灵魂。要是——要是——现在没有罗伯塔的问题——一个可怕的、无法解决的问题。但是，要是没有这个问题，没有桑德拉父母的反对（这个难题她认为自己能够克服），等待他的难道不是天堂吗？桑德拉、第十二号湖、上流社会、财富、她的爱情和美丽。想到这所有一切他就变得异常狂热起来。一旦他们结婚了，桑德拉的亲戚们又能怎样呢？只能是默许了，让他们住在他们在莱克格斯光荣显赫的家里或者以其他方式供养他们——毫无疑问，他最后会进芬赤利电器吸尘器公司做事。然后，就算他不是吉尔伯特·格里菲斯和这里起初轻视他的那些人的上级，也不会是和他们一样的身份了——他跟斯图尔特是芬赤利全部财产的继承人。并且，桑德拉的出现，对他而言无异于一颗骤然出现的闪耀着阿拉丁般光彩的加冕宝石。

他没有去思考该如何熬过从现在到十月份的这一段时间，也没有认真考虑罗伯塔当时向他提出的结婚要求。他想，自己还可以再拖一拖。可同时，他苦恼又提心吊胆地意识到，在他一生之中还从来没有像现在这样：危险地悬在灾难的边缘。在世人看来，而且他母亲也会这样认为；他至少有责任把罗伯塔解救出来。但拿爱斯塔这事来说吧，谁来拯救她了吗？她的情人？他决绝地离开了她，她也还没死吧。而罗伯塔的情形并不比他的妹妹糟糕，她为什么要用这种方式来毁灭他呢？为什么要强迫他做一些无异于谋杀他的社会地位、艺术感、热情和情感的事情呢？而如果她放过他，之后他可以为她做更多事——当然是用桑德拉的钱。他不能也不会让她得逞。不然，他的生活就毁了！

——选自《美国的悲剧》第2卷第39章

注释

① amoral [ei'mɔrəl] *adj.* 无道德感的

② censorship ['sensəʃɪp] *n.* 审查制度

③ bellboy ['bel,bɔi] *n.* 男侍者

④ seduce [sɪ'dju:s] *vt.* 引诱，诱奸
⑤ aristocracy [ˌærɪ'stɔkrəsɪ] *n.* 贵族
⑥ disarranging [ˌdɪsə'reindʒɪŋ] *adj.* 紊乱的
⑦ acquiesce [ˌækwi'es] *vt.* 默许，勉强同意
⑧ resplendent [rɪ'splendənt] *adj.* 辉煌的，华丽灿烂的
⑨ splendor ['splendə(r)] *n.* 华丽
⑩ brink [brɪŋk] *n.* 边缘
⑪ assassination [əˌsæsɪ'neiʃən] *n.* 暗杀

《嘉莉妹妹》*完成于1900年，共50章，是德莱塞创作的第一部小说，也是美国文学史上最著名的作品之一。目前国内最普遍的是潘庆舲译本和王克非译本。

Sister Carrie
嘉莉妹妹

A man's fortune or material progress is very much the same as his bodily growth. Either he is growing stronger, healthier, wiser, as the youth approaching manhood, or he is growing weaker, older, less incisive mentally, as the man approaching old age.

一个人的财富或者物质上的发展好比他身体的发育一样。要么像青少年过渡到成年时期那样，变得更加强壮，更加健康，更加聪明；要么像壮年迈入老年时期那样，变得更加虚弱，更加衰老，头脑也会更加迟钝。

——*Sister Carrie*《嘉莉妹妹》

名著导读

Sister Carrie tells the story of two characters: Carrie Meeber, an ordinary girl who rises from a low-paid wage earner to a high-paid actress, and George Hurstwood, a member of the upper middle class who falls from his comfortable lifestyle to a life on the streets. Neither Carrie nor Hurstwood earn their fates through virtue or vice, but rather through random circumstance. Their successes and failures have no moral value.

《嘉莉妹妹》讲的是两个人物的故事：嘉莉·米贝是一个平凡的女孩，她从一个低薪打工妹变成了一个高收入的女演员；乔治·赫斯渥是中上层阶级的一员，他最初生活安逸，后来却沦落街头。嘉莉和赫斯渥都不是通过美德或恶行获得他们的命运的，而是随波逐流。他们的成功和失败都没有道德价值。

名段选读

During all this time—a period rapidly approaching three years—Hurstwood had been moving along in an even path. There was no apparent slope downward, and distinctly none upward, so far as the casual observer might have seen. But psychologically there was a change, which was marked enough to suggest the future very distinctly indeed. This was in the mere matter of the halt his career had received when he departed from Chicago. A man's fortune or material progress is very much the same as his bodily growth. Either he is growing stronger, healthier, wiser, as the youth approaching manhood, or he is growing weaker, older, less incisive mentally, as the man approaching old age. There are no other states. Frequently there is a period between the **cessation**① of youthful **accretion**② and the setting in, in the case of the middle-aged man, of the tendency toward decay when the two processes are almost perfectly balanced and there is little doing in either direction. Given time enough, however, the balance becomes a **sagging**③ to the grave side. Slowly at first, then with a modest momentum, and at last the graveward process is in the full swing. So it is frequently with man's fortune. If its process of accretion is never halted, if the balancing stage is never reached, there will be no toppling. Rich men are, frequently, in these days, saved from this dissolution of their fortune by their ability to hire younger brains. These younger brains look upon the interests of the fortune as their own, and so steady and direct its progress. If each individual were left absolutely to the care of his own interests, and were given time enough in which to grow exceedingly old, his fortune would pass as his strength and will. He and his would be utterly dissolved and scattered unto the four winds of the heavens.

在这段时间里——很快就三年了——赫斯渥一直路途平坦。迄今为止，正如一般的旁观者看到的那样，他没有明显的大起大落。但是他的心理上产生了一些变化，而这确实足够清楚地暗示了他的未来。这个变化仅仅是因为他离开芝加哥导致了事业的停滞。一个人的财富或者物质上的发展就好比他身体的发育一样。要么像青少年过渡到成年时期那样，变得更加强壮，更加健康，更加聪明；要么像壮年迈入老年时期那样，变得更加虚弱，更加衰老，头脑也会更加迟钝。除此之外就没有其他的情况了。对中年人来说，通常在青年期成长停顿之后和开始出现衰退迹象之前存在着一个时期，在这一时期中两个进程达到完美的平衡，两个都无增减。然而，经过足够长的时间后，这个平衡就会向境况黯淡的那头倾斜。起初很缓慢，然后适当地加速，最后，就全速向黯淡行进了。人的财富通常也都是这样。如果财富的增长过程从没停顿过，如果它从没达到过之前所说的平衡状态，那么也就不会有财富的衰退。通常，在这段时期，有钱人可以通过雇佣年轻的人才，从而将自己从财产的瓦解中解救出来。这些年轻的人才把财产收益看成是自己的收益，所以财富的增长是稳定而直接的。如果每一个人都完全依靠自己的力量来管理自身收益，那么等到他老态龙钟的时候，他的财富就会像他的力气和意志一样消逝。他和他的财富将会全部消散，散落到四面八方。

——选自《嘉莉妹妹》第47章

注释

★“在《嘉莉妹妹》中，德莱塞像巴尔扎克、托尔斯泰一样，创造了一个真实的世界，场面壮阔，构思宏伟，其中的人物各具面貌，真实可信。”

——（美）亚历山大·克恩

① cessation [se'seiʃən] *n.* 停止

② accretion [ə'kriːʃən] *n.* 增长，积聚

③ sagging [sæɡiŋ] *n.* 倾斜

《金融家》出版于1947年，是德莱塞著名的长篇小说《欲望三部曲》中的第1部。目前国内最普遍的是许汝祉的译本和裘柱常的译本。

The Financier
金融家

A real man—a financier—was never a tool. He used tools. He created. He led.

一个真正的男人——一个金融家——决不能是一个工具。他是工具的使用者、创造者和领导者。

——*The Financier*《金融家》

名著导读

In Philadelphia, Frank Cowperwood, whose father is a banker, makes his first money by buying cheap soaps on the market and selling it back with profit to a grocer. Later, he gets a job in Henry Waterman & Company, and leaves it for Tighe & Company. He also marries an affluent widow, in spite of his young age. Things begin to crumble when he falls in love with, Aileen Butler, the daughter of a politically prominent Irish industrialist. They have an affair, which is discovered just when Cowperwood's business is under great duress as a result of a financial panic caused by the great Chicago fire. Pressed to cover large loans, Cowperwood engages in some legally questionable acts. Cowperwood is put on trial for larceny. He is convicted and sent to prison, but pardoned after a year. He then proceeds to recoup his fortune, eventually leaving

Philadelphia with Aileen for the greater promise of the west.

故事发生在费城，法兰克•柯帕乌是一个银行家的儿子。他在集市上买了一些廉价的肥皂，然后加价转卖给了杂货店，以此赚到了他人生的第一桶金。后来，他在亨利•华脱曼公司工作，之后又离开去了泰依公司。他还和一位有钱的寡妇结了婚，尽管他很年轻。当他爱上了艾琳•巴德勒——一个在政界很知名的企业家的女儿——之后，事情开始变得糟糕起来。在因芝加哥大火产生的金融恐慌影响下，柯帕乌的公司受到了严重的压制，而此时，他和艾琳私通的事被人发现。为了偿还巨额的贷款，柯帕乌参与了一些违法行为。他因盗窃罪被起诉并被判入狱，但一年之后被赦出狱。之后，他开始着手重新获得自己的财富，最终，他和艾琳离开了费城，去西部追寻更远大的前程。

名段选读

Yet in time he also asked himself, who was it who made the real money—the stock-brokers? Not at all. Some of them were making money, but they were, as he quickly saw, like a lot of **gulls**[①] or stormy petrels, hanging on the **lee**[②] of the wind, hungry and anxious to snap up any unwary fish. Back of them were other men, men with **shrewd**[③] ideas, subtle resources. Men of immense means whose enterprise and holdings these stocks represented, the men who **schemed**[④] out and built the railroads, opened the mines, organized trading enterprises, and built up immense manufactories. They might use brokers or other agents to buy and sell on change; but this buying and selling must be, and always was, **incidental**[⑤] to the actual fact—the mine, the railroad, the wheat crop, the flour mill, and so on. Anything less than straight-out sales to realize quickly on assets, or buying to hold as an investment, was gambling pure and simple, and these men were gamblers. He was nothing more than a gambler's agent. It was not troubling him any just at this moment, but it was not at all a mystery now, what he was. As in the case of Waterman & Company, he sized up these men shrewdly, judging some to be weak, some foolish, some clever, some slow, but in the main all small-minded or deficient because they were agents, tools, or gamblers. A man, a real man, must never be an agent, a tool, or a gambler—acting for himself or for others—he must employ such. A real man—a financier—was never a tool. He used tools. He created. He led.

Clearly, very clearly, at nineteen, twenty, and twenty-one years of age, he saw all this, but he was not quite ready yet to do anything about it. He was certain, however, that his day would come.

但是他及时地反问自己，谁才真正赚了钱——股票经纪人？不完全是。他们有一部分人的确赚钱了，但是他很快发现，他们就像是暴风雨中一群依靠风的庇护的海鸥和海燕，饥饿而渴望地争抢任何疏忽大意的鱼。他们背后另有其人，那是一群有着聪明头脑和巨大财力的人。那些人有通天的手段，这些股票代表的是他们自己的公司和持有的所有股份，他们设计并建造铁路、开办矿场、组建贸易公司、建立大型工厂。他们可能利用经纪人或其他代理人根据市场变化进行买和卖；但这些买卖必须总是附属于实际资产的——矿产、铁路、小麦作物、面粉厂等等。除了旨在变现资产的坦诚销售和将股票作为投资的买入之外的任何买卖行为都是纯粹的赌博，而这些人都是赌徒。而他自己只不过是一个赌徒的代理人罢了。在这个时刻，这些想法已经不会对他造成任何困扰了，他的身份也不再是神秘的事了。他会精明地揣摩华脱曼公司的那些人，去判断哪些人脆弱，哪些人愚蠢，哪些人聪明，哪些人迟钝，但基本上那都是心胸狭窄或有缺点的人，因为他们是代理人，是工具，或是赌徒。一个男人，一个真正的男人决不能是一个代理人、一个工具或是一个赌徒——不管他是为自己还是为别人工作——他必须利用这些代理人、工具和赌徒。一个真正的男人——一个金融家——决不能是一个工具。他得是工具的使用者、创造者和领导者。

当他十九岁、二十岁、二十一岁的时候，便清楚地明白了这点，非常清楚，但是他还没有完全准备好去做些什么。然而，他确信，属于他的那天终会到来。

——选自《金融家》第6章

注释

① gull [gʌl] *n.* 海鸥

② lee [liː] *n.* 保护，背风处

③ shrewd [ʃruːd] *adj.* 精明的，聪明的

④ scheme [skiːm] *vi.* 计划，策划

⑤ incidental [ˌɪnsɪˈdentl] *adj.* 附带发生的，伴随而来的

2 美利坚民族的精神丰碑——欧内斯特·米勒·海明威

Ernest Miller Hemingway (July 21, 1899—July 2, 1961) was an American novelist, short-story writer and journalist. His distinctive writing style, characterized by economy and understatement, influenced 20th-century fiction, as did his life of adventure and public image. He won Pulitzer Prize for Fiction in 1953 and the Nobel Prize in Literature in 1954. Many of his works are classics of American literature, such as *The Sun Also Rises, A Farewell to Arms, For Whom the Bell Tolls, The Old Man and the Sea, True at First Light. The Old Man and the Sea* was one of his most famous works and the last major work of fiction to be produced by Hemingway and published in his lifetime.

欧内斯特·米勒·海明威（1899年7月21日—1961年7月2日）是一位美国小说家、短篇小说家和新闻记者。他的作品简洁含蓄，文风独特，其语言风格以及他一生的冒险经历和公众形象对20世纪的小说界产生了重大影响。1953年，他获得普利策小说奖；1954年，他获得诺贝尔文学奖。他的许多作品都成为美国文学中的经典，比如《太阳照常升起》、《永别了，武器》、《丧钟为谁而鸣》、《老人与海》和《曙光示真》。其中，《老人与海》是他最著名的作品之一，也是海明威一生中创作和发表的最后一部主要作品。

《老人与海》*发表于1952年，共30章。大海和鲨鱼象征着与人作对的社会与自然力量，而老人在与之进行的殊死搏斗中，表现了无与伦比的力量和勇气，不失人的尊严，虽败犹荣，精神上并没有被打败。目前国内最好的译本是余光中的译本。

The Old Man and the Sea
老人与海

"But man is not made for defeat," he said. "A man can be destroyed but not defeated."

"但是人不是为了失败而生，"他说。"一个人可以被摧毁但不可以被打败。"

——*The Old Man and the Sea*《老人与海》

名著导读

The Old Man and the Sea recounts an epic battle of wills between an old, an aging experienced Cuban fisherman, Santiago, and a giant marlin far out in the Gulf Stream said to be the largest catch of his life. Santiago spends three days fighting a giant marlin before he catches it. Despite his noble victory, by the time Santiago drags the fish back to his village, sharks have eaten the entire fish, leaving only the skeleton.

《老人与海》讲述的是一位年迈而又经验丰富的古巴渔夫圣地亚哥与一条巨大的枪鱼在离岸很远的墨西哥湾流进行了一场惊心动魄的意志之战，据说这条鱼是他有生以来捕获的最大的一条。圣地亚哥与这条巨大的枪鱼连续搏斗了三天才捕捉到它。虽然他赢得了巨大的胜利，但当圣地亚哥把这条鱼拖回村子时，整条鱼都已经被鲨鱼吃了，只留了下一副鱼骨架。

名段选读

"But man is not made for defeat," he said. "A man can be destroyed but not defeated." I am sorry that I killed the fish though, he thought. Now the bad time is coming and I do not even have the harpoon. The dentuso is cruel and able and strong and intelligent. But I was more intelligent than he was. Perhaps not, he thought. Perhaps I was only better armed.

"Don't think, old man," he said aloud. "Sail on this course and take it when it comes."

But I must think, he thought. Because it is all I have left. That and baseball. I wonder how the great DiMaggio would have liked the way I hit him in the brain? It was no great thing, he thought. Any man could do it. But do you think my hands were as great a **handicap**① as the bone spurs? I cannot know. I never had anything wrong with my heel except the time the sting ray stung it when I stepped on him when swimming and **paralyzed**② the lower leg and made the **unbearable**③ pain.

"Think about something cheerful, old man," he said. "Every minute now you are closer to home. You sail lighter for the loss of forty pounds."

He knew quite well the pattern of what could happen when he reached the inner part of the current. But there was nothing to be done now.

"Yes there is," he said aloud. "I can lash my knife to the **butt**④ of one of the oars."

So he did that with the tiller under his arm and the sheet of the sail under his foot.

"Now," he said, "I am still an old man. But I am not unarmed."

"但是人不是为了失败而生，"他说。"一个人可以被摧毁但不可以被打败。"虽然我很遗憾杀死了这条鱼，他心想。现在倒霉的时候到了，而我甚至连鱼叉都没有。尖吻鲭鲨既凶残又能干，而且强壮聪明，但是我比他更聪明。也许不是，他心想，也许只是我的装备更好。

“别再想了，老头儿，”他大声叫道。“沿着这条路线航行，碰到什么再想办法对付吧。”

但我必须得好好想想，他思索着。因为我只剩下这个了，这个和棒球。我想知道伟大的迪马乔觉得我打中他头部的方式如何呢？他想，这也不是什么大不了的事。任何人都可能做到。但是你认为我的双手是如骨刺那般的大障碍吗？我无从知晓。我的脚跟从来没有出过任何问题，除了有一次我在游泳时踩到一条鳐鱼，被它刺了一下脚跟，我的小腿感到一阵麻痹并且疼痛难忍。

“想想高兴的事吧，老头儿，”他说。“现在每过一分钟你就离家更近。因为少了四十磅的重量，所以你航行得更轻快。”

他非常明白当他到达漩涡内时将会发生什么事。

但是现在却什么都不能做。

“对了，”他大声说。“我可以把我的刀和其中一只船桨绑在一起。”

于是他腋下夹着舵柄、脚踩着船帆便照做了。

“现在，”他说，“我仍然是一个老头儿。但是我不再手无寸铁了。”

——选自《老人与海》第18章

注释

★“这个朴素的故事里充满了并非故意卖弄的寓意……作为一篇干净利落的陈述性散文，它在海明威的全部作品中都是无与伦比的。每一个词都有它的作用，没有一个词是多余的。”

——英国当代著名小说家、评论家　安东尼·伯吉斯

① handicap ['hændɪkæp] *n.* 障碍

② paralyze ['pærəlaiz] *vt.* 使麻痹

③ unbearable [ʌn'beərəbl] *adj.* 无法忍受的

④ butt [bʌt] *n.* 较粗的一端

《太阳照常升起》★发表于1926年，共19章，成功地塑造了一战后生活在巴黎的“迷惘的一代”的人物形象。目前国内最好的译本是冯涛的译本。

The Sun Also Rises
太阳照常升起

Enjoying living was learning to get your money's worth and knowing when you had it.

享受生活就是学会让你的钱花得值并且懂得何时花才划算。

——*The Sun Also Rises*《太阳照常升起》

名著导读

The narrator of The Sun Also Rises is Jake Barnes, an expatriate journalist in his mid-twenties who lives in Paris. Barnes is impotent because of a war wound, though the nature of his wound is never explicitly described. He loves Lady Brett Ashley, a twice-divorced Englishwoman in her thirties who gained a title from her most recent marriage. Brett wears her hair short and embodies the new sexual freedom of the 1920s, having had numerous love affairs.

《太阳照常升起》的讲述者是杰克·巴恩斯，他是一名二十多岁就移居巴黎的外籍记者。他因为战争创伤失去了性能力，虽然小说中从来都明确地描述是什么性质的创伤。他深爱着布莱特·阿什利夫人——一位三十多岁、离过两次婚的英国女人，这个头衔是从她最近的一次婚姻中所获得的。布莱特夫人留一头短发，这象征着20世纪20年代新兴的性解放和性自由，在她身上的确有不少情爱纠葛。

名段选读

Women made such **swell**① friends. Awfully swell. In the first place, you had to be in love with a woman to have a basis of friendship. I had been having Brett for a friend. I had not been thinking about her side of it. I had been getting something for nothing. That only delayed the presentation of the bill. The bill always came. That was one of the swell things you could count on.

I thought I had paid for everything. Not like the woman pays and pays and pays. No idea of **retribution**② or punishment. Just exchange of values. You gave up something and got something else. Or you worked for something. You paid some way for everything that was any good. I paid my way into enough things that I liked, so that I had a good time. Either you paid by learning about them, or by experience, or by taking chances, or by money. Enjoying living was learning to get your money's worth and knowing when you had it. You could get your money's worth. The world was a good place to buy in. It seemed like a fine **philosophy**③. In five years, I thought, it will seem just as silly as all the other fine philosophies I've had.

Perhaps that wasn't true, though. Perhaps as you went along you did learn something. I did not care what it was all about. All I wanted to know was how to live in it. Maybe if you found out how to live in it you learned from that what it was all about.

女人可以是很棒的朋友。特别棒。要和一个女人建立友谊，你首先必须得爱上她。我曾经和布莱特是朋友关系，但我没有站在她的立场去考虑问题。我并没有付出，但却得到了一些回报。而那只不过是推迟了账单的出现时间，账单总是会来的。那是你能够指望的好事之一。

我认为我已经为这所有的一切付出了代价，不是像女人那样一味地付出，也丝毫不觉得这是报答或惩罚，仅仅只是价值交换罢了。有失必有得。或者你努力追求某些东西，你会为所有有益于自己的东西付出某种方式的代价。我以自己的方式来为我喜欢的东西付出，所以我很快乐。你的付出方式可以是你对你所钟爱的东西的了解，也可以是经验、冒险和金钱。享受生活就是学会让你的钱花得值并且懂得何时花才划算。你能够让你的钱花得有价值。因为这个世界是一个买东西的好地方。这看起来似乎是一种很不错的哲理。但是我想，五年后，它将会变得和我曾经有过的所有其他哲理一样愚蠢可笑。

但是或许那也不正确。也许当你继续走下去，你真的会有所领悟。我不在乎它的具体内容是什么，我只想知道该如何在其中生活。可能如果你发现了如何在其间生活，你就会从中知晓它到底是怎么回事了。

——选自《太阳照常升起》第14章

注释

★“你们都是迷惘的一代。”

——美国先锋派作家　格特鲁德·斯坦因

① swell [swel] *adj.* 很棒的

② retribution [ˌretrɪ'bjuːʃən] *n.* 报答

③ philosophy [fə'lɔsəfɪ] *n.* 哲理，哲学

《丧钟为谁而鸣》发表于1940年，共43章，凭借其深沉的人道主义力量感动了一代又一代人。目前国内最流行的译本是程中瑞的译本。

For Whom the Bell Tolls
丧钟为谁而鸣

There will always be people who say it does not exist because they cannot have it. But I tell you it is true and that you have it and that you are lucky even if you die tomorrow.

总有人说爱情是不存在的，因为他们无法拥有爱情。可是我要告诉你，爱情确实存在，当你拥有爱情，即使明天就会死去你也是幸运的。

——*For Whom the Bell Tolls*《丧钟为谁而鸣》

名著导读

For Whom the Bell Tolls tells the story of Robert Jordan, a young American in the

International Brigades attached to a republican **guerilla**① unit during the Spanish Civil War. As an expert in the use of explosives, he is assigned to blow up a bridge during an attack on the city of Segovia. Jordan dynamites the bridge but he is hit by a shell and is unable to escape. He fights pain and suicidal thoughts with the hope that he can buy time for the fleeing guerillas. The novel closes here, as Jordan awaits his certain death on the pine-covered ground he appeared on in the first scene.

《丧钟为谁而鸣》讲的是一位年轻的美国人罗伯特·乔丹的故事，在西班牙内战期间，他隶属于共和国游击队的国际纵队。作为一名爆破专家，在攻击塞哥维亚城时，他被派往炸毁一座大桥。乔丹完成了任务，但他被炮弹壳击中而没能脱身。他在自杀的念头与心中的希望之间做着痛苦的挣扎与斗争，他的希望是能为正在撤退的游击队争取时间。最后，乔丹躺在小说第一幕出现过的覆满松针的地面上，等待着他必然将至的死亡。

名段选读

Even if there isn't supposed to be any such thing as love in a purely **materialistic**② conception of society?

Since when did you ever have any such conception? Himself asked. Never. And you never could have. You're not a real Marxist and you know it. You believe in Liberty, Equality and **Fraternity**③. You believe in Life, Liberty and the Pursuit of Happiness. Don't ever kid yourself with too much **dialectics**④. They are for some but not for you. You have to know them in order not to be a sucker. You have put many things in abeyance to win a war. If this war is lost all of those things are lost.

But afterwards you can discard what you do not believe in. There is plenty you do not believe in and plenty that you do believe in.

And another thing. Don't ever kid yourself about loving some one. It is just that most people are not lucky enough ever to have it. You never had it before and now you have it. What you have with Maria, whether it lasts just through today and a part of tomorrow, or whether it lasts for a long life is the most important thing that can happen to a human being. There will always be people who say it does not exist because they cannot have it. But I tell you it is true and that you have it and that you are lucky even if you die tomorrow.

难道在社会纯粹的唯物主义观念里，就不该有爱情这回事吗？

你是从什么时候开始有这种观念的？他问自己。从来没有，并且你永远也不可能会有。你不是真正的马克思主义者，你知道的。你信仰自由、平等和博爱。你信仰生活、自由、追求幸福。永远不要拿过多的辩证法来戏弄自己。它们对某些人有用，但对你却不行。你不得不学习辩证只是为了不当一个傻瓜。为了赢得这场战争，你已经把很多事情都先搁置一旁了。如果这场战争失利，你就会失去一切。

但是以后你可以抛弃那些你不相信的东西。这个世界上有很多东西是你不信仰的，但也有很多东西是你信仰的。

还有一件事情。永远别拿爱上某人来跟你自己开玩笑。因为大多数人都不足以幸运到拥有爱情。之前你从不曾拥有而现在你拥有了。你和玛利亚的爱情，不管是只能持续到今天或明天的某个时候，还是会持续长久的一生，这都是发生在人类身上最重要的事情。总有人说爱情是不存在的，因为他们无法拥有爱情。可是我要告诉你，爱情确实存在，当你拥有爱情，即使明天就会死去你也是幸运的。

——选自《丧钟为谁而鸣》第26章

注释

① guerilla [gə'rɪlə] *n.* 游击队

② materialistic [məˌtɪəriə'lɪstɪk] *adj.* 贪图享乐的

③ fraternity [frə'tɜːnətɪ] *n.* 博爱

④ dialectic [ˌdaiə'lektɪk] *n.* 辩证法

3 近代幽默文学的泰斗——马克·吐温

Mark Twain (November 30, 1835—April 21, 1910) was an American author and humorist. He is noted for his novels *Adventures of Huckleberry Finn* (1885), called "the Great American Novel", and *The Adventures of Tom Sawyer* (1876). Twain was popular, and his wit and satire earned praise from critics and peers. Upon his death he was lauded as the "greatest American humorist of his age", and William Faulkner called Twain "the father of American literature".

马克·吐温（1835年11月30日—1910年4月21日），美国作家和幽默大师。因小说《哈克贝里·费恩历险记》（1885）和《汤姆·索亚历险记》（1876）而成名，前者被誉为"伟大的美式小说"。吐温很受欢迎，他的机智风趣和讽刺风格赢得了批评家和同龄人的赞赏。去世后，他被世人称赞为"他那一时期最伟大的美国幽默大师"，威廉·福克纳称他为"美国文学之父"。

《哈克贝里·费恩历险记》*发表于1885年，共43章。作者讴歌一个卑贱的黑奴的优秀品质，正是对种族主义者的"白人优越论"的严正批判，对种族歧视、美化蓄奴制的"文明"社会的公开挑战，在哈克和吉姆这两个人物身上闪耀着作者人道主义思想和民主思想的光辉。国内比较著名的译本是张万里的译本。

Adventures of Huckleberry Finn
哈克贝里·费恩历险记

The average man don't like trouble and danger.

一般人都不爱惹麻烦，做危险的事。

——*Adventures of Huckleberry Finn*《哈克贝里·费恩历险记》

名著导读

Adventures of Huckleberry Finn tells the story of a teenaged misfit who finds himself floating on a raft down the Mississippi River with an escaping slave, Jim. In the course of their perilous journey, Huck and Jim meet adventure, danger, and a cast of characters who are sometimes menacing and often hilarious.

《哈克贝里·费恩历险记》讲的是一个不愿接受教化的少年和一个逃亡的黑奴——吉姆，乘着竹筏顺着密西西比河顺流而下，在他们危机重重的旅途中，哈克和吉姆了遭遇各种危险，还遇到了许多或凶恶或搞笑的人物。

名段选读

"Do I know you? I know you clear through was born and raised in the South, and I've lived in the North; so I know the average all around. The average man's a coward. In the North he lets anybody walk over him that wants to, and goes home and prays for a humble spirit to bear it. In the South one man all by himself, has stopped a stage full of men in the daytime, and robbed the lot. Your newspapers call you a brave people so much that you think you are braver than any other people—whereas you're just AS brave, and no braver. Why don't your juries hang murderers? Because they're afraid the man's friends will shoot them in the back, in the dark—and it's just what they WOULD do."

"So they always **acquit**①; and then a MAN goes in the night, with a hundred masked cowards at his back and **lynches**② the **rascal**③. Your mistake is, that you didn't bring a man with you; that's one mistake, and the other is that you didn't come in the dark and fetch your masks. You brought PART of a man—Buck Harkness, there—and if you hadn't had him to start you, you'd a taken it out in blowing."

"You didn't want to come. The average man don't like trouble and danger. YOU don't like trouble and danger. But if only HALF a man—like Buck Harkness, there—shouts 'Lynch him! lynch him!' you're afraid to back down—afraid you'll be found out to be what you are—COWARDS—and so you raise a yell, and hang yourselves on to that half-a-man's coat-tail, and come raging up here, swearing what big things you're going to do. The **pitifulest**④ thing out is a mob; that's what an army is—a mob; they don't fight with courage that's born in them, but with courage that's borrowed from their mass, and from their officers. But a mob without any MAN at the head of it is BENEATH pitifulness. Now the thing for YOU to do is to droop your tails and go home and crawl in a hole. If any real lynching's going to be done it will be done in the dark, Southern fashion; and when they come they'll bring their masks, and fetch a MAN along. Now LEAVE—and take your half-a-man with you"—**tossing**⑤ his gun up across his left arm and **cocking**⑥ it when he says this.

“我认识你吗？我在南方出生和长大的时候就清楚地了解你了，而我又在北方生活过；所以我了解各个地方一般人的情况。一般人都是胆小鬼。在北方，大家会随意地让别人践踏自己，然后回到家，祈祷自己卑微的灵魂可以忍受这一切。在南方，如果一个人在光天化日之下拦下一辆装满人的马车，然后进行抢劫，报纸就会夸你为勇士，以至于你真的就认为自己比其他任何人都勇敢——然而你只是和他们一样，并不是更加勇敢。为什么陪审团不处死杀人犯呢？因为他们害怕这个人的朋友会在暗地里从背后向他们开枪——而这也正是他们会做的事情。”

“所以他们总是无罪释放；然后在一个夜晚，一个男人走出来，身后跟着上百个戴着面具的胆小鬼，将恶棍‘就地正法’了。你错在没有带一个男人；这是一个失误，而另一个失误就是你不是在晚上来，而且没有戴面具。你带了半个男人——在那边的巴克·哈克尼斯——如果不是他让你来，你早就飞快地逃走了。”

“你不想来。一般人都不爱惹麻烦，做危险的事，你也不例外。但要是半个男人——像那边的巴克·哈克尼斯一样——大喊‘处死他！处死他！’你恐怕就不敢后退了——害怕别人会发现你是个——胆小鬼——所以你也高声叫喊起来，躲在半个男人的身后猖狂起来，发誓自己要准备干一件大事。最可怜的事就是围攻；这就是军队的作风——一群暴徒；他们打仗靠的不是自己与生俱来的胆量，而是狐假虎威，依仗整体和长官们的力量。但是对于一群暴徒来说，如果他的前面没有先锋坐镇，那么他就会显得更加可怜。现在你要做的事情就是夹起尾巴回家，钻进洞里躲起来。如果真的要动用私刑，那也会是在晚上，这是南方的习俗；而且他们来的时候会戴着面具，还得带上一个男人来。现在，带着你的半个男人——走开。”他一边说，一边从左臂上方抡起他的枪，并扳起扳机。

——选自《哈克贝里·费恩历险记》第22章

注释

★“《哈克贝利·费恩历险记》是我们的文学的最佳典范，所有的美国作品都源于此，可以说是前无古人，后无来者。”

——美国著名小说家　海明威

① acquit [ə'kwɪt] *vt.* 宣判……无罪

② lynch [lɪntʃ] *vt.* 用私刑处死

③ rascal ['rɑːskl] *n.* 流氓，无赖

④ pitiful ['pɪtɪfl] *adj.* 可怜的

⑤ toss [tɔs] *vi.* 扔，掷

⑥ cock [kɔk] *vt.* 扣，扳

《汤姆·索亚历险记》*共35章，发表于1876年。小说通过主人公的冒险经历，对美国虚伪庸俗的社会习俗、伪善的宗教仪式和刻板陈腐的学校教育进行了讽刺和批判，以欢快的笔调描写了少年儿童自由活泼的心灵。海豚出版社张志利的译本比较完整。

The Adventures of Tom Sawyer
汤姆·索亚历险记

Men's misfortunes are forgotten in the excitement of new enterprises.

在新动力的不断刺激下，人们就会忘掉眼前的不快。

——*The Adventures of Tom Sawyer*《汤姆·索亚历险记》

名著导读

The Adventures of Tom Sawyer is about a young boy growing up in a small town along the Mississippi River. Tom Sawyer's bold spirit, winsome smile, and inventive solutions to the problems of everyday life in fictional St Petersburg—whether getting his friends to whitewash a fence for him, or escaping the demands of his vigilant Aunt Polly—have won him the hearts of generations.

《汤姆·索亚历险记》讲的是一个在密西西比河流域的一个小镇里长大的小伙子的故事。不管是要求朋友帮忙粉刷围墙，还是摆脱他城府极深的姨母波莉的使唤，在作者虚构的圣彼得堡里，汤姆·索亚勇敢的精神、迷人的微笑和解决生活中琐碎问题的谋略让他赢得了几代人的心。

名段选读

He was not the Model Boy of the village. He knew the model boy very well though—and loathed[①] him.

Within two minutes, or even less, he had forgotten all his troubles. Not because his troubles were one whit less heavy and bitter to him than a man's are to a man, but because a new and powerful interest bore them down and drove them out of his mind for the time—just as men's misfortunes are forgotten in the excitement of new enterprises. This new interest was a valued novelty in whistling, which he had just acquired from a negro, and he was suffering to practise it undisturbed. It consisted in a peculiar bird-like turn, a sort of liquid warble, produced by touching the tongue to the roof of the mouth at short intervals in the midst of the music—the reader probably remembers how to do it, if he has ever been a boy. Diligence and attention soon gave him the knack of it, and he strode down the street with his mouth full of harmony and his soul full of gratitude. He felt much as an astronomer feels who has discovered a new planet—no doubt, as far as strong, deep, unalloyed② pleasure is concerned, the advantage was with the boy, not the astronomer.

他并不是这个村子里的模范男孩，虽然他非常了解那个模范男孩，——而且讨厌他。

在两分钟内，或者更短的时间里，他就已经忘记了他所有的烦恼。不是因为他的烦恼与一般人相比显得无足轻重，或者没有那么苦涩，而是因为当时，一股新生的、强烈的热情把它们给了压下去，并且把它们从他的头脑中驱逐了出去——就好比在新动力的不断刺激下，人们就会忘掉眼前的不快。这股新热情就是一种珍贵新颖的口哨吹法，这是他从一个黑人那里学到的，他在那里安静地练习着吹口哨。哨声中有鸟儿般婉转的曲调，有潺潺流水似的声音，他吹着口哨，不时用舌头接触上腭，就会发出这些声音——如果读者也曾是个毛头小孩的话，那么也应该知道怎么吹。通过专心致志地观察，他很快就抓住了诀窍，然后他大步地走在街上，嘴里吹着调子，心里充满着感激。他感觉自己就像是一位发现了新天体的天文学家——毫无疑问的是，就强烈、浓厚、纯粹的程度而言，小男孩的喜悦无疑比天文学家更胜一筹。

——选自《汤姆·亚历险记》第1章

注释

★“《汤姆·索亚历险记》有诚挚的真情：它描写的事件和感情从不虚假，且既恰到好处又完美和谐。”

——20世纪美国著名批评家　莱昂内尔·特里林

① loathe [ləʊð] *vt.* 厌恶

② unalloyed [ˌʌnəˈlɔid] *adj.* 纯粹的

《王子与贫儿》共30章，发表于1882年，描写一个贫苦儿童汤姆和一个富贵王子爱德华交换社会地位的童话故事。小说虽然取材于16世纪的英国，但其批评的矛头是指向19世纪的美国。国内流行的译本是辛红娟的译本。

The Prince and the Pauper
王子与贫儿

When I am king, they shall not have bread and shelter only, but also teachings out of books; for a full belly is little worth where the mind is starved, and the heart.

等我当上了国王，他们将不仅有吃有住，还能接受到一些教育学习知识；因为如果一个人没有思想、没有良心，那么他就算吃得再饱也没有意义。

——*The Prince and the Pauper*《王子与贫儿》

名著导读

The novel tells the story of two young boys who are identical in appearance: Tom Canty, a pauper who lives with his abusive father in Offal Court off Pudding Lane in London, and Edward VI of England, son of Henry VIII of England. One day they meet and as a jest, switch clothes. However, the boys look remarkably alike and because they switch clothes, the palace guards throw the prince out into the street. Edward runs into Tom's family and a gang of thieves and Twain illustrates England's unfair and barbaric justice system. After the death of Henry VIII, Edward interrupts Tom's coronation and switch places, and Edward is crowned King of England.

小说讲的是两个长得一模一样的小男孩的故事：汤姆·康第（一个被父亲虐待，住在伦敦布丁巷一个废弃的院子里的贫民）和英格兰的爱德华六世（国王亨利八世的儿子）。一天，他们阴差阳错地相遇了，并且互换了衣服。然而，两个人长得实在是太像了，因为互换了衣服，结果皇宫侍卫把王子扔到了街上。爱德华遇到了汤姆的家人，还有一群小偷。吐温以这种形式揭露着英格兰不公平而且残暴的司法体制。亨利八世去世后，爱德华阻止了汤姆的加冕礼，并且交换了身份，最后爱德华成为了英格兰的国王。

名段选读

As night drew to a close that day, the prince found himself far down in the close-built portion of the city. His body was bruised, his hands were bleeding, and his rags were all **besmirched**① with mud. He wandered on and on, and grew more and more **bewildered**②, and so tired and faint he could hardly drag one foot after the other. He had ceased to ask questions of anyone, since they brought him only **insult**[3] instead of information. He kept muttering to himself, "Offal Court—that is the name; if I can but find it before my strength is wholly spent and I drop, then am I saved—for his people will take me to the palace and prove that I am none of theirs, but the true prince, and I shall have mine own again." And now and then his mind reverted to his treatment by those rude Christ's Hospital boys, and he said, "When I am king, they shall not have bread and shelter only, but also teachings out of books; for a full **belly**[4] is little worth where the mind is starved, and the heart. I will keep this diligently in my remembrance, that this day's lesson be not lost upon me, and my people suffer thereby; for learning softeneth the heart and breedeth gentleness and charity.

The lights began to twinkle, it came on to rain, the wind rose, and a raw and **gusty**[5] night set in. The houseless prince, the homeless heir to the throne of England, still moved on, drifting deeper into the maze of **squalid**[6] alleys where the **swarming**[7] hives of poverty and misery were massed together.

夜幕降临时，王子发现自己来到了一个遥远的地方，这里的房屋十分密集。他身体受了伤，双手正流着血，身上破烂的衣服也全沾满了泥。他漫无目的地走着，越来越迷茫，他疲惫无力，几乎一步都挪不动脚。他再也不想询问任何人了，因为他从别人那里得到的回答都是辱骂。他仍然喃喃自语着："废弃的院子——这就是它的名字；如果我能够在精疲力竭地倒下之前找到它的话，那我就得救了——因为他的亲友会把我带到皇宫，并且证明我不是他们的家人，而是真正的王子，那我就能成为我自己了。"他脑子里不时想起被那些基督教医院里的男孩粗鲁对待时的场景，他说："等我当上了国王，他们将不仅有吃有住，还能接受一些教育学习知识；因为如果一个人没有思想、没有良心，那么他就算吃得再饱也没有意义。我要牢牢记住这一点，不能忘了今天的教训，让我的人民遭受不幸；学习会让他们心地善良、礼貌和仁慈。

闪电划过夜空，似乎要下雨了，起风了，野性、狂风暴雨的夜晚来临了。无家可归的王子，无家可归的英格兰皇位继承人，仍然继续前行着，游走在一条曲折肮脏幽深的巷子里，那条肮脏的巷子里密密麻麻地住着许许多多穷苦的人。

——选自《王子与贫儿》第4章

注释

① besmirch [bɪ'smɜːtʃ] *vt.* 弄脏

② bewildered [bɪ'wɪldə(r)d] *adj.* 迷惑的

③ insult ['ɪnsʌlt] *n.* 辱骂

④ belly ['belɪ] *n.* 肚子

⑤ gusty ['gʌstɪ] *adj.* 起大风的，阵风的

⑥ squalid ['skwɔlɪd] *adj.* 污秽的，肮脏的

⑦ swarm [swɔːm] *vi.* 成群地来回移动

4 美国现代短篇小说之父——欧·亨利

O. Henry was the **pseudonym**① of the American writer William Sydney Porter (September 11, 1862—June 5, 1910). O. Henry's short stories are well known for their wit, **wordplay**②, warm characterization and clever twist endings. Henry's stories are famous for their surprise endings, to the point that such an ending is often referred to as an "O. Henry ending." He was called the American answer to Guy de Maupassant. Among his most famous stories are: The Gift of the Magi, The Cop and the Anthem, A Service of Love and The Last Leaf.

欧·亨利是美国作家威廉·悉尼·波特（1862年9月11日—1910年6月5日）的笔名。欧·亨利的短篇小说因机智诙谐的语言、双关语的运用、温情的描述和巧妙曲折的结局而闻名。他的故事以出人意料的结局而著称，因此常常被称为"欧·亨利式结局"。他有"美国的莫泊桑"之称。欧·亨利最著名的小说有《麦琪的礼物》、《警察和赞美诗》、《爱的牺牲》和《最后一片叶子》。

《麦琪的礼物》发表于1906年，欧·亨利的代表作，其创作动因，通常都以为是为了反映美国下层人民生活的艰难，揭示美国贫富悬殊的社会现实。其实，还有一个重要的原因，那就是作家欧·亨利在缅怀其爱妻——阿索尔·艾斯帝斯。最佳译本是人民文学出版社王永年的译本。

The Gift of the Magi
麦琪的礼物

Being wise, their gifts were no doubt wise ones, possibly bearing the privilege of exchange in case of duplication.

聪明的人，毫无疑问他们的礼物也是聪明的，如果礼物碰巧相同，那么他们仍保留有交换礼物的权利。

——*The Gift of the Magi*《麦琪的礼物》

名著导读

The Gift of the Magi is about a young couple who are short of money but desperately want to buy each other Christmas gifts. Unbeknownst to Jim, Della sells her most valuable possession, her beautiful hair, in order to buy a platinum fob chain for Jim's watch; while unbeknownst to Della, Jim sells his own most valuable possession, his watch, to buy jeweled combs for Della's hair.

《麦琪的礼物》讲的是一对缺钱但是非常想给对方买圣诞礼物的年轻夫妻。吉姆不知黛拉为了给自己买一条白金表链以陪衬金表而卖掉了自己最珍贵的秀发；同样，黛拉也不知道吉姆卖掉了最珍贵的金表，为自己买来了一套镶着宝石的梳子。

名段选读

For there lay The Combs—the set of combs, side and back, that Della had worshipped long in a Broadway window. Beautiful combs, pure tortoise shell, with jewelled rims—just the shade to wear in the beautiful vanished hair. They were expensive combs, she knew, and her heart had simply craved and yearned over them without the least hope of possession. And now, they were hers, but the tresses that should have adorned the **coveted**[③] **adornments**[④] were gone.

But she hugged them to her bosom, and at length she was able to look up with dim eyes and a smile and say: "My hair grows so fast, Jim!"

And then Della leaped up like a little singed cat and cried, "Oh, oh!"

Jim had not yet seen his beautiful present. She held it out to him eagerly upon her open palm. The dull precious metal seemed to flash with a reflection of her bright and **ardent**[⑤] spirit.

"Isn't it a dandy, Jim? I hunted all over town to find it. You'll have to look at the time a hundred times a day now. Give me your watch. I want to see how it looks on it."

Instead of obeying, Jim tumbled down on the couch and put his hands under the back of his head and smiled.

"Dell," said he, "let's put our Christmas presents away and keep'em a while. They're too nice to use just at present. I sold the watch to get the money to buy your combs. And now suppose you put the **chops**[⑥] on."

The magi, as you know, were wise men—wonderfully wise men—who brought gifts to the Babe in the manger. They invented the art of giving Christmas presents. Being wise, their gifts were no doubt wise ones, possibly bearing the **privilege**[⑦] of exchange in case of duplication. And here I have **lamely**[⑧] related to you the uneventful chronicle of two foolish children in a flat who most unwisely sacrificed for each other the greatest treasures of their house. But in a last word to the wise of these days let it be said that of all who give gifts these two were the wisest. O all who give and receive gifts, such as they are wisest. Everywhere they are wisest. They are the magi.

因为那些梳子就放在那里——一整套梳子，装饰头发侧面和后面的梳子，黛拉曾经在百老汇的一个橱窗前仰慕了好久。精美的梳子、纯正的玳瑁、周边镶着宝石——刚好陪衬那已经失去的美丽秀发。她知道这套梳子很昂贵，以前她的心里只是渴求，却从不敢奢望能拥有它们。而现在它们是属于她的了，然而可以使这渴慕已久的装饰品熠熠生辉的长发却已经不见了。

然而她把它们紧紧抱在怀里，终于她能够抬起头用失落的眼神看着吉姆，微笑着说："吉姆，我的头发很快就会长起来的！"

马上黛拉像一只烫伤的小猫一样跳起来，叫道，"哦，哦！"

吉姆还没看见他漂亮的礼物。她急切地摊开手，把礼物呈给他。那暗淡又珍贵的金属似乎闪耀着她的欢快和热忱。

"吉姆，好看吗？我跑遍了整个市镇才买到的。以后你可以一天看一百次时间。把你的表给我，让我看看配上去怎么样。"

吉姆没有遵从，却倒在了沙发上，他把手放在脑后，微笑着。

"黛拉，"他说，"把我们的圣诞礼物都收起来吧，保存一段时间。它们都太漂亮了，可是现在不能马上用。我把表卖了，用这个钱给你买了梳子。现在你去把肉排盛来吧。"

正如你知道的，麦琪是聪明人——聪明绝顶的人——他们给马厩里的耶稣带来了礼物。他们开始了赠送圣诞礼物的传统。聪明的人，毫无疑问他们的礼物也是聪明的，如果礼物碰巧相同，那么他们仍保留有交换礼物的权利。在这里，我笨拙地给你们讲述了一所公寓里的两个傻孩子的平凡故事，他们很不明智地为对方牺牲了这所房子里各自拥有的最宝贵的东西。但是最后，我想对如今的聪明人说，在所有送礼物的人中，他们两个是最聪明的。在所有礼物的给予者和接受者中，他们也是最聪明的。不管在哪，他们都是最聪明的。他们就是麦琪。

——选自《麦琪的礼物》

注释

①pseudonym ['su:dənɪm] *n.* 笔名

② wordplay ['wɜ:dplei] *n.* 双关语，文字游戏

③ coveted ['kʌvətɪd] *adj.* 梦寐以求的

④ adornment [ə'dɔ:nmənt] *n.* 装饰品

⑤ ardent ['ɑ:dənt] *adj.* 热情的

⑥ chop [tʃɔp] *n.* 肋骨肉

⑦ privilege ['prɪvəlɪdʒ] *n.* 特权

⑧ lamely ['leimlɪ] *adv.* 不完全地

《警察和赞美诗》发表于1904年，小说的矛头直指当时的美国社会，真实地反映了不明是非、颠倒黑白的社会现实。王永年翻译的经典译本最好。

The Cop and the Anthem
警察和赞美诗

And also in a moment his heart responded thrillingly to this novel mood. An instantaneous and strong impulse moved him to battle with his desperate fate.

而且他的心立刻就对这个新情绪做出了激动的反应。瞬间的强烈冲动驱使着他去和自己绝望的命运抗争。

——*The Cop and the Anthem*《警察和赞美诗》

名著导读

The Cop and the Anthem is about a New York City **hobo**① named Soapy, who sets out to get arrested so he can avoid sleeping in the cold winter as a guest of the city jail. Despite efforts at petty theft, vandalism, disorderly conduct, and "mashing" with a young prostitute, Soapy fails to draw the attention of the police. Disconsolate, he pauses in front of a church, where an organ anthem inspires him to clean up his life—and is ironically charged for loitering and sentenced to three months in prison.

《警察和赞美诗》讲述的是纽约市流浪汉索比的故事，他千方百计地希望被捕入狱以避免在寒冷的冬天露宿街头。虽然他尝试了种种方法，譬如小偷小摸，故意破坏公物，扰乱治安以及与妓女调情，却也没能引起警察的注意。他郁郁不乐地停在一所教堂前，从里面传出来的一首风琴赞美诗令他受到启示，决定改过自新——讽刺的是，就在这时，他因"街头滞留罪"被判入狱三个月。

名段选读

The moon was above, **lustrous**② and **serene**③; vehicles and pedestrians were few; sparrows **twittered**④ sleepily in the eaves—for a little while the scene might have been a country churchyard. And the anthem that the organist played cemented Soapy to the iron fence, for he had known it well in the days when his life contained such things as mothers and roses and ambitions and friends and **immaculate**⑤ thoughts and collars.

The conjunction of Soapy's receptive state of mind and the influences about the old church wrought a sudden and wonderful change in his soul. He viewed with swift horror the pit into which he had **tumbled**⑥, the **degraded**⑦days, unworthy desires, dead hopes, wrecked faculties and base motives that made up his existence.

And also in a moment his heart responded thrillingly to this novel mood. An instantaneous and strong impulse moved him to battle with his desperate fate. He would pull himself out of the mire; he would make a man of himself again; he would conquer the evil that had taken possession of him. There was time; he was comparatively young yet; he would resurrect his old eager ambitions and pursue them without faltering. Those solemn but sweet organ notes had set up a revolution in him. Tomorrow he would go into the roaring downtown district and find work. A fur importer had once offered him a place as driver. He would find him tomorrow and ask for the position. He would be somebody in the world.

月亮悬挂在高高的夜空中，明亮静谧；车辆和行人都很稀少；麻雀懒散地在屋檐上喊喊喳喳地叫——有那么一刻，他觉得这个情景就像是在一片乡村墓地。而那风琴手演奏的赞美诗把索比吸引到铁栅栏前，因为他曾经很熟悉这首曲子，那时候他的生活里还有母爱、玫瑰、雄心、朋友和纯洁无瑕的思想以及洁白的衣领。

索比那种愿意接受的心态与古老教堂周边环境交融在一起，却让他的灵魂猛然间出现了奇妙的变化。他立刻惊恐地醒悟到自己已经坠入了深渊，堕落的岁月，可耻的欲念，悲观失望，才穷智竭，动机卑鄙，心头掠过一阵战栗，这些统统构成了他现在的生活。

一瞬间，这些新的情绪立刻使他的心不安起来。瞬间的强烈冲动驱使着他去和自己绝望的命运抗争。他想要把自己从这个泥潭中拽出来；他想重新为人；他想要征服那些占领他的邪恶。为时不晚；他还不算太老；他想要恢复自己旧日的雄心壮志，并且毫不犹豫地追求它们。那些庄严而悦耳的风琴音符促成了他的转变。明天，他会去喧哗的市中心找工作，一位皮毛进口商曾经提供给他一个司机的职位，明天就去找他，恳求得到那个职位。他要成为这世上一个了不起的人。

——选自《警察和赞美诗》

注释

① hobo ['həubəu] *n.* 流浪者，无业游民

② lustrous ['lʌstrəs] *adj.* 明亮的

③ serene [sə'ri:n] *adj.* 宁静的

④ twitter ['twɪtə(r)] *vi.* 吱吱叫

⑤ immaculate [ɪ'mækjələt] *adj.* 无瑕的，纯洁的

⑥ tumble ['tʌmbl] *vi.* 摔倒

⑦ degraded [dɪ'greidɪd] *adj.* 堕落的

《最后一片叶子》故事背景是发生美国华盛顿广场附近的一个小区里，这里聚集了许多艺术家的故事，特别强调在艺术家们潦倒困顿的生活中，还能互相扶持的可贵情谊。王永年翻译的经典译本最好。

The Last Leaf
最后一片叶子

It is a sin to want to die.

想死是一种罪过。

——*The Last Leaf*《最后一片叶子》

名著导读

A young girl decides that she will die when the last leaf drops from a dying vine outside her window, as lingering pneumonia slowly takes her will to live. Her neighbor is an elderly artist frustrated by his inability to paint what is in his heart. In an attempt to save the young girl, he creates the masterpiece he has been struggling to paint.

难缠的肺炎慢慢磨灭了一个年轻女孩儿的生存意志，她断定，当最后一片叶子从窗外那棵枯死的常春藤上飘落时，自己就会死去。她的邻居是一位年长的画家，他正为画不出他心中所想的作品而沮丧不已。在挽救这个年轻女孩的努力过程中，他终于创作出了他梦寐以求的杰作。

名段选读

The ivy leaf was still there.

Johnsy lay for a long time looking at it. And then she called to Sue, who was **stirring**① her chicken broth over the gas stove.

"I've been a bad girl, Sudie," said Johnsy. "Something has made that last leaf stay there to show me how **wicked**② I was. It is a sin to want to die. You may bring me a little broth now, and some milk with a little port in it, and—no; bring me a hand-mirror first, and then pack some pillows about me, and I will sit up and watch you cook."

And hour later she said:

"Sudie, some day I hope to paint the Bay of Naples."

The doctor came in the afternoon, and Sue had an excuse to go into the hallway as he left.

"Even chances," said the doctor, taking Sue's thin, shaking hand in his. "With good nursing you'll win. And now I must see another case I have downstairs. Behrman, his name is—some kind of an artist, I believe. **Pneumonia**③, too. He is an old, weak man, and the attack is acute. There is no hope for him; but he goes to the hospital today to be made more comfortable."

The next day the doctor said to Sue: "She's out of danger. You won. Nutrition and care now—that's all."

And that afternoon Sue came to the bed where Johnsy lay, contentedly knitting a very blue and very useless woollen shoulder scarf, and put one arm around her, pillows and all.

"I have something to tell you, white mouse," she said. "Mr. Behrman died of pneumonia today in the hospital. He was ill only two days. The janitor found him the morning of the first day in his room downstairs helpless with pain. His shoes and clothing were wet through and icy cold. They couldn't imagine where he had been on such a **dreadful**[④] night. And then they found a lantern, still lighted, and a ladder that had been dragged from its place, and some **scattered**[⑤] brushes, and a palette with green and yellow colours mixed on it, and—look out the window, dear, at the last ivy leaf on the wall. Didn't you wonder why it never fluttered or moved when the wind blew? Ah, darling, it's Behrman's masterpiece—he painted it there the night that the last leaf fell."

那片常春藤叶子依然在那儿。

琼西躺在床上长久地凝视着它。然后她叫了苏一声，苏正在煤气炉旁搅拌鸡汤。

"苏蒂，我是个坏女孩儿，"琼西说。"上帝把最后一片叶子留在那儿就是要告诉我我以前有多坏。想死是一种罪过。给我端点肉汤和牛奶来吧，牛奶里面加一点波堤葡萄酒，还有——不；先给我拿一面小镜子，再给我垫几个枕头，我要坐起来看你做饭。"

一个小时后她说：

"苏蒂，有朝一日我希望能画那不勒斯海湾。"

下午医生来了，当他离开后苏便找借口去了走廊。

"有一半的机会，"医生握着苏瘦弱而发抖的手说。"如果护理得好，你们就会成功。现在我要下楼去看另一个病人了。他叫贝尔曼，我想他是个艺术家，也得的肺炎。他年老又虚弱，而且病得很重，已经没有任何希望了；但他今天去医院可以让自己更好受一些。"

第二天，医生对苏说："她已经脱离危险了，你们成功了，只需保证她的营养再小心看护就行了。"

那个下午苏来到琼西床边，她正安心地织着一条蓝色的并不实用的羊毛披肩围巾，苏将琼西连着枕头和其他东西一起抱住。

"我有事情要告诉你，小白鼠，"她说，"贝尔曼先生因为肺炎今天在医院去世了。他只病了两天就走了。第一天早上，管理员发现他疼痛无助地躺在楼下自己的房间里。他的鞋子和衣服都湿透了，冰冷冰冷的。他们无法想象在那样一个可怕的夜晚他去了哪里。后来他们发现了一个还亮着的灯笼和一架从原地移动过的梯子，还有一些散乱的画笔，以及一个混着绿色和黄色颜料的调色盘，而且——亲爱的，看看窗外那常青藤叶子。你没有想过为什么刮风的时候，它也从不摆动和移动吗？啊，亲爱的，这是贝尔曼先生的杰作——是当天晚上最后一片叶子飘落时他画在那里的。"

——选自《最后一片叶子》

注释

① stir [stɜː(r)] *vt.* 搅拌

② wicked ['wɪkɪd] *adj.* 坏的

③ pneumonia [njuː'məʊniə] *n.* 肺炎

④ dreadful ['dredfl] *adj.* 可怕的

⑤ scattered ['skætəd] *adj.* 散乱的

5 “爵士时代”最重要的代表人——弗·司各特·菲茨杰拉德

Francis Scott Key Fitzgerald (September 24, 1896—December 21, 1940) was an American author of novels and short stories, whose works are the **paradigm**★ writings of the Jazz Age, a term he **coined**★ himself. He is widely regarded by many as one of the greatest American writers of the 20th century. Fitzgerald is considered a member of the "Lost Generation" of the 1920s. He finished four novels, *This Side of Paradise*, *The Beautiful and Damned*, *Tender Is the Night* and his most famous, the celebrated classic, The Great Gatsby. Fitzgerald also wrote many short stories that treat themes of youth and promise along with despair and age.

弗·司各特·菲茨杰拉德(1896年9月24日—1940年12月21日)是美国的长篇和短篇小说家。他的作品是“爵士时代”的典范，“爵士时代”这个词也是由他创造的。他被公认为是20世纪最伟大的作家之一。菲茨杰拉德被认为是20世纪20年代“迷惘的一代”的代表人物之一。他创作了4部小说，包括《天堂的这一边》、《美女和被诅咒的人》、《夜色温柔》和他最著名、最经典的作品《了不起的盖茨比》。此外，菲茨杰拉德也写了很多短篇小说，其主题不仅涵盖青春与希望，同时还涉及绝望与岁月。

《了不起的盖茨比》★全文共9章，是菲茨杰拉德1925年所写的一部短篇小说，背景设在20世纪20年代的纽约市及长岛。本书的问世，奠定了作者在现代美国文学史上的地位，使他成为20年代“爵士时代”的发言人和“迷惘的一代”的代表作家之一。目前国内较著名的译本是巫宁坤、姚乃强以及王晋华的版本。

The Great Gatsby
了不起的盖茨比

He had come a long way to this blue lawn, and his dream must have seemed so close that he could hardly fail to grasp it. He did not know that it was already behind him, somewhere back in that vast obscurity beyond the city, where the dark fields of the republic rolled on under the night.

他经过长途跋涉才来到这片蓝色海域，他的梦想似乎近在咫尺，想错过都难。但他不知道这个梦已经被他丢在身后了，丢在这座城市某个广袤昏暗的角落，夜色中，这个国家的黑暗地带延伸开来。

——*The Great Gatsby*《了不起的盖茨比》

名著导读

The novel is written in the first person by Nick, a young Midwesterner who comes east to New York to enter the bond business. On Long Island he becomes involved in the lives of his neighbors, Jay Gatsby, his cousin Daisy and her husband Tom. Five years ago, Gatsby fell helplessly in love with Daisy. However, Daisy married with Tom for his wealth. Since then, Gatsby decides to win his wealth and his love in whatever ways. While making up his fame with his wealth, he gets Daisy's heart back. In a car accident, Daisy kills Tom's mistress. In order to protect Daisy, Gatsby is murdered by the victim's husband.

小说是以第一人称叙述的。叙述者尼克是一位来自美国中西部的青年，他东迁来到纽约经营债券生意。在长岛，尼克被卷入到他的周围人——杰伊·盖茨比、表妹黛西和她的丈夫汤姆三人的生活中来。5年前，盖茨比无法自拔地爱上了黛西。然而黛西为了钱嫁给了汤姆。从此以后，盖茨比立志要不惜一切代价成为富翁，赢回黛西。当他功成名就时，他终于赢回了黛西的芳心。在一次交通事故中，黛西误杀了汤姆的情妇。盖茨比为了保护黛西，惨遭死者丈夫的杀害。

名段选读

Most of the big shore places were closed now and there were hardly any lights except the shadowy, moving glow of a ferryboat across the Sound. And as the moon rose higher the **inessential**[①] houses began to melt away until gradually I became aware of the old island here that flowered once for Dutch sailors' eyes—a fresh, green breast of the new world. Its vanished trees, the trees that had made way for Gatsby's house, had once **pandered**[②] in whispers to the last and greatest of all human dreams; for a **transitory**[③] **enchanted**[④] moment man must have held his breath in the presence of this continent, compelled into an aesthetic contemplation he neither understood nor desired, face to face for the last time in history with something **commensurate**[⑤] to his capacity for wonder.

And as I sat there brooding on the old, unknown world, I thought of Gatsby's wonder when he first picked out the green light at the end of Daisy's dock. He had come a long way to this blue lawn, and his dream must have seemed so close that he could hardly fail to grasp it. He did not know that it was already behind him, somewhere back in that vast **obscurity**[⑥] beyond the city, where the dark fields of the republic rolled on under the night.

Gatsby believed in the green light, the **orgastic**⑦ future that year by year **recedes**⑧ before us. It eluded us then, but that's no matter—tomorrow we will run faster, stretch out our arms further...And one fine morning—so we beat on, boats against the current, borne back **ceaselessly**⑨ into the past.

海滨的那些大房子大多都已关闭了，除了海湾中一只渡船上远远发出的微弱、摇晃不定的萤火之光外，四周没有一丝灯火。月亮越升越高，那些渺小得微不足道的房屋慢慢消融在夜色里，直到我逐渐意识到这是一座曾经在荷兰水手的眼里那么繁盛的古岛——它是一片清新、碧绿的新世界。那些消失了的树木，那些因为要为盖茨比的房子腾出地方而被砍伐了的树木，曾低声迎合人类最后也是最伟大的梦想；在看见这片土地的时候，有那么一瞬，美妙而短暂的一瞬，他们会摒气凝神，身不由己地进入一种他们难以理解也从未想过的审美形态中。这是人们在历史上最后一次亲眼看到这种美，它美得达到他们想象的极限。

当我坐在那里思索着这个古老的、未知的世界的时候，也想起了盖茨比第一次发现黛西的码头尽头那束绿色灯光时惊讶的表情。他经过长途跋涉才来到这片蓝色地域，他的梦想似乎近在咫尺，想错过都难。但他不知道这个梦已经被他丢在身后了，丢在这座城市某个广袤昏暗的角落，夜色中，这个国家的黑暗地带延伸开来。

那绿色的灯光曾经是盖茨比的信仰，它是一年一年渐渐离我们远去的那个欢乐的未来。它躲开了我们，不过那没关系——明天我们会跑得更快，把双臂张得更开……然后就在一个晴朗的早晨——我们奋力前行，逆流而上，不断倒退，回到过去。

——选自《了不起的盖茨比》第9章

注释

★ paradigm ['pærəˌdaim] *n.* 范例，模范

★ coin [kɔin] *vt.* 杜撰，创造

★ "《了不起的盖茨比》是自亨利·詹姆斯以来美国小说迈出的第一步，因为菲茨杰拉德在其中描写了宏大、熙攘、轻率和寻欢，凡此种种，曾风靡一时。"

——英国著名现代派诗人和文艺评论家　T. S. 艾略特

① inessential [ˌɪnɪ'senʃl] *adj.* 无关紧要的

② pander ['pændə(r)] *vi.* 迎合，怂恿

③ transitory ['trænsətrɪ] *adj.* 暂时的，瞬息的

④ enchanted [ɪn'tʃɑːntɪd] *adj.* 被施魔法的，陶醉的

⑤commensurate [kə'menʃərət] *adj.* 相称的，同量的

⑥ obscurity [əb'skjʊrətɪ] *n.* 昏暗，晦涩

⑦ orgastic [ɔː'gæstɪk] *adj.* 极度兴奋的，美妙的

⑧ recede [rɪ'siːd] *vi.* 后退，变模糊

⑨ ceaselessly ['siːsləslɪ] *adv.* 不停地，持续地

《夜色温柔》*发表于1934年，是菲茨杰拉德生前所完成的最后一部长篇小说。小说共3卷，61章，背景被安排在作者所熟悉的欧洲大陆，时间跨度为1917年到1930年间。目前国内较著名的译本是巫宁坤的版本和陈丽的版本。

Tender is the Night
夜色温柔

There was some element of loneliness involved—so easy to be loved—so hard to love.

这之中还包含些孤独的意味——被爱很容易，而爱人很难。

——*Tender is the Night*《夜色温柔》

名著导读

Dick and Nicole Diver live pleasant, **idyllic**① lives on the French Riviera as American expatriates. Rosemary Hoyt, a young rising actress joins them for the summer, falling "in love" with the Divers and their way of life. Piningly attached to Dick, Rosemary coaxes Dick into a casual affair, then seperates from the couple as she witnesses Nicole in a state of mental illness. The next part dives back into time, explaining the Divers' history; Dick was a psychiatrist to Nicole (once sexually abused by her father), and is essentially "bought" into marriage to care for her. Though Nicole's recovery is successful, her strength comes from Dick, no longer working, and no longer dependent. After a series of angry outbursts and Dick's drinking into depression, Nicole breaks away from her broken husband.

作为移居海外的美国人，迪克·戴弗和尼科尔·戴弗在法国维埃拉过着快乐悠闲的生活。罗斯玛丽·霍伊特是一个当红的女演员，她来和戴弗夫妇一起消暑。罗斯玛丽"爱"上了戴弗夫妇和他们的生活方式。她渴望能够依附迪克，于是她引诱迪克，两人产生了感情纠葛。之后当她亲眼看到尼科尔处于癫狂状态时，就离开了这对夫妇。接下来的故事就回到了从前，向我们讲述了戴弗夫妇的过去。迪克是尼科尔（曾经被父亲性侵犯）的精神病医生，被雇来与尼科尔结婚以照料她。尼科尔恢复得很好，她不再需要从迪克那里获得力量，也不再依赖他。在一系列愤怒的争吵和迪克酗酒消沉之后，尼科尔与她伤心的丈夫决裂了。

名段选读

"If you're happy in this mess, then I can't help you and I'm wasting my time."

"No, let's talk—I despise most of the others so." There was some manliness in the boy, perverted now into an active resistance to his father. But he had that typically roguish [2] look in his eyes that homosexuals assume in discussing the subject.

"It's a hole-and-corner [3] business at best," Dick told him. "You'll spend your life on it, and its consequences, and you won't have time or energy for any other decent or social act. If you want to face the world you'll have to begin by controlling your sensuality [4]—and, first of all, the drinking that provokes it—"

He talked automatically [5], having abandoned the case ten minutes before. They talked pleasantly through another hour about the boy's home in Chili and about his ambitions. It was as close as Dick had ever come to comprehending such a character from any but the pathological [6] angle—he gathered that this very charm made it possible for Francisco to perpetrate [7] his outrages, and, for Dick, charm always had an independent existence, whether it was the mad gallantry of the wretch who had died in the clinic this morning, or the courageous grace which this lost young man brought to a drab old story. Dick tried to dissect [8] it into pieces small enough to store away—realizing that the totality of a life may be different in quality from its segments, and also that life during the forties seemed capable of being observed only in segments. His love for Nicole and Rosemary, his friendship with Abe North, with Tommy Barban in the broken universe of the war's ending—in such contacts the personalities had seemed to press up so close to him that he became the personality itself—there seemed some necessity of taking all or nothing; it was as if for the remainder of his life he was condemned to carry with him the egos of certain people, early met and early loved, and to be only as complete as they were complete themselves. There was some element of loneliness involved—so easy to be loved—so hard to love.

"如果你觉得这样混乱地生活也很快乐的话，我就没办法帮你了，我是在浪费自己的时间。"

"不，我们谈谈吧——我鄙视大多数这样的人。"男孩身上有着一种男子气概，现在已经扭曲成了对他父亲的一种积极的反抗。但是他的眼神中却流露出同性恋者在讨论类似话题时展现出的典型无赖神色。

"它充其量也只是一件见不得光的勾当，"迪克告诉他。"你会在它上面浪费你的生命，然后最终，你将没有时间或者精力去做其他体面的社交活动。如果你想正视这个世界，你就得从控制你的欲望开始——而且，首先，就是导致纵欲的酗酒——"

他又不由自主地打开话匣，而十分钟之后他才闭上自己的嘴。在接下来的一个小时里，他们愉快地聊着男孩在智利的家以及他的梦想。这种情况就好像迪克之前曾经从其他各种角度分析了这样一个人，唯独没有从病理学的角度去分析——他推测正是由于性格中的魔力让弗郎西斯科胡作非为。对迪克来说，性格的魔力总是脱离人的自身而独立存在的，无论是今天早上在诊所死去的那个可怜人那超凡的勇气，还是这个迷失的年轻人为这个沉闷的老故事带来的一丝无畏气质。迪克试图将生活分割成很小的片段以便储存起来——他意识到，从本质上讲，生活的整体和片段是不同的，而人活到四十岁的时候，他的生活似乎又只能以片段的形式进行分析。他对尼科尔和罗斯玛丽的爱，以及他与亚伯·诺斯、汤米·巴比在战争末期破碎世界中的友谊——在这些联系中，各种性格似乎紧逼着他，以至于他化身为了这些性格——这其中似乎存在着一种必然：对于这些性格，要么全部接收，要么全部摈弃。好像在他的余生，他注定要带着某些人的性格生活，或是早年遇到的人，或是早年爱过的人，这些性格原来就是个整体，现在仍旧是整体。这之中还包含些孤独的意味——被爱很容易，而爱人很难。

——选自《夜色温柔》第3卷第2章

注释

★ "这部小说的绝大部分内容写得都很精彩，令人拍案叫绝，这是一部令人越读越感到趣味无穷的小说。"

——美国小说家　海明威

① idyllic [ai'dɪlɪk] *adj.* 田园般的，平和欢畅的

② roguish ['rəugɪʃ] *adj.* 无赖的，欺骗的

③ hole-and-corner [ˌhəulənd'kɔ:nə] *adj.* 偷偷摸摸的，秘密的

④ sensuality [ˌsenʃu'æləti:] *n.* 好色

⑤ automatically [ˌɔ:tə'mætɪklɪ] *adv.* 自动地，无意识地

⑥ pathological [ˌpæθə'lɔdʒɪkl] *adj.* 病理学的

⑦ perpetrate ['pɜ:pətreit] *vt.* 做（坏事），犯（罪）

⑧ dissect [dɪ'sekt] *vt.* 切碎，剖析

《本杰明的奇幻旅程》创作于1922年，2008年同名电影上映。这部短篇小说讲述了本杰明·巴顿奇幻的一生，收录在菲茨杰拉德的短篇小说集《本杰明的奇幻旅程》中，目前国内较著名的译本是张力慧和汤永宽合译的版本以及柔之、林惠敏和郑天恩合译的版本。

The Curious Case of Benjamin Button
本杰明的奇幻旅程

All these had faded like unsubstantial dreams from his mind as though they had never been. He did not remember.

所有这些如同虚无飘渺的梦，在他的记忆里渐渐褪色，就好像从来不曾发生过。他一点也不记得了。

——*The Curious Case of Benjamin Button*《本杰明的奇幻旅程》

名著导读

Benjamin is born with the physical appearance of a 70-year-old man, but already able to speak. When Benjamin turns 12, the Button family realizes that he is aging backward. In 1910, Benjamin turns over control of his company to his son, Roscoe, and enrolls at Harvard University. After graduation, Benjamin returns home, only to learn his wife has moved to Italy. He lives with Roscoe, who treats him very sternly. Benjamin slowly begins to lose memory of his earlier life. His memory fades away to the point where he cannot remember anything except his nurse. Then everything fades off to dark.

本杰明一出生就能说话了，他模样老态龙钟，像个70岁的老头。当本杰明12岁的时候，家人意识到他的年龄变化与正常人是相反的。1910年，本杰明将公司交给儿子罗斯科管理，而自己进入哈佛大学学习。毕业后，本杰明回到家，得知妻子已经移居到意大利了。于是他与儿子罗斯科一起生活，但儿子对他并不好。本杰明慢慢地开始遗忘早期的生活经历。他的记忆逐渐退化，最后除了他的护士，什么都不记得了。最后他所有的记忆消溺在一片黑暗之中。

名段选读

There were no troublesome memories in his childish sleep; no token came to him of his brave days at college, of the **glittering**① years when he **flustered**② the hearts of many girls. There were only the white, safe walls of his crib and Nana and a man who came to see him sometimes, and a great big orange ball that Nana pointed at just before his **twilight**③ bed hour and called "sun". When the sun went his eyes were sleepy—there were no dreams, no dreams to **haunt**④ him.

The past—the wild charge at the head of his men up San Juan Hill; the first years of his marriage when he worked late into the summer dusk down in the busy city for young Hildegarde whom he loved; the days before that when he sat smoking far into the night in the gloomy old Button house on Monroe Street with his grandfather—all these had faded like unsubstantial dreams from his mind as though they had never been. He did not remember.

He did not remember clearly whether the milk was warm or cool at his last feeding or how the days passed—there was only his crib and Nana's familiar presence. And then he remembered nothing. When he was hungry he cried—that was all. Through the noons and nights he breathed and over him there were soft **mumblings**⑤ and murmurings that he scarcely heard, and faintly differentiated smells, and light and darkness.

Then it was all dark, and his white crib and the dim faces that moved above him, and the warm sweet **aroma**⑥ of the milk, faded out altogether from his mind.

在他孩童般的睡眠中，没有任何惹人讨厌的记忆；大学那段意气风发的日子，以及让众多女孩子芳心暗许的辉煌岁月在他的脑海里已经荡然无存。他只记得自己婴儿床边的白色护栏，他的护士娜娜，一个偶尔会来看他的男人，还有一个巨大的橙色的圆球——黄昏时刻，他快要睡觉的时候，娜娜会指着它并叫它"太阳"。当太阳下山以后，他就会变得睡眼惺忪——他不做梦，不会因为梦而烦恼。

过去——他在圣胡安山上冲锋陷阵，叱咤风云；结婚的第一年，他为了自己深爱的小希尔德加德，在这繁华的城市里努力工作直至夏日黄昏降临；还有更早以前，在门罗街巴顿家阴暗的老房子里，坐着和爷爷抽烟抽到深夜——所有这些如同虚无飘渺的梦，在他的记忆里渐渐褪色，就好像从来不曾发生过。他一点也不记得了。

他已经记不清他喝的最后一口牛奶是热的还是冷的了，他也不记得一天一天是怎么过去的——他只记得婴儿床和熟悉的娜娜。其他的就什么也不记得了。他饿的时候就哭——只是这样而已。在他捱过的每一天，他的四周有着他几乎都听不见的喃喃细语和他分辨不出来的淡淡的不同气味、微弱的光以及黑暗。

然后，一切都黑了下来，他白色的婴儿床，在他头顶上移动的模糊的脸，温暖香甜的牛奶，所有这一切都慢慢模糊，从他的脑海里消失了。

——选自《本杰明的奇幻旅程》第14章

注释

① glittering [ˈglɪtərɪŋ] *adj.* 闪闪发亮的

② fluster [ˈflʌstə(r)] *vt.* 使慌乱，使紧张不安

③ twilight [ˈtwailait] *n.* 黄昏，薄暮

④ haunt [hɔːnt] *vt.* 使困扰，萦绕在……心头

⑤ mumbling [ˈmʌmblɪŋ] *n.* 含含糊糊的话

⑥ aroma [əˈrəumə] *n.* 浓香，香气

6 美国无产阶级文学之父——杰克·伦敦

Jack London (January 12, 1876—November 22, 1916) was an American author, journalist, and social activist. He was a pioneer in the then-**burgeoning**① world of commercial magazine fiction and was one of the first fiction writers to obtain worldwide celebrity and a large fortune from his fiction alone. He is best remembered as the author of *White Fang and the Call of the Wild*, set in the Klondike Gold Rush, as well as the short stories *To Build a Fire*, *An Odyssey of the North, and Love of Life*. He also wrote of the South Pacific in such stories as *The Pearls of Parlay* and *The Heathen*, and *The Sea Wolf*, of the San Francisco Bay area.

杰克·伦敦（1876年1月12日—1916年11月22日）是一位美国作家、记者和社会活动家。他是当时蓬勃发展的商业杂志小说界的先驱，同时也是最早的一批仅凭小说而举世闻名并获得大笔财富的小说家之一。他最知名的作品是以克朗代克地区的淘金热为背景的《白牙》和《野性的呼唤》，以及短篇小说《生火》、《北方故事》和《热爱生命》。他在《帕尔拉伊的珍珠》和《异教徒》等作品中描写了南太平洋，在《海狼》中提到了旧金山海湾地区。

《野性的呼唤》共10章，发表于1903年，是一部以阿拉斯加淘金热为背景、体现人的意志与生命之美的小说。目前国内比较著名的译本是刘荣跃的译本。

The Call of the Wild
野性的呼唤

He was beaten (he knew that); but he was not broken.

他被打败了（他明白这一点），可是他并没有崩溃。

——*The Call of the Wild*《野性的呼唤》

名著导读

The Call of the Wild concerns a previously domesticated dog named Buck, whose primordial instincts return after a series of events leads to his serving as a sled dog in the Yukon during the 19th-century Klondike Gold Rush, in which sled dogs were bought at generous prices. Buck eventually kills the Indians to avenge John Thornton. After that, his old life is a thing of the past, Buck follows the wolf into the forest and answers the call of the wild.

《野性的呼唤》是关于一只早前被驯化、名叫巴克的狗。在19世纪克朗代克地区淘金热时期，雪橇犬出售价格十分高昂。经历一系列事件后巴克在育空(加拿大西北部地区)成为了一条雪橇犬，之后他才恢复了原始的本能。为了替约翰·桑顿报仇，他杀死了印第安人。以前的生活从此成为了过去，巴克跟随着狼群回到了深林，回应了野性的呼唤。

名段选读

He was beaten (he knew that); but he was not broken. He saw, once for all, that he stood no chance against a man with a club. He had learned the lesson, and in all his after life he never forgot it. That club was a **revelation**②. It was his introduction to the reign of primitive law, and he met the introduction halfway. The facts of life took on a fiercer aspect; and while he faced that aspect uncowed, he faced it with all the latent cunning of his nature aroused. As the days went by, other dogs came, in crates and at the ends of ropes, some **docilely**③, and some raging and roaring as he had come; and, one and all, he watched them pass under the dominion of the man in the red sweater. Again and again, as he looked at each brutal performance, the lesson was driven home to Buck: a man with a club was a lawgiver, a master to be obeyed, though not necessarily **conciliated**④. Of this last Buck was never guilty, though he did see beaten dogs that fawned upon the man, and wagged their tails, and licked his hand. Also he saw one dog, that would neither conciliate nor obey, finally killed in the struggle for mastery.

Now and again men came, strangers, who talked excitedly, **wheedlingly**⑤, and in all kinds of fashions to the man in the red sweater. And at such times that money passed between them the strangers took one or more of the dogs away with them. Buck wondered where they went, for they never came back; but the fear of the future was strong upon him, and he was glad each time when he was not selected.

Yet his time came, in the end, in the form of a little weazened man who spat broken English and many strange and **uncouth**⑥ exclamations which Buck could not understand.

他被打败了(他明白这一点)，可是他并没有崩溃。他彻底地明白他没有机会对抗一个手持木棍的人类。他吸取了这个教训，而且在他以后的生命中都不曾忘记这一点。那根木棍就是个启示，令他在生命的半途中领教了被原始法则统治的滋味。生活的现实呈现出更残酷的一面；当他毫不畏缩地面对这一面时，他本性里潜伏的狡诈也被激起。随着日子一天天过去，其他的狗来了，他们被装在木桩箱里并用绳子牵着；他们有些很温顺，而有些就像他来这里时一样发怒咆哮。他看着他们在那个穿红毛衣的人的指挥下走过去。当他一次又一次地看到那残酷的场面时，巴克更加深刻地懂得了这个教训：手拿木棍的人就是立法者，是他们必须服从的主人，虽然他们不一定会得到安抚。巴克也从不因此感到内疚，虽然他的确看到那些挨打的狗对那个人讨好奉承，摇着尾巴，舔他的手。他还见过一只狗，既不温顺，也不服从，最后在争夺控制权时被杀死了。

不时会有一些陌生人过来，他们兴奋地并甜言蜜语地用各种方式跟那个穿红毛衣的人交谈。这种时候，他们之间就会有金钱交易，那些陌生人就会带走一条或几条狗。巴克想知道他们到底去了哪里，因为他们再也没回来过；但是，他对未来有着强烈的恐惧，每当没被选中时，他就会很高兴。

然而最后还是轮到他了，选中他的是一个身材矮小干瘪的男人，说着蹩脚的英语，还满嘴都是巴克听不懂的古怪粗俗的惊叹词。

——选自《野性的呼唤》第1章

注释

① burgeoning ['bɜːdvənɪŋ] *adj.* 迅速发展的

② revelation [ˌrevə'leɪʃn] *n.* 启示

③ docilely ['dəusaɪlli] *adv.* 温顺地

④ conciliate [kən'sɪlieit] vt. 驯服

⑤ wheedlingly ['wiːdlɪŋlɪ] *adv.* 用甜言蜜语哄骗地

⑥ uncouth [ʌn'kuːθ] *adj.* 粗俗的

《马丁·伊登》共46章，发表于1909年。在这部带有自传色彩的长篇小说中，杰克·伦敦写下了自己如何在平庸的资产阶级鄙夷下含辛茹苦地读书和写作的经历，也尽情阐释了他个人的混杂着马克思主义的阶级观、斯宾塞的社会达尔文主义和尼采的“超人”说的社会见解。国内比较流行的译本是吴劳、张经浩的译本。

Martin Eden
马丁·伊登

It shows us that a man with will may rise superior to his environment.

这向我们表明一个意志坚定的人可以超脱环境，获得成功。

——*Martin Eden*《马丁·伊登》

名著导读

Martin Eden is a novel about a struggling young writer. Living in Oakland at the dawn of the 20th century, Martin Eden struggles to rise far above his **destitute**① circumstances through an intense and passionate pursuit of self-education in order to achieve a coveted place among the literary elite. The main driving force behind Martin Eden's efforts is his love for Ruth Morse. Because Eden is a sailor from a working class background, and the Morses are a bourgeois family, a union between them would be impossible until he reaches their level of wealth and perceived cultural, intellectual refinement.

《马丁·伊登》是一部关于一名努力奋斗的年轻作家的小说。20世纪初期，住在奥克兰的马丁·伊登发奋自学，想借此努力摆脱贫困的环境，并实现在文学界他梦寐以求的地位。马丁·伊登发奋的主要动力是他对露丝·莫尔斯的爱。因为他只是一名工人阶层的水手，而莫尔斯是一个资产阶级家族。如果他没有能跟莫尔斯家相匹敌的财富、智慧和文化修养，他们俩的结合是不可能的。

名段选读

"But I have not finished my story," she said. "He worked, so father says, as no other office boy he ever had. Mr. Butler was always eager to work. He never was late, and he was usually at the office a few minutes before his regular time. And yet he saved his time. Every spare moment was devoted to study. He studied book-keeping and type-writing, and he paid for lessons in shorthand by dictating at night to a court reporter who needed practice. He quickly became a clerk, and he made himself invaluable. Father appreciated him and saw that he was bound to rise. It was on father's suggestion that he went to law college. He became a lawyer, and hardly was he back in the office when father took him in as junior partner. He is a great man. He refused the United States Senate several times, and father says he could become a justice of the Supreme Court any time a **vacancy**② occurs, if he wants to. Such a life is an inspiration to all of us. It shows us that a man with will may rise superior to his environment."

"He is a great man," Martin said sincerely. But it seemed to him there was something in the recital that **jarred**③ upon his sense of beauty and life. He could not find an adequate motive in Mr. Butler's life of pinching and **privation**④. Had he done it for love of a woman, or for attainment of beauty, Martin would have understood. God's own mad lover should do anything for the kiss, but not for thirty thousand dollars a year. He was dissatisfied with Mr. Butler's career. There was something **paltry**[5] about it, after all. Thirty thousand a year was all right, but **dyspepsia**[6] and inability to be humanly happy robbed such princely income of all its value.

“但我的故事还没说完呢，” 她说。“我父亲说他工作起来跟他办公室的任何勤杂工都不一样。巴特勒先生总是非常热切地工作，他从不迟到，而且总是比规定时间提前几分钟到办公室，并能将时间节约出来。他把一切空闲时间都专心用于学习，学习簿记和打字，他在晚上给一个需要训练的法庭书记官做听写，赚了钱去上速记课程。他很快变成了办事员，让自己变得非常有价值。爸爸很欣赏他，认为他势必会节节高升。他听从父亲的建议去上法律学院并成了一名律师，他刚回到办公室工作，父亲就让他做了他年轻的合作伙伴。他是一个了不起的人，曾经几次拒绝做美国参议员。父亲说只要他愿意，一有空缺他就可能做最高法院的法官。这样的人生对我们所有人来说都是一种鼓舞。这向我们表明一个意志坚定的人可以超脱环境，获得成功。”

“他是个了不起的人，” 马丁诚恳地说道。但是对他来说，故事里似乎有些东西扰乱了他对美和人生的理解。他不能为巴特勒先生那种清苦而艰辛的生活找到一个充分的动机。如果他是出于对一个女人的爱情，或是为了得到美，马丁倒是能理解。上帝自己那疯狂的情人为了一个吻可以做任何事情，但不是为了一年三万美元的收入。他对巴特勒先生的事业并不满意，说到底，他总觉得有某种不足之处。一年三万是不错，但是消化不良，并且不能像一般人那样快乐，那么即便如此丰厚的收入也没有任何价值可言。

——选自《马丁·伊登》第8章

注释

① destitute ['destɪtjuːt] *adj.* 贫穷的，贫困的

② vacancy ['veɪkənsi] *n.* 空缺

③ jar [dʒɑː(r)] *vi.* 撞击

④ privation [praiˈveiʃən] *n.* 贫穷

⑤ paltry ['pɔːltrɪ] *adj.* 无价值的

⑥ dyspepsia [dɪs'pepsiə] *n.* 消化不良

《白牙》共5卷，发表于1906年。背景是加拿大西北边陲的冰封地带，叙述了一只幼狼如何从荒野中进入人类的文明世界。国内比较流行的译本是王勋和纪飞的译本，以及孙毅兵的译本。

White Fang
白牙

One cannot violate the promptings of one's nature without having that nature recoil upon itself.

任何人都不可能违背了天性的指示而不受到天性的惩罚。

——*White Fang*《白牙》

名著导读

The story takes place in Yukon Territory, Canada, during the Klondike Gold Rush at the end of the 19th-century, and details a wild wolfdog's journey to domestication. White Fang examines the violent world of wild animals and the equally violent world of humans. The book also explores complex themes including morality and **redemption**①.

故事发生在19世纪末克朗代克地区淘金热时期加拿大的育空地区，它详细讲述了一只狼狗被驯养的过程。《白牙》这部小说审视了野生动物凶残的世界和同样残酷的人类世界，同时也探讨了道德和救赎等复杂的主题。

名段选读

One cannot violate the promptings of one's nature without having that nature recoil upon itself. Such a **recoil**② is like that of a hair, made to grow out from the body, turning unnaturally upon the direction of its growth and growing into the body—a **rankling**③, **festering**④ thing of hurt. And so with White Fang. Every urge of his being impelled him to spring upon the pack that cried at his heels, but it was the will of the gods that this should not be; and behind the will, to enforce it, was the whip of cariboo-gut with its biting thirty-foot lash. So White Fang could only eat his heart in bitterness and develop a hatred and malice commensurate with the ferocity and indomitability of his nature.

If ever a creature was the enemy of its kind, White Fang was that creature. He asked no **quarter**⑤, gave none. He was continually marred and scarred by the teeth of the pack, and as continually he left his own marks upon the pack. Unlike most leaders, who, when camp was made and the dogs were unhitched, huddled near to the gods for protection, White Fang disdained such protection. He walked boldly about the camp, inflicting punishment in the night for what he had suffered in the day. In the time before he was made leader of the team, the pack had learned to get out of his way. But now it was different. Excited by the day-long pursuit of him, swayed subconsciously by the insistent iteration on their brains of the sight of him fleeing away, mastered by the feeling of mastery enjoyed all day, the dogs could not bring themselves to give way to him. When he appeared amongst them, there was always a squabble. His progress was marked by snarl and snap and growl. The very atmosphere he breathed was **surcharged**[6] with hatred and malice, and this but served to increase the hatred and malice within him.

任何人都不可能违背了天性的指示而不受到天性的惩罚。这种惩罚就根本是往身体外长出的一根毛发，却不自然地朝着与生长方向相反的方向生长，长进了身体里——化脓，引起疼痛。白牙也是一样的。体内的每一股冲动都驱使他扑向那群在他后面大叫的狗，但神的旨意却告诉他不应该这样做。身后那根抽得人生疼的三十英尺长的鹿肠鞭子，实施着神的旨意。所以白牙只能将痛苦埋在心里，酝酿着与他天性中的凶猛和不屈不挠相称的仇恨和恶毒。

如果有一种生物是他的同类的敌人的话，那么它就是白牙。他不要求同情，也不给予怜悯。狗群的牙齿不断地在他身上留下累累伤痕，他也不断地给他们留下印记。一旦营地建好，绳子一解开，大部分领头狗就会挤作一团寻求神的保护，但白牙蔑视这样的保护。他在营地周围大胆地走来走去，他要在夜晚报复白天所遭受的痛苦。在他还没有成为队里的领头狗的时候，狗群已经学会了给他让路。但现在却不同了。那群狗因为追了他一整天而兴奋不已，脑海中反复出现的白牙逃跑时的情景在潜意识里影响着他们，享受了一整天的征服感支配着他们，他们无法令自己给他让路。只要白牙在他们中出现，争吵声就会不断，他前进的每一步都伴随着咆哮、撕咬和怒吼。就连他呼吸的空气都充斥着憎恨和恶毒，而这些只不过进一步增长了他体内的仇恨和恶毒。

——选自《白牙》第1卷第1章

注释

① redemption [rɪ'dempʃən] *n.* 赎回，拯救

② recoil ['riːkɔil] *n.* 反冲

③ rankling ['ræŋklɪŋ] *adj.* 化脓的

④ fester['festə] *vi.* 化脓，溃烂

⑤ quarter ['kwɔːtə(r)] *n.* 同情

⑥surcharge ['sɜːtʃɑːdʒ] *vt.* 使装载过多

美国"南方文学"派创始人——威廉·福克纳

William Cuthbert Faulkner (September 25, 1897—July 6, 1962) was a Nobel Prize-winning American novelist and short story writer. One of the most influential writers of the 20th century, his reputation is based mostly on his novels, **novellas***, and short stories. He was also a published poet and an occasional screenwriter. From the early 1920s to the outbreak of World War Ⅱ, when Faulkner left for California, he published 13 novels and numerous short stories, the body of work that grounds his reputation and for which he was awarded the Nobel Prize at the age of 52. This prodigious output includes his most celebrated novels such as *The Sound and the Fury* (1929), *As I Lay Dying* (1930), *Light in August* (1932), and *Absalom, Absalom!* (1936).

威廉·卡斯伯特·福克纳（1897年9月25日—1962年7月6日）是一名曾获诺贝尔文学奖的美国小说家。他是20世纪最有影响力的作家之一，主要因其长篇、中篇和短篇小说而闻名于世。同时，他也是诗人和业余编剧家。从20世纪20年代初到第二次世界大战爆发的这段时间，福克纳来到了加利福尼亚州，他发表了13部小说和大量的短篇小说。这些作品为他赢得世界声誉打下了基础，并且也因此在52岁时获得诺贝尔文学奖。他的文学巨著包括最著名的小说《喧哗与骚动》（1929）、《我弥留之际》（1930）、《八月之光》（1932）、《押沙龙，押沙龙！》（1936）等等。

《我弥留之际》*发表于1930年，共59章，篇章长短不一，有15个不同的叙述者。该小说采用意识流的写作手法。威廉·福克纳凭借这部小说获得诺贝尔文学奖。目前国内最常见的该小说的翻译版本是上海译文出版社李文俊的译本。

As I Lay Dying
我弥留之际

It's because I am alone. If I could just feel it, it would be different, because I would not be alone. But if I were not alone, everybody would know it. And he could do so much for me, and then I would not be alone. Then I could be all right alone.

因为我是孤单的。如果我能感受到它，情况就会不一样了，因为那样我就不再孤单了。但是如果我不是孤单的，那么所有的人都会知道。他能为我做很多事情，那样我就不孤单了，即使孤单也没关系。

——*As I Lay Dying*《我弥留之际》

名著导读

As I Lay Dying by William Faulkner consists of strange happenings throughout the story. One of the most **awkward**① settings in the book is the relationship between husband and wife that occurred between Anse and Addie Bundren. What is seen in the beginning is that of a wife on her deathbed and a caring husband who wants to make everything better for his wife by making her wishes come true. However, this was just a masking technique Faulkner used to give the readers the wrong impression on how things were run.

威廉·福克纳的《我弥留之际》是由很多奇异事件构成的一个故事。小说中最尴尬的布局之一就是安斯和艾迪·本德仑之间的夫妻关系。故事开头展现的是在妻子临终时，体贴入微的丈夫想尽一切办法实现妻子遗愿的场景。然而，这只是福克纳采用的障眼法，目的是让读者对故事的情节发展产生误解。

名段选读

He could do so much for me if he just would. He could do everything for me. It's like everything in the world for me is inside a **tub**② full of **guts**③, so that you wonder how there can be any room in it for anything else very important. He is a big tub of guts and I am a little tub of guts and if there is not any room for anything else important in a big tub of guts, how can it be room in a little tub of guts. But I know it is there because God gave women a sign when something has happened bad.

It's because I am alone. If I could just feel it, it would be different, because I would not be alone. But if I were not alone, everybody would know it. And he could do so much for me, and then I would not be alone. Then I could be all right alone.

I would let him come in between me and Lafe, like Darl came in between me and Lafe, and so Lafe is alone too. He is Lafe and I am Dewey Dell, and when mother died I had to go beyond and outside of me and Lafe and Darl to **grieve**④ because he could do so much for me and he don't know it. He don't even know it.

From the back porch I cannot see the barn. Then the sound of Cash's sawing comes in from that way. It is like a dog outside the house, going back and forth around the house to whatever door you come to, waiting to come in. He said I worry more than you do and I said you don't know what worry is so I can't worry. I try to but I can't think long enough to worry.

只要他愿意，他可以为我做很多事情。他可以为我做任何事情。对我来说，世上的一切就像是装在一只满是内脏的桶里，于是你会怀疑那里面怎么还会有空间容下其他重要的东西。他是一只装满内脏的大桶，而我是一只装满内脏的小桶，如果大桶都没有空间能容下其他重要的东西，那么小桶又怎么会有呢。但是我知道还是有空间的，因为一旦发生了不好的事情，上帝就会给女人一个信号。

因为我是孤单的。如果我能感受到它，情况就会不一样了，因为那样我就不再孤单了。但是如果我不是孤单的，那么所有的人都会知道。他能为我做很多事情，那样我就不孤单了，即使孤单也没关系。

我会让他像达尔那样来到我和莱夫中间，这样一来莱夫就孤单了。他是莱夫，我是杜威·德尔。母亲去世的时候，我不得不退出以我、莱夫和达尔之间的三人关系来哀悼，因为他能为我做很多事，可是他却不知道。他压根就不知道。

站在后面的走廊上我看不见谷仓。接着卡什拉锯的声音从那边传了过来。这声音就像是屋外的一条狗，在屋子周围转来转去，守候在你要去的任何一个门口，然后伺机从你打开的门里冲进来。他说他担心的事情比我多，我说他根本不知道什么是担心，所以我不担心。我确实想担心，但是我没法长久地思考，因此也不知该从何担心起。

——选自《我弥留之际》“杜威·德尔”

注释

★ novella [nə'velə] *n.* 中篇小说

★“福克纳的主要目的更像是迫使读者以比书中的人物与行动第一眼看去所需要或值得的更高一层、更有普遍意义的角度来读这本小说，来理解本德仑一家及其历险记。还有，尽管这个故事读来让人不愉快，它经常具有一种阴阴惨惨的狂想曲的气氛，但是它使我们逐渐领会，在某种意义上它是关于人类忍受能力的一个原始的寓言，是整个人类经验的一幅悲喜剧式的图景。”

——英国批评家　迈克尔·米尔盖特

① awkward ['ɔːkwəd] *adj.* 尴尬的，棘手的

② tub [tʌb] *n.* 桶，浴盆

③ gut [gʌt] *n.* 肠，内脏

④ grieve [griːv] *vi.* 哀悼，悲伤

《押沙龙，押沙龙！》发表于1936年，是福克纳最重要，也是最复杂、最深奥、最具史诗风格的一部作品。本书书名源自《圣经》典故，书中描述的亲子之间的爱与恨、兄妹之间的暧昧感情等，具有《圣经》故事的色彩。目前国内最常见的该小说的翻译版本是上海译文出版社李文俊的译本。

Absalom, Absalom!
押沙龙，押沙龙！

They lead beautiful lives—women. Lives not only divorced from, but irrevocably excommunicated from, all reality.

她们拥有美好的人生——我是说女人。这种人生不仅脱离了一切现实，甚至彻底地被现实驱逐出来。

——*Absalom, Absalom!*《押沙龙，押沙龙！》

名著导读

It is a story about three families of the American South, taking place before, during, and after the Civil War, with the focus of the story on the life of Thomas Sutpen. Thomas Sutpen arrives in Jefferson, Mississippi, in 1833. An enigmatic figure, he never reveals much about his past or his reasons for choosing Jefferson as the site for his home. He comes with a group of "wild" slaves (presumably from Haiti), a French architect, and construction tools. Rumors abound about the mysterious Sutpen...

故事以托马斯·塞德潘的生活为主线，讲述了美国南方的三个家庭在南北战争前、中、后三个时期所发生的故事。1833年，托马斯·塞德潘来到密西西比州的杰斐逊，他是一个像谜一样的人物，从来没有透露过他的过去，也从没说过他选择在杰斐逊安家的原因。他带着一群野蛮的奴隶（据推测来自于海地），一个法国建筑师，还有一大堆建筑设备来到这里。关于神秘塞德潘的传闻渐渐多了起来……

名段选读

"Yes. They lead beautiful lives—women. Lives not only divorced from, but irrevocably **excommunicated**① from, all reality. That's why although their deaths, the instant of dissolution, are of no importance to them since they have a courage and **fortitude**② in the face of pain and **annihilation**③ which would make the most **spartan**④ man resemble a pulling boy, yet to them their funerals and graves, the little puny affirmations of **spurious**⑤ immortality set above their **slumber**⑥, are of incalculable importance. You had an aunt once (you do not remember her because I never saw her myself but only heard the tale) who was faced with a serious operation which she became convinced she would not survive, at a time when her nearest female kin was a woman between whom and herself there had existed for years one of those bitter **inexplicable**⑦ (to the man mind) **amicable**⑧ **enmities**⑨ which occur between women of the same blood, whose sole worry about departing this world was to get rid of a certain brown dress which she owned and knew that the **kinswoman**⑩ knew she had never liked, which must be burned, not given away but burned in the back yard beneath the window where, by being held up to the window (and suffering **excruciating**⑪ pain) she could see it burned with her own eyes, because she was convinced that after she died the kinswoman, the logical one to take charge, would bury her in it."

"是的。她们拥有美好的人生——我是说女人。这种人生不仅脱离了一切现实，甚至彻底地被现实驱逐出来。这就是为什么尽管她们会死，但那一瞬间的死亡对她们来说并不重要。因为她们有直面痛苦和毁灭的勇气和坚毅，而这种痛苦和毁灭却能让一个最刚强的男人变成手足无措的小孩。但是对她们而言，在葬礼和坟墓以及墓志铭上对她们虚假永生的丝毫肯定都至关重要。你曾经有一个姑妈(你不记得她，因为我也没有亲眼见过她，只是听过她的故事而已)，她曾经要做一个大手术，她确信自己活不下来了，当时，与她血缘关系最近的亲属是一位女性，她们之间多年来便已经存在着某种痛苦又令人费解(对于男人而言)的"友善的敌意"，这通常是发生在同一血缘的女性之间。你姑妈对于离开人世唯一的担心就是要处理掉自己那件棕色衣服。她确信那个女性亲戚知道她一直都不喜欢那件衣服，所以必须把它烧掉，不能丢掉，而且一定要在窗子下面的后院里烧掉。她让人把她搀扶到窗边(承受着难以忍受的痛苦)，这样她就可以亲眼看到那件衣服被烧掉了，因为她确信在她死后，葬礼会由这个女亲戚负责，而且她会让自己穿着那件衣服入土。"

——选自《押沙龙，押沙龙！》第6章

注释

① excommunicate [ˌekskəˈmjuːnɪkeit] *vi.* 逐出

② fortitude [ˈfɔːtɪtjuːd] *n.* 刚毅，不屈不挠

③ annihilation [əˌnaiəˈleiʃn] *n.* 毁灭，消灭

④ spartan [ˈspɑːtən] *adj.* 刚硬的

⑤ spurious [ˈspjuəriəs] *adj.* 假的，伪造的

⑥ slumber [ˈslʌmbə(r)] *n.* 沉睡，休眠

⑦ inexplicable [ˌɪnɪkˈsplɪkəbl] *adj.* 最费解的

⑧ amicable [ˈæmɪkəbl] *adj.* 友好的

⑨ enmity [ˈenmətɪ] *n.* 敌意

⑩ kinswoman [ˈkɪnzwʊmən] *n.* 女性亲戚

⑪ excruciating [ɪkˈskruːʃieitɪŋ] *adj.* 极其痛苦的

《喧哗与骚动》*发表于1929年，分为4个部分，全篇采用多个不同的叙事风格。本书的书名出自莎士比亚的悲剧《麦克白》第5幕第5场麦克白的有名的台词："人生如痴人说梦，充满了喧哗与骚动，却没有任何意义。"目前国内最常见的该小说的翻译版本是上海译文出版社李文俊的译本。

The Sound and the Fury
喧哗与骚动

Because if it were just to hell; if that were all of it. Finished. If things just finished themselves. Nobody else there but her and me.

因为如果仅仅只是要下地狱的话，事情就了结了。如果事情要自行了结的话，就只会是她和我，没有别人。

——*The Sound and the Fury*《喧哗与骚动》

名著导读

The Sound and the Fury is set in the fictional Yoknapatawpha County. The general outline of the story is the decline of the Compson family, a once noble Southern family descended from U.S. Civil War hero General Compson. The family falls victim to those vices which Faulkner believed were responsible for the problems in the reconstructed South: racism, **avarice**①, selfishness, and the psychological inability of individuals to become determinants. Over the course of the thirty years or so related in the novel, the family falls into financial ruin, loses its religious faith and the respect of the town of Jefferson, and many of them die tragically.

《喧哗与骚动》的故事背景设在虚构的约克纳帕塔法县，主要讲述了康普生家族的没落，它曾是赫赫有名的南方望族，是美国南北战争时期的英雄康普生将军的后裔。福克纳认为这个家族衰败的原因应该归咎于美国在南方重建问题上的种种恶行：种族歧视、贪婪、自私和个人内心的无能和懦弱。在小说里，三十年来，这个家族彻底破产，背弃了宗教信仰，失去了杰斐逊小镇上人们的尊敬，有很多人悲惨地死去了。

名段选读

It was a while before the last stroke ceased **vibrating**②. It stayed in the air, more felt than heard, for a long time. Like all the bells that ever rang still ringing in the long dying light-rays and Jesus and Saint Francis talking about his sister. Because if it were just to hell; if that were all of it. Finished. If things just finished themselves. Nobody else there but her and me. If we could just have done something so dreadful that they would have fled hell except us. I have committed **incest**③ I said Father it was I it was not Dalton Ames And when he put Dalton Ames. Dalton Ames. Dalton Ames. When he put the **pistol**④ in my hand I didn't. That's why I didn't. He would be there and she would and I would. Dalton Ames. Dalton Ames. Dalton Ames. If we could have just done something so dreadful and Father said That's sad too people cannot do anything that dreadful they cannot do anything very dreadful at all they cannot even remember tomorrow what seemed dreadful today and I said, You can **shirk**⑤ all things and he said, Ah can you. And I will look down and see my murmuring bones and the deep water like wind, like a roof of wind, and after a long time they cannot distinguish even bones upon the lonely and **inviolate**⑥ sand. Until on the Day when He says Rise only the flat-iron would come floating up. It's not when you realise that nothing can help you—religion, pride, anything—it's when you realise that you don't need any aid.

过了一会儿，最后一击产生的震动才停下来。余音久久萦绕在空气中，与其说是听到的，不如说是感觉到的。就像在最后的光束快要熄灭，耶稣和圣弗朗西斯谈论着他妹妹的时候，那些已经停止的钟声仍然响彻耳畔。因为如果仅仅只是要下地狱的话，事情就了结了。如果事情要自行了结的话，就只会是她和我，没有别人。如果我们做了什么罪大恶极的事情，其他人就会逃离地狱，只剩下我们俩。我犯了乱伦的罪，当神父怪罪道尔顿·艾姆斯时，我告诉他这是我的错，不是她的错。道尔顿·艾姆斯，道尔顿·艾姆斯，道尔顿·艾姆斯。他把手枪放在我手里，但我并没有开枪。我之所以不开枪，是因为他要是下地狱的话，她也会，我也会。道尔顿·艾姆斯，道尔顿·艾姆斯，道尔顿·艾姆斯。如果我们做了什么可怕的事情，神父会说太可悲了，一般人不会做出这么可怕的事情，他们根本不会做出这么可怕的事情，他们甚至明天就不记得今天那些觉得可怕的事情了。我说你可以躲开一切，他说，啊？你可以吗？然后我低下头去看微微作响的骨头，还有像风一样，像风汇成的屋顶一样的深深的水流，很久以后，人们甚至都不能把骨头与孤寂、纯洁的沙石分辨开来。直到有一天，他说起来吧，只有烙铁才会浮起来。那一天，不是你意识到宗教、自尊以及其他任何东西都不能帮助你的时候，而是意识到你自己根本不需要任何帮助的时候。

——选自《喧哗与骚动》“1910年6月2日”

注释

★ “从《喧哗与骚动》中，我们可以看到福克纳对生活与历史的高度的认识、概括能力。尽管他的作品显得扑朔迷离，有时也的确如痴人说梦，但是实际上还是通过一个旧家庭的分崩离析和趋于死亡，真实地呈现了美国南方历史性变化的一个侧面。”

——中国著名翻译家　李文俊

① avarice [ˈævərɪs] *n.* 贪婪

② vibrate [vai'breit] *vi.&vt.* 振动，颤动

③ incest ['ɪnsest] *n.* 乱伦

④ pistol ['pɪstl] *n.* 手枪

⑤ shirk [ʃɜːk] *vt.* 逃避

⑥ inviolate [ɪn'vaiələt] *adj.* 未亵渎的，无污染的

8 美国首位诺贝尔文学奖得主——哈利·辛克莱·刘易斯

Harry Sinclair Lewis (February 7, 1885—January 10, 1951) was an American novelist, short-story writer, and playwright. In 1930, he became the first writer from the United States to be awarded the Nobel Prize in Literature, "for his vigorous and graphic art of description and his ability to create, with wit and humor, new types of characters." His works are known for their insightful and critical views of American society and capitalist values, as well as for their strong characterizations of modern working women, such as *Free Air, Main Street, Babbitt, Arrowsmith,* and *Elmer Gantry.*

哈利·辛克莱·刘易斯（1885年2月7日—1951年1月10日），美国小说家、短篇小说家、剧作家。1930年，"由于他生动形象的叙述风格，以及机智幽默地创造新角色的才华"，刘易斯成为美国第一位获得诺贝尔文学奖的作家。他的作品凭着对美国社会与资本主义价值观的深刻见解与批评，以及对现代女强人鲜明个性的描述而闻名于世，如《自由的空气》、《大街》、《巴比特》、《阿罗史密斯》以及《埃尔默·甘特利》。

《巴比特》发表于1922年，共34章，是一部反映美国商业文化繁盛时期城市商人生活的小说。湖南人民出版社王仲年译本是最好的版本。

Babbitt
巴比特

He had enormous and poetic admiration, though very little understanding, of all mechanical devices. They were his symbols of truth and beauty.

尽管对机械所知甚少，但他对所有机械设备都充满了浪漫的幻想，在他看来，它们是真与美的象征。

——*Babbitt*《巴比特》

名著导读

The central character, George Follansbee Babbitt, is a middle-aged realtor living in Zenith. He is unimaginative, self-important, and hopelessly middle class. Vaguely dissatisfied with his position, he tries to alter the pattern of his life by flirting with liberalism and by having an affair with an attractive widow, only to find that his dread of ostracism is greater than his desire for escape.

主人公乔治·福兰斯比·巴比特是泽尼斯市的一个中年房地产经纪人。他是一个无趣、妄自尊大、生活无望的中产阶级。因为突然对现状感到茫然和不满，他想方设法改变生活模式，他玩弄自由主义，与一个迷人的寡妇私通，结果却发现他对放逐生活的恐惧更胜于他想逃离现实的渴望。

名段选读

He forgot Paul Riesling in an afternoon of not unagreeable details. After a return to his office, which seemed to have **staggered**① on without him, he drove a "prospect" out to view a four-flat **tenement**② in the Linton district. He was inspired by the customer's admiration of the new cigarlighter. Thrice its novelty made him use it, and thrice he hurled halfsmoked cigarettes from the car, protesting, "I got to quit smoking so blame much!"

Their **ample**③ discussion of every detail of the cigar-lighter led them to speak of electric flat-irons and bed-warmers. Babbitt apologized for being so shabbily old-fashioned as still to use a hot-water bottle, and he announced that he would have the sleeping-porch wired at once. He had enormous and poetic admiration, though very little understanding, of all mechanical devices. They were his symbols of truth and beauty. Regarding each new intricate mechanism—metal lathe, two-jet carburetor, machine gun, oxyacetylene welder—he learned one good realistic-sounding phrase, and used it over and over, with a delightful feeling of being technical and initiated.

The customer joined him in the **worship**④ of machinery, and they came **buoyantly**⑤ up to the tenement and began that examination of plastic slate roof, kalamein doors, and seven-eighths-inch blind-nailed flooring, began those diplomacies of hurt surprise and readiness to be persuaded to do something they had already decided to do, which would some day result in a sale.

在那个没有太多令人不快的琐事的下午，他忘掉了保罗·里斯林。回了一趟办公室，他发现没有他，事务所里的一切似乎举步维艰。之后，他开车带一个“潜在买家”去看了在林顿区的一栋四套间的房子。客户很欣赏那个新的雪茄打火机，这使得他非常兴奋。由于太喜欢这个新奇的小玩意了，以至于他连用了三次，并且三次都把抽了一半的香烟用力扔出车外，并坚决申明："我非得戒掉这该死的烟不可了！"

他们详细地讨论了雪茄打火机的每一个细节，然后又说到电熨斗和床上取暖器。巴比特为自己不体面的守旧而表示歉意，因为他还在用热水袋，于是他宣布要立即在凉台装上电线。尽管对机械所知甚少，但他对所有机械设备都充满了浪漫的幻想，在他看来，它们是真与美的象征。对于每一个新的、复杂的机械装置——金属车床、双喷嘴汽化器、机关枪、氧炔焊接机——他每学到一个实用而响亮的名词都会反复地使用，内心充满了一种懂得技术和学到新知识的愉悦之情。

客户跟他一起赞美着机器，然后他们愉快地来到了那所房子，开始检查塑料板瓦屋顶、外包金属门和八分之七英寸厚的暗钉地板。然后他们用起那些交际手段，装出受打击或惊讶的样子，接着假装勉强被说服做出他们早已做好的决定，最后在某一天成交。

——选自《巴比特》第6章

注释

① stagger ['stægə(r)] *vi.* 摇摇晃晃，蹒跚而行

② tenement ['tenɪmənt] *n* 房屋

③ ample ['æmpl] *adj.* 丰富的，充足的

④ worship ['wɜːʃɪp] *n.* 崇拜，尊敬

⑤ buoyantly ['bɔiəntlɪ] *adv.* 心情愉快地

《大街》发表于1920年，共39章。小说以第一次世界大战前后美国一个小镇为背景，描写一位城市女知识分子卡罗尔嫁到小镇上成为一名乡村医生太太后的遭遇。译林出版社樊培绪的译本和上海译文出版社的译本最好。

Main Street
大街

There are two insults which no human being will endure: the assertion that he hasn't a sense of humor, and the doubly impertinent assertion that he has never known trouble.

有两种侮辱是任何人都不能忍受的：一是有人断言；你没有一点儿幽默感；一是有人更加蛮横无理地说；你从来都不知道什么是痛苦。

——*Main Street*《大街》

名著导读

In this classic satire, beautiful young Carol Kennicott comes to a small town in Gopher Prairie, Minnesota, with dreams of transforming the provincial old town into a place of beauty and culture. But she runs into a wall of bigotry, hypocrisy and complacency. In her unhappiness, Carol leaves her husband and moves for a time to Washington, D.C., but she eventually returns.

在这篇经典的讽刺小说中，年轻貌美的卡罗尔•肯尼柯特来到明尼苏达州戈弗草原的一个小镇上，梦想着把这个偏僻的老镇改造成一个文明美丽的地方。但是她却遭遇了由人们的偏执、虚伪和自满形成的阻力。卡罗尔很不开心，因此她离开了自己的丈夫，去华盛顿特区住了一阵，但最终还是回到了小镇上。

名段选读

"What have you been hearing?"

"Nothing, really. I just heard Mrs. Bogart say she'd seen you and Valborg walking together a lot." Vida's chirping **slackened**①. She looked at her nails. "But—I suspect you do like Valborg. Oh, I don't mean in any wrong way. But you're young; you don't know what an innocent liking might drift into. You always pretend to be so **sophisticated**② and all, but you're a baby. Just because you are so innocent, you don't know what evil thoughts may **lurk**③ in that fellow's brain."

"You don't suppose Valborg could actually think about making love to me?"

Her rather cheap sport ended abruptly as Vida cried, with **contorted**④ face, "What do you know about the thoughts in hearts? You just play at reforming the world. You don't know what it means to suffer."

There are two insults which no human being will endure: the assertion that he hasn't a sense of humor, and the doubly impertinent assertion that he has never known trouble. Carol said furiously, "You think I don't suffer? You think I've always had an easy—"

"No, you don't. I'm going to tell you something I've never told a living soul, not even Ray." The dam of **repressed**⑤ imagination which Vida had builded for years, which now, with Raymie off at the wars, she was building again, gave way.

"I was—I liked Will terribly well. One time at a party—oh, before he met you, of course—but we held hands, and we were so happy. But I didn't feel I was really suited to him. I let him go. Please don't think I still love him! I see now that Ray was predestined to be my mate. But because I liked him, I know how sincere and pure and noble Will is, and his thoughts never straying from the path of rectitude, and—If I gave him up to you, at least you've got to appreciate him! We danced together and laughed so, and I gave him up, but—This IS my affair! I'm NOT intruding! I see the whole thing as he does, because of all I've told you. Maybe it's shameless to bare my heart this way, but I do it for him—for him and you!"

"你听到什么了？"

"什么也没听到，真的。我只是听到博加特太太说她经常看到你和瓦尔博格一起散步。"维达唧唧喳喳的声音慢慢变弱了，她看着自己的手指甲。"但是——我怀疑你确实喜欢瓦尔博格。哦，我并不是说那个意思，只是你还年轻，还不知道这种单纯的喜欢可能会逐渐陷入怎样的境地。你总是装作一副世故的样子，但你还是个孩子。正因为你太天真了，所以你不知道那个家伙脑子里可能藏着什么邪恶的想法。”

“你不会是认为瓦尔博格其实是在想向我求爱吧？”

她尖刻的戏谑突然停了下来，因为这时维达的脸扭曲着，大叫起来：“你怎么知道别人心里的想法呢？你只会假装要改造世界，却根本不知道改造世界意味着要承受怎样的痛苦。”

有两种侮辱是任何人都不能忍受的：一是有人断言你没有一点儿幽默感；一是有人更加蛮横无理地评论你从来都不知道什么是痛苦。于是，卡罗尔怒气冲冲地说：“你以为我不痛苦吗？你以为我一直过着轻松的——”

“是的，你确实没有痛苦过。我要告诉你一件事，这件事我从来都没有告诉过任何人，对雷也没说过。”维达多年来构建的压抑自己思想的堤坝（现在，随着雷米在战争中的离开，她再次修建着的堤坝），顷刻间坍塌。

“我曾经——我曾经深爱着威尔。一次在聚会上——噢，那是在他遇到你之前——那时我们手牵着手，那么的开心。但是我觉得自己并不适合他，于是我放他走了。请不要认为我依旧爱着他。我现在明白雷是我命中注定的伴侣。但是因为我爱过威尔，我知道他是个多么真诚、纯洁和高尚的人，他从来都是正直的。而且，如果是我的放弃成全了你和他，那么你至少应该学会欣赏他！我们一起跳舞，开怀大笑，然后我放弃了他，但——但那是我的事！我并不是想插入你们之间！我只是从他的角度来看待整个事情，我这么做的原因我已经说过了。我这样将心事袒露给你，可能有点不知廉耻，但是我这么做是为了他——为了你们俩！”

——选自《大街》第31章

注释

① slacken [ˈslækən] *vi.* 减弱

② sophisticated [səˈfɪstɪkeitid] *adj.* 久经世故的

③ lurk [lɜːk] *vi.* 潜伏

④ contorted [kənˈtɔːtɪd] *adj.* 扭曲的

⑤ repressed [rɪˈprest] *adj.* 受压制的

《阿罗史密斯》发表于1925年。作者通过马丁·阿罗史密斯的坎坷一生，揭露和讽刺了当时美国医学界的弊病，深入细致地剖析了当时美国的社会现象。江苏人民出版社译本最好。

Arrowsmith
阿罗史密斯

I make many mistakes. But one thing I keep always pure: the religion of a scientist.

我犯过很多错。但有一点我始终保持着它的纯洁：一个科学家的信仰。

——*Arrowsmith*《阿罗史密斯》

名著导读

Arrowsmith tells the story of bright and scientifically minded Martin Arrowsmith as he makes his way from a small town in the Midwest to the upper echelons of the scientific community. He is born in Elk Mills, the same fictional state in which several of Lewis's other novels are set. Along the way he experiences medical school, private practice as the only doctor in North Dakota, various stints as regional health official, and the lure of high-paying hospital jobs. Finally, Arrowsmith is recognized by his former medical school mentor, Max Gottlieb, for a scientific paper he has written and is invited to take a post with a prestigious research institute in New York.

《阿罗史密斯》讲述了聪明、颇具科学头脑的马丁·阿罗史密斯从美国中西部的一个小镇逐渐步入科学领域上层社会的故事。他出生于埃尔克米尔斯州（辛克莱·刘易斯其他好几部小说都以这个虚构的州为背景）。一路上，他在医学院学习过，开过私人诊所——成为了北达科他州唯一的医生，被分配去地方卫生部做各种各样的工作，也遇到过医院高薪职位的诱惑。最后，阿罗史密斯以一篇科学著作得到了他以前的医学院老师马克思·戈特利布的认可，并受邀去纽约一所很有名望的研究所任职。

名段选读

"Perhaps I am a **crank**[①], Martin. There are many who hate me. There are plots against me—oh, you think I imagine it, but you shall see! I make many mistakes. But one thing I keep always pure: the religion of a scientist.

"To be a scientist—it is not just a different job, so that a man should choose between being a scientist and being an explorer or a bond-salesman or a physician or a king or a farmer. It is a **tangle**[②] of very obscure emotions, like mysticism, or wanting to write poetry; it makes its victim all different from the good normal man. The scientist is intensely religious—he is so religious that he will not accept quarter-truths, because they are an insult to his faith.

"He wants that everything should be subject to **inexorable**③ laws. He is equal opposed to the capitalists who think their silly money-grabbing is a system, and to liberals who think man is not a fighting animal; he takes both the American booster and the European aristocrat, and he ignores all their blithering. Ignores it! All of it! He hates the preachers who talk their fables, but he is not too kindly to the anthropologists and historians who can only make guesses, yet they have the nerf to call themselves scientists! Oh, yes, he is a man that all nice good-natured people should naturally hate!

"He speaks no meaner of the ridiculous faith-healers and chiropractors than he does of the doctors that want to snatch our science before it is tested and rush around hoping they heal people, and spoiling all the clues with their footsteps; and worse than the men like hogs, worse than the imbeciles who have not even heard of science, he hates pseudo-scientists, guess-scientists—like these psycho-analysts; and worse than those comic dream-scientists he hates the men that are allowed in a clean kingdom like biology but know only one text-book and how to lecture to nincompoops all so popular! He is the only real revolutionary, the authentic scientist, because he alone knows how little he knows.

"可能我是个怪人，马丁，很多人都恨我。有很多阴谋诡计都针对我——哦，你肯定会认为是我自己胡思乱想了，但你以后会明白的！我犯过很多错。但有一点我始终保持着它的纯洁：一个科学家的信仰。

当一名科学家——它不仅仅是一项特别的工作，好让一个人在当科学家和探险家、商人、内科医生、国王或是农民中进行选择。那是一种难以说清的情感纠结，就像神秘论，或者是想要写诗的欲望，它让人变得与正常人不一样。科学家是非常虔诚的——他是如此的虔诚，以至于他不会接受任何欺人之谈，因为那是对他的信仰的侮辱。

"他希望一切都遵守无情的法律。同时，他反对那些把自己愚蠢的抢钱行为当成一种制度的资本家，反对那些认为人不是好战动物的自由主义者。他既接受美国的支持者又接受欧洲贵族，却忽略他们所有的胡扯。忽略它，所有的！他厌恶那些满嘴无稽之谈的传教士，但对那些只会做出猜测的人类学家和历史学家也不太和善，尽管他们厚着脸皮称自己为科学家！哦，是的，他就是这样一个人，所有性格和善的人都会自然而然地恨他！

他认为，那些想在我们的科学成果通过检验之前就夺走它们并四处游走希望这些成果能够治愈疾病的医生同荒谬的信仰治疗者和脊椎按摩指压治疗者一样卑鄙无耻，他们用自己的足迹毁掉了一切线索；他痛恨伪科学家和只会推测的科学家(如精神分析学家)，这种痛恨更甚于他对像猪一样的蠢人和那些甚至没有听说过科学的低能者的憎恶；在生物学这样纯净的王国里，有人只懂一本教科书，只知道给遍地皆是的傻瓜们讲课，他痛恨这种人，这种人比可笑的、整天做梦的科学家还要糟糕。他是唯一的一个真正的革命者和可靠的科学家，因为只有他才知道自己的知识是多么匮乏。"

——选自《阿罗史密斯》第26章第1节

注释

① crank [kræŋk] *n.* 怪人

② tangle ['tæŋgl] *n.* 混乱状态

③ inexorable [ɪn'eksərəbl] *adj.* 无情的

9 美国文学之父——华盛顿·欧文

Washington Irving (April 3, 1783—November 28, 1859) was an American author, essayist, biographer and historian of the early 19th century. He was best known for his short stories *The Legend of Sleepy Hollow* and *Rip Van Winkle*, both of which appear in his book *The Sketch Book of Geoffrey Crayon, Gent*. His historical works include *biographies of George Washington, Oliver Goldsmith and Muhammad*, and several histories of 15th-century Spain, dealing with subjects such as Christopher Columbus, the Moors, and the Alhambra.

华盛顿·欧文(1783年4月3日—1859年11月28日)是19世纪初期美国作家、散文家、传记作者、历史学家。他因短篇小说《睡谷的传说》和《瑞普·凡·温克尔》而声名远扬，这两篇小说都收集在他的《见闻札记》里面。他的历史著作包括《华盛顿传》、《哥尔德斯密斯传》、《穆罕默德传》和几部涉及15世纪的西班牙的历史书籍，故事涵盖了克里斯托弗·哥伦布、摩尔人以及阿尔汉布拉宫殿等主题。

《瑞普·凡·温克尔》出版于1819年6月。以荷兰殖民地时期哈德逊河畔的一个山村为背景，描写了贫苦农民瑞普·凡·温克尔的奇特遭遇。目前国内较著名的译本是沈利人的版本。

Rip Van Winkle
瑞普·凡·温克尔

In a word, Rip was ready to attend to anybody's business but his own; but as to doing family duty, and keeping his farm in order, he found it impossible.

总而言之，瑞普非常乐意帮助任何人，除了他自己；要是让他做自家的事情，经营自己的农场，他就觉得办不到了。

——*Rip Van Winkle*《瑞普·凡·温克尔》

名著导读

Some years before the American Revolution, Rip Van Winkle lives in a pleasant village at the foot of the Catskill Mountains. One day he wanders into the mountains and happens upon the ghosts of Henry Hudson and his crew playing nine pins in a mysterious hollow. He drinks their brew and falls asleep. Twenty years later, he wakes as an aged man and wanders back to his village, where he is astonished by the changes that have taken place. After some ado, he is reunited with his now-grown daughter and her children.

美国独立战争前几年，瑞普·凡·温克尔住在卡茨基尔山脚一个风景宜人的村子里。一天，他漫步走进了山里，碰巧遇到亨利·哈得逊和他手下的鬼魂在一个神秘的山谷里玩九柱戏。他喝下他们的酒便睡着了。二十年后，他醒来时已经是个老人，再回村里时，却惊讶地发现那里发生了很大的变化。几经波折，他终于和已长大成人的女儿以及她的孩子们重聚了。

名段选读

The great error in Rip's composition was an **insuperable**① **aversion**② to all kinds of profitable labor. It could not be from the want of **assiduity**③ or perseverance; for he would sit on a wet rock, with a rod as long and heavy as a Tartar's lance, and fish all day without a murmur, even though he should not be encouraged by a single nibble. He would carry a fowling piece on his shoulder for hours together, trudging through woods and swamps, and up hill and down dale, to shoot a few squirrels or wild pigeons. He would never refuse to assist a neighbor even in the roughest toil, and was a foremost man at all country **frolics**④ for husking Indian corn, or building stone-fences; the women of the village, too, used to employ him to run their errands, and to do such little odd jobs as their less obliging husbands would not do for them. In a word, Rip was ready to attend to anybody's business but his own; but as to doing family duty, and keeping his farm in order, he found it impossible.

In fact, he declared it was of no use to work on his farm; it was the most **pestilent**⑤ little piece of ground in the whole country; every thing about it went wrong, and would go wrong, in spite of him. His fences were continually falling to pieces; his cow would either go **astray**⑥, or get among the cabbages; weeds were sure to grow quicker in his fields than anywhere else; the rain always made a point of setting in just as he had some outdoor work to do; so that though his patrimonial estate had dwindled away under his management, acre by acre, until there was little more left than a mere patch of Indian corn and potatoes, yet it was the worst-conditioned farm in the neighborhood.

瑞普性格中有一个很大的缺点：他从心理上讨厌所有赚钱的活儿。这并不是因为他不勤快，没有耐性；因为他可以坐在一块潮湿的岩石上，手里拿着一根象鞑靼人的长矛一样又长又重的竿子钓上一整天，即使没有一点收获，他也毫无怨言。为了猎捕几只松鼠或野鸽子，他会背上一把猎枪，连续几个小时穿越树林和沼泽，翻山越岭。他从不会拒绝帮助邻居，即使是最辛苦的活儿也不例外。在所有的全村聚会上，他总是第一个剥印度玉米或砌石墙的人；村庄里的妇女们也经常差遣他为她们跑腿，叫他做一些自己不够体贴的丈夫所不愿做的零碎活。总而言之，瑞普非常乐意帮助任何人，除了他自己；要是让他做自家的事情，经营自己的农场，他就觉得办不到了。

事实上，他宣称他在自己的农地里干活是没有用的；那是整个村庄最折腾人的一小块地，跟这块地有关的所有事情都会出现问题，尽管他一次次纠正，可还是会出问题。他的篱笆总是坍塌；他的母牛不是迷了路，就是跑到了卷心菜地里；地里的杂草肯定比别处长得都快；他要出门干活的时候，就会很凑巧地下起雨来；于是，这块祖传的地在他的管理下，一英亩一英亩地减少下去，直到最后仅剩下一小块玉米和马铃薯地，但是这块地仍然是附近最糟糕的地。

——选自《瑞普·凡·温克尔》

注释

① insuperable [ɪn'suːpərəbl] *adj.* 无法克服的

② aversion [ə'vɜːʃən] *n.* 厌恶，讨厌的人

③ assiduity [ˌæsɪ'djuːətɪ] *n.* 勤勉

④ frolic ['frɔlɪk] *n.* 欢乐的聚会

⑤ pestilent ['pestɪlənt] *adj.* 恼人的

⑥ astray [ə'strei] *adv.* 迷途地

《睡谷的传说》创作于19世纪初，它与欧文的另外两篇短篇小说《瑞普·凡·温克尔》、《鬼新郎》被称为"最早的现代短篇小说"。目前国内较著名的译本是顾韶阳的版本和李淑敏的版本。

The Legend of the Sleepy Hollow
睡谷的传说

I profess not to know how women's hearts are wooed and won. To me they have always been matters of riddle and admiration.

我承认，我不懂如何追求女人并赢得她们的芳心。对我来说，她们总是神秘而迷人的。

——*The legend of the Sleepy Hollow*《睡谷的传说》

名著导读

The story is set circa 1790 in the Dutch settlement of Tarry Town, in a **secluded glen**[①] called Sleepy Hollow. It tells the story of Ichabod Crane, a superstitious schoolmaster from Connecticut, who competes with Brom the hand of Katrina Van Tassel. As Crane leaves a party, he is pursued by the Headless Horseman. Ichabod mysteriously disappears from town, leaving Katrina to marry Brom. Although the nature of the Headless Horseman is left open to interpretation, the story implies that the Horseman was really Brom in disguise.

该故事发生在1790年左右荷兰人聚居的塔里敦村庄，这是一个与世隔绝的幽谷，名叫睡谷。它讲述的是来自康涅狄格州的一位迷信教师的故事，他叫伊卡包德·克兰，和布鲁姆同是卡特琳娜·凡·塔塞尔的追求者。当克兰从一个聚会返回时，受到一名无头骑士的追赶，伊卡包德从此神秘地从镇上消失了，卡特琳娜就嫁给了布鲁姆。虽然无头骑士的身份还有待说明，但故事暗示了无头骑士其实就是布鲁姆假装的。

名段选读

I profess not to know how women's hearts are **wooed**[②] and won. To me they have always been matters of riddle and admiration. Some seem to have but one **vulnerable**[③] point, or door of access; while others have a thousand avenues, and may be captured in a thousand different ways. It is a great triumph of skill to gain the former, but a still greater proof of generalship to maintain possession of the latter, for man must battle for his fortress at every door and window. He who wins a thousand common hearts is therefore **entitled**[④] to some renown; but he who keeps undisputed sway over the heart of a coquette is indeed a hero. Certain it is, this was not the case with the redoubtable Brom Bones; and from the moment Ichabod Crane made his advances, the interests of the former evidently declined: his horse was no longer seen tied to the palings on Sunday nights, and a deadly **feud**[⑤] gradually arose between him and the preceptor of Sleepy Hollow.

Brom, who had a degree of rough **chivalry**[⑥] in his nature, would fain have carried matters to open warfare and have settled their pretensions to the lady, according to the mode of those most concise and simple reasoners, the knights-errant of yore,—by single combat; but Ichabod was too conscious of the superior might of his adversary to enter the lists against him; he had overheard a boast of Bones, that he would "double the schoolmaster up, and lay him on a shelf of his own schoolhouse;" and he was too wary to give him an opportunity. There was something extremely provoking in this **obstinately**[⑦] pacific system; it left Brom no alternative but to draw upon the funds of rustic **waggery**[8] in his disposition, and to play off **boorish**[9] practical jokes upon his rival. Ichabod became the object of **whimsical**[10] persecution to Bones and his gang of rough riders. They harried his hitherto peaceful domains; smoked out his singing school by stopping up the chimney; broke into the schoolhouse at night, in spite of its **formidable**[11] fastenings of withe and window stakes, and turned everything **topsy-turvy**[12], so that the poor schoolmaster began to think all the witches in the country held their meetings there. But what was still more annoying, Brom took all opportunities of turning him into **ridicule**[13] in presence of his mistress, and had a scoundrel dog whom he taught to whine in the most ludicrous manner, and introduced as a rival of Ichabod's, to instruct her in **psalmody**[14].

我承认，我不懂如何追求女人并赢得她们的芳心。对我来说，她们总是神秘而迷人的。有些女人的心似乎只有一个突破口，或者说只有一扇可进入的门，而有些女人的心则有上千条路，可以被上千种方法俘获。要赢得前者，必须有高超的技巧；但要永久地拥有后者，却需要更大的才能，因为男人必须保卫好自己堡垒的每一扇门和窗。因此，一个赢得一千个普通女人的心的男人是令人敬佩的，但是能够牢牢占据一个风情女子的心的男人，才是真的英雄。当然了，可敬的布鲁姆·伯恩斯并不是这种人。从伊卡包德·克兰开始追求卡特琳娜那一刻开始，布鲁姆的优势便明显下降了：再也没有人在星期天晚上的时候看见他的马拴在篱笆上了，他对那位睡谷教师的恨意也与日俱增。

布鲁姆天性中就有一种鲁莽的骑士精神。他原本希望能将此事转化为公开战斗，沿用古时候游侠骑士们最简单明了的方式——一对一进行决斗，以解决他们对这位女士的争夺；但是，伊卡包德非常清楚对手的强大力量，坚决不肯应战。他曾无意中听到伯恩斯吹牛说“要把这个教师对折起来，放在他自己校舍里的一个书架上”，于是他更加小心谨慎，不让他有可乘之机。这样相持的局面实在让人愤怒至极；于是布鲁姆别无选择，只好利用他的质朴诙谐来取悦卡特琳娜，并粗野地捉弄他的情敌。伊卡包德成了伯恩斯和他那帮粗野的骑士们用各种古怪方法迫害的对象。他们进攻他一向和平的生活，堵住烟囱用烟熏他的音乐学校；不管柳条绕得多紧，顶窗多么坚固，他们都会在晚上闯进校舍，把东西弄得乱七八糟，弄得这位可怜的教师开始认为村子里所有的坏蛋都来这里汇集过。但更可气的是，布鲁姆利用一切机会让伊卡包德在卡特琳娜面前出丑，布鲁姆养了一条恶狗，他教它以一种最滑稽的方式哀嚎，并且介绍说这条狗跟伊卡包德差不多，可以教她唱赞美诗。

——选自《睡谷的传说》

注释

① secluded glen【词组】隐蔽幽谷，隐秘幽谷

② woo [wuː] *vt.* 追求

③ vulnerable ['vʌlnərəbl] *adj.* 易受攻击的，有弱点的

④ entitle [ɪn'taitl] *vt.* 使享有权利
⑤ feud [fju:d] *n.* 夙怨
⑥ chivalry ['ʃɪvəlrɪ] *n.* 骑士精神
⑦ obstinately ['ɔbstɪnətlɪ] *adv.* 固执地
⑧ waggery ['wægərɪ] *n.* 滑稽，消化
⑨ boorish ['buərɪʃ] *adj.* 粗野的，粗鄙的
⑩ whimsical ['wɪmzɪkl] *adj.* 古怪的，异想天开的
⑪ formidable ['fɔ:mɪdəbl] *adj.* 难对付的
⑫ topsy-turvy [ˌtɔpsɪ'tə:vɪ] *adj.* 颠倒的，乱七八糟的
⑬ ridicule ['rɪdɪkju:l] *n.* 嘲笑，愚弄
⑭ psalmody ['sɑ:mədɪ] *n.* 赞美诗

《破碎的心》发表于1819年7月，是优美的散文名篇，收录在华盛顿·欧文的《见闻札记》中。目前国内最有名的译本是刘荣跃的《见闻札记》和林纾的《拊掌录》。

The Broken Heart
破碎的心

But a woman's whole life is a history of the affections. The heart is her world; it is there her ambition strives for empire—it is there her avarice seeks for hidden treasures.

但女人的一生却是一部爱情史，心灵就是她的世界，在这里，她立志建造自己的王国；在这里，她贪婪地搜寻隐藏的宝藏。

——*The Broken Heart*《破碎的心》

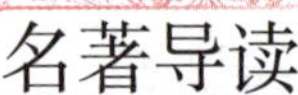

名著导读

It was included in *the Sketch Book of Geoffrey Crayon, Gent*, a collection of 34 essays and short stories. In it the Geoffrey Crayon relates the story of a young Irish woman who wasted away "in a slow but hopeless decline" following the death of her true love.

本文收录于《见闻札记》——一本包含了34篇散文和短篇小说的集子。在文中，杰弗里·科瑞讲述了一个年轻的爱尔兰女人的故事，在她真心爱着的人去世之后，她在“缓慢且无望的老去”中日渐消瘦。

名段选读

Man is the creature of interest and ambition. His nature leads him forth into the struggle and bustle of the world. Love is but the **embellishment**① of his early life, or a song piped in the **intervals**② of the acts. He seeks for fame, for fortune for space in the world's thought, and dominion over his fellow-men. But a woman's whole life is a history of the affections. The heart is her world; it is there her ambition strives for empire—it is there her avarice seeks for hidden treasures. She sends forth her sympathies on adventure; she embarks her whole soul in the traffic of affection; and if shipwrecked, her case is hopeless—for it is a bankruptcy of the heart.

To a man, the disappointment of love may occasion some bitter pangs; it wounds some feelings of tenderness—it blasts some prospects of felicity; but he is an active being—he may dissipate his thoughts in the whirl of varied occupation, or may plunge into the tide of pleasure; or, if the scene of disappointment be too full of painful associations, he can shift his abode at will, and taking, as it were, the wings of the morning, can "fly to the uttermost parts of the earth, and be at rest."

But woman's is comparatively a fixed, a **secluded**③, and **meditative**④ life. She is more the companion of her own thoughts and feelings; and if they are turned to ministers of sorrow, where shall she look for consolation? Her lot is to be wooed and won; and if unhappy in her love, her heart is like some fortress that has been captured, and sacked, and abandoned, and left desolate.

男人是野心勃勃、追求利益的生物。天性引导他们进入世界的争斗和喧闹之中。爱情只不过是他早年生活的一件装饰品，或是中场休息时吹奏的一支乐曲。男人追逐名望、财富，希望在这个世界的思想中占据一席之地，并统领他的追随者。但女人的一生却是一部爱情史，心灵就是她的世界。在这里，她立志建造自己的王国；在这里，她贪婪地搜寻隐藏的宝藏。在爱的冒险中，她付出同情与怜悯；在爱的旅程中，她全身心的投入。一旦受挫了，她便会陷入绝望——因为心彻底碎了。

对于男人而言，失恋可能带来一些苦闷和悲痛，它会伤害到某些细腻的感情，毁灭某些对幸福的憧憬；但他是积极的个体——他可以通过各种的方式来驱散心中的苦闷，或投身于欢乐的浪潮之中，或者，假如失恋的场面太令人痛苦，他可以随心所欲地搬家，然后乘着清晨的翅膀，“飞往天涯海角，让心静下来”。

但是相对而言，女人却过着一种固定不变、与世隔绝、冥思苦想的生活。她更多的是与自己的思想和感情作伴；如果这些思想和感情全变成了最大的悲伤，那她该去哪里寻找心灵的慰藉呢？她天生是要被追求、被俘虏的，如果她的爱情是不幸的，她的心就会像是某个堡垒：被占领过、掠夺过，最后却被抛弃，变得荒芜寂寥。

——选自《破碎的心》

注释

① embellishment [ɪm'belɪʃmənt] *n.* 装饰

② interval ['ɪntəvl] *n.* 间歇

③ secluded [sɪ'klu:dɪd] *adj.* 与世隔绝的

④ meditative ['medɪtətɪv] *adj.* 沉思的，冥想的

10 西方现代心理小说的开拓者——亨利·詹姆斯

Henry James (April 15, 1843—February 28, 1916) was an American-born writer, regarded as one of the key figures of 19th-century literary realism. He is primarily known for the series of novels in which he portrays the encounter of Americans with Europe and Europeans. His method of writing from the point of view of a character within a tale allows him to explore issues related to consciousness and perception, and his style in later works hasfs been compared to impressionist painting. Among James's masterpieces are *The American* (1877), *Daisy Miller* (1879) and *The Portrait of a Lady* (1881).

亨利·詹姆斯(1843年4月15日—1916年2月28日)，美国著名作家，被认为是19世纪现实主义文学主要代表人物之一。他在一系列小说中刻画了美国人与欧洲文化以及欧洲人之间的冲突，他也因此为众人所知。他的写作手法是通过故事中人物的角度来探讨意识和认识的问题。他后期的作品风格被比作印象画派。詹姆斯的杰作包括《美国人》(1877)、《黛西·米勒》(1879)和《贵妇的画像》(1881)。

《贵妇的画像》完成于1881年，是亨利·詹姆斯的早期代表作，也是他的杰作之一，被西方批评家看成是美国现代小说的一个发端。目前国内流行的译本是章汝雯的《贵妇画像》，洪增流和尚晓进的《贵妇人画像》以及项星耀的《一位女士的画像》。

The Portrait of a Lady
贵妇的画像

You must have suffered first, have suffered greatly, have gained some miserable knowledge. In that way your eyes are opened to it.

你必须先忍受痛苦，并从中积累一些惨痛的教训。这样你才能够开阔视野，才可以看见它。

——*The Portrait of a Lady*《贵妇的画像》

名著导读

The Portrait of a Lady is the story of a spirited young American woman, Isabel Archer, who "**affronts**[①] her destiny" and finds it overwhelming. She inherits a large amount of money and subsequently becomes the victim of machiavellian scheming by two American expatriates . Isabel arrives in Europe hoping to broaden her **experiences**[②] and find maturity and happiness. As she is a fiercely independent woman, she encounters many conflicts between how she perceives herself and how she is expected to behave. Ultimately, Isabel succumbs to the pressure to marry, but she finds herself in a loveless marriage, her freedom sacrificed to society's conventions.

《贵妇的画像》讲述的是一位勇敢激进的美国少女——伊莎贝尔·阿切尔的故事，她敢于挑战自己的命运，最后却发现它是不可战胜的。她继承了一大笔财产，却接着成为两个美国侨民策划的政治阴谋中的牺牲品。伊莎贝尔来到欧洲，希望增长见识，使自己成熟并追求自己的幸福。伊莎贝尔是一位非常独立的女性，在她所希望的自己与他人所期待的自己之间，她产生了诸多矛盾。最终，她迫于压力结婚了，但她发现这是一场没有爱情的婚姻，她的自由也成了社会陈规的牺牲品。

名段选读

Ralph shook his head sadly. "I might show it to...you, but you'd never see it. The privilege isn't given to every one; it's not enviable. It has never been seen by a young, happy, innocent person like you. You must have suffered first, have suffered greatly, have gained some miserable knowledge. In that way your eyes are opened to it. I saw it long ago," said Ralph.

"I told you just now I'm very fond of knowledge," Isabel answered.

"Yes, of happy knowledge—of pleasant knowledge. But you haven't suffered, and you're not made to suffer. I hope you'll never see the ghost!"

She had listened to him **attentively**[③], with a smile on her lips, but with certain gravity in her eyes.

Charming as he found her, she had struck him as rather **presumptuous**[④]—indeed it was a part of her charm; and he wondered what she would say. "I'm not afraid, you know," she said, which seemed quite presumptuous enough.

"You're not afraid of suffering?"

"Yes, I'm afraid of suffering. But I'm not afraid of ghosts. And I think people suffer too easily," she added.

"I don't believe you do," said Ralph, looking at her with his hands in his pockets.

"I don't think that's a fault," she answered. "It's not absolutely necessary to suffer; we were not made for that."

拉尔夫伤心地摇了摇头说："我可以展示给你看，但是你可能永远都不想看见它。这种特权并不是每个人都有的，不过也没什么好羡慕的。从来没有一个像你这样年轻、快乐、天真的人看见过它。你必须先忍受痛苦，并从中积累一些惨痛的教训。这样你才能够开阔视野，才可以看见它。而我已在很久之前就见过它了。"

"我刚才告诉过你我喜欢经历生活，"伊莎贝尔回答。

"是的，你喜欢快乐的经历——愉快的经历。但是你还没有经历过痛苦的，不过你也没有必要去经历。我希望你永远都不会遇到可怕的事！"

她聚精会神地听着，嘴角带着微笑，但眼神却庄严而肃穆。

他发现她很迷人，她肆无忌惮地闯进了他的世界，扣动着他的心弦——其实这也正是她的一种魅力；他很好奇她会说什么。"你知道的，我不害怕。"她说。这似乎显得更加放肆了。

"你不怕受苦？"

"不，我害怕承受痛苦，但是我不害怕可怕的事，因为我觉得令人感到痛苦的事情太多了。"她接着说。

"我不信你是这样想的，"拉夫尔说。他看着她，将手放在口袋里。

"我觉得这话也没有错，"她回答说，"生活不一定要经历苦难，我们也不是为了受苦才活在这世上。"

——选自《贵妇的画像》第5章

注释

① affront[ə'frʌnt] *vt.* 面对，冒犯

② expatriate [eks'pætriət] *n.* 移居海外者

③ attentively [ə'tentɪvlɪ] *adv.* 聚精会神地，周到地

④ presumptuous [prɪ'zʌmptʃuəs] *adj.* 放肆的，冒失的

《黛西·米勒》于1878年以连载的形式出现，接着在1879年以书籍的形式出版，是亨利·詹姆斯最受欢迎的小说之一。目前国内比较普遍的译本是巫宁坤和赵萝蕤的译本。

Daisy Miller
黛西·米勒

I believe that it makes very little difference whether you are engaged or not!

我认为你有没有订婚其实并没有多大区别！

——*Daisy Miller*《黛西·米勒》

名著导读

Daisy Miller is the story of the exuberant and naive Daisy Miller, a young American girl who flirts and partakes of young life to its fullest while visiting Europe. Daisy meets the more subtle and self-aware Winterbourne and their romance ends in misfortune. The portrait of Daisy is a quintessential exploration of the social mores of her era. And her flirtatious disregard of them is simultaneously a breath of fresh air and the heart of tragedy.

《黛西·米勒》讲述的是一位天真无邪、充满活力的美国女孩黛西·米勒在欧洲尽情挥霍自己青春年华的故事。黛西遇到了更加难以捉摸、更加自我的温特伯恩，他们的爱情以悲剧收场。作者对黛西的刻画是对她那个时代社会道德的精辟剖析。她对社会道德观念的漠视是一股清新的空气，同时也是她悲剧的根源。

名段选读

"I should advise you," said Winterbourne, "to drive home as fast as possible and take one!"

"What you say is very wise," Giovanelli rejoined. "I will go and make sure the carriage is at hand." And he went forward rapidly.

Daisy followed with Winterbourne. He kept looking at her; she seemed not in the least embarrassed. Winterbourne said nothing; Daisy chattered about the beauty of the place. "Well, I have seen the Colosseum by moonlight!" she exclaimed. "That's one good thing." Then, noticing Winterbourne's silence, she asked him why he didn't speak. He made no answer; he only began to laugh. They passed under one of the dark **archways**①; Giovanelli was in front with the carriage. Here Daisy stopped a moment, looking at the young American. "Did you believe I was engaged, the other day?" she asked.

"It doesn't matter what I believed the other day," said Winterbourne, still laughing.

"Well, what do you believe now?"

"I believe that it makes very little difference whether you are engaged or not!"

He felt the young girl's pretty eyes fixed upon him through the thick gloom of the archway; she was **apparently**② going to answer. But Giovanelli hurried her forward. "Quick! Quick!" he said; "if we get in by midnight we are quite safe."

"我建议你，"温特伯恩说，"尽快驾车回家拿一个！"

"你说的很对，"焦瓦内利回答道。"我去看看马车准备好了没。"他疾步往前走去。

黛西跟随着温特伯恩。他一直看着她，她似乎一点儿也不尴尬。温特伯恩没有说话，黛西喋喋不休地赞叹这个地方有多么美。"我看到月光下的罗马圆形大剧场啦！"她叫嚷着，"确实很美妙。"这时，她意识到了温特伯恩的沉默，于是问他为什么不说话。他没有回答，只是大笑起来。他们穿过了暗处的一座拱门，焦瓦内利和马车就在前面。黛西突然停了一会，看着这个年轻的美国小伙子，问道："那天你相信我订婚了吗？"

"我相不相信并不重要，"温特伯恩说道。他仍然面带笑容。

"那么，你现在怎么想呢？"

"我认为你有没有订婚其实并没有多大区别！"

他感觉到这个年轻女孩漂亮的眼睛正穿过拱门浓浓的幽暗注视着他；显然，她正要回答什么，但是焦瓦内利在催她。"赶快！快点！"他说，"如果能够在午夜之前赶到那里，我们就安全了。"

——选自《黛西·米勒》第4章

注释

① archway[ˈɑːtʃwei] *n.* 拱门，拱道

② apparently [əˈpærəntlɪ] *adv.* 显然地

《德莫福夫人》出版于1874年，是亨利·詹姆斯最长的小说之一。目前国内流行的译本是聂华苓的译本。

Madame De Mauves
德莫福夫人

Deep experience is never peaceful.

深刻的经历永远是不平静的。

——*Madame De Mauves*《德莫福夫人》

名著导读

Outside Paris a wealthy American man named Longmore is introduced to his countrywoman Euphemia de Mauves. She is the sweet but **austere**① wife of Comte

Richard de Mauves, a cynical, womanizing Frenchman who hints that Longmore should take an amorous interest in his wife. Longmore resists the suggestion, even though he spots Richard with his latest mistress in a Paris cafe. Longmore finally leaves for America. Two years later he hears that Richard has committed suicide because Euphemia wouldn't forgive his adulteries and reconcile with him, though Richard promised to be faithful to her in the future. Although Euphemia is now free, Longmore is undecided about returning to Europe to pursue her.

在巴黎郊外，富有的美国人朗莫尔经人介绍认识了与他同样是美国人的尤菲米亚·德莫福。她是理查德·德莫福伯爵的妻子，不仅漂亮且品行端正，而理查德是一个愤世嫉俗、荒淫无度的人。他暗示朗莫尔去勾引自己的妻子。虽然朗莫尔在巴黎咖啡馆撞见了理查德和他的新情人，但他还是拒绝了这个请求。朗莫尔后来去了美国。两年后，他听说理查德自杀了，因为虽然他保证以后会忠诚于尤菲米亚，但她还是不愿宽恕他的浪荡行径，不肯与他重归于好。尤菲米亚现在自由了，但朗莫尔还没有决定重返欧洲去追求她。

名段选读

She neither smiled nor looked flattered; it seemed indeed to Longmore that she took his reappearance with no pleasure. But he was uncertain, for he immediately noted that in his absence the whole character of her face had changed. It showed him something **momentous**[②] had happened.

It was no longer self-contained **melancholy**[③] that he read in her eyes, but grief and **agitation**[④] which had lately struggled with the passionate love of peace ruling her before all things else, and forced her to know that deep experience is never peaceful. She was pale and had evidently been shedding tears. He felt his heart beat hard—he seemed now to touch her secret. She continued to look at him with a clouded brow, as if his return had surrounded her with **complications**[⑤] too great to be disguised by a colorless welcome. For some moments, as he turned and walked beside her, neither spoke; then abruptly, "Tell me truly, Mr. Longmore," she said, "why you've come back." He inclined himself to her, almost pulling up again, with an air that startled her into a certainty of what she had feared. "Because I've learned the real answer to the question I asked you the other day. You're not happy—you're too good to be happy on the terms offered you. Madame de Mauves," he went on with a gesture which protested against a gesture of her own, "I can't be happy, you know, when you're as little so as I make you out. I don't care for anything so long as I only feel helpless and sore about you. I found during those dreary days in Paris that the thing in life I most care for is this daily privilege of seeing you. I know it's very brutal to tell you I admire you; it's an insult to you to treat you as if you had complained to me or appealed to me. But such a friendship as I waked up to there"—and he tossed his head toward the distant city—"is a **potent** [⑥] force, I assure you. When forces are stupidly **stifled** [⑦] they explode. However," he went on, "if you had told me every trouble in your heart it would have mattered little; I couldn't say more than I—that if that in life from which you've hoped most has given you least, this devoted respect of mine will refuse no service and betray no trust."

她的眼神里既没有笑意，也没有谄媚。朗莫尔觉得自己的再次到来似乎并没有给她带来惊喜。但是他并不确定是否如此，因为他注意到自己不在的时候她的整个表情都变了。他看得出来一定发生过什么重大的事情。

从她的眼睛里，他读到的不再是沉默寡言、郁郁寡欢，而是一种悲伤和焦虑。最近，这些情绪与她对平静生活的热爱较量起来（这种热爱曾经是她生活的唯一主导），并且让她明白：深刻的经历永远是不平静的。她脸色苍白，很显然刚才哭过了。他感觉到自己的心跳得很快，现在他似乎已经触及到她的心事了。她继续用忧愁的表情面对他，似乎他的再次出现是件极其麻烦的事情，以至于她无法只是用一句漠然的问候来掩饰。在一段时间里，他在她身旁走来走去，两个人都没有说话，突然她开口了，"请你诚实地告诉我，朗莫尔先生，"她说，"你为什么回来？"他向她凑拢过去，脸上那个曾经一度使她感到害怕的神情，差点儿又一次吓坏她。"因为我知道了那天我问你的那个问题的真正答案。德莫福夫人，你并不快乐，你太善良了，你拥有的一些并不能使你快乐。"他继续以一种对她的姿势表示抗议的姿态说道："你知道的，我对你了解得如此之少，所以我无法快乐。我什么都不在乎，只是对你感到无助和痛心。在巴黎那段沉闷的日子里，我最期待的就是每天都能看见你。我知道向你倾诉我对你的爱慕显得很无礼。你向我抱怨什么，或者说我喜欢你之类的话对你来说就是耻辱。但是我在这里察觉到的情感——"他抬头看了看远方的城市说，"是一种强大的力量，我向你保证。这种力量如果被不合理的压抑就会爆发。"他继续说道："但是，如果你肯告诉我你的心事，那么它们就不会再困扰你了。我只能说，如果你对生活期望的太多，得到的太少，那么我会随时为你效劳，永不背叛你。"

——选自《德莫福夫人》第5章

注释

① austere [ɔ'stɪə] *adj.* 朴素的，严峻的

② momentous [mə'mentəs] *adj.* 重要的，重大的

③ melancholy ['melənkəlɪ] *n.* 忧郁，愁思

④ agitation [ˌædʒɪ'teiʃən] *n.* 激动，煽动

⑤ complication [ˌkɔmplɪ'keiʃən] *n.* 复杂化，复杂的因素

⑥ potent ['pəutənt] *adj.* 有力的，有效的

⑦ stifle ['staifl] *vt.* 受抑制，受阻止

Chapter 3

法国名家名著榜

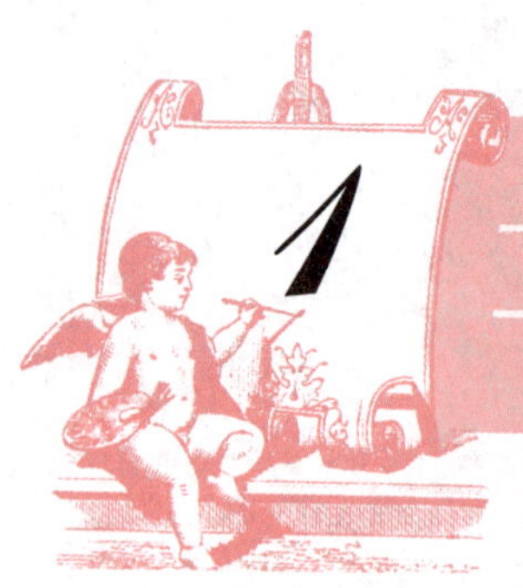

1 十九世纪法国伟大批判现实主义作家——奥诺雷·德·巴尔扎克

Honoré de Balzac (May 20, 1799—August 18, 1850) was a French novelist and playwright. His **magnum opus**① was a sequence of short stories and plays collectively entitled *La Comédie humaine*, which presents a panorama of French life in the years after the fall of Napoleon I in 1815. Due to his keen observation of detail and unfiltered representation of society, Balzac is regarded as one of the founders of realism in European literature. He is renowned for his multi-faceted characters; even his lesser characters are complex, morally ambiguous and fully human. This prodigious output includes his most celebrated novels such as *Eugenie Grandet* (1833), *Id Goriot* (1835) and *Lost Illusions* (1837—1843).

奥诺雷·德·巴尔扎克(1799年5月20日—1850年8月18日)是法国小说家和剧作家。他的代表作是由一系列短篇小说和戏剧集合而成的《人间喜剧》，反映了1815年拿破仑一世下台后法国的社会全貌。由于他敏锐细致的观察力和对社会面貌的真实再现，巴尔扎克被认为是欧洲现实主义文学的奠基者之一。他因擅于刻画多重人物性格而闻名，甚至他作品中的小角色都是复杂而道德模糊的鲜活人物。他的伟大著作包括《欧也妮·葛朗台》(1833)、《高老头》(1835)、《幻灭》(1837—1843)等等。

《欧也妮·葛朗台》发表于1833年，共7章，是巴尔扎克《人间喜剧》中“最出色的画幅之一”。葛朗台是小说着力刻画的人物，作者笔下的这一形象被刻画得栩栩如生，成为世界文学史上四大吝啬鬼形象之一。该小说目前在国内最常见的翻译版本是翻译家傅雷和长江文艺出版社余启应的译本。

Eugenie Grandet
欧也妮·葛朗台

Misers have no belief in a future life; the present is their all in all.

守财奴并不相信有来世，现世拥有的就是他们的一切。

——*Eugenie Grandet*《欧也妮·葛朗台》

名著导读

Eugenie Grandet is set in the town of Saumur. The Grandet household, oppressed by the exacting **miserliness**[②] of Felix Grandet himself, is jerked violently out of routine by the sudden arrival of Eugénie's cousin Charles, recently orphaned and penniless. Eugénie's emotional awakening, stimulated by her love for her cousin, brings her into direct conflict with her father, whose cunning and financial success are matched against her determination to rebel. Felix's banker des Grassins wishes Eugenie to marry his son Adolphe, and his lawyer Cruchot wishes Eugenie to marry his nephew Cruchot des Bonfons. The two families constantly visit the Grandets to get Felix's favour, and Felix in turn plays them off against each other for his own advantage.

《欧也妮·葛朗台》的故事场景设在索漠镇。菲力克斯·葛朗台非常吝啬，家人都在他的这种压迫下生活。然而，欧也妮的堂弟查尔斯的到来突然打破了这种看似正常的生活轨道。查尔斯最近成了孤儿，而且身无分文。欧也妮沉睡的感情被唤醒，她爱上了她的堂弟，但这直接激起了她与父亲的矛盾。为了自己的财富，老奸巨猾的菲力克斯不允许女儿反抗他。菲力克斯的银行家德·拉格桑希望欧也妮嫁给自己的儿子阿道夫，而他的律师克罗旭则希望欧也妮嫁给自己的外甥特·蓬风。这两家为此经常来讨好菲力克斯，而反过来，菲力克斯却通过在他们之间挑拨离间来为自己捞好处。

名段选读

Hearing these words, mother and daughter slipped back into their rooms and burrowed in their beds, with the celerity of frightened mice getting back to their holes.

"Madame Grandet, have you found a mine?" said the man, coming into the chamber of his wife.

"My friend, wait; I am saying my prayers," said the poor mother in a trembling voice.

"The devil take your good God!" **growled**[③] Grandet in reply.

Misers have no belief in a future life; the present is their all in all. This thought casts a terrible light upon our present epoch, in which, far more than at any former period, money sways the laws and politics and morals. Institutions, books, men, and **dogmas**[④], all **conspire**[⑤] to

undermine[⑥] belief in a future life,—a belief upon which the social **edifice**[⑦] has rested for eighteen hundred years. The grave, as a means of transition, is little feared in our day. The future, which once opened to us beyond the **requiems**[⑧], has now been imported into the present. To obtain a **terrestrial**[⑨] paradise of luxury and earthly enjoyment, to harden the heart and **macerate**[⑩] the body for the sake of **fleeting**[⑪] possessions, as the martyrs once suffered all things to reach eternal joys, this is now the universal thought—a thought written everywhere, even in the very laws which ask of the legislator, "What do you pay?" instead of asking him, "What do you think?" When this doctrine has passed down from the bourgeoisie to the **populace**[⑫], where will this country be?

听了这些话，母亲和女儿立马溜回了自己的房间，钻进床上的被子里，就像受到惊吓的老鼠敏捷地逃回自己的洞里一样。

"葛朗台太太，你是找到一个金库了吗？"走进妻子房间的男人说道。

"等一下，老朋友，我正在祈祷呢，"这位可怜的母亲用颤抖的声音回答道。

"魔鬼把你善良的上帝赶走啦！"葛朗台咆哮着。

守财奴并不相信有来世，现世拥有的就是他们的一切。比起以往任何一个时代，这种观念在现今这个时代尤为盛行，钱财可以支配法律、政治和道德。制度、书籍、人、教条，所有这些都削弱着人们对来生的信仰，而这种信仰作为社会赖以生存的根基已经存在了1800年。死亡，对我们来说不过是一种过渡的方式，已经没什么可害怕的了。来世，它曾经只会在我们安息后才向我们敞开大门，而如今，已被牵涉进了现世。追求奢靡淫乐的人间天堂，追求转瞬即逝的财富，哪怕要为此变成铁石心肠，付出健康的代价，就像以前烈士们为了追求永恒的快乐甘愿忍受一切痛苦一样。这种想法随处可见，甚至被写进了法律，法律向立法者提出的问题是"你付多少钱？"而不是"你怎么想？"当这种教条从中产阶级传到平民中去时，这个国家的未来会变成怎样呢?

——选自《欧也妮·葛朗台》第6章

注释

① magnum opus ['mægnəm'əupəs] 代表作，巨著

② miserliness ['maizəlınıs] *n.* 贪婪，吝啬

③ growl [graul] *vi.* 咆哮着说

④ dogmas ['dɔgməz] *n.* 教条

⑤ conspire [kən'spaiə(r)] *vi.* 图谋，共谋

⑥ undermine [ˌʌndə'main] *vt.* 破坏

⑦ edifice ['edıfıs] *n.* 大厦，建筑物

⑧ requiem ['rekwiəm] *n.* 安魂曲

⑨ terrestrial [tə'restriəl] *adj.* 地球的，人间的

⑩ macerate ['mæsəreit] *vt.* 使身体衰弱

⑪ fleeting ['fli:tɪŋ] *adj.* 转瞬即逝的

⑫ populace ['pɔpjələs] *n.* 平民，大众

《高老头》发表于1834年，共6章。它是《人间喜剧》的序幕，也是《人间喜剧》中最优秀的作品之一。傅雷先生在1963年首译的《高老头》版本后由人民文学出版社，在1977年重新出版，至今无人企及。

Old Goriot
高老头

Money brings everything to you; even your daughters.

钱可以买到一切，甚至包括女儿。

——*Old Goriot*《高老头》

名著导读

In Maison Vauquer, there lives an elderly retired vermicelli-maker named Jean-Joachim Goriot. The old man is ridiculed frequently by the other boarders, who soon learn that he has bankrupted himself to support his two well-married daughters. Rastignac, who moved to Paris from the south of France, becomes attracted to the upper class. Goriot, supportive of Rastignac's interest in his daughter Delphine and furious with her husband's tyrannical control over her, finds himself unable to help. When his other daughter, Anastasie, informs him that she has been selling off family jewelry to pay her lover's debts, the old man is overcome with grief at his own **impotence**① and suffers a stroke. Neither Delphine nor Anastasie will visit Goriot as he lies on his deathbed, and before dying he rages about their disrespect toward him.

在伏盖公寓里住着一位年老退休的面粉商人，名叫杰·乔基姆·戈里奥。这个老头为了供养两个已婚的女儿，弄得自己身无分文，公寓其他住客知道后经常嘲笑他。从法国南部来到巴黎的拉斯蒂涅被上流社会深深吸引，高老头支持他追求自己的一个女儿戴尔芬，因为女婿对女儿非常专制，他因此而感到极其恼怒，却又无能为力。他另外一个女儿——安纳斯塔西则告诉他，她变卖了家传的珠宝为情人还债，高老头对自己的无能感到悲恸，并因此得了中风。高老头临终前，戴尔芬和安纳斯塔西这两个女儿都没有来看望他，他对于女儿的不孝愤慨不已。

名段选读

"Ah! If I were rich still, if I had kept my money, if I had not given all to them, they would be with me now; they would **fawn**[②] on me and cover my cheeks with their kisses! I should be living in a great **mansion**[③]; I should have grand apartments and servants and a fire in my room; and they would be about me all in tears, and their husbands and their children. I should have had all that; now—I have nothing. Money brings everything to you; even your daughters. My money. Oh! Where is my money? If I had plenty of money to leave behind me, they would nurse me and tend me; I should hear their voices, I should see their faces. Ah, God! Who knows? They both of them have hearts of stone. I loved them too much; it was not likely that they should love me. A father ought always to be rich; he ought to keep his children well in hand, like **unruly**[④] horses. I have gone down on my knees to them. Wretches! This is the crowning act that brings the last ten years to a proper close. If you but knew how much they made of me just after they were married. (Oh! This is cruel torture!) I had just given them each eight hundred thousand francs; they were bound to be civil to me after that, and their husbands too were civil. I used to go to their houses: it was 'My kind father' here, 'My dear father' there. There was always a place for me at their tables. I used to dine with their husbands now and then, and they were very respectful to me. I was still worth something, they thought. How should they know? I had not said anything about my affairs. It is worth while to be civil to a man who has given his daughters eight hundred thousand francs apiece; and they showed me every attention then—but it was all for my money. Grand people are not great. I found that out by experience!"

"唉！如果我仍然富裕，如果我之前能把自己的钱攒起来，如果我没有把钱全都给她们，她们现在就会来看我了，她们会奉承我，会不断亲吻着我的脸颊！我现在本应该是住在一所豪宅里，我本应该有豪华的公寓、仆人、火炉。如果是这样，她们、她们的丈夫和孩子就都会团团围在我身旁，伤心地流眼泪。那一切都是我本该拥有的，但是现在——我却一无所有。钱可以买到一切，甚至包括女儿。我的钱。啊！我的钱去哪了？如果我能留下一大笔遗产，她们就会来伺候我，照料我；那样，我就可以听到她们的声音，看到她们的脸庞。唉！老天！谁知道她们都是铁石心肠呢？我太爱她们，而她们却不能同样地爱我。做父亲的应该永远都有钱，应该把孩子紧紧地攥在手里，就像对待任性的马儿一样。可我却对她们卑躬屈膝，可怜的家伙！现在，她们这一过分的行为，为过去的10年划上了一个彻底的句号。你不知道她们刚结婚时是怎样讨好我的(哦！回想这些真是一种折磨！)，我给了她们每人80万法郎；自此以后，她们和她们的丈夫都对我很好，我过去经常到她们家里去，他们总是"好爸爸"前"好爸爸"后的。他们的餐桌旁总是会给我留一个位子，我偶尔与她们的丈夫一起用餐，他们都很尊敬我。他们觉得我还有一些可利用的价值。他们怎么知道呢？我对自己的事情只字未提。一个给他每个女儿80万法郎的人是值得被讨好的；那时候，他们对我无微不至——但都是为了我的钱。达官贵人并不高尚。我从自己的经历中知道了这一点。”

——选自《高老头》第6章

注释

① impotence [ˈɪmpətəns] *n.* 无效，无力
② fawn [fɔːn] *vi.* 奉承，讨好
③ mansion [ˈmænʃən] *n.* 大宅，大厦
④ unruly [ʌnˈruːlɪ] *adj.* 不受拘束的，蛮横的

《幻灭》* 创作于1837年至1843年间，共分3个部分。在表现作家本人的思想感情和直接的生活体验方面，《幻灭》比其他小说更具代表性。目前，这部作品在国内最常见的翻译版本有傅雷和郑永慧的译本。

Lost Illusions
幻灭

I thought that if you meant to make my successes yours, you would surely make my adversity yours also, and here we are going to part already.

我原本以为，如果你能把我的成功当作是自己的成功，那么，你也一定会把我的逆境当成是自己的逆境，但是现在我们却已经要分手了。

——*Lost Illusions*《幻灭》

名著导读

Lucien Chardon, a young poet from Angouleme, tries desperately to make a name for himself in Paris. Handsome and ambitious but naive, Lucien is patronized by the beau monde as represented by Madame de Bargeton and her cousin, only to be duped by them. Denied the social rank he thought would be his, Lucien discards his poetic aspirations and turns to hack journalism; his descent into Parisian low life ultimately leads to his own death.

吕西安·查顿是一位来自安格雷姆的年轻诗人，他一心想在巴黎成名。他英俊，有抱

负，但很天真。吕西安接受以德·巴日东太太和她的表妹为代表的上流社会的资助，却被她们所操控，失去了自我。他原以为上流社会是自己的归属，在被上流社会抛弃后，吕西安放弃了当诗人的梦想，转而成为了一名新闻界的无耻之徒；最后，他沦为巴黎社会的底层人物，这最终导致了他的死亡。

名段选读

Towards six o'clock that evening, when dinner was over, Mme. de Bargeton **beckoned**① Lucien to sit beside her on the shabby sofa, covered with a flowered chintz—a yellow pattern on a red ground.

"Lucien mine," she said, "don't you think that if we have both of us done a foolish thing, suicidal for both our interests, it would only be common sense to set matters right? We ought not to live together in Paris, dear boy, and we must not allow anyone to suspect that we traveled together. Your career depends so much upon my position that I ought to do nothing to spoil it. So, to-night, I am going to remove into **lodgings**② near by. But you will stay on here, we can see each other every day, and nobody can say a word against us."

And Louise explained conventions to Lucien, who opened wide eyes. He had still to learn that when a woman thinks better of her **folly**③, she thinks better of her love; but one thing he understood—he saw that he was no longer the Lucien of Angouleme. Louise talked of herself, of her interests, her reputation, and of the world; and, to veil her egoism, she tried to make him believe that this was all on his account. He had no claim upon Louise thus suddenly transformed into Mme. de Bargeton, and, more serious still, he had no power over her. He could not keep back the tears that filled his eyes.

"If I am your glory," cried the poet, "you are yet more to me—you are my one hope, my whole future rests with you. I thought that if you meant to make my successes yours, you would surely make my adversity yours also, and here we are going to part already."

"You are judging my conduct," said she, "you do not love me."

那天晚餐将近六点钟的时候结束，之后，德·巴日东太太示意吕西安坐在她旁边一个罩着红底黄花的棉布的破旧沙发上。

“我亲爱的吕西安，”她说，“如果我们两个做了一件愚蠢的事，这件事会毁了我们的利益，难道你不认为把事情纠正过来是一种常识吗？在巴黎，我们不能再住在一起了，亲爱的，关于我们一起去旅行的事情，也不能引起任何人的怀疑。你的前途主要取决于我的地位，所以，我决不能做任何有损我地位的事。所以今晚我要去附近借宿，但你要继续留在这里，我们依然可以每天见面，并且没有人会对我们说三道四。”

当露易丝向吕西安解释这些约定时，吕西安把眼睛睁得大大的。他还不知道，当一个女人重新考虑自己所做的蠢事的时候，她也会重新定位自己的爱人。但是，有一点他很明白——他再也不是安格雷姆的那个吕西安了。露易丝谈论着她自己、她的利益、她的声誉以及这个世界；为了掩盖她的一己私利，她试图让他相信这一切都是在为他考虑。突然间，露易丝变成了德·巴日东太太，他不再拥有她了，而且更严格地讲，他已经没有权力管束她了。想到这些，他便无法控制自己满眼的泪水。

“如果我是你的荣耀，”诗人叫道，“那么你对我的意义更加重大——你是我唯一的希望，我把整个未来都拴在你身上。我原本以为，如果你能把我的成功当作是自己的成功，那么，你也一定会把我的逆境当成是自己的逆境，但是现在我们却已经要分手了。”

“你是在指责我的所作所为，”她说，“你根本就不爱我。”

——选自《幻灭》第2部分第1章

注释

★“《幻灭》一书所描写的虽是理想的破灭，却并不给人以悲观的印象。因为作者在揭露黑暗的同时，也着力刻画了一些追求正义者、自强不息者，时刻让读者感觉到有一股不与恶浊环境同流合污的对抗力量，也就是说，巴尔扎克认为：人是可以与社会较量的。”

——人民文学出版社外国文学编审　艾珉

① beckon [ˈbekən] *vt.* 召唤，示意

② lodging [ˈlɔdʒɪŋ] *n.* 住宿，寓所

③ folly [ˈfɔlɪ] *n.* 愚蠢，荒唐事

2 十八世纪法国大革命的思想先驱——让·雅克·卢梭

Jean-Jacques Rousseau (June 28, 1712—July 2, 1778) was a major Genevois philosopher, writer, and composer of 18th-century Romanticism. His political philosophy heavily influenced the French Revolution, as well as the American Revolution and the overall development of modern political, sociological and educational thought. His novel, *Émile, or On Education* is a seminal treatise on the education of the whole person for citizenship. His Discourse on the Origin *of Inequality* and his *On the Social Contract* are cornerstones in modern political and social thought and make a strong case for democratic government. Rousseau also made important contributions to music as a theorist.

让·雅克·卢梭(1712年6月28日—1778年7月2日)是一位举足轻重的日内瓦哲学家、作家以及18世纪浪漫主义作曲家。他的政治哲学思想深深地影响了法国大革命、美国独立战争以及现代政治、社会和教育思想的全面发展。他的小说《爱弥儿》(或《论教育》)是对公民进行完整的个人教育的创新论述。他的《论不平等的起源》以及《社会契约论》是现代政治和社会思想的基石，建立了一个民主政府的模型。作为一个理论家，卢梭也为音乐界做出了重要的贡献。

《爱弥儿》发表于1762年，全书共分5卷，卢梭通过对他所假设的教育对象爱弥儿的教育，来反对封建教育制度，阐述他的资产阶级教育思想。上海人民出版社彭正梅译本是最好的版本。

Émile
爱弥儿

We are born weak, we need strength; helpless, we need aid; foolish, we need reason.

我们生来就很脆弱，我们需要力量；我们生来就很无助，我们需要帮助；我们生来就很愚蠢，我们需要理性。

——*Émile*《爱弥儿》

名著导读

Émile, or On Education is a treatise on the nature of education and on the nature of man. The work tackles fundamental political and philosophical questions about the relationship between the individual and society. The text is divided into five books: the first three are dedicated to the child Émile, the fourth to an exploration of the adolescent, and the fifth to outlining the education of his female counterpart Sophie, as well as to Émile's domestic and civic life.

《爱弥儿》（或《论教育》）一书是对教育的性质和人性的论述。这部著作主要论述了有关个人与社会之间关系的基本政治和哲学问题。原书分为五个分册：前三本书主要讲述的是孩童时期的爱弥儿，第四本书是对其青少年时期的探究，第五本书概述了爱弥儿的女伴索菲的教育，以及爱弥儿的家庭生活和公民生活。

名段选读

We are born weak, we need strength; helpless, we need aid; foolish, we need reason. All that we lack at birth, all that we need when we come to man's **estate**①, is the gift of education. This education comes to us from nature, from men, or from things. The inner growth of our organs and **faculties**② is the education of nature, the use we learn to make of this growth is the education of men, what we gain by our experience of our surroundings is the education of things. Thus we are each taught by three masters. If their teaching conflicts, the scholar is ill-educated and will never be at peace with himself; if their teaching agrees, he goes straight to his goal, he lives at peace with himself, he is well-educated.

Now of these three factors in education nature is wholly beyond our control, things are only partly in our power; the education of men is the only one controlled by us; and even here our power is largely **illusory**③, for who can hope to direct every word and deed of all with whom the child has to do.

Viewed as an art, the success of education is almost impossible, since the essential conditions of success are beyond our control. Our efforts may bring us within sight of the goal, but fortune must favour us if we are to reach it.

我们生来就很脆弱，我们需要力量；我们生来就很无助，我们需要帮助；我们生来就很愚蠢，我们需要理性。所有我们出生时缺乏的东西，所有我们长大成人所必需的东西，都承蒙教育的馈赠。这种教育源于自然界，源于一切人或物。我们内在器官发育和才能的增长是大自然教育的结果。我们学会对这些增益加以利用，属于人类教育的范畴，而我们通过与周围环境的接触所学到的东西，则属于事物教育的范畴。因此，我们每个人都有三位老师。如果他们在教学上发生了冲突，那么，学习者就不能受到良好的教育，而且永远不能保持平和的心态；如果他们的教学和谐一致，那么，学习者就会直奔目标，并能保持平和的心态，受到良好的教育。

现在，就教育的这三个因素来说，自然界是完全不受我们控制的，而世间万物只有一部分是受人类支配的；人的教育是唯一一个我们可以控制的因素；而且即使是这个因素，我们的对它的控制在很大程度上也都是虚幻的，因为，没有人能完全指挥自己孩子的一言一行。

从艺术的角度来看，成功的教育几乎是不可能做到的，因为我们无法掌控成功所需的基本条件。我们的努力可能会让我们一步步接近目标，但是，如果我们要真正地达到目标，就必须依赖好运气了。

——选自《爱弥儿》第1卷

注释

① estate [ɪ'steit] *n.* 时期

② faculty ['fækltɪ] *n.* 才能

③ illusory [ɪ'lu:sərɪ] *adj.* 虚幻的

《社会契约论》发表于1762年，全书共分4卷。《社会契约论》中主权在民的思想，是现代民主制度的基石，深刻地影响了逐步废除欧洲君主绝对权力的运动和18世纪末北美殖民地摆脱英帝国统治、建立民主制度的斗争。商务印书馆何兆武的译本最好。

On the Social Contract
社会契约论

The strongest is never strong enough to be always the master, unless he transforms strength into right, and obedience into duty.

哪怕是最强大的人也不可能永远做主人，除非他把力量转化成权利，把服从转化为责任。

——*On the Social Contract*《社会契约论》

名著导读

It is the book in which Rousseau theorized about the best way in which to set up a political community in the face of the problems of commercial society. *The Social*

Contract was a progressive work that helped inspire political reforms or revolutions in Europe, especially in France. *The Social Contract* argued against the idea that monarchs were divinely empowered to legislate; as Rousseau asserts, only the people, in the form of the sovereign, have that all powerful right.

在这本书中，卢梭论述了在面对商业社会的问题时，建立一个政治团体的最好方法。《社会契约论》是一部具有革新意义的著作，它鼓舞了欧洲，尤其是法国的政治改革和革命。《社会契约论》反驳了“君权神授”的观点；正如卢梭断言的那样：只有主宰国家的人民才能拥有所有这些强大的权利。

名段选读

The strongest is never strong enough to be always the master, unless he transforms strength into right, and **obedience**① into duty. Hence the right of the strongest, which, though to all seeming meant ironically, is really laid down as a fundamental principle. But are we never to have an explanation of this phrase? Force is a physical power, and I fail to see what moral effect it can have. To yield to force is an act of necessity, not of will—at the most, an act of **prudence**②. In what sense can it be a duty?

Suppose for a moment that this so-called "right" exists. I maintain that the sole result is a mass of inexplicable **nonsense**③. For, if force creates right, the effect changes with the cause: every force that is greater than the first succeeds to its right. As soon as it is possible to disobey with **impunity**④, disobedience is legitimate; and, the strongest being always in the right, the only thing that matters is to act so as to become the strongest. But what kind of right is that which **perishes**⑤ when force fails? If we must obey perforce, there is no need to obey because we ought; and if we are not forced to obey, we are under no obligation to do so. Clearly, the word "right" adds nothing to force: in this connection, it means absolutely nothing.

哪怕是最强大的人也不可能永远做主人的，除非他把力量转化成权利，把服从转化为责任。因此，虽然看似有些讽刺，但最强大的人所拥有的权利确实被作为一项基本原则定下来了。然而，我们对此从来都没有一个解释吗？武力只是一种外在的力量，我没有看到它带来什么道德上的影响。向武力屈服是一种逼不得已的行为，而并不是出于自愿——顶多算得上是一种谨慎的行为。怎么能说服从是一种责任呢？

让我们暂时假设这种所谓的“权利”是存在的。我还是认为，它所带来的唯一结果就是一大堆令人费解的胡言乱语。因为，如果武力可以创造权利，那么动机改变了，其影响也会发生变化：任何一种超越前者的强大武力都可以承袭前者的权利。只有当免受惩罚的反抗变为可能，反抗才能变成合法的；而且，最强大的人永远都是对的，唯一重要的事情就是去行动，使自己变成最强大的人。然而，随着武力削弱而消亡的权利又是什么样的呢？如果我们必须服从强制性的武力，那么，我们就没有服从它的责任，因为我们是被迫的；如果我们不是被迫服从的，那么，我们就没有服从它的义务。很明显，“权利”这个词不能巩固武力：从这个角度上来说，权利绝对什么也不是。

——选自《社会契约论》第1卷

注释

① obedience [ə'biːdiəns] *n.* 服从

② prudence ['pruːdəns] *n.* 谨慎

③ nonsense ['nɔnsəns] *n.* 荒谬的言行

④ impunity [ɪm'pjuːnətɪ] *n.* 不受惩罚

⑤ perish ['perɪʃ] *vi.* 消亡，毁灭

《忏悔录》发表于1782年，全书共12章，分上下两卷。前6章为上卷，后6章为下卷。《忏悔录》是一个激进的平民思想家与反动统治激烈冲突的结果。它是一个平民知识分子在封建专制压迫面前维护自己不仅是作为一个人，更重要的是作为一个普通人的人权和尊严的作品，是对统治阶级迫害和污蔑的反击。人民文学出版社黎星、范希衡的译本较著名。

The Confessions
忏悔录

While endeavoring to rise too high we are in danger of falling.
当我们力图要爬得过高的时候，就会有掉下来的危险。

——*The Confessions*《忏悔录》

名著导读

The Confessions was one of the first autobiographies in which an individual wrote of his own life mainly in terms of his worldly experiences and personal feelings. *The Confessions* is also noted for its detailed account of Rousseau's more humiliating and shameful moments. In addition, Rousseau explains the manner in which he disposes of his five illegitimate children, whom he had with his world-wide known companion, Therese Levasseur.

《忏悔录》是卢梭最早的自传之一。在这本自传中，作者主要以自己世俗的经历和个人的感受来书写他自己的一生。《忏悔录》也因卢梭毫不避讳详述自己做过的那些不光

彩、令人羞愧的事情而著称。此外，卢梭解释了自己对待他的五个私生子的态度，他们是卢梭和他众所周知的伴侣泰瑞莎·雷瓦索所生的。

名段选读

In the successive order of my **inclinations**① and ideas, I had ever been too high or too low. **Achilles**② or **Thersites**③; sometimes a hero, at others a villain. M. Gaime took pains to make me properly acquainted with myself, without **sparing**④ or giving me too much discouragement. He spoke in advantageous terms of my disposition and talents, adding, that he foresaw obstacles which would prevent my profiting by them; thus, according to him, they were to serve less as steps by which I should mount to fortune, than as resources which might enable me to exist without one. He gave me a true picture of human life, of which, **hitherto**⑤, I had formed but a very erroneous idea, teaching me, that a man of understanding, though destined to experience adverse fortune, might, by skillful management, arrive at happiness; that there was no true felicity without virtue, which was practicable in every situation. He greatly diminished my admiration of **grandeur**⑥, by proving that those in a superior situation are neither better nor happier than those they command. One of his maxims has frequently returned to my memory: it was, that if we could truly read the hearts of others we should feel more inclination to descend than rise: this reflection, the truth of which is striking without extravagance, I have found of great utility, in the various exigences of my life, as it tended to make me satisfied with my condition. He gave me the first just conception of relative duties, which my high-flown imagination had ever pictured in extremes, making me sensible that the enthusiasm of **sublime**⑦ virtues is of little use in society; that while endeavoring to rise too high we are in danger of falling; and that a virtuous and uniform discharge of little duties requires as great a degree of fortitude as actions which are called heroic, and would at the same time procure more honor and happiness. That it was infinitely more desirably to possess the lasting esteem of those about us, than at intervals to attract admiration.

在我一连串的想法和倾向中，我对自己的评价不是过高就是过低。有时是阿喀琉斯，有时成了忒耳西忒斯；有时是一个英雄，有时又是个坏蛋。盖姆费尽苦心，让我能够正确地认识自己，他既不纵容我也不给我过多的打击。他夸赞我的性情和才华，此外，他也预见了那些将使我无法从中获益的障碍；因此，根据他所说的，性格和才能不是我通向财富的阶梯，而是使我能够在没有财富的情况下生存下来的动力和源泉。他给我描绘了生活的真实场景，而我至今对人生的想法仍是非常错误的。他让我知道，一个洞察人生的人虽然注定要经历逆境，但是也可能通过巧妙经营达到幸福的终点；没有美德就不会有真正的幸福，在任何情况下都是如此。他大大打消了我对显赫地位的崇拜，因为他证明了那些高高在上的人并不比那些普通人过得更好、更幸福。他的一句格言常常在我的脑海中浮现：如果我们真正读懂了别人的心，那么，我们应该会更倾向于低就而不是攀高。这句话毫不夸张，让我惊醒，也让我获益良多。在我遇到各种各样危机的时候，它使我能够安于自己的现状。他让我第一次对相关责任有了正确的概念，曾经，我那夸张的想象力对责任的理解是非常极端的，这让我认识到，对崇高美德的狂热在社会上基本没有用处；当我们力图要爬得过高的时候，就会有掉下来的危险；有德行并始终如一地去履行琐碎的职责，与英雄的行为一样需要坚持不懈的精神，并且会让人获得更多的荣誉和幸福。拥有持久的尊重比偶尔得到赞赏更加令人向往。

——选自《忏悔录》第3章

注释

① inclination [ˌɪnklɪ'neiʃən] *n.* 倾向

② Achilles，阿喀琉斯。海洋女神忒提斯(Thetis)与国王佩琉斯(Peleus)的儿子，他是所有英雄之中最耀眼的一位，战无不胜。

③ Thersites，忒耳西忒斯。荷马史诗中的人物，希腊军中最丑陋者，多言而好斗，后为阿喀琉斯所杀。

④ spare [spɛə(r)] *vt.* 宽容，饶恕

⑤ hitherto [ˌhɪðə'tuː] *adv.* 到目前为止，迄今

⑥ grandeur ['grændʒə(r)] *n.* 显赫的地位，伟大

⑦ sublime [sə'blaim] *adj.* 崇高的

3 法兰西的莎士比亚——维克多·雨果

Victor-Marie Hugo (February 26, 1802—May 22, 1885) was a French poet, playwright, novelist, essayist, visual artist, statesman, human rights activist and exponent of the Romantic Movement in France. In France, Hugo's literary fame comes first from his poetry but also rests upon his novels and his dramatic achievements. Among many volumes of poetry, *Les Contemplations* and *La Légende des siècles* stand particularly high in critical esteem, and Hugo is sometimes identified as the greatest French poet. Outside France, his best-known works are the novels *Les Misérables* and *Notre-Dame de Paris* (known in English also as *The Hunchback of Notre-Dame*).

维克多·雨果(1802年2月26日—1885年5月22日)是一位法国诗人、剧作家、小说家、散文作家、视觉艺术家、政治家、人权活动家以及法国浪漫主义运动的楷模。在法国，雨果在文学上的名声最初来源于他的诗歌，但也有赖于他的小说作品和戏剧成就。在他的众多诗集中，《沉思集》和《世纪传说》尤其受到世人的好评，雨果也一度被认为是最伟大的法国诗人。他的声名远播国外，最著名的作品要数长篇小说《悲惨世界》和《巴黎圣母院》(英文也译作《钟楼怪人》)。

《巴黎圣母院》出版于1931年，是法国作家维克多·雨果第一部大型浪漫主义小说。全书共2部，11卷，59节，艺术地再现了400多年前法王路易十一统治时期的真实历史。目前国内较著名的译本是管震湖、李玉民和施康强的版本。

Notre-Dame de Paris
巴黎圣母院

"Oh! love!" said she, and her voice trembled, and her eye beamed. "That is to be two and to be but one. A man and a woman mingled into one angel. It is heaven."

"啊！爱情！"她的声音颤抖起来，眼中闪烁着光芒，"爱情是两个人结合为一体。一个男人和一个女人结合成一个天使。爱情就是天堂。”

——*Notre-Dame de Paris*《巴黎圣母院》

名著导读

The story dates back to 1482 in Paris, France. Esmeralda, a beautiful Gypsy with a kind and generous heart, captures the hearts of many men, including that of a Captain Phoebus, but especially those of Quasimodo and his adopted father, Claude Frollo, the Archdeacon of Notre Dame. Esmeralda is later charged with the attempted murder of Phoebus, whom Frollo attempted to kill in jealousy, and is sentenced to death by hanging. Quasimodo then goes to a mass grave, lies next to her corpse, crawls off to Esmeralda's tomb with his arms around her body and eventually dies of starvation.

故事追溯到1482年的法国巴黎。爱斯梅拉尔达，是一位心地善良、慷慨大方、美丽动人的吉布赛女孩，她俘获了众多男人的心，包括卫队长弗比斯，特别是伽西莫多和他的养父——巴黎圣母院副主教克罗德·弗罗洛。之后，爱斯梅拉尔达被指控企图谋杀弗比斯，其实是弗罗洛因为嫉妒想杀死他，但爱斯梅拉尔达却因此被判处绞刑。伽西莫多跑到墓地，躺在她的尸体旁，并用双臂抱着她的遗体缓缓爬向她的坟墓，他最终在饥饿中死去。

名段选读

Esmeralda began to **crumble**① some bread, which Djali ate gracefully from the hollow of her hand.

Moreover, Gringoire did not give her time to resume her **revery**②. He hazarded a delicate question.

"So you don't want me for your husband?"

The young girl looked at him intently, and said, "No."

"For your lover?" went on Gringoire.

She pouted, and replied, "No."

"For your friend?" pursued Gringoire.

She gazed fixedly at him again, and said, after a momentary reflection, "Perhaps."

This "perhaps," so dear to philosophers, emboldened Gringoire.

"Do you know what friendship is?" he asked.

"Yes," replied the gypsy; "it is to be brother and sister; two souls which touch without mingling, two fingers on one hand."

"And love?" pursued Gringoire.

"Oh! love!" said she, and her voice **trembled**③, and her eye **beamed**④. "That is to be two and to be but one. A man and a woman mingled into one angel. It is heaven."

The street dancer had a beauty as she spoke thus, that struck Gringoire **singularly**⑤, and seemed to him in perfect keeping with the almost oriental exaltation of her words. Her pure, red lips half smiled; her serene and candid brow became troubled, at intervals, under her thoughts, like a mirror under the breath; and from beneath her long, drooping, black eyelashes, there escaped a sort of **ineffable**⑥ light, which gave to her profile that ideal serenity which Raphael found at the mystic point of intersection of virginity, maternity, and divinity.

Nevertheless, Gringoire continued,—

"What must one be then, in order to please you?"

"A man."

"And I—" said he, "what, then, am I?"

"A man has a helmet on his head, a sword in his hand, and golden spurs on his heels."

"Good," said Gringoire, "without a horse, no man. Do you love any one?"

"As a lover?—"

"Yes."

She remained thoughtful for a moment, then said with a peculiar expression: "That I shall know soon."

"Why not this evening?" resumed the poet tenderly. "Why not me?"

She cast a grave glance upon him and said,—

"I can never love a man who cannot protect me."

爱斯梅拉尔达开始撕碎一些面包，贾利斯文地在她手心里吃起来。

而格兰瓜尔根本没有再给她想入非非的时间。他只是冒险地问了她一个颇为棘手的问题。

"这样说来，你不想让我做你的丈夫？"

这个年轻女孩注视着他，说，"是的。"

"做你的情人呢？"格兰瓜尔继续问。

她有些不快，回答说，"不行。"

"朋友呢？"格兰瓜尔穷追不舍地问道。

她凝视着他，略微思索了一下说，"也许吧。"

"也许"对哲学家们来说是很珍贵的，这让格兰瓜尔有了勇气。

"你知道什么是友谊吗？"他问。

"知道。"吉布赛女孩回答；"友谊就像是哥哥和妹妹，像是两颗不用结合就能相互触碰的心灵，像是一只手上的两根手指。"

"那爱情呢？"格兰瓜尔追问。

"啊！爱情！"她的声音颤抖起来，眼中闪烁着光芒，"爱情是两个人结合为一体。

一个男人和一个女人结合成一个天使。爱情就是天堂。”

这个街头舞女在说这些话时，身上有一种让格兰瓜尔心动不已的美，对他而言，似乎这种美和她话语中东方人的欣喜神情有着完美的一致。她那纯洁而红润的嘴唇半带着微笑；在她思考问题时，她那宁静而率真的额头会偶尔紧皱，像一面被吹过一口气的镜子；在她长长的、垂下的黑色睫毛下面，闪过一道无法形容的目光，使得她整个人有一种沁人的娴静感，这只有在拉斐尔描绘纯洁、母性和神圣的神秘交汇点的时候才会出现。

不过，格兰瓜尔继续问，——

“什么样的男人才能讨得你的欢心呢？”

“一个真正的男人。”

“那我——”他说，“那我是什么样的男人呢？”

“我钟情的男人是一个头戴钢盔，手握利剑，鞋跟上有金马刺的男人。”

“很好，”格兰瓜尔说，“不骑马的男人就不叫真正的男人。你爱上谁了吗？”

“你是说恋爱？——”

“是的。”

她继续深思了片刻，然后表情古怪地说道：“我很快就会知道了。”

“为什么不是今晚？”诗人温和地继续说。“为什么不是我呢？”

她严肃地瞥了他一眼说，——

“我绝不会爱上一个不能保护我的男人。”

——选自《巴黎圣母院》第2卷第7节

注释

① crumble ['krʌmbl] *vt.* 弄碎

② revery ['revərɪ] *n.* 空想，思考

③ tremble ['trembl] *vi.* 战栗，微动

④ beam [biːm] *vi.* 照耀，流露

⑤ singularly ['sɪŋgjələlɪ] *adv.* 异常地，令人无法理解地

⑥ ineffable [ɪn'efəbl] *adj.* 不可言喻的，难以形容的

《悲惨世界》*是雨果于1862年所发表的一部长篇小说，是19世纪最著名的小说之一。小说跨越了拿破仑战争和之后的十几年的时间，共5部48卷。目前国内较著名的译本是李玉民的版本、郭文华的版本以及李丹、方于合译的版本。

Les Mis é rables
悲惨世界

There is a spectacle more grand than the sea; it is heaven: there is a spectacle more grand than heaven; it is the inmost recesses of the soul.

有一种景象比大海更壮观，那就是天空；有一种景象比天空更壮观，那就是心灵的最深处。

——*Les Misérables*《悲惨世界》

名著导读

The novel focuses on the life of the ex-convict Jean Valjean who regenerated after 19 years of military prison. Valjean, having broken his parole and changed his name to Monsieur Madeleine, has risen to become mayor of Montreuil. To keep his promise to Fantine, a dying woman, Valjean is again in disguise and lives a quiet life in Paris with Cossette. He rescues Marius, a revolutionist who is in love with Cossette. Finally, Valjean died in peace.

小说主要讲的是有犯罪前科的冉·阿让的生活，他在军事监狱呆了19年之后重获新生。阿让撕毁了假释令，化名马德兰先生，后来荣升为蒙特勒伊市长。为了实现对一位垂死妇女芳汀的承诺，阿让再次隐姓埋名，与珂赛特一起在巴黎过着安静的生活，他还救了与珂赛特相爱的革命者马吕斯。最后，阿让安详地死去了。

名段选读

The reader has, no doubt, already **divined**① that M. Madeleine is no other than Jean Valjean. We have already gazed into the depths of this conscience; the moment has now come when we must take another look into it. We do so not without emotion and **trepidation**②. There is nothing more terrible in existence than this sort of **contemplation**③. The eye of the spirit can nowhere find more dazzling brilliance and more shadow than in man; it can fix itself on no other thing which is more formidable, more complicated, more mysterious, and more infinite. There is a spectacle more grand than the sea; it is heaven: there is a spectacle more grand than heaven; it is the inmost recesses of the soul.

To make the poem of the human conscience, were it only with reference to a single man, were it only in connection with the basest of men, would be to blend all epics into one superior and definitive epic. Conscience is the chaos of chimeras, of **lusts**④, and of temptations; the furnace of dreams; the lair of ideas of which we are ashamed; it is the **pandemonium**⑤ of sophisms; it is the battlefield of the passions. Penetrate, at certain hours, past the **livid**⑥ face of a human being who is engaged in reflection, and look behind, gaze into that soul, gaze into that obscurity. There, beneath that external silence, battles of giants, like those recorded in Homer, are in progress; skirmishes of dragons and hydras and swarms of phantoms, as in Milton; visionary circles, as in Dante. What a **solemn**⑦ thing is this infinity which every man bears within him, and which he measures with despair against the caprices of his brain and the actions of his life!

Alighieri one day met with a sinister-looking door, before which he hesitated. Here is one before us, upon whose threshold we hesitate. Let us enter, nevertheless.

毫无疑问，读者已经发现了马德兰先生恰恰就是冉·阿让。我们曾经仔细审视过这颗心灵的最深处；现在，我们必须用另一种眼光去审视他。我们这样做的时候并不是不带感情、不感到恐惧的。世界上没有什么东西比这种审视更加可怕。人类精神的眼睛能透过人的肉体，看到最多耀眼的光芒和最多晦暗的阴影；人类的心灵比任何东西都更强大、更复杂、更神秘、更具有无限性。有一种景象比大海更壮观，那就是天空；有一种景象比天空更壮观，那就是心灵的最深处。

要创作关于人类良知的诗篇，就算只涉及一个人，就算只涉及一个最卑微的人，也得将所有的史诗融合成一篇卓越的、权威性的史诗。良知是狂想、贪欲和诱惑的混合体，是梦想的熔炉，是我们令人羞耻的思想藏身之处；良知是各种诡辩的较量，也是激情的战场。在某些时候，透过沉思之人的铁青脸色，我们可以看到他的灵魂，看到他不为人知的一面。在那里，在表面的平静下面，有荷马史诗中那样的巨灵在格斗；有弥尔顿诗歌中那样的龙、九头蛇以及一大群幽灵的在混战；也有但丁诗歌中的幻想在盘旋萦绕。这是我们每个人的内心都存在的东西，它是那样的神圣，又是那么深不可测。正是因为有了良知，我们才能衡量自己的每一个贪念和每一次行动，才能与绝望抗衡！

一天，阿利吉耶里遇见了一扇看上去很凶险的门，于是，他在门前踌躇着。现在挡在我们面前也有这样一扇门，我们在门前徘徊不定。不管怎样，我们还是进去吧。

——选自《悲惨世界》第1部第7卷第3章

注释

★ “我当时所读到的《悲惨世界》虽只是片段，但震撼力强劲无比，以文学价值而言，远远在大仲马、梅里美等人之上。文学风格与价值的高下，即使对于当时我这个没有多大见识的少年人，其间的对比也是十分明显的。”

——中国武侠小说宗师　金庸

① divine [dɪ'vain] *vt.* 推测，发现

② trepidation [ˌtrepɪ'deiʃən] *n.* 恐惧，忧虑

③ contemplation [ˌkɔntəm'pleiʃən] *n.* 注视，沉思

④ lust [lʌst] *n.* 贪欲

⑤ pandemonium [ˌpændə'məuniəm] *n.* 喧哗吵闹

⑥ livid ['lɪvɪd] *adj.* 铁青的
⑦ solemn ['sɔləm] *n.* 严肃的，庄严的

《海上劳工》*创作于1866年，共分3个部分。在该小说中，雨果把普通人的劳动英雄化，使得这部小说有了重大的社会意义。目前国内较著名的译本是陈筱卿的版本、陈乐的版本和许钧的版本。

Les Travailleurs sur la mer
海上劳工

Life is a voyage; the idea is the itinerary.

如果生活是一段航行，那么，思想就是航行的指南针。

——*Les Travailleurs sur la mer*《海上劳工》

名著导读

The story concerns a Guernseyman named Gilliatt, a social outcast who falls in love with Deruchette, the niece of a local shipowner, Mess Lethierry. When Lethierry's ship is wrecked on the Roches Douvres, a perilous reef, Deruchette promises to marry whoever can salvage the ship's steam engine. Gilliatt eagerly volunteers, and the story follows both his physical trials and tribulations (which includes a battle with an octopus), as well as the undeserved opprobrium of his neighbours.

故事的主人公是一个被社会所遗弃的水手吉利亚特，他爱上了当地船主梅斯·勒蒂埃利的侄女黛吕谢特。当勒蒂埃利的船在危险的多佛尔礁遇险时，黛吕谢特许诺嫁给任何一个能挽救船上的蒸汽机的人，于是吉利亚特自告奋勇。紧接着，故事以他身体受到的考验和磨难(包括与章鱼的斗争)，以及邻居对他的非难展开。

名段选读

Sometimes he remained all the afternoon at the window of his room, which looked out upon the port, with his head **drooping**①, his elbows on the stone, his ears resting on his fists, his back turned to the whole world, his eye fixed on the old massive iron ring fastened in the wall of the house, at only a few feet from his window, where in the old days he used to moor the Durande. He was looking at the rust which gathered on the ring.

He was reduced to the mere mechanical habit of living.

The bravest men, when deprived of their most cherished idea, will come to this. His life had become a void. Life is a voyage; the idea is the itinerary. The plan of their course gone, they stop. The object is lost, the strength of purpose gone. Fate has a secret **discretionary**[②] power. It is able to touch with its rod even our moral being. Despair is almost the destitution of the soul. Only the greatest minds resist, and for what?

Mess Lethierry was always **meditating**[③], if absorption can be called meditation, in the depth of a sort of cloudy abyss. Broken words sometimes escaped him like these: "There is nothing left for me now but to ask yonder for leave to go."

There was a certain **contradiction**[④] in that nature, complex as the sea, of which Mess Lethierry was, so to speak, the product. Mess Lethierry's grief did not seek relief in prayer.

To be powerless is a certain strength. In the presence of our two great expressions of this blindness—destiny and nature—it is in his powerlessness that man has found his chief support in prayer.

Man seeks **succour**[⑤] from his terror; his anxiety bids him kneel.

But Mess Lethierry prayed not.

有时整个下午他都呆在他房间的窗前，从这里能看到港口，他垂着头，双肘压在石头上，双拳托着耳朵，背对着整个世界。他的目光注视着系在房子墙上的那个巨大的旧铁圈。在离窗子只有几英尺的那个位置，就是昔日他停泊“迪朗德号”的地方。他正看着那个布满铁锈的铁圈。

他很颓废，每天只是机械地生活。

即使是最勇敢的人，如果被剥夺了最珍贵的思想，也会沦落到这一地步。他的生活变得空虚。如果生活是一段航行，那么，思想就是航行的指南针。航程计划都没有了，他们也就停下来了。失去了目标，也就没有了追逐的力量。命运有一种神秘的决定权。它凭借它的权杖甚至能触及我们的道德观。绝望几乎就是灵魂的致命弱点，只有最伟大的人才能抵抗，而那是为什么呢?

如果全神贯注可以被称之为沉思的话，梅斯·勒蒂埃利则总是深陷在无止境的沉思中。他有时会断断续续地说一些话：“我现在一无所有，只能请求那边的人将我带走。”

他的天性中存在着像大海一样复杂的矛盾，这样说来，梅斯·勒蒂埃利就是这一矛盾的产物。梅斯·勒蒂埃利的痛苦并没有因为祷告而减轻。

无能为力也能产生某种力量。一旦一个人陷入到这种归咎于“命运”和“本性”的盲目性中——当他变得无能为力时，他会从祷告中寻找到自己最重要的精神寄托。

人因恐惧而寻求救援；这时，他的焦虑会将他击垮。

但是，梅斯·勒蒂埃利祈祷自己不会这样。

——选自《海上劳工》第3部分

注释

★ “作品表现了自由自在的心灵和无拘无束的想象力。他不再说教，也不再争辩……我们身临其境地看到了这个强有力的作家所做的宏伟的梦，他让人与茫茫自然短兵相接。”

——法国作家、自然主义创始人　左拉

① droop ['dru:p] *vi.* 低垂，垂落

② discretionary [dɪ'skreʃ ənərɪ] *adj.* 任意的，无条件的

③ meditate ['medɪteit] *vi.* 深思

④ contradiction [ˌkɔntrə'dɪkʃ ən] *n.* 矛盾

⑤ scuttle ['skʌtl] *n.* 救援

4 世界三大短篇小说巨匠之一——莫泊桑

Guy de Maupassant (August 5, 1850—July 6, 1893) was a popular 19th-century French writer, generally considered one of the three fathers of the modern short story. Maupassant took the subjects for his pessimistic stories and novels chiefly from the behavior of the bourgeoisie, the Franco-Prussian War, and the fashionable life of Paris. Among his short story masterpiece are *Boule De Suif* (1880), *My Uncle Jules* (1883) and *The Necklace* (1884).

居伊・德・莫泊桑(1850年8月5日—1893年7月6日)是19世纪法国著名作家，被认为是“三大现代短篇小说之父”之一。莫泊桑的短篇故事和小说主要取材于资产阶级、普法战争以及巴黎上流社会的生活。他最著名的短篇小说是《羊脂球》(1880)、《我的叔叔于勒》(1883)和《项链》(1884)。

《羊脂球》★发表于1880年，是莫泊桑公开发表的第一篇重要的短篇小说，并一举成名，收录在《羊脂球》短篇小说集中，现在国内著名的《羊脂球》小说集译本是柳鸣九的译本和高临的译本。

Boule de Suif
羊脂球

She felt herself swallowed up in the scorn of these virtuous creatures, who had first sacrificed, then rejected her as a thing useless and unclean.

她觉得自己已被这群道貌岸然的家伙们的轻蔑所吞噬，他们先是牺牲了她，接着又把她当做一样毫无用处并且不干不净的东西，抛弃了她。

——*Boule de Suif*《羊脂球》

名著导读

The story is set in the Franco-Prussian War. Ten French residents of Rouen decide to leave Rouen and flee to Le Havre in a stagecoach. Sharing the carriage is the prostitute Boule de Suif. The travelers are detained by a Prussian officer until Boule de Suif agrees to sleep with the officer. The travelers use various examples of logic and morality to convince her it is the right thing to do; she finally gives in and sleeps with the officer, who allows them to leave the next morning. As they continue on their way to Le Havre, these "representatives of Virtue" ignore Boule de Suif and refuse to share their food with her. Boule de Suif weeps for her lost dignity.

故事以普法战争为背景展开。十位法国鲁昂市的居民决定离开鲁昂，乘马车逃到勒阿弗尔。车上有一名名叫"羊脂球"的妓女。一位普鲁士军官把旅客们拦截住了，他要求羊脂球与他过夜。旅客们用逻辑和道德的例子劝说她这么做是正确的。最终，羊脂球被说服，与军官过夜了。军官第二天早晨就放他们离开了。在他们继续前往勒阿弗尔的路上，这些"美德的代表"们完全忽略了羊脂球，并拒绝和她分享食物。羊脂球只能为她失去的尊严哭泣。

名段选读

Boule de Suif, in the haste and confusion of her departure, had not thought of anything, and, stifling with rage, she watched all these people placidly eating. At first, ill-suppressed wrath shook her whole person, and she opened her lips to **shriek**① the truth at them, to overwhelm them with a volley of insults; but she could not utter a word, so choked was she with indignation.

No one looked at her, no one thought of her. She felt herself swallowed up in the scorn of these virtuous creatures, who had first sacrificed, then rejected her as a thing useless and unclean. Then she remembered her big basket full of the good things they had so greedily devoured: the two chickens coated in jelly, the pies, the pears, the four bottles of claret; and her fury broke forth like a cord that is overstrained, and she was on the verge of tears. She made terrible efforts at self-control, drew herself up, swallowed the sobs which choked her; but the tears rose nevertheless, shone at the brink of her eyelids, and soon two heavy drops coursed slowly down her cheeks. Others followed more quickly, like water **filtering**② from a rock, and fell, one after another, on her rounded bosom. She sat upright, with a fixed expression, her face pale and rigid, hoping desperately that no one saw her give way.

离开时，羊脂球很匆忙、很混乱，脑子里一片空白。现在，她看着这些人若无其事地吃着东西，愤怒得差点窒息。一开始，无法克制的愤怒使得她浑身颤抖，她张开嘴想对他们喊出真相，用辱骂来淹没他们，但她被愤怒堵住了喉咙，一句话也说不出来。

没有人关注她，没有人想到她。她觉得自己已经被这群道貌岸然的家伙们的轻蔑所吞噬，他们先是牺牲了她，接着又把她当做一样毫无用处并且不干不净的东西，抛弃了她。她又想起了自己的那只大篮子，里面本来装满了好吃的食物，现在都已经被他们狼吞虎咽地吃掉了：两只涂满了胶冻的鸡、馅饼、梨子和四瓶红葡萄酒；她的愤怒仿佛过度拉紧的绳子一样爆发出来。她就快哭出来了。她尽力地克制自己，挺直身体，咽下噎住自己的呜咽，尽管如此，眼泪还是流了出来，在她眼角闪烁着，很快，两大滴眼泪慢慢地从她脸颊滑落，另外一些紧随其后，越流越多，就像从岩石中渗出的水一样，一滴接一滴地滑落到她丰满的胸上。她笔直地坐在那里，表情僵硬，脸色发白，神情呆滞，绝望地希望没有人看见她情绪失控。

——选自《羊脂球》

注释

★“《羊脂球》这部杰作，这满含柔情、讥嘲和勇气的完美无缺的作品，爆响了。他开始就拿出一部具有决定意义的作品，使自己跻身于大师的行列。”

——法国作家、自然主义创始人左拉

① shriek [ʃri:k] *vt.* 尖声发出

② filter [ˈfɪltə(r)] *vi.* 走漏

《项链》发表于1884年，是莫泊桑短篇小说中脍炙人口的名篇，收录在中短篇小说集《项链》中。目前国内最著名的《项链》小说集的译本是资深翻译家郝运和王振孙先生的译本。

The Necklace
项链

How strange life is, how fickle! How little is needed to ruin or to save!

人生是多么的奇妙和变幻无常啊!有时，仅仅是一件很小的事，就能决定人生是毁灭还是救赎!

——*The Necklace*《项链》

名著导读

Mathilde always imagined herself in a high social position with wonderful jewels. However she has nothing and marries a low paid clerk. Mathilde borrows a fancy jewel necklace from her friend Jeanne to attend the party held by the minister. After the party,

Mathilde discovers that she has lost the necklace. Mathilde and her husband have to take out loans to buy a necklace that looks just like the one that was lost. It takes them ten years of hard labor to come up with the 36,000 francs necessary to pay them back. Toward the end, Mathilde meets Jeanne and confesses how she worked so hard to return her necklace. Jeanne, deeply moved, tells Mathilde that the one she had borrowed was fake and that it was worth at most 500 francs.

玛蒂尔德常常幻想自己身处上层社会，戴着华丽的珠宝。但她一无所有，和一个薪水很低的职员结了婚。为了参加部长举办的晚会，玛蒂尔德向她的朋友珍妮借了一条漂亮的钻石项链。舞会结束后，玛蒂尔德发现她弄丢了项链。她和丈夫只好借高利贷买了一条看起来和丢失的项链一样的项链。他们为此付出了十年艰苦的劳动来偿还的3600法郎的债务。最后，玛蒂尔德遇到珍妮，坦白了自己是怎样辛苦工作来偿还那条项链的。珍妮被深深地感动，告诉她，借给她的项链是假的，最多值500法郎。

名段选读

Every month notes had to be paid off, others renewed, time gained.

Her husband worked in the evenings at putting straight a merchant's accounts, and often at night he did copying at twopence-halfpenny a page.

And this life lasted ten years.

At the end of ten years everything was paid off, everything, the **usurer's**① charges and the accumulation of **superimposed**② interest.

Madame Loisel looked old now. She had become like all the other strong, hard, **coarse**③ women of poor households. Her hair was badly done, her skirts were awry, her hands were red. She spoke in a **shrill**④ voice, and the water slopped all over the floor when she **scrubbed**⑤ it. But sometimes, when her husband was at the office, she sat down by the window and thought of that evening long ago, of the ball at which she had been so beautiful and so much admired.

What would have happened if she had never lost those jewels. Who knows? Who knows? How strange life is, how fickle! How little is needed to ruin or to save!

One Sunday, as she had gone for a walk along the Champs-Elysees to freshen herself after the labours of the week, she caught sight suddenly of a woman who was taking a child out for a walk. It was Madame Forestier, still young, still beautiful, still attractive.

Madame Loisel was conscious of some emotion. Should she speak to her? Yes, certainly. And now that she had paid, she would tell her all. Why not?

每个月都必须付清一些借据，然后重新立一些借据来拖延一段时间。

她的丈夫要在晚上为一个商人整理账目，在夜里还经常得抄书，报酬是两个半便士一页。

这样的生活持续了十年。

十年快要结束的时候，高利贷的费用以及层层叠加的利息，一切都还清了。

卢瓦泽尔太太现在看起来老了。她已经变得像其他贫困家庭里那些强壮、坚强、粗俗的妇人一样了。她的头发乱糟糟的，裙子歪斜，双手通红。她说话时声音尖锐刺耳，擦地时，满屋都是溅出的水。不过，有的时候，当她的丈夫去上班时，她会坐在窗前，想起很久以前那个晚上，想起那次舞会，舞会上的她是那么美丽，那么令人羡慕。

如果她从来没有弄丢那条项链，她的人生又该是怎样一种境况呢？谁知道？谁知道？人生是多么的奇妙和变幻无常啊!有时，仅仅是一件很小的事，就能决定人生是毁灭还是救赎!

一个星期天，她正沿着香榭丽舍大街散步，好缓解一下一周来的疲劳。突然，她看见一个带着孩子出来散步的女人。那是弗雷斯蒂尔太太，她还是那么年轻，那么漂亮，那么有魅力。

卢瓦泽尔太太的情绪有些激动。她应该上前和她说话吗？是的，当然。现在她已经还清了债务，她要告诉她所有的事情。为什么不呢？

——选自《项链》

注释

① usurer [ˈjuʒərə(r)] *n.* 高利贷者

② superimposed [ˌsuːpərɪmˈpəuzd] *adj.* 叠加的

③ coarse [kɔːs] *adj.* 粗糙的，粗俗的

④ shrill [ʃrɪl] *adj.* 尖锐的，刺耳的

⑤ scrub [skrʌb] *vt.* 用力擦洗

《我的叔叔于勒》发表于1883年，是莫泊桑最著名的短篇小说名篇之一，收录在中短篇小说集《项链》中。目前国内最著名的《项链》小说集的译本是资深翻译家郝运和王振孙先生的译本。

My Uncle Jules
我的叔叔于勒

Jules, who up to that time had not been worth his salt, suddenly became a good man, a kind-hearted fellow, true and honest like all the Davranches.

从那时起，一直是吃白饭的于勒叔叔，突然变成了一个好人，一个心地善良的人，就像所有达夫朗什家的人一样忠诚可靠。

——*My Uncle Jules*《我的叔叔于勒》

名著导读

The uncle Jules was the family's terror. He went to America and in his last letter he said that he would come back once he would have made fortune. This letter had helped a man to get married with Joseph's most beautiful sister. The family decided that after the marriage, she would make a journey in Jersey. During the journey, in the boat, a poor people, who sold oysters, looked like Jules. The captain told the father that this man was called Jules. Their dream of making a fortune reduced to zero and his sister's marriage was at risk. At last, the family came back by boat quietly.

于勒叔叔曾经是家里的噩梦。他去了美国，在最后一封家书里他写道，一旦发财了就会回家。这封信让约瑟夫最美丽的姐姐找到了丈夫。家里决定在他们结婚后，让她去泽西岛旅行。在他们乘坐的船上，有一个卖牡蛎的可怜人长得很像于勒。船长告诉父亲说，那人就叫于勒。他们发财的梦想化为乌有，他姐姐的婚姻也岌岌可危。最后，全家人不动声色地乘船回来了。

名段选读

Once there, my uncle began to sell something or other, and he soon wrote that he was making a little money and that he soon hoped to be able to **indemnify**[①] my father for the harm he had done him. This letter caused a profound emotion in the family. Jules, who up to that time had not been worth his salt, suddenly became a good man, a kind-hearted fellow, true and honest like all the Davranches.

One of the captains told us that he had rented a large shop and was doing an important business.

Two years later a second letter came, saying: "My dear Philippe, I am writing to tell you not to worry about my health, which is excellent. Business is good. I leave to-morrow for a long trip to South America. I may be away for several years without sending you any news. If I shouldn't write, don't worry. When my fortune is made I shall return to Havre. I hope that it will not be too long and that we shall all live happily together…"

This letter became the **gospel**[②] of the family. It was read on the slightest **provocation**[③], and it was shown to everybody.

For ten years nothing was heard from Uncle Jules; but as time went on my father's hope grew, and my mother, also, often said: "When that good Jules is here, our position will be different. There is one who knew how to get along!"

And every Sunday, while watching the big steamers approaching from the horizon, pouring out a stream of smoke, my father would repeat his **eternal**[④] question: "What a surprise it would be if Jules were on that one! Eh?"

We almost expected to see him waving his handkerchief and crying: "Hey! Philippe!"

一到那儿，我的叔叔开始卖些这样或那样的东西，很快，他就写信说自己赚了一点钱，希望能尽快补偿他对父亲造成的伤害。这封信对家里人产生了不小的影响。从那时起，一直是吃白饭的于勒叔叔，突然变成了一个好人，一个心地善良的人，就像所有达夫朗什家的人一样忠诚可靠。

有位船长告诉我们，于勒叔叔已经租了一间大商店，并且正在做一笔很重要的买卖。

两年后第二封信到了，信上写道："我亲爱的菲利普，我写信是告诉你别担心我的健康，我身体很好，生意也不错。明天我就要动身去遥远的南美洲了，也许要离开好几年，不能给你写信了。万一我没有写信，也不用担心我。等我赚钱了就会回哈佛尔。我希望这不会要太久，那时，我们所有人就可以一起快乐地生活了……"

这封信成了家里的福音书。一有机会就被拿出来念，还给每个人都看过。

十年里我们都没有收到于勒叔叔的消息；但是父亲的希望却与日俱增，母亲也经常说："等到那个好心的于勒回来的时候，我们的境况就会不同了。他可是一个很会过日子的人！"

于是，每个星期天，每当看见大汽船冒着烟从天边驶过来时，父亲就会重复他那永恒不变的话："如果于勒就在那条船上该多让人惊喜啊！是吧？"

几乎我们所有人都指望着看见他挥舞着手帕喊："嗨！菲利普！"

——选自《我的叔叔于勒》

注释

① indemnify [ɪn'demnɪfai] *vt.* 补偿

② gospel ['gɔspl] *n.* 福音

③ provocation [ˌprɔvə'keiʃən] *n.* 挑拨，刺激

④ eternal [ɪ'tɛːnl] *adj.* 永恒的

5 天才的小说家——亚历山大·仲马

Alexandre Dumas, père (July 24, 1802—December 5,1870) was a French writer, best known for his historical novels of high adventure which have made him one of the most widely read French authors in the world. Many of his novels, including *The Count of Monte Cristo, The Three Musketeers, Twenty Years After,* and *The Vicomte de Bragelonne* were originally serialized. He also wrote plays and magazine articles and was a prolific correspondent. Duma was called by Belinsky as "a talented novelist"; and he is also one of Marxist's favorite writers.

亚历山大·仲马(1802年7月24日—1870年12月5日)，法国作家，他因著有多部脍炙人口的历史性冒险小说而闻名于世，这也使他成为了世界知名的法国作家之一。他的很多作品，包括《基督山伯爵》、《三个火枪手》、《二十年后》、《布拉热洛纳子爵》等，在初步起草时就开始连载出版了。同时，他也创作戏剧和报刊文章，是一位多产的记者。别林斯基称大仲马为“天才小说家”，他也是马克思最喜爱的作家之一。

大仲马于1844年写就《三个火枪手》，并于当年的3至7月间在巴黎《世纪》报纸上连载。全书分为上、下两卷，共66章。这部小说目前国内最常见的翻译版本是上海译文出版社1978李青崖译制的版本。

The Three Musketeers
三个火枪手

All for one, one for all.

人人为我，我为人人。

——*The Three Musketeers*《三个火枪手》

名著导读

Young D'Artagnan arrives in Paris at the tender age of 18, and almost immediately offends three musketeers, Porthos, Aramis, and Athos. Instead of dueling, the four are attacked by five of the Cardinal's guards, and the courage of the youth is made apparent during the battle. The four become fast friends, and, embark upon an adventure that takes them across both France and England in order to thwart the plans of the Cardinal Richelieu. Along the way, they encounter a beautiful young spy, named simply Milady, who will stop at nothing to disgrace Queen Anne of Austria before her husband, Louis XIII, and take her revenge upon the four friends.

年仅18岁的达塔尼昂初到巴黎就冒犯了3位火枪手：波尔托斯、阿拉米斯和阿托斯。他们正要动武的时候却被5个红衣主教的卫兵袭击，在与卫兵的交锋中，达塔尼昂过人的胆识彰显出来。这4个人很快成为了莫逆之交，为了阻止红衣主教黎塞留的计划，他们开始了穿越法国和英国的冒险之旅。路上，他们遇到了米拉迪——一位年轻漂亮的女间谍，她不择手段地想让奥地利的安妮皇后在丈夫路易十三面前受辱，并且利用她的四个朋友实施复仇计划。

名段选读

The officers were full of thanks, and took away their prey. As they were going down d'Artagnan laid his hand on the shoulder of their leader.

"May I not drink to your health, and you to mine?" said d'Artagnan, filling two glasses with the Beaugency wine which he had obtained from the liberality of M. Bonacieux.

"That will do me great honor," said the leader of the posse, "and I accept thankfully."

"Then to yours, monsieur—what is your name?"

"Boisrenard."

"Monsieur Boisrenard."

"To yours, my gentlemen! What is your name, in your turn, if you please?"

"d'Artagnan."

"To yours, monsieur."

"And above all others," cried d'Artagnan, as if carried away by his enthusiasm, "to that of the king and the cardinal."

The leader of the posse would perhaps have doubted the sincerity of d'Artagnan if the wine had been bad; but the wine was good, and he was convinced.

"What **diabolical**① **villainy**② you have performed here," said Porthos, when the officer had rejoined his companions and the four friends found themselves alone. "Shame, shame, for four Musketeers to allow an unfortunate fellow who cried for help to be arrested in their midst! And a gentleman to **hobnob**③ with a **bailiff**④!"

"Porthos," said Aramis, "Athos has already told you that you are a **simpleton**⑤, and I am quite of his opinion. D'Artagnan, you are a great man; and when you occupy Monsieur de Treville's place, I will come and ask your influence to secure me an **abbey**⑥."

"Well, I am in a maze," said Porthos; "do YOU approve of what d'Artagnan has done?"

"PARBLEU! Indeed I do," said Athos; "I not only approve of what he has done, but I congratulate him upon it."

"And now, gentlemen," said d'Artagnan, without stopping to explain his conduct to Porthos, "All for one, one for all—that is our motto, is it not?"

"And yet—" said Porthos.

"Hold out your hand and swear!" cried Athos and Aramis at once.

Overcome by example, **grumbling**⑦ to himself, nevertheless, Porthos stretched out his hand, and the four friends repeated with one voice the formula dictated by d'Artagnan:

"All for one, one for all."

"That's well! Now let us everyone retire to his own home," said d'Artagnan, as if he had done nothing but command all his life; "and attention! For from this moment we are at feud with the cardinal."

军官们连声道谢，押走了他们的犯人。他们正要下去的时候，达塔尼昂拍了拍他们长官的肩膀。

“如果我没有向您敬酒，祝您身体健康的话，那么，您会向我敬酒吗？”达塔尼昂一边说，一边往两个杯子里倒满了博让西酒，这酒是慷慨的波那斯先生送过来的。

“我荣幸之至啊，”长官说，“那我就恭敬不如从命啦！”

“那么，先生，让我们为了您的健康干杯，对了，敢问您尊姓大名？”

“布瓦勒纳。”

“布瓦勒纳先生。”

“那么先生，为您的健康干杯！能告诉我您的大名吗？”

“达塔尼昂。”

“也为您的健康干杯，先生。”

“除了为你我的健康干杯外，”达塔尼昂似乎一时性起，他大声地说道，“也为国王和红衣主教的健康干杯。”

如果酒不好喝，长官也许还会怀疑达塔尼昂的诚意；但是因为酒很好喝，所以他也不好怀疑了。

“你们在这儿做了一件多么邪恶的事情！”波尔托斯说。这时，那个长官已经和他的那伙士兵离开了，只剩下他们四个朋友。“可耻！真可耻！堂堂的四个火枪手让一个喊救命的可怜人在他们眼前被抓走！而这个绅士却在这里跟军官喝酒！”

“波尔托斯，”阿拉米斯说，“阿托斯说过你是个笨蛋，你还真是。达塔尼昂，你真了不起；当你攀升到特雷维尔先生的位子的时候，我一定得沾你的光，让你给我弄所修道院。”

“好吧，我有些糊涂了，”波尔托斯说，“你们两个都赞成达塔尼昂的做法吗？”

“是的，我确实同意，”阿托斯说，“我不仅赞成，我还要向他表示祝贺。”

“现在，先生们，”达塔尼昂并没有向波尔托斯解释他为什么这样做，继续说道，“人人为我，我为人人，这是我们的座右铭，对吧？”

“可是——”波尔托斯说。

“举起手宣誓吧！”阿托斯和阿拉米斯立刻异口同声地说道。

尽管有些不满，在伙伴们的带动下，波尔托斯还是伸出了手。这四个朋友一齐照着达塔尼昂样子誓言：

“人人为我，我为人人。”

“很好！现在大家各自回去，”达塔尼昂说，好像他这一辈子都在发号施令似的，“注意！从现在开始，我们要和红衣主教展开长期的较量了。”

——选自《三个火枪手》第9章

注释

① diabolical [ˌdaiə'bɔlɪkl] *adj.* 恶魔的

② villainy ['vɪlənɪ] *n.* 恶行，坏事

③ hobnob ['hɔbnɔb] *vi.* 共饮

④ bailiff ['beilɪf] *n.* 执行官，法警

⑤ simpleton ['sɪmpltən] *n.* 笨蛋，傻子

⑥ abbey ['æbɪ] *n.* 修道院

⑦ grumble ['grʌmbl] *vi.* 牢骚

《基督山伯爵》★完成于1844年，共117章。《基督山伯爵》主要讲述的19世纪一位名叫爱德蒙·唐泰斯的大副受到陷害后的悲惨遭遇以及日后以基督山伯爵身份成功复仇的故事。这部小说目前国内最著名的翻译版本是长江文艺出版社高临的译本。

The Count of Monte Cristo
基督山伯爵

There is neither happiness nor misery in the world; there is only the comparison of one state with another, nothing more.

这世上既没有快乐也没有痛苦；它们都是相对的，除此之外，别无其他。

——*The Count of Monto Cristo*《基督山伯爵》

名著导读

Dashing young sailor Edmond Dantes is a guileless and honest man, whose peaceful life and plans to marry the beautiful Mercedes are abruptly shattered when his best friend Fernand, who wants Mercedes for himself, deceives him. Set up to be unlawfully sentenced to the infamous island prison of Chateau D'If, Edmond is trapped in a nightmare that lasts for thirteen years. With the help of an equally innocent fellow inmate, Dantes escapes from prison, whereupon he transforms himself into the mysterious and wealthy Count of Monte Cristo. With cunning ruthlessness, he cleverly insinuates himself into the French nobility and systematically destroys the men who manipulated and enslaved him.

年轻勇敢的水手爱德蒙·唐泰斯是一个正直、诚实的人。他过着平静的生活，正打算和美丽的心上人默西迪丝结婚。然而，他最好的朋友费尔南德为了得到默西迪丝而欺骗了他，从此，他原来的生活完全被打乱了。由于非法判决，爱德蒙被送去臭名昭著的岛上监狱——逸夫岛城堡服刑，他在那里被困了13年之久。在另一名同样无辜的罪犯的帮助下，唐泰斯逃出了监狱，之后，他摇身变成了神秘而富有的基督山伯爵。凭着机智和冷酷无情，他顺利地进入了法国贵族社会，一步一步毁灭了那个曾经利用自己并使自己遭受牢狱之灾的费尔南德。

名段选读

"There is a **felucca**① for you at anchor. Jacopo will carry you to Leghorn, where Monsieur Noirtier awaits his granddaughter, whom he wishes to bless before you lead her to the **altar**②. All that is in this **grotto**③, my friend, my house in the Champs Elysees, and my chateau at Treport, are the marriage gifts **bestowed**④ by Edmond Dantes upon the son of his old master, Morrel. Mademoiselle de Villefort will share them with you; for I **entreat**⑤ her to give to the poor the immense fortune reverting to her from her father, now a madman, and her brother who died last September with his mother. Tell the angel who will watch over your future destiny, Morrel, to pray sometimes for a man, who like Satan thought himself for an instant equal to God, but who now acknowledges with Christian humility that God alone possesses supreme power and infinite wisdom. Perhaps those prayers may soften the **remorse**⑥ he feels in his heart. As for you, Morrel, this is the secret of my conduct towards you. There is neither happiness nor misery in the world; there is only the comparison of one state with another, nothing more. He who has felt the deepest grief is best able to experience supreme happiness. We must have felt what it is to die, Morrel, that we may appreciate the enjoyments of living."

"Live, then, and be happy, beloved children of my heart, and never forget that until the day when God shall **deign**⑦ to reveal the future to man, all human wisdom is summed up in these two words, 'Wait and hope.'

Your friend,

Edmond Dantes, Count of Monte Cristo."

"岸边停着一艘小船，那是为你准备的。雅各布会带你们到来亨去，诺瓦迪埃先生会在那里等着他的孙女，他希望在你们领她去圣坛之前先为她祝福。我的朋友，这个山洞里的一切，还有我在香榭丽舍大街的房子，以及我在特雷波特的别墅，都是爱德蒙·唐泰斯送给他的老船长之子——莫雷尔的结婚礼物，特维尔福小姐将和你共同拥有这些财产；因为，她的父亲现在疯了，她的弟弟和母亲在去年九月一同去世了，我恳求她把从父亲和弟弟那里继承的财产捐献给穷人。莫雷尔，告诉那位将守护你未来命运的天使，请她时常为一个人祈祷，那个人，像撒旦一样，曾一度认为自己与上帝平起平坐，但现在，他怀着基督徒的谦卑承认：只有上帝才拥有至高无上的权力和无限的智慧。也许这些祈祷可以抚慰他心里的内疚。至于你，莫雷尔，我跟你说的都是知心话。这世上既没有快乐也没有痛苦；它们都是相对的，除此之外，别无其他。只有体验过最深悲痛的人才能够体会到最大的快乐。莫雷尔，我们必须认识到死亡的痛苦，那样，我们才会珍惜活着的幸福。"

"所以，我心爱的孩子们，你们不仅要活着，还要快乐地活着；永远不要忘记，在上帝向我们透露人类未来命运的信息之前，人类的智慧都可以总结为两个词：'等待'和'希望'。

你们的朋友，

基督山伯爵　爱德蒙·唐泰斯。"

——选自《基督山伯爵》第117章

注释

★ "这是一部令人精神焕发的小说。"

——前苏联无产阶级作家　高尔基

① felucca [fe'lʌkə] *n.* 小帆船

② altar ['ɔːltə(r)] *n.* 圣坛

③ grotto ['grɔtəu] *n.* 洞穴
④ bestow [bɪ'stəu] *vt.* 给予
⑤ entreat [ɪn'tri:t] *vt.* 恳求
⑥ remorse [rɪ'mɔ:s] *n.* 懊悔，同情
⑦ deign [dein] *vi.* 赐予

《黑郁金香》创作于1850年，共33章。作品以17世纪荷兰资产阶级革命时期的激烈政治斗争和动荡生活为背景。目前，这部小说在国内最著名的翻译版本是江西人民出版社1979年郝运的译本。

The Black Tulip
黑郁金香

"Sometimes one has suffered so much that he has the right never to be able to say, 'I am too happy.'"

"有时候，当一个人经历了太多的痛苦后，他有权利永远不说，'我太幸福了。'"

——*The Black Tulip*《黑郁金香》

名著导读

The city of Haarlem, Netherlands has set a prize of 100,000 guilders to the person who can grow a black tulip, sparking competition between the country's best gardeners to win the money, honour and fame. The young and bourgeois Cornelius van Baerle has almost succeeded, but is suddenly thrown into the Loevestein prison. There he meets the prison guard's beautiful daughter Rosa, who will be his comfort and help, and at last his rescuer.

在荷兰的哈勒姆市，政府设置了10万荷兰盾的奖金给能够种出黑色郁金香的人，这立刻吸引了全国优秀园丁的争相参加——为了金钱、荣誉和名望。正当来自中产阶层的年轻人科尼利厄斯·范·巴尔勒眼看就要赢得比赛的时候，他突然被关进了卢费斯坦城堡监狱。在那里，他遇到了监狱看守女儿美丽的罗莎，罗莎不断地安慰他、帮助他，甚至最终帮他逃出了监狱。

名段选读

It was indeed a sight to see him watching the **obnoxious**① **moths**② and butterflies, killing **slugs**③, and driving away the hungry bees.

As he had heard Boxtel's story, and was furious at having been the **dupe**④ of the pretended Jacob, he destroyed the **sycamore**⑤ behind which the envious Isaac had spied into the garden; for the plot of ground belonging to him had been bought by Cornelius, and taken into his own garden.

Rosa, growing not only in beauty, but in wisdom also, after two years of her married life, could read and write so well that she was able to undertake by herself the education of two beautiful children which she had borne in 1674 and 1675, both in May, the month of flowers.

As a matter of course, one was a boy, the other a girl, the former being called Cornelius, the other Rosa.

Van Baerle remained faithfully attached to Rosa and to his tulips. The whole of his life was devoted to the happiness of his wife and the culture of flowers, in the latter of which occupations he was so successful that a great number of his varieties found a place in the catalogue of Holland. The two principal **ornaments**⑥ of his drawing-room were those two leaves from the Bible of Cornelius de Witt, in large golden frames; one of them containing the letter in which his godfather **enjoined**⑦ him to burn the correspondence of the Marquis de Louvois, and the other his own will, in which he **bequeathed**⑧ to Rosa his bulbs under condition that she should marry a young man of from twenty-six to twenty-eight years, who loved her and whom she loved, a condition which was **scrupulously**⑨ fulfilled, although, or rather because, Cornelius did not die.

And to ward off any envious attempts of another Isaac Boxtel, he wrote over his door the lines which Grotius had, on the day of his flight, scratched on the walls of his prison: "Sometimes one has suffered so much that he has the right never to be able to say, 'I am too happy.'"

看着他观察那些讨厌的飞蛾和蝴蝶，杀死粘叶蜂，赶走饥饿的蜜蜂，确实是不错的风景。

他在听说博克斯特尔的故事以后，为自己受到这个假装雅各布的人的欺骗而暴跳如雷，他愤怒地砍掉了那棵藏匿艾萨克并让他得以窥视花园的枫树；因为科尼利厄斯买下了那块地，并延伸到了他自己的花园里。

罗莎不仅越来越美丽，还越来越聪明了；结婚两年后，她不仅学会了阅读，还学会了写字，这样，她就可以指导她那两个漂亮孩子学习了，他们都是在繁华盛开的五月出生的——一个出生于1674年，一个出生于1675年。

一个是男孩，一个是女孩，所以理所当然的是，男孩叫科尼利厄斯，而女孩叫罗莎。

范·巴尔勒深爱着他的妻子和他的郁金香。他生活的全部就是让妻子幸福以及培育郁金香，他培育了很多新品种，都刊登在荷兰的花卉目录上。他客厅里的两个主要装饰物是从科尼利厄斯·德·威特的《圣经》上撕下来的两页纸，用金色的大相框裱着；其中一页是他的教父留给他的信，信中嘱咐他把与德·路瓦斯的通信全部烧掉，另外一页是他的遗嘱，内容是把郁金香球茎留给罗莎，条件是她必须嫁给一个26岁至28岁与她真心相爱的年轻人。虽然科尼利厄斯还没有死，但他的遗嘱已经在严谨地执行中了，其实，还不如说正是因为科尼利厄斯还没有死，才这样的。

为了防止其他像艾萨克·博克斯特尔那样嫉妒的人，他在门上写下了格劳秀斯在逃走那天刻在牢房墙上的话："有时候，当一个人经历了太多的痛苦后，他有权利永远不说，'我太幸福了。'"

——选自《黑郁金香》第33章

注释

① obnoxious [əb'nɔkʃəs] *adj.* 可憎的，讨厌的

② moth [mɔθ] *n.* 蛾，蛀虫

③ slug [slʌg] *n.* 粘叶蜂

④ dupe [dju:p] *n.* 易上当的人

⑤ sycamore ['sɪkəmɔ:(r)] *n.* 枫树

⑥ ornament ['ɔ:nəmənt] *n.* 装饰品

⑦ enjoin [ɪn'dʒɔin] *vt.* 嘱咐，命令

⑧ bequeath [bɪ'kwi:ð] *vt.* 遗赠

⑨ scrupulously ['skru:pjələslɪ] *adv.* 谨慎地

6 现代主义"鼻祖"——居斯塔夫·福楼拜

Gustave Flaubert (December 12, 1821—May 8, 1880) was a French writer who is counted among the greatest Western novelists. His masterpiece, *Madame Bovary* (1857), is a sharply realistic portrayal of **provincial**★ **bourgeois**★ boredom and **adultery**★. His other novels include the exotic *Salammbô* (1862), set in ancient Carthage; *A Sentimental Education* (1869), a classic **bildungsroman**★ of **disillusionment**★ in a time of social and political change; and *The Temptation of Saint Anthony* (1874), notable for its depiction of spiritual torment. *Trois Contes* (1877) contains three novellas set in the ancient, medieval, and contemporary periods. Renowned for his lapidary style, he is regarded as the foremost exponent of French realism..

居斯塔夫·福楼拜(1821年12月12日—1880年5月8日)是一位法国作家，他被认为是西方最伟大的小说家之一。他的代表作《包法利夫人》是一部尖锐地揭露乡村中产阶级的空虚和荒淫的现实主义著作。他的其他小说包括有着异国情调的《萨朗波》(1862年)，它的故事发生在古代迦太基；《情感教育》(1869年)，一部描绘社会政治动荡时期幻想破灭的经典教育小说；以及《圣安东尼的诱惑》(1874年)，该书因其对精神折磨的描写而著称。《三个故事》(1877年)包括了三个短篇故事，背景分别设在古代、中世纪以及当代。福楼拜的作品以考究的写作手法著称，被认为是法国现实主义流派的先驱。

《包法利夫人》★ 出版于1856年,共分3部分，35章。作者以简洁而细腻的文笔，通过一个富有激情的妇女爱玛的经历，再现了19世纪中期法国的社会生活。目前国内较著名的译本是许渊冲的版本和李健吾的版本。

Madame Bovary
包法利夫人

This nature, positive in the midst of its enthusiasms, that had loved the church for the sake of the flowers, and music for the words of the songs, and literature for its passional stimulus, rebelled against the mysteries of faith as it grew irritated by discipline, a thing antipathetic to her constitution.

这是她的热情中一种积极的天性——她喜欢教堂是因为教堂里的花朵，她喜欢音乐是因为优美的歌词，她喜欢文学是因为它充满热情的感染力——当这种天性渐渐被各种戒律（她生来就讨厌的一种东西）所烦扰时，它就会奋起反抗信仰的神秘。

——*Madame Bovary*《包法利夫人》

名著导读

The story focuses on a doctor's wife, Emma Bovary, who has adulterous affairs and lives beyond her means in order to escape the **banalities**[①] and emptiness of provincial life. Finally, in despair, Emma swallows **arsenic**[②] and dies an agonizing death. Emma's husband Charles, heartbroken, abandons himself to grief and dies, leaving his young daughter Berthe to live with distant relatives and she is eventually sent to work at a cotton mill.

故事讲述了爱玛·包法利，一个医生的妻子，为了摆脱平庸、空虚的乡村生活，而与人通奸并过着入不敷出的生活。最后，绝望的爱玛吞下砒霜，在极度痛苦中结束了自己的生命。爱玛的丈夫查尔斯悲痛欲绝，郁郁寡欢，伤心而死。失去双亲的女儿贝尔特被寄养在一个远方亲戚家里，后来进入纱厂工作。

名段选读

The good nuns, who had been so sure of her **vocation**[③], perceived with great astonishment that Mademoiselle Rouault seemed to be slipping from them. They had indeed been so lavish to her of prayers, retreats, **novenas**[④], and sermons, they had so often preached the respect due to saints and **martyrs**[⑤], and given so much good advice as to the modesty of the body and the salvation of her soul, that she did as tightly reined horses; she pulled up short and the bit slipped from her teeth. This nature, positive in the midst of its enthusiasms, that had loved the church for the sake of the flowers, and music for the words of the songs, and literature for its passional stimulus, rebelled against the mysteries of faith as it grew irritated by discipline, a thing **antipathetic**[⑥] to her constitution. When her father took her from school, no one was sorry to see her go. The Lady Superior even thought that she had latterly been somewhat irreverent to the community.

Emma, at home once more, first took pleasure in looking after the servants, then grew disgusted with the country and missed her convent. When Charles came to the Bertaux for the first time, she thought herself quite disillusioned, with nothing more to learn, and nothing more to feel.

But the uneasiness of her new position, or perhaps the disturbance caused by the presence of this man, had sufficed to make her believe that she at last felt that wondrous ⑦ passion which, till then, like a great bird with rose-coloured wings, hung in the splendour of the skies of poesy; and now she could not think that the calm in which she lived was the happiness she had dreamed.

那些好心的修女们一开始以为鲁奥小姐受了上帝的感召，但是后来她们非常惊讶地发现她好像离她们越来越远。修女们对她确实无微不至，她们让她祈祷、静修、祷告、布道，她们经常向她宣扬要尊重圣人先烈，还给了她很多克制肉欲、拯救灵魂的建议，而她也就像被缰绳紧紧拉住的马一样照做了；然而没过多久，她就不干了，所有的清规戒律都被她甩到脑后。这是她的热情中一种积极的天性——她喜欢教堂是因为教堂里的花朵，她喜欢音乐是因为优美的歌词，她喜欢文学是因为它充满热情的感染力——当这种天性渐渐被各种戒律(她生来就讨厌的一种东西)所烦扰时，它就会奋起反抗信仰的神秘。所以当她的父亲把她从修道院接回家时，没人感到遗憾。修道院长甚至认为她后来对教会有些不敬。

爱玛再一次回到家中，一开始她还觉得照管佣人们很有趣，但后来她开始厌倦乡村生活，想念起修道院来。当查尔斯第一次来贝尔托时，她觉得自己的幻想已经破灭了，没有什么可学的，也没有感觉到什么。

但是对于自己新身份的不自在，或者可能是这个男人的出现引起的骚动，足以使她相信她终于感受到了那种奇妙的爱情。在那之前，爱情对她来说就像是一只长着玫瑰色翅膀的神鸟，翱翔在广阔无垠、充满诗意的天空中；而现在，她无法想象，这样平静的生活就是她以前梦寐以求的幸福。

——选自《包法利夫人》第1部分第6章

注释

★ “在法国小说史里，《包法利夫人》具有划时代的意义，它说明某些东西的结束和某些东西的开始。”

——法国学者　布吕纳

★ provincial [prə'vɪnʃl] *adj.* 地方的，偏狭的

★ bourgeois ['buəʒwa:] *n.* 中产阶级

★ adultery [ə'dʌltərɪ] *n.* 通奸，私通

★ bildungsroman ['bɪlduŋzrəu,ma:n] *n.*（德语）教育小说

★ disillusionment [,dɪsɪ'lu:ʒənmənt] *n.* 幻灭，觉醒

① banality[bə'nɪlətɪ] *n.* 平庸，陈腐
② arsenic ['ɑːsənɪk] *n.* 砒霜
③ vocation [vəʊ'keiʃən] *n.* 天命，神召
④ novena [nəʊ'vɪːnə] *n.* 连续九天的祷告
⑤ martyr ['mɑːtə(r)] *n.* 受难者，受苦者
⑥ antipathetic [ˌæntɪpə'θetɪk] *adj.* 讨厌的，厌恶的
⑦ wondrous ['wʌndrəs] *adj.* 令人惊奇的

《萨朗波》发表于1862年，共15章，是一部历史小说。时代背景是公元前3世纪时罗马和迦太基进行激烈斗争时期，地点在迦太基。目前国内最著名的译本是上海译文出版社郑永慧的版本。

Salammbo 萨朗波

Would you rather die on the evening of a defeat, in misery beneath the shelter of a bush, or amid the outrages of the populace and the flames of funeral piles?

你是愿意在败北的夜晚、在藏身的灌木丛中悲惨地死去，还是想在民众的辱骂声中、在火化的柴火堆上离去？

——*Salammbo*《萨朗波》

名著导读

After the First Punic War, Carthage is unable to fulfil promises made to its army of **mercenaries**①, and finds itself under attack. The fictional title character, a priestess and the daughter of Hamilcar Barca, an aristocratic Carthaginian general, is the object of the obsessive lust of Matho, a leader of the mercenaries. With the help of the scheming freed slave, Spendius, Matho steals the sacred veil of Carthage, the Zaïmph, prompting Salammbô to enter the mercenaries' camp in an attempt to steal it back. The Zaïmph is an ornate bejewelled veil draped about the statue of the goddess Tanith in the sacrosanct of her temple: the veil is the city's guardian and touching it will bring death to the perpetrator.

第一次布匿战争后，迦太基无法向雇佣军兑现原来的承诺，还遭到了围攻。小说主角萨朗波是一名女祭司，同时她也是迦太基贵族统帅哈米尔卡·巴尔卡的女儿。雇佣军将领

马托深深迷恋着她。在机智多谋的自由奴隶斯庞迪斯的帮助下，马托盗走了保佑迦太基城的神衣——赞姆浮，而这使得萨朗波潜入雇佣军的军营试图把它偷回来。赞姆浮是一件镶满珠宝的面纱，它原本是搭在神殿中女神塔妮斯的神像上的，是迦太基城的守护符，碰到它的人就会有灭顶之灾。

名段选读

After leaving the gardens Matho and Spendius found themselves checked by the **rampart**[②] of Megara. But they discovered a breach in the great wall and passed through. The ground sloped downwards, forming a kind of very broad valley. It was an exposed place.

"Listen," said Spendius, "and first of all fear nothing! I shall fulfil my promise—"

He stopped abruptly, and seemed to reflect as though searching for words,—"Do you remember that time at sunrise when I showed Carthage to you on Salammbo's terrace? We were strong that day, but you would listen to nothing!" Then in a grave voice: "Master, in the **sanctuary**[③] of Tanith there is a mysterious veil, which fell from heaven and which covers the goddess."

"I know," said Matho.

Spendius resumed: "It is itself divine, for it forms part of her. The gods reside where their images are. It is because Carthage possesses it that Carthage is powerful." Then leaning over to his ear: "I have brought you with me to carry it off!"

Matho recoiled in horror. "Begone! look for some one else! I will not help you in this **execrable**[④] crime!"

"But Tanith is your enemy," retorted Spendius, "she is persecuting you and you are dying through her wrath. You will be revenged upon her. She will obey you, and you will become almost immortal and **invincible**[⑤]."

Matho bent his head. Spendius continued:

"We should succumb; the army would be **annihilated**[⑥] of itself. We have neither flight, nor succour, nor pardon to hope for! What **chastisement**[⑦] from the gods can you be afraid of since you will have their power in your own hands? Would you rather die on the evening of a defeat, in misery beneath the shelter of a bush, or amid the outrages of the populace and the flames of funeral piles? Master, one day you will enter Carthage among the colleges of the **pontiffs**[⑧], who will kiss your sandals; and if the veil of Tanith weighs upon you still, you will reinstate it in its temple. Follow me! come and take it."

Matho was consumed by a terrible longing. He would have liked to possess the veil while refraining from the sacrilege. He said to himself that perhaps it would not be necessary to take it in order to **monopolise**[9] its virtue.

He did not go to the bottom of his thought but stopped at the boundary, where it terrified him.

"Come on!" he said; and they went off with rapid strides, side by side, and without speaking.

离开花园后，马托和斯庞迪斯被墨伽拉的城墙困住了。幸好他们发现城墙上有一条裂缝，于是就从那儿穿了过去。城墙后的地面向下倾斜，形成了一个很宽的山谷。那地方无处藏身。

"听着，"斯庞迪斯说，"首先，什么都别怕！我会兑现自己的承诺的……"

他突然沉默下来，好像在思考接下来应该怎么说，"你还记得那天日出的时候，我们站在萨朗波的露台上，我指着迦太基让你看吗？那时候我们还有权有势，但是你听不进任何话！"然后他严肃地说："主人，在塔妮斯的神殿里有一件面纱，它从天而降，搭在了女神的神像上。"

"我知道，"马托说。

斯庞迪斯继续说："面纱本身就很神圣，因为它是女神的一部分。神的雕像在哪儿，神就在哪儿。迦太基会如此强大就是因为有了这件面纱。"然后他伏到马托的耳边说："我把你带到这里就是来拿走面纱的！"

马托惊恐地向后退了几步，说："走开！去找其他人吧！我不会帮你干这种坏事呢！"

"但是塔妮斯是你的敌人，"斯庞迪斯反驳道，"她在迫害你，你会死在她的淫威之下。你得找她报仇，这样她就会听从于你，你也会拥有不死之身，而且天下无敌。"

马托低下了头，斯庞迪斯继续说：

"我们可以投降，那样的话我们的军队就会自生自灭。我们既没有办法逃跑，也没有救兵，又不能幻想着得到宽恕！如果你手握神权，你还会害怕遭受神的惩罚吗？你是愿意在败北的夜晚、在藏身的灌木丛中悲惨地死去，还是想在民众的辱骂声中、在火化的柴火堆上离去？主人，终有一天你会跟一群祭司一起进入迦太基，他们将亲吻你的鞋子；如果那时你仍觉得塔妮斯的面纱很重要，就让它在神殿里恢复它的力量。跟我来！咱们把它拿出来！"

马托被一种可怕的欲望折磨着。他想拥有面纱，但是又不想亵渎圣物。他对自己说或许不一定非要占有它才能独享它的神力。

他没有深刻地思考，只是略微地想了一下，而这一下让他胆战心惊。

"来啊！"他说。他们肩并肩快步前进着，彼此都没有说话。

——选自《萨朗波》第5章

注释

① mercenary ['mɛ:sənəri:] *n.* 雇佣兵，唯利是图者

② rampart ['ræmpɑ:t] *n.* 垒，城墙

③ sanctuary ['sæŋktʃuərɪ] *n.* 教堂，圣殿
④ execrable ['eksɪkrəbl] *adj.* 拙劣的，极坏的
⑤ invincible [ɪn'vɪnsəbl] *adj.* 不能征服的，无敌的
⑥ annihilated [ə'naiə,leitɪd] *adj.* 废止的
⑦ chastisement [tʃæ'staizmənt] *n.* 惩戒，责罚
⑧ pontiff ['pɔntɪf] *n.* 罗马教皇，主教
⑨ monopolise [mə'nɔpəlaiz] *vt.* 垄断，独占

《情感教育》的第一稿写于1843年至1845年，但福楼拜并不满意，将它束之高阁。1864年9月，他着手写第二稿，于1869年5月完成。全书共21章。李健吾的译本较好。

Sentimental Education
情感教育

Love is the inspiration, and, as it were, the atmosphere of genius. Extraordinary emotions produce sublime results.

爱是动力，无论是过去还是现在，它都能够造就天才。非凡的感情会创造高尚的成就。

——*Sentimental Education*《情感教育》

名著导读

The novel describes the life of a young man, Frederic Moreau, living through the revolution of 1848 and the founding of the Second French Empire, and his love for an older woman. Frederic Moreau prepares to study law in 1840 when, on a boat trip along the Seine, he glimpses the most beautiful woman he has ever seen. She is the wife of a **philandering**① businessman, M. Arnoux. Through his studies, the coup of 1851, engagements and affairs with other women, Frederic befriends and quietly worships Mme. Arnoux.

小说描写了年轻人弗雷德里克·莫罗在1848年革命和第二法兰西帝国建立期间的经历以及他对一个年长女子的爱。1840年，弗雷德里克·莫罗正准备学习法律，然而在塞纳河上的一艘小船上，他无意中看到了他所见过的最美的女人——阿诺克丝夫人，她的丈夫是个荒淫无度的商人。他经历了学习、1851年的动乱、和其他女人的订婚及风流韵事，但是他始终默默地帮助并爱慕着阿诺克丝夫人。

名段选读

And they continued walking from one end to the other of the two bridges which rest on the narrow islet formed by the canal and the river. On the side toward Nogent they had immediately in front of them a block of houses which projected a little. At the right was the church, behind the mills, whose **sluices**② had been closed up; and, on the left, were the hedges, covered with **shrubs**③, **skirting**④ the wood, and forming a boundary for the gardens, which could scarcely be distinguished. On the side toward Paris the high road formed a sheer descending line, and the **meadows**⑤ lost themselves in the distance amid the vapours of the night. Silence reigned along this road, whose white track **gleamed**⑥ through the surrounding gloom. Odours of damp leaves ascended toward them. The waterfall, where the stream had been diverted from its course a hundred paces farther away, rumbled with that deep harmonious sound which waves make in the night time.

Deslauriers stopped, and said: "Tis droll to have all these worthy folks sleeping peacefully! Patience! A new 'eighty-nine is in the air. People are tired of constitutions, charters, subtleties, lies! Ah, if I only had a newspaper, or a platform, how I would wrestle with all these things! But, in order to undertake anything whatever, money is necessary. What a curse it is to be a tavern-keeper's son. And to waste one's youth in quest of bread!"

He hung his head, bit his lips, and shivered beneath his **threadbare**⑦ overcoat.

Frederick flung half his **cloak**⑧ over his friend's shoulders. They both wrapped themselves up in it; and, with their arms around each other, they walked down the road.

"How do you think I can possibly live over there without you?" said Frederick. His friend's bitterness had revived his own sadness. "I could have done something, with a woman to love me. Why do you laugh? Love is the inspiration, and, as it were, the atmosphere of genius. Extraordinary emotions produce sublime results. As for seeking after her whom I desire, I will not! Besides, if I should ever find her, she would repel me. I belong to the race of the disinherited, and I shall be swept under by a treasure that will be of paste or of diamond I know not which."

他们不停地在两座桥上来回走着，这两座桥架在运河和河流冲积而成的小岛上。另一端连接着诺让，映入眼帘的是几栋略微突起的房子。房子的右边是教堂，后面是磨坊，磨坊的水闸已经关了；左边是树篱，长满了矮灌木，这些矮灌木把大树围了起来，成了花园的界线，但这界线并不那么清晰。通向巴黎的那一头，高高的路面形成了一条陡峭向下的坡。在夜晚的雾气中，草地消失在远方。静谧笼罩着这条路，白色的路面在黑暗中若隐若现。潮湿叶子的香气扑鼻而来。百步开外，溪水在半路分流，形成了一个瀑布，瀑布轰隆、深沉的声音响彻夜空。

岱丝萝停下脚步说：“看着这些可敬的人们平静地安睡在这里感觉是多么奇怪啊！忍耐！新的大革命(法国大革命发生于1789年)遥遥无期。人们已经厌倦了宪法、宪章、阴谋、谎言！唉，如果我有份报纸或者其他平台，看我怎样和这些抗衡！但是想做任何事都离不开钱。作为一个酒馆老板的儿子是多么可悲啊，要为了生计浪费青春！”

岱丝萝垂下头咬着嘴唇，身体在他那破旧的外套下打起了寒战。

弗雷德里克把半边斗篷搭在朋友的肩膀上，把他们俩都裹在了斗篷里，他们互相搂着对方向前走着。

“你怎么会觉得没有了你我还能活下来呢？”弗雷德里克说。朋友的痛苦也唤醒了他的悲伤。“如果有个女人爱我的话，我也许还能做些什么。你笑什么？爱是动力，无论是过去还是现在，它都能够造就天才。非凡的感情会创造高尚的成就。说到找寻我所爱的人，我绝不会去找的！而且即使我找到她，她也可能拒绝我。我是个已经被剥夺了继承权的人，我可能会因为我不知道的人造宝石或是钻石之类的财宝而被她扫地出门的。”

——选自《情感教育》第2章

注释

① philander [fɪ'lændə] *vt.* 调戏，玩弄女性

② sluice [sluːs] *n.* 水门，水闸

③ shrub [ʃrʌb] *n.* 灌木丛

④ skirt [skɛːt] *v.* 绕开，环绕

⑤ meadow ['medəʊ] *n.* 草地，牧场

⑥ gleam [gliːm] *vi.* 闪烁

⑦ threadbare ['θredbeə(r)] *adj.* 磨破的，破旧的

⑧ cloak [kləuk] *n.* 披风，斗篷

7 现代科学幻想小说之父——儒勒·凡尔纳

Jules Gabriel Verne (February 8, 1828—March 24, 1905) was a French author who helped pioneer the science fiction genre. Verne wrote about space, air, and underwater travel before navigable aircraft and practical submarines were invented, and before any means of space travel had been devised. He is best known for his novels *A Journey to the Centre of the Earth* (1864), *From the Earth to the Moon* (1865), *Twenty Thousand Leagues Under the Sea* (1869–1870), *Around the World in Eighty Days* (1873) and *The Mysterious Island* (1875).

儒勒·加布里埃尔·凡尔纳(1828年2月8日—1905年3月24日)是法国作家，科幻小说之父。凡尔纳在可以航行的飞机和实用的潜艇发明之前，就创作了关于太空、天空以及水下旅行探险的小说。他最著名的小说包括《地心游记》(1864)、《从地球到月球》(1865)、《海底两万里》(1869—1870)、《八十天环游世界》(1873)以及《神秘岛》(1875)。

《八十天环游世界》发表于1873年，共37章，讲述的是一位绅士福格因为在改良俱乐部同牌友们打赌，而从伦敦出发，用80天的时间环游地球一周的故事。陈筱卿的译本比较好。

Around the World in Eighty Days
八十天环游世界

It is certain, not only that we shall risk our lives, but horrible tortures, if we are taken.

有一点是肯定的，我们不仅是在拿生命来冒险，而且一旦被抓就会受到可怕的折磨。

——*Around the World in Eighty Days*《八十天环游世界》

名著导读

Around the World in Eighty Days is a classic adventure novel. In the story, Phileas Fogg of London and his newly employed French valet Passepartout attempt to circumnavigate the world in 80 days on a £20,000 wager (equal to £1,324,289 today) set by his friends at the Reform Club. Accompanied by Monsieur Passepartout, he leaves London by train at 8:45 P.M. on October 2, 1872, and thus is due back at the Reform Club at the same time 80 days later, on December 21.

《八十天环游世界》是一部经典探险小说。故事讲述了菲利亚斯·福格在伦敦的改良俱乐部和朋友打赌，要在80天内和新雇佣的法国仆人路路通环游世界一圈，赌注是20万英镑(合现在的1,324,289英镑)。福格在1872年10月2日下午8：45坐火车离开伦敦，正好在80天后即11月21日准时到达改良俱乐部。

名段选读

The project was a bold one, full of difficulty, perhaps impracticable. Mr. Fogg was going to risk life, or at least liberty, and therefore the success of his tour. But he did not hesitate, and he found in Sir Francis Cromarty an enthusiastic ally.

As for Passepartout, he was ready for anything that might be proposed. His master's idea charmed him; he perceived a heart, a soul, under that icy **exterior**①. He began to love Phileas Fogg.

There remained the guide: what course would he adopt? Would he not take part with the Indians? In **default**② of his assistance, it was necessary to be assured of his **neutrality**③.

Sir Francis frankly put the question to him.

"Officers," replied the guide, "I am a **Parsee**④, and this woman is a Parsee. Command me as you will."

"Excellent!" said Mr. Fogg.

"However," resumed the guide, "it is certain, not only that we shall risk our lives, but horrible tortures, if we are taken."

"That is foreseen," replied Mr. Fogg. "I think we must wait till night before acting."

"I think so," said the guide.

这个大胆的计划充满了困难，甚至可能无法实现。福格先生将要用他的生命去冒险，或者至少是用他的自由去冒险，因此也是拿旅行的成功去冒险。但是福格先生没有丝毫犹豫，而且他发现弗朗西斯·克罗默蒂爵士是个热心的盟友。

对于路路通来说，他乐于接受任何提议。主人的想法吸引了他，他能感觉到在那冰冷的外表下是一颗炽热的心。他开始喜欢菲利亚斯·福格了。

现在只剩下向导了：他会站在哪一边呢？他不会袒护印度人吗？要是他不肯帮忙，就有必要确认他是保持中立的。

弗朗西斯爵士直截了当地问他。

“长官，”向导回答说，“我是一个帕西人，这个女人也是帕西人。我随时听从命令。”

“很好！”福格先生说。

“但是，”向导继续说，“有一点是肯定的，我们不仅是在拿生命来冒险，而且一旦被抓就会受到可怕的折磨。”

“这个可以预料得到，”福格先生回答说。“我想我们必须等到晚上再行动。”

“我也这么认为，”向导说。

——选自《八十天环游戏世界》第13章

注释

① exterior [ɪk'stɪəriə(r)] *n.* 外表，表面

② default [dɪ'fɔːlt] *n.* 缺席，不履行

③ neutrality [njuː'trælətɪ] *n.* 中立

④ Parsee [ˌpaː'siː] *n.* 帕西人，印度拜火教徒

《海底两万里》发表于1870年，共20章，是一部出色的悬念小说。中国青年出版社曾觉之的译本和陈筱卿译本比较好。

Twenty Thousand Leagues Under the Sea
海底两万里

In my selfish personal interests, could I go back on my word and be responsible for ruining the future lives of my companions?

我能为了一己私利违背自己的诺言，毁了伙伴们的未来吗？我负得起这个责任吗？

——*Twenty Thousand Leagues Under the Sea*《海底两万里》

名著导读

Twenty Thousand Leagues Under the Sea tells the story of Captain Nemo and his submarine Nautilus as seen from the perspective of Professor Pierre Aronnax. Everyone in Europe and America is talking about a mysterious creature that has been sinking and damaging ships. Finally, the United States government decides to intervene and commissions the Abraham Lincoln to capture and identify the creature. On board the ship are Pierre Aronnax, a renowned scientist along with his manservant, Conseil, and Ned Land the king of harpooners. The three men find themselves on top of the mysterious creature, which is actually a submarine vessel. They are never to leave the vessel again.

《海底两万里》从皮尔·阿龙纳斯教授的角度讲述了尼摩船长和他的鹦鹉螺号潜水艇的故事。欧洲和美洲的所有人都在谈论一个神秘生物，这个生物会摧毁和击沉船只。最后，美国当局决定介入此事，派遣亚伯拉罕·林肯号驱逐舰去捕获和确认那个生物。驱逐舰上有著名的科学家皮尔·阿龙纳斯、他的男仆康赛尔以及捕鲸好手尼德兰。三个人发现其实自己就在那只神秘生物的上面，这个神秘生物原来是一艘潜艇。他们再也没能离开潜艇。

名段选读

"The sea is rough," I said.

"Admitted," the Canadian replied, "but we've got to risk it. Freedom is worth paying for. Besides, the longboat's solidly built, and a few miles with the wind behind us is no big deal. By tomorrow, who knows if this ship won't be 100 **leagues**① out to sea? If circumstances are in our favor, between ten and eleven this evening we'll be landing on some piece of solid ground, or we' ll be dead. So we're in God's hands, and I'll see you this evening!"

This said, the Canadian withdrew, leaving me close to **dumbfounded**②. I had imagined that if it came to this, I would have time to think about it, to talk it over. My stubborn companion hadn't granted me this **courtesy**③.

But after all, what would I have said to him? Ned Land was right a hundred times over. These were near–ideal circumstances, and he was taking full advantage of them. In my selfish personal interests, could I go back on my word and be responsible for ruining the future lives of my companions? Tomorrow, might not Captain Nemo take us far away from any shore?

Just then a fairly loud hissing told me that the ballast tanks were filling, and the Nautilus sank beneath the waves of the Atlantic.

I stayed in my **stateroom**④. I wanted to avoid the captain, to hide from his eyes the agitation overwhelming me. What an agonizing day I spent, torn between my desire to regain my free will and my regret at abandoning this marvelous Nautilus, leaving my underwater research incomplete! How could I **relinquish**⑤ this ocean—"my own Atlantic," as I liked to call it—without observing its lower **strata**⑥, without wresting from it the kinds of secrets that had been revealed to me by the seas of the East Indies and the Pacific! I was putting down my novel half read, I was waking up as my dream neared its climax! How painfully the hours passed, as I sometimes **envisioned**[7] myself safe on shore with my companions, or, despite my better judgment, as I sometimes wished that some unforeseen circumstances would prevent Ned Land from carrying out his plans.

“海上充满了凶险，” 我说。

“是啊，” 加拿大人回答说， “但是我们必须去冒险。自由是值得我们为之付出代价的。而且，这艘大艇很坚固，顺风航行几英里没什么问题的。明天之前，谁知道这艘船会不会在海上100里格开外了呢？如果运气好，我们大概会在今晚十点到十一点之间在某个陆地登陆，不然我们就会死掉。所以我们的命掌握在上帝手里了，今天晚上见！”

说完后，加拿大人离开了，留下我在那里发呆。我以前想过如果真到了这一步，我还会有时间思考，找人讨论一下。但是我那固执的同伴没有给我这个机会。

但是，毕竟我又能对他说什么呢？尼德兰总是对的。这些正是接近理想的情况，他正在充分地利用它们。我能为了一己私利违背自己的诺言，毁了伙伴们的未来吗？我负得起这个责任吗？明天，尼摩船长不是可以带我们远离任何海岸吗？

正在那时，传来一阵很大的嘶嘶声，我知道是压载水舱满了，鹦鹉螺号沉入了大西洋的波涛之下。

我待在自己的舱房里。我要避开船长，我不想让他看到我的局促不安。我度过了非常痛苦的一天，在重获自由的渴望和放弃鹦鹉螺号潜水艇，丢下我没有完成的水下研究的遗憾中饱受折磨！我怎么能放弃这个海洋呢——我喜欢称它为“我的大西洋”——我还没有观察它的下层，还没有从它那里解开我已经在东印度洋和太平洋揭示的秘密！小说读到一半我就放下了，梦境快到高潮的时候我却醒来了！时间在痛苦的煎熬中过去了，我有时想象着自己和同伴安全地着陆了，或者，虽然我的判断更准确，但是有时我又希望有一些不可预知的情况可以阻止尼德兰实施他的计划。

——选自《海底两万里》第8章第2节

注释

① league [li:g] *n.* 里格(长度单位)

② dumbfounded [dʌm'faʊndɪd]] *adj.* 目瞪口呆的

③ courtesy ['kɛ:təsɪ] *n.* 礼貌，谦恭

④ stateroom ['steitru:m] *n.* 特等舱

⑤ relinquish [rɪ'lɪŋkwɪʃ] *vt.* 放弃

⑥ stratum ['strɑ:təm] *n.* 层，地层

⑦ envision [ɪn'vɪʒən] *vt.* 想象

《沙皇的信使》发表于1876年，分2部分，共32章。军事幻想小说，作品中所讲述故事的历史背景是18世纪中期爆发的鞑靼人与俄罗斯人之间的战争，以乌兹别克人反攻西伯利亚为题材。远方出版社的译本和内蒙古人民出版社石谟的译本比较好。

The Courier of the Czar
沙皇的信使

Go for God, for Russia, for my brother, and for myself!

为了上帝，为了俄罗斯，为了我的兄弟和我，出发吧！

——*The Courier of the Czar*《沙皇的信使》

名著导读

Michael Strogoff, a 30-year-old native of Omsk, is a courier for Tsar Alexander II of Russia. The Tartar Khan, Feofar, incites a rebellion and separates the Russian Far East from the mainland, severing telegraph lines. Rebels encircle Irkutsk, where the local governor, brother of the Tsar, is making a last stand. Strogoff is sent to Irkutsk to warn the governor about the traitor Ivan Ogareff. Ogareff, a former colonel, was once demoted and exiled and now seeks revenge against the royal family. He intends to destroy Irkutsk by setting fire to the huge oil storage tanks on the banks of the Angara River.

30岁的鄂木斯克人米歇尔·斯托戈夫是沙皇亚历山大二世的信使。鞑靼可汗费奥法发动叛变，把俄罗斯远东地区从大陆分离出去，并切断了电报线。叛军包围了伊尔库茨克，沙皇的弟弟是伊尔库茨克的长官，正在做最后的垂死挣扎。斯托戈夫被派往伊尔库茨克，向长官揭发叛徒伊万·奥加莱夫。奥加莱夫是前陆军上校，以前曾被降级流放，现在企图向皇室复仇。他计划通过点燃安加拉河沿岸的大油库来摧毁伊尔库茨克。

名段选读

The **Czar**①, rising, told Michael Strogoff to draw near.

Michael advanced a few steps, and then stood motionless, ready to answer.

The Czar again looked him full in the face and their eyes met. Then in an abrupt tone, “Thy name?” he asked.

“Michael Strogoff, sire.”

"Thy rank?"

"Captain in the corps of **couriers**[②] of the Czar."

"Thou dost know Siberia?"

"I am a Siberian."

"A native of?"

"Omsk, sire."

"Hast thou relations there?"

"Yes sire."

"What relations?"

"My old mother."

The Czar suspended his questions for a moment. Then, pointing to the letter which he held in his hand, "Here is a letter which I charge thee, Michael Strogoff, to deliver into the hands of the Grand Duke, and to no other but him."

"I will deliver it, sire."

"The Grand Duke is at Irkutsk."

"I will go to Irkutsk."

"Thou wilt have to **traverse**[③] a rebellious country, invaded by Tartars, whose interest it will be to **intercept**[④] this letter."

"I will traverse it."

"Above all, beware of the traitor, Ivan Ogareff, who will perhaps meet thee on the way."

"I will beware of him."

"Wilt thou pass through Omsk?"

"Sire, that is my route."

"If thou dost see thy mother, there will be the risk of being recognized. Thou must not see her!"

Michael Strogoff hesitated a moment.

"I will not see her," said he.

"Swear to me that nothing will make thee acknowledge who thou art, nor whither thou art going."

"I swear it."

"Michael Strogoff," continued the Czar, giving the letter to the young courier, "take this letter; on it depends the safety of all Siberia, and perhaps the life of my brother the Grand Duke."

"This letter shall be delivered to his Highness the Grand Duke."

"Then thou wilt pass whatever happens?"

"I shall pass, or they shall kill me."

"I want thee to live."

"I shall live, and I shall pass," answered Michael Strogoff.

The Czar appeared satisfied with Strogoff's calm and simple answer.

"Go then, Michael Strogoff," said he, "go for God, for Russia, for my brother, and for myself!"

沙皇站起来，让米歇尔·斯托戈夫走到跟前。

斯托戈夫向前走了几步，站定，准备回答沙皇的问题。

沙皇又一次面对面地盯着他看，然后冷不丁地问道："你的名字？"

"米歇尔·斯托戈夫，陛下。"

"军衔？"

"沙皇信使团上尉。"

"你了解西伯利亚吗？"

"我是西伯利亚人。"

"出生地是？"

"鄂木斯克，陛下。"

"那里有亲戚吗？"

"有，陛下。"

"什么亲戚？"

"我的老母亲。"

沙皇停止了问话。然后，他指着手里的那封信，说："这里有一封信，我委派你，米歇尔·斯托戈夫，把它送到大公手里，一定要亲手送到他手里。"

"我会送到的，陛下。"

"大公在伊尔库茨克。"

"我会去伊尔库茨克."

"你将会横穿一个发生了叛乱、被鞑靼人占领的地区，他们会拦截这封信的。"

"我会穿过它的。"

"最重要的是，你可能会在路上遇到叛徒伊万·奥加莱夫，一定要提防他。"

"我会提防他。"

"你会经过鄂木斯克吗？"

"陛下，那是我的必经之地。"

"你如果去看望你的母亲，就有可能被认出来，所以不能去看她。"

斯托戈夫犹豫了一会。

"我不会去看她。"

"向我发誓，任何情况下，你都不会泄露你的身份和你将去的地方。"

"我发誓。"

"米歇尔·斯托戈夫，"沙皇边说边把信递给年轻的信使，"带上信，整个西伯利亚地区和我兄弟大公的安危就全取决于它了。"

“这封信会被送到大公殿下手上。”

“那么不管发生什么，你都能穿过那里吗？”

“我会穿过去的，不然就让他们杀了我。”

“我要你活着。”

“我会活着，并且穿过去，” 米歇尔·斯托戈夫说。

沙皇似乎对斯托戈夫冷静、简单的回答很满意。

“那就出发吧，米歇尔·斯托戈夫，” 沙皇说，“为了上帝，为了俄罗斯，为了我的兄弟和我，出发吧！”

——选自《沙皇的信使》第1部第3章

注释

① czar [zɑː] *n.* 沙皇

② courier ['kʊriə(r)] *n.* 信差，情报员

③ traverse [trə'vɛːs] *vt.* 穿越，穿过

④ intercept [ˌɪntə'sept] *vt.* 拦截，截住

8 法国自然主义文学流派的领袖——埃米尔·左拉

Émile Zola (April 2, 1840—September 29, 1902) was an influential French writer, the most important exemplar of the literary school of naturalism and an important contributor to the development of theatrical naturalism. Among Zola's most important works is his famous *Rougon-Macquart* cycle (1871—1893), which included such novels as *L'Assommoir* (1877), about the suffering of the Parisian working-class, *Nana* (1880), dealing with prostitution, and *Germinal* (1885), depicting the mining industry.

埃米尔·左拉(1840年4月2日—1902年9月29日)是一位有影响力的法国作家，也是法国自然主义文学流派的领袖，自然主义戏剧发展的重要贡献者。他最重要的作品是著名的《卢贡-马卡尔家族》(1871—1893)，其中包括叙述巴黎工人阶级苦难的《小酒店》(1877)、关于刻画卖淫生活的《娜娜》(1880)和描写采矿业的《萌芽》等小说。

《萌芽》* 于1885年出版，小说共分7部分，共40章。属于左拉的自然主义家族史小说《卢贡——马卡尔家族》的第13部作品。是法国19世纪文学中最出色、最重要的一部描写社会主义工人运动的杰作。目前国内最普遍的中文译本是符锦勇的译本。

Germinal
萌芽

Men were springing forth, a black avenging army, germinating slowly in the furrows, growing towards the harvests of the next century, and their germination would soon overturn the earth.

人们在不断地成长、壮大，黑色的复仇军队正在田野里慢慢地萌芽，为的是下个世纪的丰收，他们的萌芽很快就会推翻旧世界。

——*Germinal*《萌芽》

名著导读

Etienne Lantier is an out-of-work railway worker who by sheer luck has secured a job in the coal mine called "Le Voreux". As the miners' working and living conditions continue to worsen, they decide to strike and Étienne, now a respected member of the community, becomes the leader of the movement. They are eventually confronted by police and the army. Disillusioned, the miners go back to work, blaming Étienne for the failure of the strike. Étienne is eventually fired but he goes on to live in Paris.

失业的铁路工人艾蒂安·朗蒂埃突然走运，在一个叫"蒙苏"的煤矿找到了一份有保障的工作。随着矿工们的工作和生活条件日益恶化，他们决定罢工。艾蒂安在这里受到大家的拥护和爱戴，因此成为了罢工行动的领导者。他们最终被警察和军队镇压了下来。矿工们的幻想破灭了，回到矿地继续干活，还把罢工失败的责任推到艾蒂安的身上。最后艾蒂安被开除了，但他后来去了巴黎生活。

名段选读

But Étienne, leaving the Vandame road, now came on to the paved street. On the right he saw Montsou, which was lost in the valley. Opposite were the ruins of the Voreux, the **accursed**① hole where three pumps worked **unceasingly**②. Then there were the other pits at the horizon, the Victoire, Saint-Thomas, Feutry-Cantel; while, towards the north, the tall chimneys of the **blast**③ **furnaces**④, and the batteries of **coke**⑤ **ovens**⑥, were smoking in the transparent morning air. If he was not to lose the eight o'clock train he must hasten, for he had still six kilometres before him.

And beneath his feet, the deep blows, those obstinate blows of the pick, continued. The mates were all there; he heard them following him at every stride. Was not that Maheude beneath the **beetroots**⑦. With bent back and hoarse respiration accompanying the **rumble**⑧ of the **ventilator**⑨? To left, to right, farther on, he seemed to recognize others beneath the wheatfields, the hedges, the young trees. Now the April sun, in the open sky, was shining in his glory, and warming the pregnant earth. From its fertile flanks life was leaping out, buds were bursting into green leaves, and the fields were **quivering**⑩ with the growth of the grass. On every side seeds were swelling, stretching out, cracking the plain, filled by the need of heat and light. An overflow of sap was mixed with whispering voices, the sound of the germs expanding in a great kiss. Again and again, more and more distinctly, as though they were approaching the soil, the mates were hammering. In the fiery rays of the sun on this youthful morning the country seemed full of that sound. Men were springing forth, a black **avenging**⑪ army, **germinating**⑫ slowly in the furrows, growing towards the harvests of the next century, and their germination would soon overturn the earth.

然而，艾蒂安离开旺达姆路，走上了铺好的大路。右边，他看着蒙苏渐渐消失在了山谷里。对面是蒙苏煤矿的废墟，三台抽水机正在不停地从那被诅咒的井中抽水。接着是维克托瓦尔矿井、圣托马斯矿井、弗特里-康泰尔矿井，一个接一个地出现在他的视野里。北边，炼铁高炉高耸的烟囱和一连串的焦炭炉，正向早晨清新的空气中吐着黑烟。如果他想赶上八点的火车，他必须加快速度，因为前面还有六公里的路程。

脚下深处，一如既往的挖矿的重击声还在继续。伙伴们都在那里；他每走一步都能听见他们跟在他后头的声音。这块甜菜地下面的人不正是马厄吗？伴随着通风机的隆隆声，他弯着腰，气喘吁吁的？左边、右边、更远处，在麦田、篱笆和小树下，他似乎能辨认出其他人。现在，四月的太阳高挂在广阔的天空上，发出耀眼的光芒，温暖着孕育万物的大地。绿芽从肥沃的土壤中破土而出，长成了新叶，随着青草的生长大地也颤抖着。每一处的种子都在隆起、发芽，为了获取生长所需的光和热，破土而出。溢出的草木汁液与飒飒的风声混合在一起，萌芽在微风的轻抚下长大。同伴们还在不断锤击，声音越来越清晰，似乎已经接近地面了。在炽热的阳光下，在这个清新的早晨，整个乡村似乎都充斥着这样的敲击声。人们在不断地成长、壮大，黑色的复仇军队正在田野里慢慢地萌芽，为的是下个世纪的丰收，他们的萌芽很快就会推翻旧世界。

——选自《萌芽》第7部第6章

注释

★“《萌芽》的风格由于强有力的缓缓进展、广阔的潮流、细节的累积和作者手法的直率而具有古代史诗的风格。”

——法国批评家　于勒·勒梅特尔

① accursed [ə'kɛːsɪd] *adj.* 受诅咒的

② unceasingly [ʌn'siːsɪŋlɪ] *adv.* 不断地

③ blast [blɑːst] *n.* 爆破，一连串

④ furnace ['fɛːnɪs] *n.* 火炉

⑤ coke [kəuk] *n.* 焦炭

⑥ oven ['ʌvən] *n.* 烤炉

⑦ beetroot ['biːtruːt] *n.* 甜菜根

⑧ rumble ['rʌmbl] *n.* 隆隆声

⑨ ventilator ['ventɪleitə(r)] *n.* 通风设备

⑩ quiver ['kwɪvə(r)] *vi.* 颤抖

⑪ avenging [ə'vendʒɪŋ] *adj.* 复仇的

⑫ germinate ['dʒɛːmɪneit] *vi.* 发芽，生长

《小酒店》于1877年出版，属于左拉的自然主义家族史小说《卢贡——马卡尔家族》的第7部作品。这部小说面世后，左拉一举成名，从此踏上了成功之路。目前国内最普遍的中文译本是王了一的译本和孙立坚的译本。

L'Assommoir
小酒店

When one was not rich one had no time for that sort of thing.
但当一个人不富裕的时候，她就没有时间去那样假装了。

——*L'Assommoir*《小酒店》

名著导读

Abandoned by Lantier, the virtuous and hard-working Gervaise marries a slater, Coupeau, and their household prospers for a while. A daughter, Anna, is born. But Coupeau has a dramatic fall and, disgruntled at his fate, turns to drink. Though her finances are depleted, Gervaise takes on a laundry of her own with the help of an admirer, Goujet. But, when Lantier returns and worms his way into the household, with Coupeau ever the worse for drink, her own indulgences and the growing hostility of her neighbours bring about Gervaise's ruin and her terrible physical and moral degradation. She also turns to drink; Coupeau dies in the throes of delirium tremens in a hospital; Anna (Nana) takes to prostitution; and Gervaise, reduced to a life of utmost squalor, dies of starvation.

勤劳善良的绮尔维丝被朗蒂埃抛弃后，嫁给了石瓦工古波，他们暂时过上了幸福稳定的生活。后来女儿安娜出生了。但是古波突然变得堕落，他不满于自己的命运，开始借酒消愁。尽管已经用光了所有的积蓄，但在自己的爱慕者克劳德的帮助下，绮尔维丝还勉强经营着自己的洗衣店。然而，这个时候朗蒂埃回来了，并且不断介入这个家庭。古波酗酒也越来越严重，自身的放纵加上邻居对她日益滋长的敌意，让绮尔维丝彻底崩溃，经历了身体和道德上的沦落。她也开始喝酒，最后古波酒后中风痛苦地死在医院里；安娜(娜娜)沦为妓女；而绮尔维丝过着极度卑劣的生活，最后饿死了。

名段选读

Coupeau did not sleep much that night. He covered up the fire in the stove. Every hour he had to get up to give the baby spoonfuls of **lukewarm**① sugar and water. That did not prevent his going off to his work in the morning as usual. He even took advantage of his lunch-hour to make a declaration of the birth at the mayor's. During this time Madame Boche, who had been informed of the event, had hastened to go and pass the day with Gervaise. But the latter, after ten hours of sleep, **bewailed**② her position, saying that she already felt pains all over her through having been so long in bed. She would become quite ill if they did not let her get up. In the evening, when Coupeau returned home, she told him all her worries; no doubt she had confidence in Madame Boche, only it put her beside herself to see a stranger installed in her room, opening the drawers, and touching her things.

On the morrow the **concierge**③, on returning from some **errand**④, found her up, dressed, sweeping and getting her husband's dinner ready; and it was impossible to persuade her to go to bed again. They were trying to make a fool of her perhaps! It was all very well for ladies to pretend to be unable to move. When one was not rich one had no time for that sort of thing. Three days after her **confinement**⑤ she was ironing **petticoats**⑥ at Madame Fauconnier's, banging her irons and all in a **perspiration**⑦ from the great heat of the stove.

古波那晚没怎么睡着。他灭了暖炉的火。每隔一小时，他就得起床给婴儿喂几勺微热的糖水。他照样还是每天早晨早起上班。他甚至要利用午餐时间去市长那里办理出生登记。在这段时间里，博斯夫人知道后立即赶了过来，陪了绮尔维丝一整天。但是绮尔维丝睡了十个小时，醒来后便哀叹自己的处境，说在床上躺了太长时间感觉浑身都疼，如果他们不让她起床，她会生病的。晚上古波回到家后，她就告诉了他自己所有的忧虑；毫无疑问，她信任博斯夫人，但是她就是看不惯一个陌生人呆在她房间，开她的抽屉，碰她的东西。

次日，办完差事回来的看门人发现绮尔维丝起床了，梳洗打扮过了，房间也清扫过了，还把丈夫的晚餐也准备好了；知道再也不可能劝服她躺回床上去了。他们也许会取笑她！妇女假装不能动完全是无可非议的！但当一个人不富裕的时候，她就没有时间去那样假装了。在分娩后的第三天，她就在福科尼耶夫人家熨衬裙了，敲打着熨斗，因为暖炉的热气，她做完这些时已经汗流浃背了。

——选自《小酒店》第4章

注释

① lukewarm [ˌluːk'wɔːm] *adj.* 微温的，不冷不热的

② bewail [bɪ'weil] *vt.* 哀叹

③ concierge [ˌkɔːnsiˈɛəʒ] *n.* 看门人
④ errand [ˈerənd] *n.* 差事
⑤ confinement [kənˈfainmənt] *n.* 分娩，产期
⑥ petticoat [ˈpetɪkəut] *n.* 衬裙
⑦ perspiration [ˌpɛːspəˈreiʃən] *n.* 汗水

《娜娜》出版于1880年，共14章，是左拉的鸿篇巨著自然主义家族史小说《卢贡——马卡尔家族》中的第9部，是一部颇有文学价值和艺术价值的长篇小说。它的问世扩大并巩固了左拉在世界文学史上的地位。目前国内比较普遍的中文译本是王了一、林如稷和郑永慧的译本。

Nana
娜娜

Paris would always picture her thus—would see her shining high up among crystal glass like the good God himself.

巴黎永远都是这样描绘她的——看到她在水晶玻璃的中间灿烂夺目，就像高高在上的上帝。

——*Nana*《娜娜》

名著导读

Nana tells the story of Nana Coupeau's rise from **streetwalker**① to high-class **cocotte**② during the last three years of the French Second Empire. She takes up with Fontan, an actor. She tries to be domestic and kind, but Fontan beats her, then abandons her and she turns to streetwalking. Nana destroys every man who pursues her. In the end, Nana catches smallpox and dies miserably, the disease ravaging her beauty. She dies in 1870 just as the Franco-Prussian War begins.

《娜娜》讲述的是娜娜·古波在法国第二帝国时期的最后三年里从拉客妓女变成高等妓女的故事。她开始与演员丰唐交往。尽管她尽力表现得百依百顺且，但丰唐却时常殴打她，之后还抛弃了她，她不得不再次沦为拉客妓女。娜娜耗尽了每一个追求她的男人的钱财。最后，娜娜染上了天花，这个疾病毁掉了她的美貌，使她在悲惨中死去。她死于1870年，正是普法战争刚刚开始的时候。

名段选读

Nana dead! It was a blow to them all. Without a word Muffat had gone back to the bench, his face still buried in his handkerchief. The others burst into **exclamations**[3], but they were cut short, for a fresh band passed by, howling, "A Berlin! A Berlin! A Berlin!" Nana dead! Hang it, and such a fine girl too! Mignon sighed and looked relieved, for at last Rose would come down. A chill fell on the company. Fontan, meditating a tragic role, had assumed a look of woe and was drawing down the corners of his mouth and rolling his eyes **askance**[4], while Fauchery chewed his cigar nervously, for despite his cheap journalistic **chaff**[5] he was really touched. Nevertheless, the two women continued to give **vent**[6] to their feelings of surprise. The last time Lucy had seen her was at the Gaite; Blanche, too, had seen her in Melusine. Oh, how stunning it was, my dear, when she appeared in the depths of the crystal **grot**[7]! The gentlemen remembered the occasion perfectly. Fontan had played the Prince Cocorico. And their memories once stirred up, they launched into **interminable**[8] particulars. How ripping she looked with that rich coloring of hers in the crystal grot! Didn't she, now? She didn't say a word: the authors had even deprived her of a line or two, because it was **superfluous**[9]. No, never a word! It was **grander**[10] that way, and she drove her public wild by simply showing herself. You wouldn't find another body like hers! Such shoulders as she had, and such legs and such a figure! Strange that she should be dead! You know, above her she had nothing on but a golden **girdle**[11] which hardly concealed her behind and in front. All round her the grotto, which was entirely of glass, shone like day. **Cascades**[12] of diamonds were flowing down; strings of brilliant pearls glistened among the **stalactites**[13] in the **vault**[14] overhead, and amid the transparent atmosphere and flowing fountain water, which was crossed by a wide ray of electric light, she gleamed like the sun with that flamelike skin and hair of hers. Paris would always picture her thus—would see her shining high up among crystal glass like the good God himself. No, it was too stupid to let herself die under such conditions! She must be looking pretty by this time in that room up there!

娜娜死了！这对所有的人都是一个打击。莫法一声不吭地回到那条长凳上坐着，脸仍埋在手帕里。其他人顿时发出一阵阵惊叹，但是很快被一群路过的人打断，他们一边走一边大声喊着："进军柏林！"，"进军柏林！"，"进军柏林！"娜娜死了！岂有此理，这么好的一个女孩！密尼翁叹了口气，似乎轻松了不少，因为罗斯终于要下来了。一种寒意笼罩在人们身上。丰唐，为自己冥想出了一个悲剧角色，他装出一副很悲伤的样子，耷拉着嘴角，翻着白眼；而浮切瑞则紧张地抽着他的雪茄，虽然平时他很爱开一些低级玩笑，但他是真的被触动了。不过，两个女人继续表达着她们的惊讶。露西最后一次看到娜娜是在盖特，布兰奇也是，她们最后一次看见她是在她出演《美人鱼》时。啊！她出现在水晶岩洞深处的时候，亲爱的，真是太美了！这几位先生都还记得很清楚。丰唐扮演的是雄鸡王子。他们的记忆匣子一旦被打开，就没完没了地谈起来。她在水晶宫出场时的浓艳妆容是多么动人啊！不是吗？她没有说一个字：甚至编剧也没有给她安排一两句台词，因为那是多余的。是的，一个字也没有！这样更具有震撼力，她只需要展示自己就足以让观众为她痴狂了。你再也找不到比谁比她身材更加迷人了：那肩膀，那双腿，那身材！她怎么会死呢？真想不通！当时她几乎什么都没穿，只系着一条金色的腰带，而这条腰带却几乎什么也没有遮住。她周围的岩洞都是玻璃做的，像透明的日光一样闪耀着。钻石帘子像瀑布一样飞泻而下，璀璨的珍珠项链在拱顶上的钟乳石间珠光四射。在透明的大气和流动的山泉之间划过了一道强烈的电光，娜娜如太阳般熠熠生辉：她的皮肤和头发闪着光芒。巴黎永远都是这样描绘她的——看到她在水晶玻璃的中间灿烂夺目，就像高高在上的上帝。她就这样死了，真是太可惜了！她现在躺在房间里，看起来一定很漂亮。

——选自《娜娜》第14章

注释

① streetwalker [ˈstriːtˌwɔːkə] *n.* 拉客妓女，娼妓
② cocotte [kəˈkɔt] *n.* 妓女
③ exclamation [ˌekskləˈmeiʃən] *n.* 感叹
④ askance [əˈskæns] *adv.* 斜眼看，瞟
⑤ chaff [tʃɑːf] *n.* 玩笑
⑥ vent [vent] *n.* 发泄
⑦ grot [grɔt] *n.* 洞穴
⑧ interminable [ɪnˈtɛːmɪnəbl] *adj.* 无限的，冗长的
⑨ superfluous [suːˈpɛːfluəs] *adj.* 多余的
⑩ grand [grænd] *adj.* 壮观的，显赫的
⑪ girdle [ˈgɛːdl] *n.* 腰带
⑫ cascade [kæˈskeid] *n.* 瀑布
⑬ stalactite [ˈstæləktait] *n.* 钟乳石
⑭ vault [vɔːlt] *n.* 拱顶

9 法兰西思想之王——伏尔泰

François-Marie Arouet (November 21, 1694—May 30, 1778), better known by the pen name Voltaire, was a French Enlightenment writer, historian and philosopher famous for his wit and for his advocacy of civil liberties, including freedom of religion and free trade. Voltaire was a prolific writer and produced works in almost every literary form including plays, poetry, novels, essays, historical and scientific works, more than 20,000 letters and more than 2,000 books and pamphlets. He wrote two book-long epic poems, including the first ever written in French, *The Henriade*, and later, *The Maid of Orleans*, besides many other smaller pieces.

弗朗索瓦·马里·阿鲁埃(1694年11月21日—1778年5月30日)，他的笔名“伏尔泰”更为人所熟知。他是法国的启蒙作家、历史学家和哲学家，以其智慧和对公民自由(包括宗教自由和贸易自由)的拥护而著称。伏尔泰是一位多产作家，他的作品几乎涉及了所有的文学体裁，包括戏剧、诗歌、小说、随笔、历史和科学作品、20,000多封信件以及超过2,000本书和小册子。除了很多其他短诗之外，他还写了两部史诗，史诗的篇幅有一本书的内容那么多：一本是《亨利亚德》，这是他第一次尝试用法语进行创作；另一本是《奥尔良少女》。

《老实人》★ 创作于1759年，是伏尔泰的代表作。全书共分为30章，其主题是批判盲目乐观主义哲学。目前国内较著名的译本是徐志摩的版本和傅雷的版本。

Candide
老实人

For private misfortunes are public benefits; so that the more private misfortunes there are, the greater is the general good.

因为个人的不幸就是公众的利益；所以，个人的不幸越多，公众获益就越大。

——*Candide*《老实人》

名著导读

It begins with a young man, Candide, who is living a sheltered life in an Edenic paradise and being indoctrinated with Leibnizian optimism (or simply Optimism) by his mentor, Pangloss. The work describes the abrupt cessation of this lifestyle, followed by Candide's slow, painful disillusionment as he witnesses and experiences great hardships in the world. Finally, Candide and his friends take to cultivating a garden in earnest. All their time and energy goes into the work, and none is left over for philosophical speculation.

故事以一个叫憨第德的年轻人展开，他在像天堂一样的地方过着受人庇护的生活，而且被他的老师邦葛罗斯灌输着莱布尼兹的乐观主义（或者简单讲就是乐观主义）思想。这本书描写了当憨第德目睹并经历了世上的艰难困苦之后，慢慢地、痛苦地醒悟了。最终，憨第德和他的朋友们开始认真地培育一片花园。他们把所有的时间和精力都投入在这项工作上，没有人再愿意去研究哲学思想了。

名段选读

As he wrote a good hand, and understood accounts **tolerably**① well, the Anabaptist made him his bookkeeper. At the expiration of two months, being obliged by some **mercantile**② affairs to go to Lisbon he took the two philosophers with him in the same ship; Pangloss, during the course of the voyage, explained to him how everything was so constituted that it could not be better. James did not quite agree with him on this point.

"Men," said he, "must, in some things, have deviated from their original **innocence**③; for they were not born wolves, and yet they worry one another like those beasts of prey. God never gave them twenty-four pounders nor **bayonets**④, and yet they have made cannon and bayonets to destroy one another. To this account I might add not only bankruptcies, but the law which seizes on the effects of bankrupts, only to cheat the creditors."

"All this was indispensably necessary," replied the one-eyed doctor, "for private misfortunes are public benefits; so that the more private misfortunes there are, the greater is the general good."

While he was arguing in this manner, the sky was overcast, the winds blew from the four quarters of the compass, and the ship was **assailed**⑤ by a most terrible **tempest**⑥, within sight of the port of Lisbon.

因为他写得一手好字，并且十分清楚账目，所以那个再洗礼派教徒让他做自己的会计员。在两个月期满之后，因为一些贸易事务，他得去里斯本，他带着两个哲学家一起上了船；在旅途中，邦葛罗斯向他解释说世间万物的构成是如此完美，堪称极致。但是詹姆斯并不是十分赞同他的观点。

“人，”他说，“有时会偏离原来的天真无邪；因为人并不是天生就是狼，然而，他们却互相提防，就像那些猎食的猛兽一样。上帝从没赐予他们24磅的大炮和刺刀，但是他们自己却制造了大炮和刺刀来互相残杀。在这个账目上，我也许不仅会写上破产，还会写上那些利用破产来欺骗债权人的法律。”

“所有这些都是绝对必要的，”独眼的医生回答说，“因为个人的不幸就是公众的利益；所以，个人的不幸越多，公众获益就越大。”

当他以这种方式争辩的时候，天阴沉了下来，风从四面八方吹来，同时他们的船也遭到了最猛烈的暴风雨的袭击，这时，里斯本的港口已经依稀可见了。

——选自《老实人》第4章

注释

★“《老实人》是值得花你们宝贵的光阴的，不容情的读者们，因为是一部西洋来的《镜花缘》，这镜里照出的却不止是西洋的丑态，我们也一样分得着体面。”

——中国现代诗人、散文家　徐志摩

① tolerably ['tɔlərəblɪ] *adv.* 可容忍地，尚好地

② mercantile ['mɛːkəntail] *adj.* 商业的，贸易的

③ innocence ['ɪnəsəns] *n.* 天真无邪，纯真

④ bayonet ['beiənət] *n.* 刺刀

⑤ assail [ə'seil] *vt.* 攻击，袭击

⑥ tempest ['tempɪst] *n.* 暴风雨

《查第格》为法国启蒙文学家伏尔泰所著的中篇小说，写于1747年，由18个章节组成。它以古代的东方为背景，富有神话色彩和异国情调，给读者展现出一个似真似假、虚实交融的奇异世界。目前国内较著名的译本是傅雷的版本。

Zadig
查第格

Nothing passes so slowly as Time to him who is in Expectation; and nothing so swift as Time to him who is in the perfect Enjoyment of his Wishes.

对于一个等待中的人来说，没有什么比时间更慢了；对于一个正在享乐的人来说，没有什么比时间更快了。

——*Zadig*《查第格》

名著导读

It tells the story of Zadig, a philosopher in ancient Babylonia. Zadig falls into favour with the king and queen of Babylonia and is eventually appointed prime minister. He is forced to flee the kingdom, because Zadig's reciprocated love for queen Astarté is discovered and he worries that the king's desire for revenge might drive him to kill Astarté. Finally, Zadig returns to Babylonia, marries Astarté, is crowned king, and rules over a prosperous kingdom.

小说讲述了查第格的故事，他是古巴比伦王国的一位哲学家。查第格得到巴比伦王国的国王和王后的赏识，最终被任命为首相。当他对王后阿斯塔蒂的爱慕之情被揭发时，他被迫逃离了巴比伦。他担心国王怒火中烧，为了报复，可能会杀了阿斯塔蒂。最终，查第格回到了巴比伦，和阿斯塔蒂结了婚，并被加冕为国王，从此统治着一个繁荣的王国。

名段选读

The first Question the Grand Magus proposed was this: What is the longest and yet the shortest thing in the World; the most swift and the most slow; the most **divisible**[1], and the most extended; the least valued, and the most regretted; And without which nothing can possibly be done: Which, in a Word, **devours**[2] every Thing how minute soever, and yet gives Life and Spirit to every Object or Being, however Great?

Itobad had the Honour to answer first. His reply was, that a Man of his Merit had something else to think on, than **idle**[3] Riddles; 'twas enough for him, that he was acknowledged the Hero of the Circus. One said, the Solution of the Ænigma proposed was Fortune; others said the Earth; and others again the Light; But Zadig pronounced it to be Time. Nothing, said he, can be longer, since 'tis the Measure of **Eternity**[4]; Nothing is shorter, since there is Time always wanting to accomplish what we aim at. Nothing passes so slowly as Time to him who is in Expectation; and nothing so swift as Time to him who is in the perfect Enjoyment of his Wishes. It's Extent is to Infinity, in the Whole; and divisible to Infinity in part. All Men neglect it in the Passage; and all regret the Loss of it when 'tis past. Nothing can possibly be done without it; it buries in Oblivion whatever is unworthy of being transmitted down to Posterity; and it renders all illustrious Actions immortal. The Assembly agreed unanimously that Zadig was in the Right.

大祭司提出的第一个问题是：世界上什么东西最长又最短，最快又最慢，最好分割又最能延展，最没价值却最让人感到后悔；没有它，可能任何事情都做不成。总之，它能摧毁所有的东西，无论它们多么渺小；然而也能赋予所有的东西生命，无论它们多么庞大，这东西是什么呢？

艾图拜德有幸第一个回答。他的回答是：高尚的人有许多其他的事情要思考，而不是把时间浪费在猜谜上；这对他来说足够了，人们把他封为竞技场上的英雄。有人说，大祭司所提出的问题答案是运气；有人说是泥土；还有人说是光：但查第格却说是时间。他说，没有什么比时间更长，因为永恒是无法估量的；没有什么比时间更短，因为在实现目标的过程中，我们总是缺少时间。对于一个等待中的人来说，没有什么比时间更慢；对于一个正在享乐的人来说，没有什么比时间更快。总的来说，它的范围是无限的；它也可被分解成无限个小块。时间匆匆流逝的时候，所有的人都忽略了它；当时光已成往事的时候，所有人都会为它的流逝而感到后悔。没有时间，我们做不了任何事情；它被埋葬在那些被遗忘的记忆中，因为我们觉得它不值得传给后代，它孕育了所有不朽的行为。大家一致认为查第格的回答是正确的。

——选自《查第格》第18章

注释

① divisible [dɪ'vɪzəbl] *adj.* 可分的

② devour [dɪ'vaʊə(r)] *vt.* 吞噬，毁灭

③ idle ['aidl] *adj.* 无用的，闲散的

④ eternity [ɪ'tɛːnətɪ] *n.* 不朽，来世

伏尔泰1751年至1753年间完成并出版了《路易十四时代》，是西方文化史中断代史研究的佳作。在该书中他高度赞扬了那个时代，认为“欧洲的文明礼貌和社交精神的产生都应归功于路易十四的宫廷”。国内有吴模信等译商务印刷出版社1982年出版的版本。

The Age of Louis XIV
路易十四时代

Every king who loves glory loves the public weal.

每一个热爱荣誉的国王都会欣然维护公众利益。

——*The Age of Louis XIV*《路易十四时代》

名著导读

Voltaire's The Age of Louis XIV established a new way of writing history. Prior to this work, history books were an account of political and military history. To these topics, Voltaire added the history of the achievements of the great artists, writers, and builders of the day in order to achieve a better understanding of the era. This new approach to writing history was adopted by many historians who later followed Voltaire's example. Voltaire was greatly impressed by Louis XIV who honored poets, writers, and artists, so he spent more than five years on the book. This work, published in 1751, was the most researched and carefully prepared of Voltaire's works.

伏尔泰的《路易十四时代》开创了一种新的记录历史的方法。在这本书之前，历史类题材的书籍都只是叙述政治和军事历史。在这本书中，为了让读者更加清晰地了解那个时代，除了这些内容之外，伏尔泰还加上了与当时伟大艺术家、作家和建筑家的成就相关的历史。很多历史学家后来也效仿伏尔泰采用了这种崭新的记述历史的方法。尊重诗人、作家和艺术家的路易十四给伏尔泰留下了十分深刻的印象，因此他花了五年多的时间来创作这本书。这本1751年出版的书是伏尔泰所有著作中在创作时研究最彻底、准备最充分的一本。

名段选读

Legislator of his people, he was no less so of his armies. It is astonishing that before his time the troops had no uniform dress. It was he who in the first year of his administration **decreed**① that each regiment should be distinguished by the color of their uniform, or by different badges—a regulation which was soon adopted by all other nations. It was he who organized the **brigadiers**② and gave the king's household troops the status they hold at the present day. He formed a company of **musketeers**③ and fixed the number of men for the two companies at five hundred.

It will be seen by this **cursory**④ glance what great changes Louis XIV brought about in the state; and that such changes were useful since they are still in force. His ministers vied with each other in their eagerness to assist him. The details, indeed the whole execution of such schemes was doubtless due to them, but his was the general organization. There can be no shadow of doubt that the **magistrates**⑤ would never have reformed the laws, the finances of the country would not have been put on a sound basis, nor discipline introduced into the army, nor a regular police force instituted throughout the kingdom; there would have been no fleets, no encouragement accorded to the arts; all these things would never have been peacefully and steadily accomplished in such a short period and under so many different ministers, had there not been a ruler to conceive of such great schemes, and with a will strong enough to carry them out.

Every king who loves glory loves the public **weal**[6]; about 1698 he commanded each comptroller to present a detailed description of his province for the instruction of the Duke of Burgundy. By this means it was possible to have an exact record of the whole kingdom and a correct census of the population.

他为群众和军队制定了法律。令人惊奇的是，在他统治之前，军队竟然没有统一的制服。在他执政的第一年里，他就颁布了法令，要求每个团都应该用不同颜色的制服或不同的徽章来区分——这项规定很快就被其他的国家采用。他赐封了准将的官职，并为全军将士设立了不同头衔，这些头衔沿用至今。他组织了一群步兵，并把他们分成两个连，每连500人。

只要粗略地一瞥，你就能看见路易十四为这个国家带来了多么伟大的改变；这些改变都起到了很大的作用，因为它们至今还被沿用。他的大臣们争先恐后地辅佐他。实际上，国家政策的细节问题，乃至整个体制的执行无疑都是他们的功劳，但路易十四却是背后的总参谋。毋庸置疑，如果没有路易十四的宏伟蓝图，没有他在实施体制时表现出的坚定毅力，法官就永远不可能革新法律，国家的经济就永远无法打下良好的基础，军队也不会有纪律可言；而全国各地也不会拥有秩序井然的警察部队，不会有舰队，不会有盛兴的艺术；这一切的一切都不可能在短时间内，在诸大臣的领导下平稳地实现。

每一个热爱荣誉的国王都会欣然维护公众利益。大约在1698年，他下令让每个审计官向他呈递一份他所统治地区的详细说明，以此来引导勃艮第公爵治理他的辖区。这样，拥有一份整个国家的详细记录以及精确的人口普查报告就成为可能。

——选自《路易十四时代》第29章

注释

① decree [dɪ'kriː] *vt.* 颁布

② brigadier [ˌbrɪgə'dɪə(r)] *n.* 陆军准将

③ musketeer [ˌmʌskə'tɪə(r)] *n.* 步兵，火枪手

④ cursory ['kɜːsərɪ] *adj.* 粗略的，仓促的

⑤ magistrate ['mædʒɪstreɪt] *n.* 长官，法官

⑥ weal [wiːl] *n.* 福利，幸福

10 存在主义文学领军人物——阿尔贝·加缪

Albert Camus (November 7, 1913—January 4, 1960) was a French Algerian author, philosopher and journalist. He was a key philosopher of the 20th-century, with his most famous work being the novel *L'Étranger (The Stranger)*. In 1949, Camus founded the Group for International **Liaisons**① within the Revolutionary Union Movement, which was opposed to some tendencies of the **Surrealist**② movement of André Breton. Camus was awarded the 1957 Nobel Prize for Literature "for his important literary production, which with clear-sighted earnestness illuminates the problems of the human conscience in our times". He was the second-youngest recipient of the Nobel Prize in Literature, after Rudyard Kipling, and the first African-born writer to receive the award.

阿尔贝·加缪(1913年11月7日—1960年1月4日)是一位拥有阿尔及利亚血统的法国作家、哲学家和新闻记者，其最有名的作品是《局外人》。1949年，加缪在革命同盟运动中成立了国际联络组，反对安德烈·布勒东的超现实主义运动倾向。"由于他在其极具影响力的文学创作中，通过清晰的视角和诚挚的笔触，揭露了这个时代所存在的有关人类良知的问题"，1957年，加缪获得诺贝尔文学奖。他是继吉卜林之后第二年轻的诺贝尔文学奖获得者，同时也是第一位获得诺贝尔文学奖的非裔作家。

《局外人》发表于1942年，分两部分，它既是加缪的成名作，同时也是存在主义文学的杰出作品之一。该书以一种客观记录式的"零度风格"，粗线条地描述了主人公默尔索在荒谬的世界中经历的种种荒谬的事情，以及自身的荒诞体验。上海译文出版社柳鸣九的译本比较好。

The Stranger
局外人

To feel it so like myself, indeed, so brotherly, made me realize that I'd been happy, and that I was happy still.

我感觉这个世界跟我自己如此相像，如此亲切，这让我意识到自己曾经很快乐，而且现在仍然快乐着。

——*The Stranger*《局外人》

名著导读

The Stranger is the story of Meursault's awakening and recovery. Early in the novel, he is unmoved by his mother's death because death itself holds no meaning for him. After murdering an Arab, Meursault progresses by degrees to a full recognition of his own purposelessness and impending death. During the long months of imprisonment, he slowly realizes that his former life was not empty. Meursault begins searching for the purpose of his existence but ends by creating one. He accepts life's absurdity and embraces his own death as a bond tying him to humanity. Meursault awaits his execution, emptied of hope, yet calm and happy because he is no longer a stranger to himself.

《局外人》讲述的是主人翁莫尔索的觉醒和重生。在小说的开头，莫尔索母亲的去世并未给他带来太大的触动，因为死对他来说根本就没有意义。在杀死一个阿拉伯人之后，莫尔索清醒地认识到自己是在漫无目的地游走于世间，也充分意识到了自己即将到来的死亡。在监狱的漫长岁月里，莫尔索逐渐意识到，以前的生活并不是毫无意义的。于是，莫尔索开始思考自己存在的意义，但最终以一个自己界定的意义结束。他接受了生活的荒谬，并认为自己的死亡是回归社会的途径。莫尔索不再抱有任何希望，平静、快乐地等待着判决的到来，因为他知道，对于他来说，自己已不再是一个局外人。

名段选读

Once he'd gone, I felt calm again. But all this excitement had exhausted me and I dropped heavily on to my sleeping **plank**③. I must have had a **longish**④ sleep, for, when I woke, the stars were shining down on my face. Sounds of the countryside came faintly in, and the cool night air, veined with smells' of earth and salt, fanned my cheeks. The marvelous peace of the sleepbound summer night flooded through me like a tide. Then, just on the edge of daybreak, I heard a steamer's siren. People were starting on a voyage to a world which had ceased to concern me forever. Almost for the first time in many months I thought of my mother. And now, it seemed to me, I understood why at her life' s end she had taken on a "fiancé"; why she'd played at making a fresh start. There, too, in that Home where lives were flickering out, the dusk came as a **mournful**⑤ **solace**⑥. With death so near, Mother must have felt like someone on the brink of freedom, ready to start life all over again. No one, no one in the world had any right to weep for her.

And I, too, felt ready to start life all over again. It was as if that great rush of anger had washed me clean, emptied me of hope, and, gazing up at the dark sky **spangled**⑦ with its signs and stars, for the first time, the first, I laid my heart open to the benign indifference of the universe. To feel it so like myself, indeed, so brotherly, made me realize that I'd been happy, and that I was happy still. For all to be accomplished, for me to feel less lonely, all that remained to hope was that on the day of my execution there should be a huge crowd of spectators and that they should greet me with howls of **execration**⑧.

他一走，我又恢复了平静。但是，所有这些刺激已经让我筋疲力尽，我重重地倒头睡在了木板床上。我一定睡了很久，因为当我醒来的时候，星光已经照在我的脸上了。我依稀可以听见村子里传来的声音，凉爽的晚风带着新鲜的泥土气息，吹拂着我的脸庞。沉睡着的夏夜异常宁静，如潮水一般悄悄涌向我，浸透了我的全身。将近黎明的时候，我听到了汽笛声，人们即将启程，前往一个再也与我无关的世界。几个月以来，我第一次想起了我的母亲。然而现在，我似乎明白了为什么她在生命最后的时间里还找了一个"未婚夫"，为什么她还想要重新开始。这里也一样，在这个屋子里，生命越来越脆弱，似乎快要走到尽头，而黄昏的到来就像是一个悲伤的安慰。当死亡来临的时候，母亲一定觉得自己站在自由的边缘，正要开始全新的生活。在这个世上，没有人，谁都没有权力为她痛哭。我也一样，正准备重新开始自己的生活。好像有股强大的怒潮将我一洗而空，也带走了我的希望。凝望那繁星点点的夜空，我第一次向这个仁慈而冷漠的世界敞开了心扉。我感觉这个世界跟我自己如此相像，如此亲切，这让我意识到自己曾经很快乐，而且现在仍然快乐着。为了让所有的一切变得圆满，为了让我不再感觉到孤单，我仍希望在我行刑的那天，会有很多人来围观，并且喊叫着诅咒我。

——选自《局外人》第2部第5章

注释

① liaison [li'eizən] *n.* 组织间的交流与合作，联络人

② surrealist [sə'rɪəlɪst] *n.* 超现实主义

③ plank [plæŋk] *n.* 厚木板

④ longish ['lɔŋɪʃ] *adj.* 稍长的

⑤ mournful ['mɔːnfl] *adj.* 悲恸的，悲哀的

⑥ solace ['sɔləs] *n.* 安慰

⑦ spangle ['spæŋgl] *vt.* 用闪光片布满(或装饰)

⑧ execration [ˌeksɪ'kreiʃən] *n.* 诅咒

《鼠疫》发表于1947年，分为5部分，是一部寓言体小说，写的是有关法西斯的寓言故事。上海译文出版社顾方济、徐志仁的译本比较好。

The Plague
鼠疫

When you see the misery it brings, you'd need to be a madman, or a coward, or stone blind, to give in tamely to the plague.

当目睹鼠疫带来的苦难时，只有疯子、懦夫或是瞎子，才会温顺地向它屈服。

——*The Plague*《鼠疫》

名著导读

The Plague is a novel that tells the story of medical workers finding solidarity in their labour as the Algerian city of Oran is swept by a plague. It asks a number of questions relating to the nature of destiny and the human condition. The characters in the book, ranging from doctors to vacationers to fugitives, all help to slow the effects the plague has on a populace.

《鼠疫》讲述的是在阿尔及利亚一座名为奥兰的城市里，医疗人员团结一致对抗鼠疫的故事。小说中提出了一系列关于命运和人类的问题。书中的人物——从医生到游客再到难民，都为防治鼠疫一起努力着。

名段选读

"I'd rather free men were employed."

"So would I. But might I ask why you feel like that?"

"I loathe men's being condemned to death."

Rieux looked Tarrou in the eyes.

"So—what?" he asked.

"It's this I have to say. I've drawn up a plan for voluntary groups of helpers. Get me empowered to try out my plan, and then let's **sidetrack**[①] **officialdom**[②]. In any case the authorities have their hands more than full already. I have friends in many walks of life; they'll form a nucleus to start from. And, of course, I'll take part in it myself."

"I need hardly tell you," Rieux replied, "that I accept your suggestion most gladly. One can't have too many helpers, especially in a job like mine under present conditions. I undertake to get your plan approved by the authorities. Anyhow, they've, no choice. But—" Rieux pondered. "But I take it you know that work of this kind may prove fatal to the worker. And I feel I should ask you this; have you weighed the dangers?"

Tarrou's gray eyes met the doctor's gaze serenely.

"What did you think of Paneloux's sermon, doctor?"

The question was asked in a quite ordinary tone, and Rieux answered in the same tone.

"I've seen too much of hospitals to **relish**③ any idea of collective punishment. But, as you know, Christians sometimes say that sort of thing without really thinking it. They're better than they seem."

"However, you think, like Paneloux, that the plague has its good side; it opens men's eyes and forces them to take thought?"

The doctor tossed his head impatiently.

"So does every ill that flesh is heir to. What's true of all the evils in the world is true of plague as well. It helps men to rise above themselves. All the same, when you see the misery it brings, you'd need to be a madman, or a coward, or stone blind, to give in **tamely**④ to the plague."

“我宁愿让志愿者们参与进来。”

“我也想啊。但是，你为什么会那样想呢？”

“我讨厌每天都有人死亡。”

里厄凝视着塔鲁的眼睛。

“所以——怎样呢？”他问。

“我要说的是，我已经为自愿救援小组拟定了一项计划。请授予我实施这个计划的权利，然后，我们就脱离政府单干。因为无论如何政府现在已经忙得焦头烂额，不可开交了。我在各界都有朋友，他们会成为行动的核心力量，当然，我自己也会加入进来。”

“不用我说你也知道，”里厄答道，“我很乐意接受你的提议。再多的志愿者也不嫌多，特别是在当前这种情况下，对于我这样一个人来说。我保证让你的计划得到政府的批准。不管怎样，他们根本没得选择。但是——”里厄若有所思地说，“但是你是知道的，我们现在的工作会有生命危险。我觉得，我还是应该跟你确认一下：你真的完全了解它的危险性了吗？”

塔鲁那双褐色的眼睛平静地与这位医生对视着。

“你是怎样看待潘鲁克神父的训诫的呢，医生先生？”

塔鲁用非常平常的语调问了这样一个问题，里厄也用同样的语调回答：

“医院里大批病人的死亡，这我见得多了，根本没心思去想什么集体惩罚。但是，你也知道，基督教徒有时候说这些话时是不假思考的。其实，他们并不像看上去那样坏。”

“然而，你也跟潘鲁克神父一样，认为鼠疫有好的一面；认为它让人们大开眼界，并迫使他们去思考吗？"

里厄医生略显不耐烦地扬起头说道：

"人类所遭受的疾病都是如此。这次鼠疫和世上其他的灾祸的在本质上都是一样，它帮助人类超越自我，迎难而上。同样的道理，当目睹鼠疫带来的苦难时，只有疯子、懦夫或是瞎子，才会温顺地向它屈服。"

——选自《鼠疫》第2部分

注释

① sidetrack ['saidtræk] *vt.* 使转移目标

② officialdom [ə'fɪʃldəm] *n.* 官场，官僚圈子

③ relish ['relɪʃ] *vt.* 喜爱，爱好

④ tamely ['teimlɪ] *adv.* 驯服地，温顺地

《误会》发表于1943年，该戏剧共分3幕，它暗含了人与隐蔽的上帝赌赛的模式，透露出其承自帕斯卡尔哲学的影响，曲折地传达出作者宗教思想的内在矛盾，是由"荒诞"系列向"反抗"系列过渡的重要中介。收录在上海译文出版李玉民翻译的《加缪全集》(戏剧卷)中。

The Misunderstanding
误会

In this world where nothing can be guaranteed some things are certain (With bitterness). And the love of a mother for her son is one of those certainties.

在这个变幻莫测的世界里，总有一些事情是一成不变的(悲痛地)。一个母亲对她儿子的爱就是其中之一。

——*The Misunderstanding*《误会》

名著导读

The Misunderstanding is a play in occupied Paris. A man who has been living overseas for many years returns home to find that his sister and widowed mother are making a living by taking in lodgers and subsequently murdering them. Since neither his sister nor his mother recognizes him, he becomes a lodger himself without revealing his identity. Ultimately, his mother and sister kill him.

《误会》这部戏剧发生在被占领的巴黎。一个久居国外的男人回家寻找他的妹妹和

守寡的母亲，却发现她们靠欺诈房客为生，之后会谋杀他们。由于他的妹妹和母亲都没有认出他，于是他隐藏自己的身份作为一名房客住了进来。最终，他被自己的母亲和妹妹杀害。

名段选读

Mother: *(in the same voice)* It's no good, Martha. I've lived too long, longer than my son. I didn't know who he was and so I killed him. The only thing left to do is join him, at the bottom of river, where the weeds are **winding** round his face.

Martha: Mother! You can't leave me on my own!

Mother: You've been a great help to me, Martha. I'll be sorry to leave you. If it still means anything to say this, I should like to put it on record that in your own way you've been a good daughter. I couldn't have asked for more. But I'm worn out. I'm much too old to take more **sorrow**. I was his mother. And when a mother fails to know her son, her function in this life has come to an end.

Martha: No, it has not! She still has a part to play in her daughter's happiness. What are you saying? I can't understand this! You of all people, who taught me not to care for anything.

Mother: *(in the same voice, devoid of all personality)* Yes, I did. But I've just learnt that I was wrong, and that in this world where nothing can be **guaranteed** some things are certain *(With bitterness)*. And the love of a mother for her son is one of those certainties.

Martha: And is there no other? What of a mother's love for her daughter?

母亲：（*用同样的声音*）这样不好，玛莎。我已经活得够久了，比我的儿子活得还要久。我刚开始并不知道他是谁，所以错杀了他。我唯一能做的事情就是去河底陪他，那儿的水草正缠绕着他的脸。

玛莎：母亲！你不能丢下我一个人！

母亲：玛莎，一直以来你帮了我太多忙，丢下你我也很难过。我不知道现在说这话还有没有意义，但我真的想告诉你，你一直都是我一个独一无二的好女儿。我已经很满足了，但是，我真的累了。我年事已高，无法再承受更多的悲痛了。我是他的母亲，当一个母亲连自己的儿子都认不出来的时候，她就已经没有资格再做母亲了。

玛莎：不，还有资格！她仍然能让她的女儿幸福。你在说什么呀？我不懂！是你教过我不要去在意任何事情的。

母亲：（*同样的声音，但已全无感情*）是的，我是这样教过你。但是我发现我错了，在这个变幻莫测的世界里，总有一些事情是一成不变的（*悲痛地*）。一个母亲对她儿子的爱就是其中之一。

玛莎：就没有其他的了吗？那母亲对女儿的爱呢？

——选自《误会》第3幕第1场

注释

① wind [waind] *vi.* 缠绕

② sorrow ['sɔrəu] *n.* 悲伤，不幸

③ guarantee [ˌgærən'tiː] *vt.* 担保

Chapter 4

中东欧国家名家名著榜

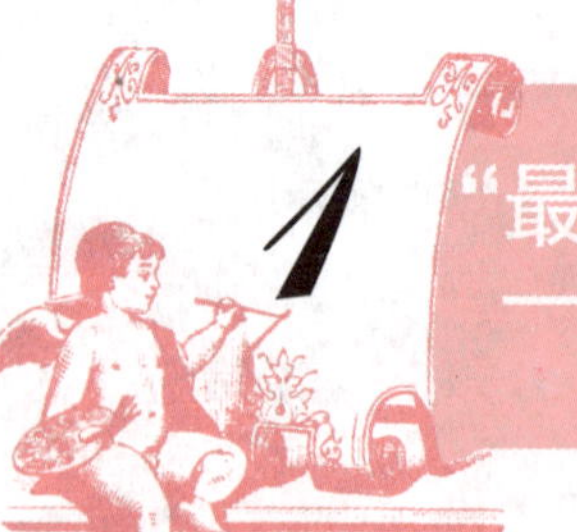

1 “最清醒的现实主义”的“天才艺术家”——列夫·尼古拉耶维奇·托尔斯泰

Leo Tolstoy, or Count Lyev Nikolayevich Tolstoy (September 9, 1828—November 20, 1910), was a Russian writer whom many consider to be the world's greatest novelist. Tolstoy's further talents as essayist, dramatist, and educational reformer made him the most influential member of the aristocratic Tolstoy family. His literary masterpieces *War and Peace and Anna Karenina* represent, in their scope, breadth and vivid depiction of 19th-century Russian life and attitudes, the peak of realist fiction.

列夫·托尔斯泰，或列夫·尼古拉耶维奇·托尔斯泰伯爵（1828年9月9日—1910年11月20日）是俄国作家，他被很多人视为世界上最伟大的小说家。同时，托尔斯泰作为散文家、戏剧家和教育改革家所表现出的天分使他成为名门托尔斯泰家族中最具影响力的成员。他的文学巨著《战争与和平》、《安娜·卡列尼娜》从不同角度生动地描写了19世纪俄国的生活现状和生活态度，达到了现实主义作品的顶峰。

《战争与和平》*写于1863年至1868年间，出版于1869年，是俄罗斯文学乃至世界文学史上公认的最光彩夺目的杰作之一。小说最突出的艺术成就是那气势磅礴、宏大复杂的结构与严整有序的布局。目前国内较著名的译本是草婴的版本和周煜山的版本。

War and Peace
战争与和平

A man in motion always devises an aim for that motion.

人一旦开始行动就会为这个行动确定一个目标。

——*War and Peace*《战争与和平》

名著导读

The novel tells the story of five aristocratic families—the Bezukhovs, the Bolkonskys, the Rostovs, the Kuragins and the Drubetskoys—and the **entanglements**[①] of their personal lives with the history of 1805—1813, principally Napoleon's invasion of Russia in 1812. Pierre and Natasha are married in 1813 and eventually have four children. Natasha grows into a solid, **frumpy**[②] Russian matron. Nicholas weds Mary, resolving his family's financial problems. He also rebuilds Mary's family's estate, which had been damaged in the war. Despite some tensions, Nicholas and Mary enjoy a happy family life.

小说的故事发生在1805年至1813年间，以1812年拿破仑入侵俄罗斯的历史为背景，讲述的是五大贵族家庭——别竺豪夫、包尔康斯基、罗斯托夫、库拉金和德鲁别茨科伊家族错综复杂的人生。1813年，皮埃尔和娜塔莎结婚，他们育有4个子女。婚后娜塔莎变成一个呆板、乏味的家庭主妇。尼古拉斯与玛丽结婚，从而解决了家族的财政危机，他还重置了玛丽家族在战争中衰退的家业。虽然偶尔会有矛盾，但尼古拉斯和玛丽还是幸福地生活在一起。

名段选读

A man in motion always devises an aim for that motion. To be able to go a thousand miles he must imagine that something good awaits him at the end of those thousand miles. One must have the prospect of a promised land to have the strength to move.

The promised land for the French during their advance had been Moscow, during their retreat it was their native land. But that native land was too far off, and for a man going a thousand miles it is absolutely necessary to set aside his final goal and to say to himself: "Today I shall get to a place twenty-five miles off where I shall rest and spend the night," and during the first day's journey that resting place **eclipses**[③] his ultimate goal and attracts all his hopes and desires. And the impulses felt by a single person are always **magnified**[④] in a crowd.

For the French retreating along the old Smolensk road, the final goal—their native land—was too remote, and their immediate goal was Smolensk, toward which all their desires and hopes, enormously intensified in the mass, urged them on. It was not that they knew that much food and fresh troops awaited them in Smolensk, nor that they were told so (on the contrary their superior officers, and Napoleon himself, knew that provisions were scarce there), but because this alone could give them strength to move on and endure their present privations. So both those who knew and those who did not know deceived themselves, and pushed on to Smolensk as to a promised land.

Coming out onto the highroad the French fled with surprising energy and **unheard-of**[5] rapidity toward the goal they had fixed on. Besides the common impulse which bound the whole crowd of French into one mass and supplied them with a certain energy, there was another cause binding them together—their great numbers. As with the physical law of gravity, their **enormous**[6] mass drew the individual human atoms to itself. In their hundreds of thousands they moved like a whole nation.

人一旦开始行动就会为这个行动确定一个目标。如果他能远行千里，那么他一定是幻想着有什么美好的东西在千里之外等着他。人必须展望到一方乐土，才会有动力为之奋进。

对于法国人来说，他们主动出军时的乐土就是莫斯科，然而败北撤退时的乐土就是自己的祖国。然而故乡这块土地太遥远了，对于踏上千里之征的人来说，暂时放下最终的目标，然后告诉自己："今天我走二十五里路后得找个地方歇一下，住一晚，"是很有必要的。然而经历了一天的旅程后，最终的目标相对那个能歇脚的地方而言，也就没那么重要了，能歇脚的地方反倒成了他所有的期待和欲望。个人的一时欲望总会在人群中膨胀起来。

对于沿着古老的斯摩棱斯克大路撤退的法国军队来说，他们的最终目的地——法国——太遥远了，于是他们眼前的目的地就成了斯摩棱斯克，在向斯摩棱斯克进发的路上，他们所有的期待和欲望都变得异常强烈起来，鞭策着他们不断前进。他们之所以奋勇向前并不是因为他们知道在斯摩棱斯克有丰盛的食物和新增的救援队伍，也没有谁跟他们这样说过(相反，他们的最高长官——拿破仑也知道斯摩棱斯克的供给不足)，而是因为只有怀着这样的希望，他们才会有前进的动力，才能熬过目前的困境。所以不管是知道的还是不知道的，都宁可欺骗自己，把斯摩棱斯克当作一方乐土，朝它奋力前行。

一踏上大路，法国军队就以惊人的活力和空前的速度向他们的目的地进发。除了共同的期待和欲望让整个法国军队凝聚在一起，赋予他们动力之外，还有另外一个起到同样作用的因素——他们庞大的数量。正如同地心引力的物理定律一样，这个偌大的军队把单个的人聚在一起。在聚集了成千上万人的军队中，他们好像是整个民族在前进。

——选自《战争与和平》第3册第19章

注释

★"更加直接和更加准确地了解俄罗斯人民的性格和气质以及整个俄国生活。"

——俄国批判现实主义作家　屠格涅夫

① entanglement[ɪn'tæŋglmənt] *n.* 纠缠，牵连

② frumpy ['frʌmpɪ] *adj.* 心底不良的，不见世面的

③ eclipse [ɪ'kɪps] *vt.* 遮蔽

④ magnify ['mægnɪfai] *vt.* 放大，夸大

⑤ unheard-of [ʌn'hɜ:d ɔv] *adj*. 前所未闻的

⑥ enormous [ɪ'nɔ:məs] *adj*. 巨大的

《安娜·卡列尼娜》创作于1873年，首版发行于1877年，是列夫·托尔斯泰的代表作品。本书描绘了俄国从莫斯科到外省乡村广阔而丰富多彩的图景，先后描写了150多个人物，是一部社会百科全书式的作品。目前国内较著名的译本是草婴的版本和周扬的版本。

Anna Karenina
安娜·卡列尼娜

Happy families are all alike; every unhappy family is unhappy in its own way.

幸福的家庭总是相似的；不幸的家庭却各有各的不幸。

——*Anna Karenina*《安娜·卡列尼娜》

名著导读

Dolly Oblonskaya has caught her husband, Stiva, having an affair with their children's former governess, and threatens to leave him. Stiva's sister, Anna Karenina, wife of the St. Petersburg government official Karenin, arrives at the Oblonskys' to mediate. Meanwhile, Dolly's younger sister, Kitty, is courted by two suitors: Konstantin Levin and Alexei Vronsky. Kitty turns down Levin in favor of Vronsky, but not long after, Vronsky meets Anna Karenina and falls in love with her instead of Kitty. Later, Levin meets Kitty at a dinner party at the Oblonsky household, and the two feel their mutual love. They become engaged and marry. Finally, at the station, despairing and dazed by the crowds, Anna throws herself under a train and dies.

多丽·奥布朗斯基发现丈夫斯基华与家庭女教师有染，威胁要离开他。斯基华的妹妹安娜·卡列尼娜是彼得斯堡官员卡列宁的妻子。她来到莫斯科为哥嫂调解。与此同时，多丽的妹妹凯蒂受到两位男士的求婚：康斯坦丁·列文和阿列克谢·渥伦斯基。而倾心于渥伦斯基的凯蒂拒绝了列文的求婚。但是不久之后，渥伦斯基遇到安娜·卡列尼娜，并且爱上了她。后来，列文在奥布朗斯基家的晚宴上碰到了凯蒂，两人互生爱慕。随后他们便订婚、结婚。故事的结尾，安娜因为这段为世人所不容的婚外情倍感绝望和茫然，最后卧轨自杀。

名段选读

Happy families are all alike; every unhappy family is unhappy in its own way.

Everything was in confusion in the Oblonskys' house. The wife had discovered that the husband was carrying on an intrigue with a French girl, who had been a governess in their family, and she had announced to her husband that she could not go on living in the same house with him.

This position of affairs had now lasted three days, and not only the husband and wife themselves, but all the members of their family and household, were painfully conscious of it. Every person in the house felt that there was no sense in their living together, and that the **stray**[①] people brought together by chance in any inn had more in common with one another than they, the members of the family and household of the Oblonskys. The wife did not leave her own room, the husband had not been at home for three days. The children ran wild all over the house; the English governess quarrelled with the housekeeper, and wrote to a friend asking her to look out for a new situation for her; the man cook had walked off the day before just at dinner-time; the kitchen-maid, and the coachman had given warning.

Three days after the quarrel, Prince Stepan Arkadyevitch Oblonsky—Stiva, as he was called in the fashionable world—woke up at his usual hour, that is, at eight o'clock in the morning, not in his wife's bedroom, but on the leather-covered sofa in his study. He turned over his stout, well-cared-for person on the **springy**[②] sofa, as though he would sink into a long sleep again; he **vigorously**[③] embraced the pillow on the other side and buried his face in it; but all at once he jumped up, sat up on the sofa, and opened his eyes.

幸福的家庭总是相似的；不幸的家庭却各有各的不幸。

奥布朗斯基家里一片混乱。妻子发现丈夫与一个法国女人有染，而且这个女人以前还是自己家的家庭教师，于是她宣布无法再跟丈夫一起生活了。

丈夫已经在外面鬼混了三天，不仅他们夫妻两人，家里的其他成员都得知了这件事情，并为此感到痛苦万分。所有人都认为他们生活在一起已经没有意义了，哪怕旅馆里偶然相遇的陌生人之间的默契都要比他们夫妻俩、他们的家庭，以及多奥布朗斯基家族之间的默契多。整整三天，妻子一直把自己关在房间里，丈夫也没有回家。孩子们在房子里到处乱窜，英国家庭女教师跟管家吵了起来，还写信让朋友帮她找份新的工作；厨子在前一天晚饭之前就辞职不干了；厨娘和马车夫也已经说过要辞职。

吵架后的第三天，斯捷潘·阿尔卡迪奇·奥布朗斯基伯爵——上流社会人士都叫他斯基华，像平常那样，在早上八点醒来。他没有睡在妻子的卧室，而是睡在了自己书房的皮沙发上。他那膀大腰圆、呵护备至的身躯在软绵绵的沙发上翻了个身，好像马上又要熟睡过去似的；他紧紧地抱住沙发另一头的枕头，把脸埋在下面；但又突然一跃而起坐在沙发上，睁开了眼睛。

——选自《安娜·卡列尼娜》第1册第1章

注释

① stray [strei] *adj.* 流浪的

② springy ['sprɪŋgɪ] *adj.* 有弹性的

③ vigorously ['vɪgərəslɪ] *adv.* 有力地

《复活》*出版于1899年，是托尔斯泰晚年的代表作。托尔斯泰通过男女主人公的遭遇以最清醒的现实主义态度对当时的全套国家机器进行了激烈的抨击。目前国内较著名的译本是草婴的版本和汝龙的版本。

Resurrection
复活

In Nekhludoff, as in every man, there were two beings: one the spiritual, seeking only that kind of happiness for him self which should tend towards the happiness of all; the other, the animal man, seeking only his own happiness, and ready to sacrifice to it the happiness of the rest of the world.

聂赫留朵夫像其他人一样，有着双重人格：一种是精神上的，追求自己幸福的同时也带给他人幸福；另一种是生理上的，只寻求自己的幸福，为了自己的幸福不惜牺牲其他所有人的幸福。

——*Resurrection*《复活》

名著导读

The story is about a nobleman named Dmitri Ivanovich Nekhlyudov, who seeks redemption for a sin committed years earlier. His brief affair with a maid, Katusha, resulted in her being fired and ending up in **prostitution**① . Framed for murder, Katusha is convicted by mistake and sent to Siberia. Realizing that he was the one who pushed Katusha onto the wrong path and feeling guilty, Nekhlyudov attempts to correct the mistake, but there is not much he can do. He decides to follow Katusha to Siberia and to marry her. When he meets with her and tells her that, she, of course, does not believe him. However, her defenses slowly go down as she sees that Nekhlyudov's change of heart is full and sincere.

小说讲述的是德米特里·伊万诺维奇·聂赫留朵夫公爵为自己年轻时所犯的罪行赎罪的故事。他与女仆卡秋莎短暂相恋后抛弃了她，从而导致卡秋莎被解雇，沦落为妓女。卡秋莎遭人陷害卷入谋杀案，然后被误判有罪，送去西伯利亚服刑。聂赫留朵夫意识到让卡秋莎误入歧途的人正是自己，感到很内疚，他尽力想帮她洗脱冤屈，但是事情已成定局，无法改变了。于是为了赎罪，他一路上跟着卡秋莎来到西伯利亚，并决定跟她结婚。当他见到卡秋莎并告诉她这一切的时候，她并不相信他。然而，当看到聂赫留朵夫确实是诚心悔过时，她慢慢地打开了心扉。

名段选读

As soon as he had seen Katusha Nekhludoff's old feelings toward her awoke again. Now, just as then, he could not see her white **apron**[②] without getting excited; he could not listen to her steps, her voice, her laugh, without a feeling of joy; he could not look at her eyes, black as sloes, without a feeling of tenderness, especially when she smiled; and, above all, he could not notice without agitation how she blushed when they met. He felt he was in love, but not as before, when this love was a kind of mystery to him and he would not own, even to himself, that he loved, and when he was persuaded that one could love only once; now he knew he was in love and was glad of it, and knew **dimly**[③] what this love consisted of and what it might lead to, though he sought to conceal it even from himself. In Nekhludoff, as in every man, there were two beings: one the spiritual, seeking only that kind of happiness for himself which should tend towards the happiness of all; the other, the animal man, seeking only his own happiness, and ready to sacrifice to it the happiness of the rest of the world. At this period of his **mania**[④] of self-love brought on by life in Petersburg and in the army, this animal man ruled supreme and completely crushed the spiritual man in him.

But when he saw Katusha and experienced the same feelings as he had had three years before, the spiritual man in him raised its head once more and began to assert its rights. And up to Easter, during two whole days, an unconscious, ceaseless inner struggle went on in him.

一见到卡秋莎，聂赫留朵夫尘封的记忆又在眼前浮现。现在还像以前一样，他看见她白色的围裙就忍不住兴奋；听见她的脚步声、说话声、笑声就会一阵欢喜；看见她那双像黑刺李似的乌黑的眼睛就觉得特别温柔，特别是她笑的时候；尤其是当他们见面的时候，她羞涩地红着脸，他就激动万分。他觉得自己恋爱了，但是这感觉跟以往不同，充满了神秘感，即使是对自己他也不愿承认是坠入爱河了，因为他认为人一生只能爱一次；现在他明白他恋爱了，尽管他极力掩饰，但还是很高兴，他隐约知道这次恋爱是怎么一回事，恋爱的结果是什么。聂赫留朵夫像其他人一样，有着双重人格：一种是精神上，追求的是自己幸福的同时也带给他人幸福；另一种是生理上，只寻求自己的幸福，为了自己的幸福不惜牺牲其他所有人的幸福。那段时期里，在圣彼得堡和军队的生活唤起了他自私自利的兽性，他的生理人格完全战胜了精神人格。

但是当他再次见到卡秋莎，再度回忆起了三年前对她的热恋，他的精神人格再次挺身而出，开始维护自己的主张。快要到复活节的这两天里，虽然他没有意识到，但内心却进行着不断的挣扎和斗争。

——选自《复活》第1册第14章

注释

★ “托尔斯泰在情节安排上一向尊重情理，从不生造偶然巧合或误会冲突，但又注意曲折细腻，引人入胜。这种创作特色在《复活》中可说达到了高峰。”

——中国著名文学翻译家　草婴

① prostitution [ˌprɔstɪ'tju:ʃən] *n.* 卖淫，作践自己

② apron ['eiprən] *n.* 围裙

③ dimly ['dɪmlɪ] *adv.* 朦胧地，模糊地

④ mania ['meiniə] *n.* 狂热

2 十九世纪末俄国伟大的批判现实主义作家——安东·巴甫洛维奇·契诃夫

Anton Pavlovich Chekhov (January 29, 1860—July 15, 1904) was a Russian short-story writer, playwright and physician, considered to be one of the greatest short-story writers in the history of world literature. His career as a dramatist produced four classics and his best short stories are held in high esteem by writers and critics. Among his masterpieces are *Three Sisters*, *The Cherry Orchard*, *Uncle Vanya*, and *The Man in a Case*.

安东·巴甫洛维奇·契诃夫（1860年1月29日—1904年7月15日），俄罗斯短篇小说家、剧作家、内科医生，他被认为是有史以来文学界最伟大的短篇小说家之一。作为一名剧作家，他创造了四部经典戏剧，而他创作的一系列最佳短篇小说也深得作家和评论家推崇，其中包括《三姊妹》、《樱桃园》、《万尼亚舅舅》和《装在套子里的人》。

《樱桃园》*是契诃夫晚年的一部力作，创作于1903年。这部4幕剧揭示了贵族阶层不可避免的没落及其被新兴资产阶级所代替的历史过程，同时，也表现了人们毅然同过去告别和向往幸福未来的乐观情绪。目前国内较著名的译本是童道明的版本。

The Cherry Orchard
樱桃园

I'm rich now, with lots of money, but just think about it and examine me, and you'll find I'm still a peasant down to the marrow of my bones.

现在，我有钱了，而且有很多钱，但是，只要你好好想想，再仔细地打量一下我，你就会发现，我骨子里仍是个农民。

——*The Cherry Orchard*《樱桃园》

名著导读

The play concerns an aristocratic Russian woman and her family as they return to the family's estate (which includes a large and well-known cherry orchard) just before it is auctioned to pay the mortgage. While presented with options to save the estate, the family essentially does nothing and the play ends with the estate being sold to the son of a former serf, and the family leaving to the sound of the cherry orchard being cut down.

这部戏剧讲述的是一个俄罗斯贵族女人和她家人的故事。他们在房产(包括一座有名的大樱桃园)被抵押拍卖前回到家。在面对挽救樱桃园的选择时，这家人实际上什么都没有做，在戏剧的最后，樱桃园被卖给他们曾经一个农奴的儿子，而这家人在樱桃林被砍倒的声音中离开。

名段选读

Lopakhin: (Listens) No…They've got to collect their luggage and so on…(Pause) Lubov Andreyevna has been living abroad for five years; I don't know what she'll be like now…She's a good sort—an easy, simple person. I remember when I was a boy of fifteen, my father, who is dead—he used to keep a shop in the village here—hit me on the face with his **fist**①, and my nose bled…We had gone into the yard together for something or other, and he was a little drunk. Lubov Andreyevna, as I remember her now, was still young, and very thin, and she took me to the **washstand**② here in this very room, the **nursery**③. She said, "Don't cry, little man, it'll be all right in time for your wedding" *(Pause)* "Little man"…My father was a peasant, it's true, but here I am in a white waistcoat and yellow shoes…a pearl out of an **oyster**④. I'm rich now, with lots of money, but just think about it and examine me, and you'll find I'm still a peasant down to the marrow of my bones. *(Turns over the pages of his book)* Here I've been reading this book, but I understood nothing. I read and fell asleep. *(Pause)*

Dunyasha: The dogs didn't sleep all night; they know that they're coming.

Lopakhin: What's up with you, Dunyasha…?

Dunyasha: My hands are **shaking**⑤. I shall faint.

Lopakhin: You're too sensitive, Dunyasha. You dress just like a lady, and you do your hair like one too. You oughtn't. You should know your place.

罗伯兴：*(听着)*不……他们得去拿行李等东西……*(停顿)*柳苞芙·安德列耶芙娜在国外生活了五年，我不知道她现在长成什么样了……她是个好人——一个随和且很单纯的人。我记得在我十五岁时，先父在这个村子里开着一家小店铺，有次他朝我脸上打了一拳，我鼻子流血了……忘了为什么，我们一起走进了院子里，他有点醉了。那时，柳苞芙·安德列耶芙娜就跟我现在所记得的一样：年轻，并且非常瘦弱。她把我带到盥洗台那里，就是在这个房间，这个保育室里。她说："不要哭，小鬼，到你结婚时就没事啦……"*(停顿)*"小鬼"……我父亲是个乡下人，真的，但我现在穿着白色马甲，黄色鞋子……我整个人就像刚出壳的珍珠般光彩夺目。现在，我有钱了，而且有很多钱，但是，只要你好好想想，再仔细地打量一下我，你就会发现，我骨子里仍是个农民。*(他翻了翻他的书)*我一直在看这本书，但我什么也看不懂。我会看着看着就睡着了。*(停顿)*

杜尼雅莎：狗一整夜都没有睡，它们知道他们要来了。

罗伯兴：你怎么啦，杜尼雅莎……?

杜尼雅莎：我的手在发抖，我快要晕倒了。

罗伯兴：你太敏感了，杜尼雅莎。你穿得像一位淑女，而且你的样式也像。你不应该这样，你应该知道自己的地位。

——选自《樱桃园》第1幕

注释

★ "《樱桃园》的戏剧结构削弱了戏剧冲突和戏剧悬念，这种戏剧结构无法靠戏剧性来取胜，这同契诃夫追求戏剧生活化的美学思想是一致的。"

——广州大学人文学院中文系教授冉东平《淡化戏剧冲突显现生活真实》

① fist [fɪst] *n.* 拳头

② washstand [ˈwɔʃstænd] *n.* 盥洗架

③ nursery [ˈnɜːsəri] *n.* 保育室

④ oyster [ˈɔɪste(r)] *n.* 牡蛎

⑤ shake [ʃeɪk] *vi.* 摇动

《装在套子里的人》出版于1898年，是契诃夫最杰出的短篇小说之一。故事的主人公别里科夫反对一切新生事物，扼杀自由与进步。他是沙皇专制制度的维护者，他的死象征着一切反动势力必然灭亡。目前国内较著名的译本是汝龙的版本和李靖民的版本。

The Man in a Case
装在套子里的人

The merest hint, the faintest hope of its possibility gives wings to the soul.

就算自由给我们最微不足道的线索、最微弱的希望，也能让灵魂插上翅膀。

——*The Man in a Case*《装在套子里的人》

名著导读

Byelikov, the Greek teacher at a provincial school, was extraordinarily orderly both in his personal and professional lives. A strict disciplinarian, he never made exceptions to the rules. Byelikov became **enamored**① of Varinka, the sister of a new teacher at the school. Byelikov saw Varinka and her brother bicycling in the park. Outraged, Byelikov went to the brother to complain about this scandalous② behavior, but was pushed down the steps. Byelikov then became depressed, took to his bed, and died.

别里科夫是一所省立学校的希腊语老师，不管是在自己的私人生活上还是在事业上，他都非常循规蹈矩。他是一个严格遵守规矩的人，从不破例。别里科夫爱上了瓦莲卡——学校一位新教师的妹妹。他看到瓦莲卡和她的哥哥在公园里骑自行车，愤怒的别里科夫走向她的哥哥，指责他们的丢脸行为，但他被推下了楼梯。此后，别里科夫变得消沉，卧床不起，最后一命呜呼了。

名段选读

"A month later Byelikov died. We all went to his funeral—that is, both the high-schools and the **seminary**③. Now when he was lying in his **coffin**④ his expression was mild, agreeable, even cheerful, as though he were glad that he had at last been put into a case which he would never leave again. Yes, he had attained his ideal! And, as though in his honour, it was dull, rainy weather on the day of his funeral, and we all wore **goloshes**⑤ and took our umbrellas. Varinka, too, was at the funeral, and when the coffin was lowered into the grave she burst into tears. I have noticed that Little Russian women are always laughing or crying—no **intermediate**⑥ mood."

"One must confess that to bury people like Byelikov is a great pleasure. As we were returning from the **cemetery**⑦ we wore **discreet**⑧ Lenten faces; no one wanted to display this feeling of pleasure—a feeling like that we had experienced long, long ago as children when our elders had gone out and we ran about the garden for an hour or two, enjoying complete freedom. Ah, freedom, freedom! The merest hint, the faintest hope of its possibility gives wings to the soul, does it not?"

"We returned from the cemetery in a good humour. But not more than a week had passed before life went on as in the past, as gloomy, oppressive, and senseless—a life not forbidden by government prohibition, but not fully permitted, either: it was no better. And, indeed, though we had buried Byelikov, how many such men in cases were left, how many more of them there will be!"

"That's just how it is," said Ivan Ivanovitch and he lighted his pipe.

"How many more of them there will be!" repeated Burkin.

"一个月后别里科夫死了。我们都参加了他的葬礼——也就是说，高中和神学院的人都去了。现在，他躺在棺材里：表情温和，和蔼可亲，甚至有些愉悦，他似乎很高兴自己终于被装在了一个套子里，再也不会离开了。是的，他实现了自己的理想！而且，好像是为了向他表示敬意，葬礼那天，连天都是阴沉的，还下着雨，我们都穿着橡胶套鞋、带着雨伞。瓦莲卡也参加了葬礼，当棺材放进坟墓里时，她哭了。我注意到，那个俄罗斯小女人一直不是在笑就是在哭——基本没有其他的情绪。"

"我们必须承认埋葬像别里科夫这样的人是一件很荣幸的事情。从墓地里回来的时候，我们脸上的表情谨慎而简单；没有人愿意流露出喜悦的情绪——这种感觉就像很久以前，当我们还是小孩子的时候，大人都出门了，而我们在花园里跑来跑去，足足玩了一两个小时，尽情地享受自由。啊，自由，自由！就算自由给我们最微不足道的线索、最微弱的希望，也让灵魂插上翅膀，不是吗？"

"我们心情愉快地从墓地回来。但还不到一个星期，我们的生活就恢复原样了，沉闷、压抑、毫无生气——这样的生活不受政府禁令的限制，但也没有完全的自由：这种生活也好不到哪里去。而且，尽管我们埋葬了别里科夫，但还有多少这种装在套子里的人呢，将来还会有多少这样的套中人呢！"

"生活本来就是这样。"伊凡·伊凡内奇说道，接着，他点了一支烟。

"将来还会有多少这样的套中人呢！"布尔金重复道。

——选自《装在套子里的人》

注释

① enamored [ɪ'næməd] *adj.* 倾心的，被迷住的

② scandalous ['skændələs] *adj.* 可耻的

③ seminary ['semɪnəri] *n.* 神学院

④ coffin ['kɔfɪn] *n.* 灵柩

⑤ golosh [ɡə'lɔʃ] *n.* 橡胶套鞋

⑥ intermediate ['ɪntə'miːdiət] *adj.* 中间的

⑦ cemetery ['semətri] *n.* 墓地

⑧ discreet [dɪ'skriːt] *adj.* 小心的，谨慎的

《万尼亚舅舅》是俄国剧作家契诃夫的名剧，创作于1896年，1897年出版。它是一部四幕剧。本剧叙述的是一个没有崇高理想和生活目标的知识分子的悲剧命运，他遭遇到精神危机并开始重新思考自己的生活道路，充满了富有戏剧性意味的心理内容和人生哲理。目前国内较著名的译本是丽尼版本。

Uncle Vanya
万尼亚舅舅

It may be that posterity, which will despise us for our blind and stupid lives, will find some road to happiness; but we—you and I—have but one hope, the hope that we may be visited by visions, perhaps by pleasant ones, as we lie resting in our graves.

那些鄙视我们盲目而愚蠢地生活的后人，可能会找到通向幸福的道路，但是我们——你和我——只有一个希望，就是希望当我们躺在坟墓安息时还能做梦，也许还是美梦。

——Uncle Vanya《万尼亚舅舅》

名著导读

For many years Uncle Vanya—who once worshipped the professor Serebryakov—has sent the farm's proceeds to the professor, while reserving only a beggar's salary for himself, only to find him a **charlatan**[①] . He shoots him in rage. Fortunately, Serebryakov manage to escape. After a long absence with his beautiful young wife, Serebryakov returns. Finally, Serebryakov and Uncle Vanya have reconciled.

万尼亚舅舅曾一度崇拜谢列布利雅可夫教授，并把庄园多年来的收入都交给了他，而自己只留一小部分可怜的薪水，结果却发现他是个骗子。一怒之下，万尼亚舅舅对他开了枪，所幸谢列布利雅可夫逃脱了。很久之后，谢列布利雅可夫又带着他那年轻貌美的妻子回来了。最后，谢列布利雅可夫和万尼亚舅舅和解了。

名段选读

Voitski: You must tell me something! Oh, my God! I am forty-seven years old. I may live to sixty; I still have thirteen years before me; an eternity! How shall I be able to endure life for thirteen years? What shall I do? How can I fill them? Oh, don't you see? *(He presses Astroff's hand* ***convulsively***[②] *)* Don't you see, if only I could live the rest of my life in some new way! If I could only wake some still, bright morning and feel that life had begun again; that the past was forgotten and had **vanished**[③] like smoke. *(He weeps)* Oh, to begin life anew! Tell me, tell me how to begin.

Astroff: *(Crossly)* What nonsense! What sort of a new life can you and I look forward to? We can have no hope.

Voitski: None?

Astroff: None. Of that I am convinced.

Voitski: Tell me what to do. *(He puts his hand to his heart)* I feel such a burning pain here.

Astroff: *(Shouts angrily)* Stop! *(Then, more gently)* It may be that posterity, which will despise us for our blind and stupid lives, will find some road to happiness; but we—you and I—have but one hope, the hope that we may be visited by visions, perhaps by pleasant ones, as we lie resting in our graves. *(Sighing)* Yes, brother, there were only two respectable, intelligent men in this county, you and I. Ten years or so of this life of ours, this miserable life, have **sucked**[④] us under, and we have become as contemptible and petty as the rest. But don't try to talk me out of my purpose! Give me what you took from me, will you?

Voitski: I took nothing from you.

Astroff: You took a little bottle of **morphine**[⑤] out of my medicine case. *(A pause)* Listen! If you are positively determined to make an end to yourself, go into the woods and shoot yourself there. Give up the morphine, or there will be a lot of talk and guesswork; people will think I gave it to you. I don't fancy having to perform a post-mortem on you. Do you think I should find it interesting?

伏依尼茨基：你必须得告诉我点什么！哦，天呐！我现在四十七岁了，我可能会活到六十岁，也就是说我还要活十三年，多么漫长的时间啊！我该如何熬过这十三年呢？我该怎么办？我要怎样才能度过这十三年啊？哦，难道你没看到吗？*(痉挛地按着阿斯特罗夫的手)*你难道没看到，要是我能用新的方式度过余生就好了！要是我能在某个静寂、明亮的早晨醒来，感觉生活又重新开始了，而那些往事已经被忘在了九霄云外，那该多好。*(流泪)*哦，重新开始生活！告诉我，告诉我要怎样开始。

阿斯特罗夫：*(生气地)*胡言八道！你和我能够指望什么样的新生活呢？我们没有希望了。

伏依尼茨基：一点也没有？

阿斯特罗夫：一点也没有，我很确定。

伏依尼茨基：告诉我该怎么做。*(把手放在心上)*我感到这里灼痛得厉害。

阿斯特罗夫：*(愤怒地大喊)*住嘴！*(稍微温和地)*那些鄙视我们盲目而愚蠢地生活的后人，他们可能会找到通向幸福的道路，但是我们——你和我——只有一个希望，就是希望当我们躺在坟墓安息时还能做梦，也许还是美梦。*(叹息)*是的，兄弟，这个村子里只有两个值得尊敬的智者，那就是你和我。这十多年来，我们的生活，这种悲惨的生活已经吞噬了我们，我们和其他人一样卑鄙可耻。但不要试着转移话题！把你从我这里拿走的东西还给我，好吗？

伏依尼茨基：我没有从你这里拿走任何东西啊。

阿斯特罗夫：你从我的药箱里拿走了一小瓶吗啡。*（停顿）*听着！如果你确实下决心要结束自己的生命，那么就到树林里去开枪自杀吧。不要用吗啡，否则，将会有很多闲言闲语和揣测；人们会认为是我给你的。我可不喜欢不得不去给你验尸的情景，你认为我会觉得那很有趣吗？

——选自《万尼亚舅舅》第4幕

注释

① charlatan [ˈʃɔːlətən] *n.* 骗子

② convulsively [kənˈvʌlsɪvli] *adv.* 痉挛性地

③ vanish [ˈvænɪʃ] *vi.* 消除

④ suck [sʌk] *vt.* 吞没

⑤ morphine [ˈmɔːfiːn] *n.* 吗啡

3 无产阶级艺术最杰出的代表——玛克西姆·高尔基

Maxim Gorky (March 28, 1868—June 18, 1936), Soviet novelist, playwright and essayist, who was a founder of social realism. Although known principally as a writer, he was closely associated with the tumultuous revolutionary period of his own country. Twenty-Six Men and a Girl (1899), is often regarded as his best short story. Song of the Stormy Petrel is a short revolutionary poem by Gorky. My Childhood (1913–14), In the World (1915–16), and My Universities (1923) are the autobiographical trilogy of Gorky.

玛克西姆·高尔基（1868年3月28日—1936年6月18日），前苏联小说家，剧作家和散文家，是社会现实主义文学的奠基人。虽然他主要是作为一名作家而为世人所知，但他个人是与前苏联纷乱的革命时期紧密联系在一起的。《二十六男和一女》(1899)通常被认为是他最好的短篇小说。《海燕之歌》是高尔基的一篇短篇革命诗。《童年》（1913－14）、《在人间》（1915－16）、《我的大学》（1923）是高尔基自传三部曲。

《童年》共13章，单行本发表于1914年，《童年》是高尔基自传体三部曲中的第一部，主要描写阿廖沙(高尔基的乳名)三岁到十岁这一时期的童年生活。北京燕山出版社秋原译本比较好。

My Childhood
童年

Grown-up people are given responsibilities and they have to answer for them to God; but it is not so with you yet; you live by a child's conscience.

大人们肩负着各种责任，他们必须得向上帝有所交代；但这与你还没有多大关系；你该按照一个孩子的想法去生活。

——*My Childhood*《童年》

名著导读

Coloured by poverty and horrifying **brutality**[①], Gorky's childhood equipped him to understand the life of the ordinary Russian. After his father, a paperhanger and upholsterer, died of cholera, five-year-old Gorky was taken to live with his grandfather, a polecat-faced tyrant who would regularly beat him unconscious, and with his grandmother, a tender mountain of a woman and a wonderful storyteller, who would kneel beside their bed and give God her views on the day's happenings, down to the last fascinating details.

高尔基的童年充满了贫困和令人毛骨悚然的暴力，这让他体会到了普通俄国人的生活。他的父亲是一位裱糊工和室内装潢商，因霍乱去世，之后五岁的高尔基被接去和外祖父母一起生活。他的外祖父是一个残暴专横的人，长着一副臭鼬一样的脸孔，经常把高尔基打到不省人事。他的外祖母是一位相当温柔的女人，特别擅长讲故事，她常常跪在床边对上帝讲述自己对白天所发生的一些事情的看法，连细节都十分精彩。

名段选读

Grandmother dragged me back to the kitchen by the collar. "Why did you do that?" she asked.

"Because she threw a carrot at you."

"That means that you did it for me? Very well! This is what I will do for you I will **horsewhip**[②] you and put you amongst the mice under the oven. A nice sort of protector you are! 'Look at a bubble and it will burst directly.' If I were to tell grandfather he would skin you. Go up to the attic and learn your lesson."

She would not speak to me for the rest of the day, but before she said her prayers that night she sat on the bed and uttered these memorable words in a very impressive tone:

"Now, Lenka, my darling, you must keep yourself from **meddling**[③] with the doings of grown-up persons. Grown-up people are given responsibilities and they have to answer for them to God; but it is not so with you yet; you live by a child's conscience. Wait till God takes possession of your heart, and shows you the work you are to do, and the way you are to take. Do you understand? It is no business of yours to decide who is to blame in any matter. God judges, and punishes; that is for Him, not for us."

She was silent for a moment while she took a pinch of snuff; then, half-closing her right eye, she added:

"Why, God Himself does not always know where the fault lies."

"Doesn't God know everything?" I asked in astonishment.

"If He knew everything, a lot of things that are done would not be done. It is as if He, the Father, looks and looks from Heaven at the earth, and sees how often we weep, how often we sob④, and says: 'My people, my dear people, how sorry I am for you!' "

She was crying herself as she spoke; and drying her wet cheeks, she went into the corner to pray.

From that time her God became still closer and still more comprehensible to me.

外祖母抓着我的衣领把我拖回到厨房里。"你为什么那样做？"她问。

"因为她向你扔胡萝卜。"

"你的意思是说你那样做是为了我？非常好！那我要为你做的事情就是：用马鞭抽你，然后把你塞到炉子下面的老鼠堆里。你可真是个好样的保护者呢！'看着一个肥皂泡，它就会破掉。'如果我把这件事告诉外祖父，他会剥了你的皮。到阁楼去，好好反省。"

那天剩下的时间，她都不愿意跟我说话，但在晚上祈祷前，她坐在床上，用感人的语调说了这些让我铭记终身的话：

"现在，莲卡，我亲爱的孩子，你必须要克制自己，不要去干涉大人们的事情。大人们肩负着各种责任，他们必须得向上帝有所交代；但这与你还没有多大关系；你该按照一个孩子的想法去生活。等等吧，上帝会掌管你的心，告诉你将要做的工作，指引你将要走的路。你明白吗？在任何情况下，你都无权决定谁要受到责备。上帝会做出判断和惩罚；那是他的事，不是我们该管的。"

她剪了一下烛花，沉默了片刻；然后，半闭着右眼，补充道：

"上帝自己也不是总知道错误在哪。"

"上帝不是无所不知的吗？"我惊讶地问。

"如果他真的无所不知，那么很多事情也就不会发生了。这就像当他，圣父，从天堂看向人间时，看见我们那么频繁地哀悼和哭泣，他会说：'我的子民，我亲爱的子民，我真为你们感到难过！'"

她说这些的时候流泪了；然后她擦干湿润的脸颊，走到角落里去祈祷。

从那次起，我觉得她的上帝对我而言更加亲切了，也更容易理解了。

——选自《童年》第7章

注释

① brutality [bruː'tæləti:] *n.* 野蛮，暴虐行为

② horsewhip ['hɔːswɪp] *vt.* 用马鞭抽打

③ meddle ['medl] *vi.* 干涉，管闲事

④ sob [sɔb] *vi.* 啜泣

《母亲》*发表于1907年，分2部，共39章，它以巨大的艺术力量阐述了俄国工人阶级和广大革命群众在革命斗争中不断觉悟、成长的过程，特别是描写了巴维尔逐渐成为有高度觉悟和理论修养的成熟革命者的经历，揭示了马克思主义和工农运动相结合是俄国无产阶级革命的必由之路。人民文学出版社夏衍译本比较好。

Mother
母亲

Poverty, hunger, and sickness—that's what work gives to the poor people.

贫穷、饥饿、疾病——那就是工作给穷人们的回报。

——*Mother*《母亲》

名著导读

It tells the story of a mother who takes after her son to socialism and works for it. She is kind and affectionate to her son and all his comrades. She has seen her son mature into a leader, thoughtful, stern and respected. In disguise, she goes to many places taking leaflets. At her son's arrest and exile she goes to distribute his last speech in the court to the common people but is caught, arrested and dies in her struggle to be a message to the masses.

小说讲的是一位跟随她的儿子从事社会主义运动的母亲。她对儿子和他所有的同志都非常友善和关爱。她见证了儿子成熟地转变成为一位有思想、严格、受敬重的领导人。她乔装打扮去很多地方散发传单。在儿子被捕和流放时，她在法庭上向公众分发他的最后一篇演讲，但她被抓捕并拘留了，她在努力给群众传递消息时牺牲。

名段选读

The mother saw that the papers were being snatched up, were being hidden in breasts and pockets.

This again put her firmly on her feet; more composed than forceful, straining herself to her utmost, and feeling how **agitated**① pride grew in her raising her high above the people, how subdued joy flamed up in her, she spoke, snatching bundles of papers from the valise and throwing them right and left into some person's quick, greedy hands.

"For this they sentenced my son and all with him. Do you know? I will tell you, and you believe the heart of a mother; believe her gray hair. Yesterday they sentenced them because they carried to you, to all the people, the honest, sacred truth. How do you live?"

The crowd grew silent in amazement, and noiselessly increased in size, pressing closer and closer together, surrounding the woman with a ring of living bodies.

"Poverty, hunger, and sickness—that's what work gives to the poor people. This order of things pushes us to theft and to corruption; and over us, **satiated**② and calm, live the rich. In order that we should obey the police, the authorities, the soldiers, all are in their hands, all are against us, everything is against us. We perish all our lives day after day in toil, always in filth, in deceit. And others enjoy themselves and **gormandize**③ themselves with our labor; and they hold us like dogs on chains, in ignorance. We know nothing, and in terror we fear everything. Our life is night, a dark night; it is a terrible dream. They have poisoned us with strong intoxicating poison, and they drink our blood. They glut themselves to **corpulence**④, to **vomiting**⑤ —the servants of the devil of greed. Is it not so?"

母亲看到传单被人们一把夺过去，藏在各自的胸前和口袋里。

这情景再一次坚定了她的脚步；她变得更加沉着冷静，力图发挥自己的极限，她感觉体内一股异常强烈的自豪感油然升起，使自己变得高大起来；她感受到被压抑的喜悦是如何在她心中燃烧，她一边从小提箱里拿出几捆传单，把它们丢向四周一双双敏捷、充满渴望的双手中，一边说着：

"因为这个，他们判决了我的儿子和他的同志们。你们知道吗？我要告诉你们，你们要相信一位母亲的心，相信她花白的头发。昨天他们判决了他们，因为他们向你们——向所有人民——传递了一个可靠、神圣的真相。你们是如何生活的？"

人群在一片惊愕中沉默了，人们在沉默中越聚越多，越靠越近，他们团团围住这位母亲，形成了一个人环。

"贫穷、饥饿、疾病——那就是工作给穷人们的回报。这种秩序迫使我们去偷窃，去堕落；而踩在我们头上的都是些酒足饭饱、生活安逸的富人。在这种秩序下，我们要服从警察、政府当局和军队，所有一切都掌握在他们手中，所有一切都对我们不利，任何事都对我们不利。我们在日复一日的苦力中，在肮脏和欺骗中，毁掉了自己的生活。而其他人靠我们的劳动来吃喝享受；他们像给狗拴上链子一样操控着我们，让我们处在无知之中。我们一无所知，我们惊慌地害怕每件事情。我们的生活就是黑夜，伸手不见五指的黑夜；我们的生活就是一场噩梦。他们用烈性的、醉人的毒药毒害我们，然后再吸干我们的血。他们狼吞虎咽直到肥胖不堪，直至呕吐——他们是贪婪的恶魔的仆人。难道不是这样吗？"

——选自《母亲》第2部第19章

注释

★"《母亲》以对新的革命现实的真实描写，以对时代本质的深刻概括，以具有高度思想性和艺术性的英雄人物形象以及新的创作方法开创了无产阶级文学的新纪元。"

——首届全国优秀外国文学国书奖特别奖获得者　谭得伶

① agitated ['ædʒɪteitɪd] *adj.* 激动的，焦虑不安的
② valise [və'lɪ:z] *n.* 小提箱
③ satiated ['seiʃieɪtɪd] *adj.* 吃饱的，饱足的
④ gormandize ['gɔ:məndaiz] *vt.* 使……拼命吃
⑤ corpulence ['kɔ:pjələns] *n.* 肥胖，发福
⑥ vomiting ['vɔmɪtɪŋ] *n.* 呕吐

《海燕之歌》发表于1901年，是著名的散文诗，它塑造了象征大智大勇革命者搏风击浪的勇敢的海燕形象，预告革命风暴即将到来，鼓舞人们去迎接伟大的战斗，这是一篇无产阶级革命战斗的檄文与颂歌，受到列宁的热情称赞。戈宝权译本比较好。

The Song of the Stormy Petrel
海燕之歌

Let it break in all its fury!
让暴风雨来得更猛烈些吧！

——*The Song of the Stormy Petrel*《海燕之歌》

名著导读

The Song of the Stormy Petrel is a short piece of revolutionary literature written by the Russian writer Maxim Gorky in 1901. Written in a variation of unrhymed trochaic tetrameter with occasional Pyrrhic substitutions, it is considered poetry. The poem calling for revolution is coded—the proud stormy petrel, unafraid of the storm (that is, revolution), as all other animals cower. The poem was later referred to as "the battle anthem of the revolution", and the epithet "the Storm Petrel of the Revolution" soon became attached to Gorky himself. According to Nadezhda Krupskaya, "The Song" became one of Lenin's favorite works by Gorky.

《海燕》是俄国作家玛克西姆·高尔基在1901年写的一篇短小的革命散文。散文是以无韵扬抑格四音步的一种变体的形式创作的，并偶尔使用了抑抑格替代，因此它也被认为是诗歌。这首呼吁革命的诗歌暗含讽喻——骄傲的海燕无畏面对暴风雨（即革命），而其他所有的动物则在暴风雨面前退缩了。后来，这首诗被称作"革命的战歌"，而"革命的海燕"也很快成为人们对高尔基的称呼。据娜德斯达·克鲁普斯卡娅（列宁的终身革命伴侣）称，这首诗歌是列宁最欣赏的高尔基的作品之一。

名段选读

Strikes the thunder. Now the waters fiercely battle with the winds. And the winds in fury seize them in **unbreakable**[①] embrace, **hurtling**[②] down the emerald masses to be shattered on the cliffs.

Like a streak of sable lightning wheels and cries the Stormy Petrel, **piercing**[③] storm-clouds like an arrow, cutting swiftly through the waters.

He is coursing like a Demon, the black Demon of the tempest, ever laughing, ever sobbing—he is laughing at the storm-clouds, he is sobbing with his rapture.

In the crashing of the thunder the wise Demon hears a **murmur**[④] of exhaustion. And he knows the storm will die and the sun will be **triumphant**[⑤]; the sun will always be triumphant!

The waters roar. The thunder crashes. Livid lightning flares in storm-clouds high above the seething ocean, and the flaming darts are captured and extinguished by the waters, while the serpentine reflections writhe, expiring, in the deep.

It's the storm! The storm is breaking!

Still the valiant Stormy Petrel proudly wheels among the lightning, o'er the roaring, raging ocean, and his cry resounds **exultant**[⑥], like a prophecy of triumph.

Let it break in all its fury!

雷声大作。海水与狂风猛烈地激战。狂风愤怒地将海水牢牢围困，然后卷起它们猛烈地冲向悬崖，将这些翡翠撞成粉碎。

海燕像一道黑色的闪电，在空中盘旋着，呼喊着，像一支箭冲入暴风雨里，迅速地劈开海水。

它飞翔着，像一个精灵，暴风雨中的黑色精灵，它时而大笑，时而呜咽——它是在嘲笑那乌云，它是在欢天喜地呜咽着。

在雷声的撞击中，这聪明的精灵听到了一种筋疲力尽的低怨。它知道暴风雨会消失，太阳会获得胜利；太阳总会胜利！

海水在咆哮。雷声在轰鸣。在翻滚的大海上空的乌云里，铁青的闪电闪耀着，这只燃烧的箭——闪电光——被海水捕获了，消灭了，像蛇一样痛苦地扭曲着，消失在大海深处。

这就是暴风雨！暴风雨正在摧毁一切！

仍然是那勇敢的海燕，骄傲地盘旋在闪电之间，越过那咆哮的、怒吼的海水，它欢快的叫声重新回荡在大海上空，像是凯旋的预言。

让暴风雨来得更猛烈些吧！

——选自《海燕之歌》

注释

① unbreakable [ʌn'breikəbl] *adj.* 牢不可破的

② hurtle ['hɜːtl] *vi.* 猛冲，飞驰

③ pierce [pɪəs] *vt.* 刺穿

④ murmur ['mɜːmə(r)] *n.* 低语，喃喃细语

⑤ triumphant [trai'ʌmfənt] *adj.* 胜利的，狂欢的

⑥ exultant [ɪg'zʌltənt] *adj.* 欢跃的

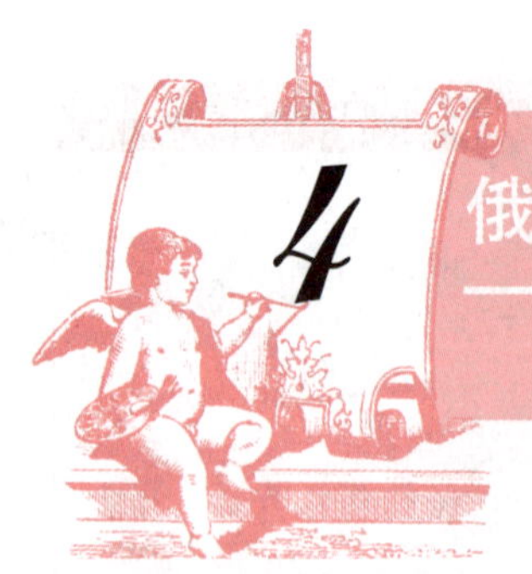

4 俄国著名现实主义艺术大师——伊凡·谢尔盖耶维奇·屠格涅夫

Ivan Sergeyevich Turgenev (November 9, 1818—September 3, 1883) was a Russian novelist, short story writer, and playwright. His first major publication, a short story collection entitled *A Sportsman's Sketches*, is a milestone of Russian Realism, and his novel *Fathers and Sons* is regarded as one of the major works of 19th-century fiction. Turgenev's artistic purity made him a favorite of like-minded novelists of the next generation, such as Henry James and Joseph Conrad, both of whom greatly preferred Turgenev to Tolstoy and Dostoyevsky.

伊凡·谢尔盖耶维奇·屠格涅夫（1818年11月9日—1883年9月3日）是俄国小说家，短篇小说家和剧作家。他发表的首部重要作品是短篇小说集《猎人笔记》，这是俄国现实主义的里程碑。小说《父与子》被认为是19世纪小说作品中最重要的作品之一。屠格涅夫艺术手法上的纯正使他成为下一代志趣相投的小说家们最喜爱的作家，比如亨利·詹姆斯、约瑟夫·康拉德，与托尔斯泰和陀思妥耶夫斯基相比，他们都更喜欢屠格涅夫。

《父与子》写于1860年8月至1861年8月间，出版于1862年，篇幅不长，共28章。这部经典小说描写的是父与子冲突的主题，这一冲突在屠格涅夫笔下着上了时代的色彩。目前国内较著名的译本是丽尼、巴金合译的版本和俞兴保的版本。

Fathers and Sons
父与子

Everyone should educate himself, as I've done, for instance... And as for the age, why should I depend upon it? Let it rather depend on me. No, my dear fellow, that's all emptiness and loose living.

每个人都应该进行自我教育，就像我所做的一样……至于时代，为什么我们要依附于时代？让时代来依附我。不，我亲爱的朋友，那只是空虚放纵的生活。

——*Fathers and Sons*《父与子》

名著导读

Set in 1859 at the moment when the Russian **autocratic**① state began to move hesitantly towards social and political reform, the novel explores the conflict between the liberal-minded fathers of Russian **reformist**② sympathies and their free-thinking intellectual sons whose revolutionary ideology threatened the stability of the state. Arkady Kirsanov is the son of Nikolai Petrovich Kirsanov, part of the landed Russian gentry—liberal but still traditionalist in most things. Evgeny Vasilev Bazarov is the son of a retired Russian military doctor and a friend of Arkady's tagging along as the recent graduate returns home to his family. Bazarov and Arkady are young intellectuals who have rejected the social and political norms of their elders. Bazarov in particular is portrayed as the nihilist, rejecting anything not tied to the physical laws of nature.

1859年，俄国独裁统治开始慢慢走向社会和政治改革。小说以此为背景，探究了父子之间的矛盾。父亲代表俄国贵族自由主义思想改革的拥护者，儿子代表思想自由的知识分子，但这些知识分子的革命观念威胁了国家稳定。阿尔卡·基尔萨诺夫是尼古拉·基尔萨诺夫的儿子，尼古拉·基尔萨诺夫属于拥有土地的俄国贵族——他是自由主义者，但在大多数事情上仍然是传统主义者。叶夫根尼·巴扎罗夫是一位退休俄国军医的儿子，也是阿尔卡的朋友，他跟随那些最近毕业的学生们回到了家中。巴扎罗夫和阿尔卡是年轻的知识分子，他们反对老一辈的社会和政治教条。尤其是巴扎罗夫，他被描述成虚无主义者，反对任何与自然法则不相关的事情。

名段选读

"So you see, Evgeny," remarked Arkady, as he finished his story, "how unjustly you judge my uncle. Not to mention that he has more than once helped my father out of financial troubles, given him all his money—perhaps you don't know, the property was never divided up—he's happy to help anyone; incidentally he is always doing something for the peasants; it is true, when he talks to them, he **screws**③ up his face and **sniffs**④ eau de Cologne..."

"Nerves, obviously," interrupted Bazarov.

"Perhaps, but his heart is in the right place. And he's far from stupid. What a lot of useful advice he has given me...especially...especially about relations with women."

"Aha! If you burn your mouth with hot milk, you'll even blow on water—we know that!"

"Well," continued Arkady, "in a word, he's profoundly unhappy—it's a crime to **despise**⑤ him."

"And who is despising him?" retorted Bazarov. "Still, I must say that a man who has staked his whole life on the one card of a woman's love, and when that card fails, turns sour and lets himself drift till he's fit for nothing, is not really a man. You say he's unhappy; you know better than I do; but he certainly hasn't got rid of all his foibles. I'm sure that he imagines he is busy and useful because he reads Galignani and once a month saves a peasant from being **flogged**[6] ."

"But remember his education, the age in which he grew up," said Arkady.

"Education?" **ejaculated**[7] Bazarov. "Everyone should educate himself, as I've done, for instance... And as for the age, why should I depend upon it? Let it rather depend on me. No, my dear fellow, that's all emptiness and loose living. And what are these mysterious relations between a man and a woman? We physiologists know what they are. You study the **anatomy**[8] of the eye; and where does it come in, that **enigmatic**[9] look you talk about? That's all romanticism, rubbish, and **moldy**[10] aesthetics. We had much better go and examine the beetle."

"你看到了，叶夫根尼，"阿尔卡讲完他的故事后还说，"你对我伯父的评价是多么不公平。更不用说他不只一次帮助我父亲摆脱财政困难，还把自己所有的钱都给了他——也许你不知道吧，财产从来就没有被分割——他很乐于帮助任何人；他总会不时地为农民做些事；这是事实，当他和他们交谈的时候，他会抬起头，并且闻一闻科隆香水的味道……"

"真是神经，"巴扎罗夫打断说。

"也许吧，但他的心意是好的。而且他一点也不愚蠢。他给我提过许多有用的建议……特别是……特别是和女人的关系。"

"哈哈！如果你被热牛奶烫了嘴，你甚至会吹凉它——我们都知道的！"

"好吧，"阿尔卡继续说道，"总之，他非常不快乐——轻视他是不对的。"

"谁轻视他了？"巴扎罗夫反驳道。"不过我还是得说，一个男人把他全部的生活都押在一个女人的爱情上，如果他输了，就变得闷闷不乐，并且开始让自己变得放荡不羁，直到一无是处，这样的男人算不上是真正的男人。你说他不快乐；你比我更了解他；但他确实没有克服自己所有的弱点。我敢说，他觉得自己是个忙碌而有用的人，因为他读了加利尼亚尼，而且每个月会帮助一个农民免受重罚。"

"但是不要忘了他所受的教育，他成长的那个时代，"阿尔卡说。

"教育？"巴扎罗夫突然说。"每个人都应该进行自我教育，就像我做的一样……至于时代，为什么我们要依附时代？让时代来依附于我。不，我亲爱的朋友，那只是空虚放纵的生活。而且一个男人和一个女人之间那些神秘的关系又是什么？我们生理学家知道那些是什么。你研究的是眼部解剖学；你所说的那种神秘的样子是从哪里来的？无非就是浪漫主义、无聊的想法和陈腐的美学。我们还不如去观察甲壳虫呢。"

——选自《父与子》第7章

注释

① autocratic [ˌɔːtəˈkrætɪk] *adj.* 独裁的，专制的

② reformist [rɪ'fɔːmɪst] *adj.* 改革主义的，改革运动的
③ screw [skruː] *vi.* 抬
④ sniff [snɪf] *vt.* 闻，吸
⑤ despise [dis'paiz] *vt.* 轻视
⑥ flog [flɪg] *vt.* 重罚，鞭打作为惩罚
⑦ ejaculate [i'dʒækjuleit] *vt.* 突然说
⑧ anatomy [ə'nætəmɪ] *n.* 解剖学
⑨ enigmatic ['enɪg'mætɪk] *adj.* 神秘的
⑩ moldy ['məuldɪ] *adj.* 陈腐的，发霉的

《罗亭》是屠格涅夫的第一部长篇小说，于1855年夏着手创作，于1856年发表于《现代人》杂志的第一、第二期。取自现实内部的形象经过作家之手后而成为典型，罗亭这个人物有血有肉、真实可信，成为俄国文学史上一个光彩照人的多余人形象。目前国内较著名的译本是王健夫的版本和徐振亚的版本。

Rudin
罗亭

I must act. I must not bury my talent, if I have any; I must not squander my powers on talk alone—empty, profitless talk—on mere words.

我必须行动。我决不能埋没我的任何天资，如果我有的话；我决不能把我的能力仅仅浪费在谈论上——空洞的、毫无益处的谈话上。

——*Rudin*《罗亭》

名著导读

Rudin is a well-educated, intellectual and extremely eloquent nobleman. His finances are in a poor state and he is dependent on others for his living. He lives at Dar'ya Mikhailovna's estate and falls in love with her daughter, Natalya. But, Rudi later left behind her. The Epilogue ends with Rudin's death at the barricades during the French Revolution of 1848; even at death he is mistaken by two fleeing revolutionaries for a Pole.

罗亭是一个受过良好教育、聪明且极有口才的贵族。他穷困潦倒，依靠他人的救济生活。他住在达里娅·米哈伊洛芙娜家，并爱上了她的女儿娜塔利娅。但后来罗亭抛弃了她。最后，故事以罗亭在1848年法国大革命期间，在巴黎巷战中阵亡而告终；甚至在临死前还被两个逃跑的革命者误会。

名段选读

"I thank you for your flattering opinion," Rudin interrupted her. "To be useful...it is easy to say!" (He passed his hand over her face.) "To be useful!" he repeated. "Even if I had any firm **conviction**① , how could I be useful?—even if I had faith in my own powers, where is one to find true, sympathetic souls?"

And Rudin waved his hand so hopelessly, and let his head sink so **gloomily**② , that Natalya **involuntarily**③ asked herself, were those really his—those enthusiastic words full of the breath of hope, she had heard the evening before.

"But no," he said, suddenly tossing back his lion-like mane, "that is all folly, and you are right. I thank you, Natalya Alexyevna, I thank you truly."(Natalya absolutely did not know what he was thanking her for.) "Your single phrase has recalled to me my duty, has pointed out to me my path...Yes, I must act. I must not bury my talent, if I have any; I must not **squander**④ my powers on talk alone—empty, profitless talk—on mere words," and his words flowed in a stream. He spoke nobly, **ardently**⑤ , convincingly, of the sin of cowardice and indolence, of the necessity of action. He **lavished**⑥ reproaches on himself, maintained that to discuss beforehand what you mean to do is as unwise as to prick with a pin the swelling fruit, that it is only a vain waste of strength and sap. He declared that there was no noble idea which would not gain sympathy, that the only people who remained misunderstood were those who either did not know themselves what they wanted, or were not worthy to be understood. He spoke **at length**⑦ , and ended by once more thanking Natalya Alexyevna, and utterly unexpectedly pressed her hand, **exclaiming**⑧. "You are a noble, generous creature!"

"谢谢你的恭维，" 罗亭打断她的话。"做一个有用的人……说起来容易！"（他的手划过她的脸颊。）"做一个有用的人！" 他重复说。"即使我有坚定的信念，我怎样才能做一个有用的人呢？——即使我相信自己的能力，在哪里能找到真实的、志趣相投的心灵呢？"

罗亭无助地挥了挥手，非常沮丧地低下了头，以至于娜塔利娅不禁自问，这真的是他说的话吗？——前一天晚上他的话语还是那样满怀希望，热情洋溢。

"但是不行，" 他说，突然抬起他狮子鬃毛般的头，"那些都是蠢话，你是对的。谢谢你，娜塔利娅·亚历山德拉，真的谢谢你。"（娜塔利娅完全不知道他因为什么而感谢她）"你简短的一席话让我想起了我的责任，给我指明了道路……对，我必须行动。我决不能埋没我的任何天资，如果我有的话；我决不能把我的能力仅仅浪费在谈论上——浪费在空洞、毫无益处的谈话上。" 他的话像小溪一样流畅。他大方地、热情地说着懦弱和懒惰的罪过，说着行动的必要性，这些话说得头头是道。他毫不吝惜地责备自己，认为在行

动之前商讨就像用大头针去扎膨胀的水果那样愚蠢，那只是白白浪费精力。他表示，高尚的计划都会得到赞同，不能理解计划的人要么是不知道自己想要什么的人，要么是不值得让人了解的人。最后，他以再次感谢娜塔利娅·亚历山德拉结束他的谈话，并且完全意想不到地紧紧握住她的手，大声说："你真是一个高尚慷慨的人！"

——选自《罗亭》第5章

注释

① conviction [kən'vɪkʃən] *n.* 确信，信念
② gloomily ['glu:mɪlɪ] *adv.* 沮丧地
③ involuntarily [ɪn'vɔləntrəlɪ] *adv.* 不禁，不知不觉地
④ squander ['skwɔndə] *vt.* 浪费
⑤ ardently ['a:dəntlɪ] *adv.* 热烈地；热心地
⑥ lavish ['lævɪʃ] *vt.* 浪费，滥用
⑦ at length【词组】最后
⑧ exclaim [ɪk'skleim] *vt.* 大声说

《木木》创作于1852年，由于遭到官方的查禁，它在1885年才得以发表在《现代人》杂志上，是屠格涅夫最为出色的一部短篇小说。小说揭露了农奴主的残暴，农奴的悲惨生活。目前国内较著名的译本是冯加的版本和巴金的版本。

Mumu
木木

But man gets used to anything, and Gerasim got used at last to living in town.
但是人终究会习惯任何事情，而格拉西姆最后也习惯了住在城镇里。

——*Mumu*《木木》

名著导读

Gerasim is a deaf and dumb peasant, brought from the country to serve his mistress as caretaker of her city property on the **outskirts**① of Moscow. He doesn't like his new life, but gets used to it, especially after he rescues a little puppy with black and white spots from the riverbank. Having this dog, Mumu, he finally has love in his bitter and otherwise loveless life, and the dog worships him. However, the mistress orders Gerasim to hand Mumu over—to be destroyed. After drowning poor Mumu, Gerasim hurries homewards, to his own village, to his own country.

格拉希姆是一个又聋又哑的农民，他从乡村被带到莫斯科郊区的城市，在那里给他的女主人看守财产。他不喜欢他的新生活，但却习惯了这种生活，尤其是他在河岸边救了一只黑白斑点的小狗之后。有了这只狗——木木，他最终在那辛酸而又无爱的生活中拥有了爱，并且那只狗也很喜欢他。然而，他的女主人却命令格拉希姆把木木交出来——要杀死它。在把可怜的木木淹死后，格拉希姆马上就跑回家收拾行李，回到他自己的村子，回到他自己的乡下。

名段选读

At first he intensely disliked his new mode of life. From his childhood he had been used to field labor, to village life. Shut off by his **affliction**② from the society of men, he had grown up, dumb and mighty, as a tree grows on a fruitful soil. When he was transported to the town, he could not understand what was being done with him; he was miserable and stupefied, with the **stupefaction**③ of some strong young bull, taken straight from the meadow, where the rich grass stood up to his belly, taken and put in the truck of a railway train, and there, while smoke and sparks and gusts of steam puff out upon the **sturdy**④ beast, he is whirled onwards, whirled along with loud roar and whistle, whither—God knows! What Gerasim had to do in his new duties seemed a mere trifle to him after his hard toil as a peasant; in half an hour all his work was done, and he would once more stand stock-still in the middle of the courtyard, staring open-mouthed at all the passers-by, as though trying to **wrest**⑤ from them the explanation of his **perplexing**⑥ position; or he would suddenly go off into some corner, and **flinging**⑦ a long way off the broom or the spade, throw himself on his face on the ground, and lie for hours together without stirring, like a caged beast. But man gets used to anything, and Gerasim got used at last to living in town. He had little work to do; his whole duty consisted in keeping the courtyard clean, bringing in a barrel of water twice a day, splitting and dragging in wood for the kitchen and the house, keeping out strangers, and watching at night. And it must be said he did his duty zealously. In his courtyard there was never a shaving lying about, never a speck of dust; if sometimes, in the muddy season, the wretched nag, put under his charge for fetching water, got stuck in the road, he would simply give it a shove with his shoulder, and set not only the cart but the horse itself moving. If he set to chopping wood, the axe fairly rang like glass, and chips and chunks flew in all directions. And as for strangers, after he had one night caught two thieves and knocked their heads together—knocked them so that there was not the slightest need to take them to the police-station afterwards—every one in the neighborhood began to feel a great respect for him; even those who came in the daytime, by no means robbers, but simply unknown persons, at the sight of the terrible porter, waved and shouted to him as though he could hear their shouts.

起初，他非常不喜欢自己新的生活方式。从童年开始，他就习惯了在田间劳动，习惯了乡村生活。他在一个没有世俗烦恼的环境下成长着，虽然天生聋哑，但是强壮有力，就像一棵生长在肥沃土壤中的大树。当他被送到城里时，他不明白他要面对的是什么；因此他痛苦不堪，感到很茫然，像一头强壮的、受到惊吓的小公牛一样，从牧场被带走了。那时，牧场上茂盛的牧草已经长到他小腹那么高了，小公牛被送上了火车，在那里，烟雾、火车擦出的电火花和一阵阵水蒸气喷向那强健的公牛，他一路上都头晕目眩，被嘈杂的咆哮声和汽笛声弄得头晕目眩，去哪儿——谁知道！在经历了农民劳作的艰辛后，现在的新任务对他来说似乎是小菜一碟；半小时内，他所有的工作都做完了，他又一动不动地站在院子中间，目瞪口呆地盯着所有的过路人，好像在努力从他们那里获得对他困惑现状的解释；或者他会突然离开，躲进某个角落，把扫把或者铁锹扔得远远的，把脸贴在地上，像被关在笼子里的动物一样，安静地躺几个小时。但是人终究会习惯任何事情，而格拉西姆最后也习惯了住在城镇里。他几乎没有什么工作可做；他所有的职责就是保持院子干净，一天提两桶水，为厨房和屋里劈柴，阻止陌生人进入和守夜。他确实工作得很积极。院子的地上绝没有木屑，绝没有一点灰尘；有时在泥泞的季节，他会让可怜的老马帮他取水，如果马在途中陷入了泥巴里，他就会用肩膀推它，这不仅会让推车开始移动，连马也会开始动了。如果他开始劈木头，他的斧头听起来简直像是玻璃的声音，大片小片的木头四处乱飞。对于陌生人来说，自从他在一天夜里抓了两个小偷并且把他们的头撞在一起之后（他撞得那么重，都省得送他们去警察局了），——周围的每个人都开始对他产生一种敬畏之情；甚至那些白天来的，绝不是强盗，而仅仅是不认识的人，看到这个令人恐惧的看门人，都会向他致意并且大声叫他，好像他能够听见他们的叫喊声一样。

——选自《木木》

注释

① outskirt [ˈautskɜːt] *n.* 市郊，郊区

② affliction [əˈflɪkʃən] *n.* 烦恼，痛苦

③ stupefaction [ˌstjuːpɪˈfækʃən] *n.* 麻醉，昏迷

④ sturdy [ˈstɜːdɪ] *adj.* 强壮的

⑤ wrest [rest] *vi.* 夺得，夺取

⑥ perplexing [pəˈpleksɪŋ] *adj.* 困惑的

⑦ fling [flɪŋ] *vt.* 扔，投

5 俄国散文之父——尼古莱·瓦西里耶维奇·果戈理

Nikolai Vasilievich Gogol (March 31, 1809—March 4, 1852) was a Ukrainian-born Russian novelist, humourist, and dramatist. He is considered the father of modern Russian realism, but at the same time, his work is very much in the genre of romanticism. His early works, such as *Evenings on a Farm Near Dikanka*, were heavily influenced by his Ukrainian upbringing and identity. The novels *Taras Bul'ba* and *Dead Souls*, the play *The Inspector-General*, and the short stories *Diary of a Madman*, The *Nose* and *The Overcoat* are among his best known works. With their scrupulous and scathing realism, ethical criticism as well as philosophical depth, they remain some of the most important works of world literature.

尼古莱·瓦西里耶维奇·果戈理（1809年3月31日—1852年3月4日）是出生于乌克兰的俄国小说家、幽默家和剧作家。他被视为俄国现代现实主义之父，但同时，他的作品也颇具浪漫主义风格。他早期的作品，像《狄康卡近乡夜话》带有浓重的乌克兰人的烙印。小说《塔拉斯·布尔巴》和《死魂灵》，戏剧《钦差大臣》，以及短篇小说《狂人日记》、《鼻子》和《外套》都是他的杰出作品。他的作品带有严谨且尖锐的现实主义和道德批判主义色彩以及深刻的哲学思想，因此一直是世界文学作品中最重要的著作。

《钦差大臣》*共5幕，发表于1836年，果戈理用喜剧这面镜子照出了当时社会达官显贵们的丑恶原形，从而揭露了农奴制俄国社会的黑暗、腐朽和荒唐反动。上海译文出版社黄成来、金留春的译本最为著名。

The Inspector-General
钦差大臣

We must present ourselves to him one at a time, and do—what ought to be done, you know—so that eyes do not see and ears do not hear.

我们必须一个一个地出现在他面前，做——那些应该做的事情，你们知道的——这样一来他就会对我们的所作所为视而不见，听而不闻了。

——*The Inspector-General*《钦差大臣》

名著导读

The corrupt officials of a small Russian town, headed by the Mayor, react with terror to the news that an **incognito**[1] inspector will soon be arriving in their town to investigate them. The **flurry**[2] of activity to cover up their considerable misdeeds is interrupted by the report that a suspicious person has arrived two weeks previously from Saint Petersburg and is staying at the inn. That person, however, is not an inspector; it is Khlestakov, a foppish civil servant with a wild imagination. Officers mistakenly assume that the inspector is Khlestakov. The servility and bribery displayed by the officials betrays their fear that their misdeeds will be uncovered.

在一个俄国小镇，当听说一个匿名的钦差大臣很快就会来镇上调查他们的时候，以镇长为首的镇上的腐败官员们都诚惶诚恐。他们急忙采取行动掩盖他们的诸多罪行，但是行动被一条传闻打断：一个可疑的人已经在两星期前从圣彼得堡来到了小镇，一直住在旅馆里。然而，那个人并不是钦差大臣；他是赫列斯达可夫，一个纨绔的、异想天开的公务员。官员们误以为赫列斯达可夫是钦差大臣。官员们卑躬屈膝和极力贿赂的行为暴露了他们担心恶行被揭发的恐惧。

名段选读

Ammos: It's risky, the **deuce**[3] take it. He'll fly into a rage at us. He's a government official, you know. Perhaps it should be given to him in the form of a gift from the nobility for some sort of memorial?

Postmaster: Or, perhaps, tell him some money has been sent here by post and we don't know for whom?

Artemy: You had better look out that he doesn't send you by post a good long ways off. Look here, things of such a nature are not done this way in a well-ordered state. What's the use of a whole regiment here? We must present ourselves to him one at a time, and do—what ought to be done, you know—so that eyes do not see and ears do not hear. That's the way things are done in a well-ordered society. You begin it, Ammos Fiodorovich, you be the first.

Ammos: You had better go first. The distinguished guest has eaten in your institution.

Artemy: Then Luka Lukich, as the enlightener of youth, should go first.

Luka: I can't, I can't, gentlemen. I confess I am so educated that the moment an official a single degree higher than myself speaks to me, my heart stands still and I get as tongue-tied as though my tongue were caught in the mud. No, gentlemen, excuse me. Please let me off.

Artemy: It's you who have got to do it, Ammos Fiodorovich. There's no one else. Why, every word you utter seems to be issuing from Cicero's mouth.

Ammos: What are you talking about! Cicero! The idea! Just because a man sometimes waxes④ enthusiastic over house dogs or hunting hounds.

All: (pressing him). No, not over dogs, but the Tower of Babel, too. Don't forsake⑤ us, Ammos Fiodorovich, help us. Be our Saviour!

Ammos: Let go of me, gentlemen.

艾莫斯：这很冒险，成功率只有百分之五十。他会对我们大发雷霆的。你要知道，他可是个政府官员。或许我们应该把它作为贵族们赠送的纪念品送给他？

邮政局长：或者我们可以告诉他，有些钱被邮寄到了这儿，但是我们不知道是寄给谁的？

阿特米：你最好还是当心点，小心他因这次邮寄把你流放到千里之外。听我说，在一个秩序井然的国家里，这种事情不是这么做的。我们所有人聚集在这里有什么用呢？我们必须一个一个地出现在他面前，做——那些应该做的事情，你们知道的——这样一来他就会对我们的所作所为视而不见，听而不闻了。这才是在一个秩序井然的社会中，我们做事的方式。从你开始，艾莫斯・费奥多罗维奇，你第一个去。

艾莫斯：最好你先去。那位尊贵的客人曾经在你们机构吃过饭。

阿特米：那么洛卡・鲁基，作为年轻人的导师，你应该第一个去。

洛卡：不，我不行，先生。我承认虽然我很有教养，但跟一个比我高一级别的官员交谈的时候，我的心脏就好像停止了跳动，说话也结结巴巴的，就好像我的舌头陷入泥里一样。不，先生，抱歉得很。放过我吧。

阿特米：你必须得去，艾莫斯・费奥多罗维奇。没有人比你更合适了。为什么不呢？你说的每一个词都像是从西塞罗口中说出来的一样。

艾莫斯：你在说什么呢！西塞罗！荒谬的想法！就因为我有时对家犬和猎狗兴致勃勃，你才这么说吧。

所有人：(逼迫他)。不，不是对狗，而是对巴别塔。不要抛弃我们，艾莫斯・费奥多罗维奇，帮帮我们。做我们的救世主吧！

艾莫斯：放过我吧，先生们。

——选自《钦差大臣》第3幕

注释

★ “《钦差大臣》是‘最完备的俄国官吏病理解剖学教程’。”

——俄国杰出的革命民主主义者、唯物主义哲学家和思想家　赫尔岑

① incognito [ɪnkɔg'ni:təu] *adj.* 匿名的，隐名埋姓的

② flurry ['flʌrɪ] *n.* 慌张，骚动
③ deuce [dju:s] *n.* 平分
④ wax [wæks] *vt.* 增大
⑤ forsake [fə'seik] *vt.* 放弃，抛弃

《死魂灵》发表于1842年，分为两部，共10章，通过对形形色色的官僚、地主群像的真切、生动的描绘，有力地揭露了俄国专制统治和农奴制度的吃人本质，极大地震撼了整个俄罗斯。鲁迅先生的译本和满涛、许庆道的译本比较好。

Dead Souls
死魂灵

No matter what may be said to the contrary, the body can never dispense with the soul.

不管人们如何反驳，肉体从来就不能脱离灵魂独立存在。

——*Dead Souls*《死魂灵》

名著导读

Chichikov, a mysterious stranger, arrives in a provincial town and visits a succession of landowners to make each a strange offer. He proposes to buy the names of dead serfs still registered on the census, saving their owners from paying tax on them, and to use these "souls" as collateral to reinvent himself as a gentleman.

一个神秘的陌生人乞乞科夫来到一个乡下的镇上，拜访了很多地主，并对每个人都提出了一个奇怪的要求。他提出要购买那些在人口普查中依旧在登的死亡奴隶的名字，这样就让主人们可以不用为那些死去的奴隶上缴赋税，也可以让他用这些“灵魂”作为抵押品，把自己彻底改造成一个绅士。

名段选读

"Listen, Paul Ivanovitch," the old man said. "I bring you your freedom, but only on this condition—that you depart out of the town **forthwith**① . Therefore gather together your effects, and waste not a moment, lest worse **befall**② you. Also, of all that a certain person has **contrived**③ to do on your behalf I am aware; wherefore let me tell you, as between ourselves, that should the **conspiracy**④ come to light, nothing on earth can save him, and in his fall he will involve others rather than be left unaccompanied in the **lurch**⑤ , and not see the guilt shared. How is it that when I left you recently you were in a better frame of mind than you are now? I beg of you not to trifle with the matter. Ah me! What boots that wealth for which men dispute and cut one another's throats? Do they think that it is possible to prosper in this world without thinking of the world to come? Believe me when I say that, until a man shall have renounced all that leads humanity to contend without giving a thought to the ordering of spiritual wealth, he will never set his temporal goods either upon a satisfactory foundation. Yes, even as times of want and scarcity may come upon nations, so may they come upon individuals. No matter what may be said to the contrary, the body can never dispense with the soul. Why, then, will you not try to walk in the right way, and, by thinking no longer of dead souls, but only of your only living one, regain, with God's help, the better road? I too am leaving the town tomorrow. Hasten, therefore, lest, bereft of my assistance, you meet with some dire misfortune."

"听着，保罗·伊万诺维奇，"老人说道。"我给你自由，但条件是——你立刻离开这里。所以，收拾你的财物，一秒钟都不要耽搁，以免更坏的事情降临在你身上。另外，我知道某个听命于你的人所筹划的全部阴谋，因此让我来告诉你，作为我们之间的悄悄话，一旦那个阴谋大白于天下，就什么都救不了他了，而且还会牵连其他人，他不会独自陷入困境，默默承担所有罪名。上次我离开你的时候，你的心情比现在要好一些，这是为什么呢？我拜托你不要小看这件事。啊！天啊！是什么让人们为财富争执而割断了彼此的喉咙？他们是否认为不去想死后去到的世界会是什么样，自己在这个世界上就会生活得很好？相信我，如果一个人不能放弃那些导致人性不顾自己精神状况而盲目争斗的东西，他就永远不会把自己眼前的利益建立在满足的基础之上。是啊，即使是一个国家也会有贫困和物资匮乏的时候，个人更是如此了。不管人们如何反驳，肉体从来就不能脱离灵魂独立存在。那么，为什么你就不能试着走上一条正确的道路？别再去想死魂灵了，还是想想你自己吧，在上帝的帮助下，重新找到更好的路。我明天也要离开这个镇了。因此，快走吧，要不，失去我的帮助，你会遇到一些可怕的灾祸。"

——选自《死魂灵》第2部第4章

注释

① forthwith ['fɔːθ'wið] *adv.* 立刻，立即

② befall [bɪ'fːl] *vt.* 降临于

③ contrive [kən'traiv] *vi.* 策划，设法做到

④ conspiracy [kən'spɪrəsɪ] *n.* 阴谋

⑤ lurch [lɜːtʃ] *n.* 蹒跚，踉跄

《外套》*是果戈里的短篇小说，发表于1840年。沙皇治下的俄国等级森严，果戈里是用小说抨击那害人的官僚制度。满涛的译本比较好。

The Overcoat
外套

And the young man covered his face with his hand; and many a time afterwards, in the course of his life, shuddered at seeing how much inhumanity there is in man, how much savage coarseness is concealed beneath refined, cultured, worldly refinement, and even, O God! in that man whom the world acknowledges as honourable and upright.

年轻人用手捂住脸；在他后来的人生旅程中，许多次他都万分震惊地看到人类本性是有多么的残忍，看到在那优雅的、文质彬彬的、很有教养的外表之下——哦，天啊，甚至是一些公认的值得敬仰的、正派的人的皮囊中——潜藏着多么残忍、粗俗、低劣的本性。

——*The Overcoat*《外套》

名著导读

The story centers on the life and death of Akaky Akakievich Bashmachkin, an **impoverished**[①] government clerk and copyist in the Russian capital of St. Petersburg. His threadbare overcoat is often the butt of others' jokes. So he forces himself to live within a strict budget to save sufficient money to buy a new overcoat. Finally, Akaky buys it. On route home, two ruffians take his coat. So he asks for help from a high-ranking general. But the general scolds Akakiy. Afterward, Akaky falls deathly ill with fever and curses the general. Finally, Akaky's ghost catches up with the general and takes his overcoat, frightening him terribly; satisfied, Akaky is not seen again.

这个故事主要描述了阿卡基·阿卡基耶维奇·巴什马奇的生活和他的死亡。他是一个穷困潦倒的政府职员和抄写员，在俄国的首都圣彼得堡工作。他破旧的外套经常成为他人的笑柄。所以他逼自己节衣缩食，以便省下足够多的钱来买一件新外套。最终，阿卡基买到了外套。回家途中，两个流氓夺走了他的外套。所以，他向一个职位很高的将军请求帮助。但是，将军却责备了阿卡基。之后，阿卡基发起高烧，生了重病，他诅咒那个将军。最终，阿卡基的鬼魂缠住了上将，拿走了他的外套，还把他吓得半死；阿卡基感到很满足，就再也没出现过。

名段选读

The young officials laughed at and made fun of him, so far as their official wit permitted;

told in his presence various stories **concocted**[②] about him, and about his landlady, an old woman of seventy; declared that she beat him; asked when the wedding was to be; and **strewed**[③] bits of paper over his head, calling them snow. But Akaky Akakiyevich answered not a word, any more than if there had been no one there beside himself. It even had no effect upon his work. Amid all these annoyances he never made a single mistake in a letter. But if the joking became wholly unbearable, as when they jogged his head, and prevented his attending to his work, he would exclaim:

"Leave me alone! Why do you insult me?"

And there was something strange in the words and the voice in which they were uttered. There was in it something which moved to pity; so much so that one young man, a newcomer, who, taking pattern by the others, had permitted himself to make sport of Akaky, suddenly stopped short, as though all about him had undergone a transformation, and presented itself in a different aspect. Some unseen force **repelled**[④] him from the comrades whose acquaintance he had made, on the supposition that they were decent, well-bred men. Long afterwards, in his gayest moments, there recurred to his mind the little official with the bald forehead, with his heart-rending words, "Leave me alone! Why do you insult me?" In these moving words, other words resounded—"I am thy brother." And the young man covered his face with his hand; and many a time afterwards, in the course of his life, shuddered at seeing how much inhumanity there is in man, how much savage coarseness is concealed beneath refined, cultured, worldly refinement, and even, O God! in that man whom the world acknowledges as honourable and upright.

年轻的官员们想方设法地来取笑他，当着他的面讲各种他们捏造的关于他和他的女房东——一个70岁的老妇人——的故事；他们声称女房东打他；还问他他俩什么时候举行婚礼；并把纸片洒在他的头上，把那称作是下雪。但是阿卡基·阿卡基耶维奇对此都一言不发，表现得旁若无人的样子。这些嘲弄甚至对他的工作没有产生丝毫的影响。尽管处在这种恼人的环境下，但他在信件中却从没有出过一个错误。但如果有些玩笑实在让人忍无可忍，比如他们轻摇他的脑袋，并妨碍他工作的时候，他就会大声说：

"别来烦我！你们为什么要如此侮辱我？"

他的这句话和他说话时的语调中包含着某些奇怪的东西，包含某种让人感到怜悯的东西，它是如此强烈以至于一个新来的、学着其他人开阿卡基玩笑的年轻人突然就停止了这种行为，仿佛经历了一次脱胎换骨，呈现出了他不同的一面。某种无形的力量将他与那些相识的那些同事分离开来，他原本以为他们都是有教养的正派人士。在很久之后，在他最快乐的时刻，他总是回忆起那个前额秃顶的小公务员和他令人心碎的话："别来烦我！你们为什么要如此羞辱我？"在这心酸的话中，仿佛还伴随着另外一个意思——"我是你们的兄弟。"

年轻人用手捂住脸；在他后来的人生旅程中，许多次他都万分震惊地看到人类本性是

有多么的残忍，看到在那优雅的、文质彬彬的、很有教养的外表之下——哦，天啊，甚至是一些公认的值得敬仰的、正派的人的皮囊中——潜藏着多么残忍、粗俗、低劣的本性。

——选自《外套》

注释

★“我们所有的人都是从果戈理的《外套》中孕育出来的。”

——俄国作家　陀思妥耶夫斯基

① impoverished [ɪm'pɒvərɪʃt] *adj.* 穷困的；用尽了的，无创造性的

② concoct [kən'kɒkt] *vt.* 捏造，编造

③ strew [stru:] *vt.* 散播，撒满

④ repel [rɪ'pel] *vt.* 推开，赶走

6 德国民族文学的最杰出的代表——约翰·沃尔夫冈·冯·歌德

Johann Wolfgang von Goethe（August 28, 1749—March 22, 1832） was a German writer and polymath. Goethe is considered by many to be the most important writer in the German language and one of the most important thinkers in Western culture. Goethe's works span the fields of poetry, drama, literature, theology, philosophy, and science. His magnum opus, a peak of world literature, is the drama Faust. Goethe's other well-known literary works include his numerous poems, the Bildungsroman *Wilhelm Meister's Apprenticeship*, and the epistolary novel *The Sorrows of Young Werther.*

约翰·沃尔夫冈·冯·歌德（1749年8月28日—1832年3月22日）是一位德国作家和博学家。歌德被许多人认为是德国语言领域最重要的作家以及西方文学史上最重要的思想家之一。歌德的作品涉及诗歌、戏剧、文学著作、神学、哲学以及科学领域。他的巨著——戏剧《浮士德》，是世界文学的巅峰之作。歌德其他著名的文学作品包括他众多的诗歌、教育小说《威廉·麦斯特的学习时代》和书信体小说《少年维特之烦恼》。

《浮士德》第1部长达12111行，完成于1808年法军入侵时，第2部则完成于1831年8月31日，第2部分5幕，27场。《浮士德》以德国民间传说为题材，以文艺复兴以来的德国和欧洲社会为背景，描写了一个新兴资产阶级先进知识分子不满现实，竭力探索人生意义和社会理想的生活道路的经历。上海创造社出版郭沫若的译本以及杨武能的译本最好。

Faust
浮士德

Ah, God! but Art is long,
And Life, alas! is fleeting.

啊，上帝！艺术是永恒的，

而生命啊，哎！却是短暂的。

——*Faust*《浮士德》

名著导读

In his study, Faust, attempts and fails to gain knowledge of nature and the universe by magic means. The **dejected**[1] Faust **contemplates**[2] suicide, but is held back by the sounds of the beginning Easter celebrations. Faust, an audacious man, boldly wagers with the devil, Mephistopheles, that Faust will give up his eternal soul if the Devil can offer him a single moment that he would wish to prolong.

在学习的过程中，浮士德试图通过魔法来获得自然和宇宙的知识，但是失败了。灰心的浮士德打算自寻短见，但是当他听到刚刚开始的复活节庆典的热闹声音，又放弃了这个想法。浮士德英勇无畏，他勇敢地和恶魔靡非斯特打赌，如果魔鬼能让他获得一个他希望永恒存在的瞬间，他就会把自己不灭的灵魂交给魔鬼。

名段选读

Wagner

Yet through delivery **orators**[3] succeed;
I feel that I am far behind, indeed.

Faust

Seek thou the honest **recompense**[4]!
Beware, a tinkling fool to be!
With little art, clear wit and sense
Suggest their own delivery;
And if thou'rt moved to speak in earnest,
What need, that after words thou yearnest?
Yes, your discourses, with their glittering show,
Where ye for men twist shredded thought like paper,
Are unrefreshing as the winds that blow
The rustling leaves through chill autumnal **vapor**[5]!

Wagner

Ah, God! but Art is long,
And Life, alas! is fleeting.

And oft, with zeal my critic-duties meeting,
In head and breast there's something wrong.
How hard it is to compass the assistance
Whereby one rises to the source!
And, **haply**[6], ere one travels half the course
Must the poor devil quit existence.

瓦格纳

然而，演讲者只有通过演讲才能获得成功，
由此我觉得自己确实落在人后了。

浮士德

去追求你那应得的酬劳吧！
当心变成一个众人皆知的傻瓜！
即使没有技巧、睿智和远见卓识，
也能够使你正确地表达自己。
如果你要认真地说话，
除了你最想说的那些话外，其他的有什么必要？
是的，你的话语用词华丽，
让人们为之绞尽脑汁，百思不得其解，
但它们就像是在寒冷的秋季，
吹得树叶沙沙作响的寒风那般使人倦怠！

瓦格纳

啊，上帝！艺术是永恒的，
而生命啊，哎！却是短暂的。
我常常在满怀热情的时候却遭遇到批判，
我的思想和灵魂肯定有哪里出了问题。
在找寻智慧源泉的途中
要获得帮助真的太难！
况且，没准在半途中，
就丢失了自己的性命。

——选自《浮士德》第1部

注释

① dejected [dɪ'dʒektɪd] *adj.* 沮丧的，灰心的

② contemplate ['kɔntəm,pleit] *vi.&vt.* 沉思，苦想
③ orator ['ɔrətə(r)] *n.* 演说者
④ recompense ['rekəmpens] *n.* 报酬
⑤ vapor ['veipə(r)] *n.* 水汽，蒸汽
⑥ haply ['hæplɪ] *adv.* 偶然地

《少年维特之烦恼》*发表于1774年，分2部分，是一部书信体小说，充满着一个处在德国“狂飙突进”时代的青年人的爱和恨，对美好生活的向往和对腐朽社会的控诉。上海译文出版侯浚吉译本比较好。

The Sorrows of Young Werther
少年维特之烦恼

It is much easier to die than to bear a life of misery with fortitude.

死很容易，坚强地承受生活的苦痛就难了。

——*The Sorrows of Young Werther*《少年维特之烦恼》

名著导读

The majority of *The Sorrows of Young Werther* is presented as a collection of letters written by Werther, a young artist of highly sensitive and passionate temperament, and sent to his friend Wilhelm. In these letters, Werther gives a very intimate account of his stay in Wahlheim. He meets Lotte, a beautiful young girl who is taking care of her siblings following the death of their mother. In spite of knowing beforehand that Charlotte is already engaged to a man named Albert, who is in fact 11 years her senior, Werther falls in love with her. His pain eventually becomes so great that he is forced to leave and go to Weimar. Unable to hurt anyone else or seriously consider committing murder, Werther sees no other choice but to take his own life.

《少年维特之烦恼》的大部分情节是以维特写给他朋友威廉的信的形式呈现出来的，维特是一位极度感性、充满热情的年轻艺术家。在这些信中，维特详细叙述了他在W城的生活。他遇到了夏洛特，一个年轻漂亮的女孩儿，在母亲去世后，她一直照顾她的兄弟姐妹。虽然早已知道夏洛特已经和一个叫艾伯特的男人订了婚，而且知道那个男人比她大11岁，维特还是爱上了她。最后他痛苦之至，不得不离开去了魏玛。维特不能伤害其他任何人也不能谋杀任何人，他别无选择只能结束他自己的生命。

名段选读

"But still, my good friend," I continued, "there are some exceptions here too. Theft is a crime, but the man who commits it from extreme poverty, with no design but to save his family from perishing, is he an object of pity, or of punishment? Who shall throw the first stone at a husband, who, in the heat of just **resentment**①, sacrifices his faithless wife and her **perfidious**② **seducer**③? or at the young **maiden**④, who, in her weak hour of rapture, forgets herself in the impetuous joys of love? Even our laws, cold and cruel as they are, **relent**⑤ in such cases, and withhold their punishment."

"That is quite another thing," said Albert; "because a man under the influence of violent passion loses all power of reflection, and is regarded as **intoxicated**⑥ or **insane**⑦."

"Oh! you people of sound understandings," I replied, smiling, "are ever ready to exclaim '**Extravagance**⑧, and madness, and **intoxication**⑨!' You moral men are so calm and so **subdued**⑩! You **abhor**⑪ the drunken man, and detest the extravagant; you pass by, like the Levite, and thank God, like the Pharisee, that you are not like one of them. I have been more than once intoxicated, my passions have always bordered on extravagance: I am not ashamed to confess it; for I have learned, by my own experience, that all extraordinary men, who have accomplished great and astonishing actions, have ever been **decried**⑫ by the world as drunken or insane. And in private life, too, is it not intolerable that no one can undertake the execution of a noble or generous deed, without giving rise to the exclamation that the doer is intoxicated or mad? Shame upon you, ye sages!"

"This is another of your extravagant humours," said Albert: "you always exaggerate a case, and in this matter you are undoubtedly wrong; for we were speaking of suicide, which you compare with great actions, when it is impossible to regard it as anything but a weakness. It is much easier to die than to bear a life of misery with fortitude."

"但是，我的好朋友，"我继续说，"还存在一些例外。偷窃是犯罪，但是如果那个人因为极其贫穷而偷窃，为的只是让家人能活下去，那么他是该得到同情呢，还是受到惩罚？如果一个丈夫因一时愤怒，杀死了背叛自己的妻子和她背信弃义的奸夫，谁会朝他扔第一块石子呢？或者是一位处于为爱痴狂的脆弱年纪的少女，沉迷在激烈爱情的狂喜中，她该被扔石子吗？在这些情况下，甚至连我们国家那些冰冷、残酷的法律都会放宽对他们的惩罚。"

"那不一样，"艾伯特说，"因为人在强烈情感的影响下就会失去理智，看起来就像喝醉了，或者像个疯子。"

"哎呀！你们这些懂得一堆大道理的人，"我笑着回答说，"永远都会斥责'狂热、

疯狂和狂喜！’你们这些君子总是心平气和，压抑自己的感情！你们憎恨酒鬼，厌恶挥霍；你们像利未人那样生活，像法利赛人那样感激上苍，但你们却跟他们(法利赛人)完全不一样。我曾不止一次地烂醉如泥，我的情感总是处于泛滥的边缘：我并不觉得承认这一点有什么可耻的；因为我的自身经历告诉我但凡拥有非凡成就、做出创世之举的伟人，都会被世人诋毁为酒鬼或者神经病。在个人生活中也是一样，你们不能容忍那种对酒鬼或者疯子泰然处之的或高尚或宽宏大量的行为，对吧？真是可耻，你们这些圣人！”

“又来了，你那夸张的情绪，”艾伯特说，“你总是把事情夸大，在这一点上，毫无疑问你是错的；因为我们正在谈的是自杀，你却把它和壮举扯在了一起，它什么都不是，只是懦弱的表现。死很容易，坚强地承受生活的苦痛就难了。”

——选自《少年维特之烦恼》第1部“8月12日”

注释

★“下任何定义都不能确切地说出这本富有想象力的杰作无限丰富的内容；但是我们可以简要地说，这篇描写炽热而不幸的爱情故事，其重要意义在于，它表现的不仅是一个人孤独的感情和痛苦，而且是整个时代的感情和痛苦。”

——丹麦文学批评家　勃兰兑斯

① resentment [rɪðzentmənt] *n.* 愤慨，怨恨

② perfidious [pəðfɪdiəs] *adj.* 不忠的，背信弃义的

③ seducer [sɪ'dju:sə] *n.* 骗子，诱惑者

④ maiden ['meidən] *n.* 少女，处女

⑤ relent [rɪ'lent] *vi.* 变温和，减弱

⑥ intoxicated [ɪn'tɔksɪkeitɪd] *adj.* 喝醉的；极度兴奋的

⑦ insane [ɪn'sein] *adj.* 疯狂的；精神病的；极愚蠢的

⑧ extravagance [ɪk'strævəgəns] *n.* 奢侈；放肆的言行

⑨ intoxication [ɪnˌtɔksɪ'keiʃən] *n.* 极度兴奋

⑩ subdued [səb'dju:d] *adj.* 屈服的

⑪ abhor [əb'hɔ:] *vt.* 痛恨，厌恶

⑫ decry [dɪ'krai] *vt.* 诽谤

《歌德自传——诗与真》发表于1833年，分2部分，共9章，他是借用诗的笔调、运用想象力去写“真”的。该书以敏锐的心理洞察力陈述了他同珂莉娅之间的复杂感情，他对一个酒吧侍女格蕾欣的恋慕，随着7年战争期间法军占领而来的视野的拓宽，约瑟夫二世在法兰克福市政厅的加冕典礼及其中世纪盛观留下的不可磨灭的印象，以及虔敬派小圈子的狂热的宗教情感。人民文学出版社刘思慕的译本比较好。

Truth and Poetry
诗与真

Every bird has its decoy, and every man is led and misled in a way peculiar to himself.

每只鸟都有它难以抗拒的诱饵；每个人都会被某种特定的方式指导或误导。

——*Truth And Poetry*《诗与真》

名著导读

Covering the period from his birth in 1749 to his departure for Weimar in 1775, in *Poetry and Truth* Goethe recalls his childhood and youth as the son of a well-to-do, middle-class family, his education and literary awakening, early loves, and the creation and reception of works from his Sturm und Drang years, such as *The Sorrows of Young Werther, Goetz von Berlichingen,* and *Urfaust*. Not merely an account of Goethe's own life, this book also explores the influences on his early years—friends, mentors, famous personages of his time, intellectual movements, cities, and historical events—to draw a lifelike picture of his time.

《诗与真》讲的是从1749年歌德出生到1775年去魏玛这段时期的故事。歌德回忆了他在富裕的中产阶级家庭中童年和青年时代的生活，他的教育经历和文学觉醒，早期恋情以及他在十八世纪德国文艺运动时期的文学创作以及那段时期创作的作品获得的反响，比如《少年维特之烦恼》、《格茨·冯·伯利欣根》和《浮士德》。这本书不仅叙述了歌德自己的生活，还探寻了一些对他早期生活产生影响的人和事——朋友、老师、他所处时代的著名人物、知识分子运动、城市以及历史事件——全书整体描绘出了一幅栩栩如生的时代图画。

名段选读

Every bird has its decoy[①], and every man is led and misled in a way peculiar to himself. Nature, education, circumstances, and habit kept me apart from all that was rude; and though I often came into contact with the lower classes of people, particularly mechanics, no close connection grew out of it. I had indeed boldness enough to undertake something uncommon and perhaps dangerous, and many times felt disposed to do so; but I was without the handle by which to grasp and hold it.

Meanwhile I was quite unexpectedly involved in an affair which brought me near to a great **hazard**② , and at least for a long time into **perplexity**③ and **distress**④ . The good terms on which I before stood with the boy whom I have already named Pylades was maintained up to the time of my youth. We indeed saw each other less often, because our parents did not stand on the best footing with each other; but, when we did meet, the old **raptures**⑤ of friendship broke out immediately. Once we met in the alleys which offer a very agreeable walk between the outer and inner gate of Saint Gallus. We had scarcely returned greetings when he said to me, "I hold to the same opinion as ever about your verses. Those which you recently communicated to me, I read aloud to some pleasant companions; and not one of them will believe that you have made them."—"Let it pass," I answered: "we will make and enjoy them, and the others may think and say of them what they please."

"There comes the unbeliever now," added my friend. "We will not speak of it," I replied: "what is the use of it? one cannot convert them."—"By no means," said my friend: "I cannot let the affair pass off in this way."

每只鸟都有令它难以抗拒的诱饵；每个人都会被某种特定的方式指导或误导。本性、教育、环境和习惯让我远离了粗俗；虽然我经常和下层人民接触，尤其是修理工，但是我并没有与他们产生密切的联系。我胆子确实很大，我勇于尝试一些不寻常，有些甚至还是危险的事情，我往往会忍不住想要尝试它们；只是我总是没有办法控制事态的发展。

与此同时，我意外地卷入了一件事里，这件事把我置于危机的边缘，至少在很长一段时间里，我都沉浸在混乱和痛苦之中。我和之前我提到的一个叫皮拉得斯的男孩关系很好，我们的友谊一直持续到了我的青年时代。事实上，我们并没有常常见面，因为我们双方父母的交情不深；但是，当我们在一起的时候，曾经的快乐又会立马爆发出来。一天，我们在后街遇到了，于是我们走在后街上，在圣加伦斯教堂的内外门之间愉快地散步。我们对于路人的问候几乎是不理不睬，这时，他说："我还是像以前一样赞赏你诗歌中的观点。我跟一些好友念过你最近寄给我的诗歌；没有人相信是你写的。"——"别管它了，"我回答说："我们高兴就好，别人怎么想，怎么说都随便。"

"他们都不相信是你写的，"我的朋友补充道。"我们不说这个了吧，"我回答说，"有什么意义呢？我们没办法改变他们的观点。"——"绝不！"我的朋友说，"我不会让这件事就这样过去的。"

——选自《诗与真》第1部第5章

注释

① decoy ['di:kɔi] *n.* 引诱物

② hazard ['hæzəd] *n.* 危险

③ perplexity [pə'pleksɪti:] *n.* 困惑，混乱

④ distress [dɪ'stres] *n.* 悲痛

⑤ rapture ['ræptʃə(r)] *n.* 狂喜

7 浪漫主义派最后的幻想之王——海因里希·海涅

Christian Johann Heinrich Heine (December 13, 1797—February 17, 1856) was a journalist, essayist, literary critic, and one of the most significant German poets of the 19th century. He is best known outside Germany for his early lyric poetry, which was set to music in the form of Lieder (art songs) by composers such as Robert Schumann. Heine's later verse and prose is distinguished by its satirical wit and irony. His famous poems include *The Silesian Weavers, On Wings of Song* and so on.

克里斯蒂安·约翰·海因里希·海涅（1797年12月13日—1856年2月17日）是记者、散文家、文学评论家，同时也是19世纪德国最杰出的诗人之一。他凭借早期的抒情诗闻名世界，这些诗歌被罗伯特·舒曼等作曲家编成了民谣(一种艺术歌曲)的音乐形式。海涅后期的诗歌和散文以语言讽刺机智著称。他著名的诗作有《西里西亚的纺织工人》、《乘着歌声的翅膀》，等等。

《你好像一朵鲜花》收录在《还乡集》里，这首诗写得简洁凝练，一共只有两节，短短的8行，然而却包含了几层意思，表达了感情的多个层次，写得曲折有致，深邃含蓄，耐人寻味，给人启迪。目前国内较著名的译本是杨能武的版本和冯至的版本。

E'en as a lovely Flower
你好像一朵鲜花

E'en as a lovely flower,
So fair, so pure thou art;
你好像一朵可爱的鲜花，
那么美丽，那么无瑕；

——*E'en As A lovely Flower*《你好像一朵鲜花》

名著导读

E'en As A lovely Flower is the most famous one among Heine's love poems. The poem describes the girl's gentleness, purity and beauty in an impressionistic and intuitive way. Besides, it also implicitly shows the passion and love deep in the poet's heart.

《你好像一朵鲜花》是海涅爱情诗中最著名的一首。这首诗用一种印象主义和直觉的方式描述了女孩的温柔、纯洁和美貌。此外，它还含蓄地展现了诗人内心深处的激情和爱意。

名段选读

E'en as a lovely flower,
So **fair**① , so pure thou art;
I gaze on thee, and sadness
Comes stealing o'er my heart.

My hands I **fain**② had folded
Upon thy soft brown hair,
Praying that God may keep thee
So lovely, pure and fair.

你好像一朵可爱的鲜花，
那么美丽，那么无瑕；
每当我注视着你，
忧伤便悄悄侵占我整个心房。

在你柔软的棕色秀发旁，
我欣然双手合十，
祈求上帝
让你永远可爱，永远美丽无瑕。

——《你好像一朵鲜花》

注释

① fair [fee(r)] *adj.* 美丽的

② fain [fein] *adv.* 欣然地，乐意地

《西里西亚的纺织工人》* 是作者1844年为支援西里西亚纺织工人起义而创作的海治抒情诗。这首如投枪匕首般锋利尖锐的“时事诗”被誉为“德国工人阶级的马赛曲”。目前国内较著名的译本是黄雨石的版本和李靖民的版本。

The Silesian Weavers
西里西亚的纺织工人

“Germany, your shroud's on our loom;
And in it we weave the threefold doom...We weave; we weave.
“德国啊，我们正在织你的裹尸布；
在那上面，我们织进了三层诅咒……我们织，不停地织。

——*The Silesian Weavers*《西里西亚的纺织工人》

名著导读

This poem was written in the year Silesian Weavers had assembled to protest starvation wages. It deals directly with the issue of workers rights and how they are exploited and oppressed by the rich. Heine suggests that a day of reckoning can not be long postponed, and that sooner or later the rich will be forced to make amends. In the poem monarchy, religion and nationalism are dismissed as being of little comfort when your family is starving and your rights are crushed underfoot.

这首诗歌创作于西西里纺织工人聚集在一起反对低工资的那一年。它直接聚焦工人的权利和他们是如何被富人剥削和压迫的。海涅指出“算账”已经刻不容缓，富人迟早都会被迫向工人们提供赔偿。在诗歌中，当家人忍饥挨饿、个人权利遭到践踏时，人们抛弃了君主制、宗教信仰和民族主义，因为它们不具有任何抚慰作用。

名段选读

In gloomy eyes there wells no tear.
Grinding their teeth, they are sitting here:
“Germany, your shroud's on our loom;
And in it we weave the threefold doom...We weave; we weave.

“Doomed be the God who was deaf to our prayer
In Winter's cold and hunger's despair.
All in vain we hoped and bided;

He only **mocked**[1] us, **hoaxed**[2], **derided**[3] ...We weave; we weave.

"Doomed be the king, the rich man's king,
Who would not be moved by our suffering,
Who tore the last coin out of our hands,
And let us be shot by his blood-thirsty bands...We weave; we weave.

"Doomed be the fatherland, false name,
Where nothing thrives but **disgrace**[4] and shame,
Where flowers are crushed before they unfold,
Where the worm is quickened by rot and mold...We weave; we weave.

"The loom is creaking, the shuttle flies;
Nor night nor day do we close our eyes.
Old Germany, your shroud's on our loom,
And in it we weave the threefold doom; ...We weave; we weave!"

忧郁的眼中没有眼泪。
他们咬牙切齿地坐在这里：
"德国啊，我们正在织你的裹尸布；
在那上面，我们织进了三层诅咒……我们织，不停地织。

"我们诅咒上帝，他对我们的祈祷充耳不闻
那是我们在冬天的严寒和饥饿中绝望的祈祷。
我们的希冀和等待只是徒劳；
他只会嘲笑我们，愚弄我们，挖苦我们……我们织，不停地织。

"我们诅咒国王，那些富有的国王，
他不会为我们的遭遇黯然心伤，
他榨干了我们手中最后一枚铜板，
还让他那嗜血的军队杀害我们……我们织，不停地织。

"我们诅咒这个徒有虚名的祖国，
这里一片荒芜，只有耻辱欣欣向荣，
这里的花朵尚未开放就惨遭摧残，
这里的蛆虫在腐烂的尸体和发霉的粪土中肆虐……我们织，不停地织。

"织机嘎吱作响，梭子飞快运转；
我们日夜织布，不曾合眼。
年老的德国啊，我们正在织你的裹尸布，
在那上面，我们织进了三层诅咒……我们织，不停地织。"

——《西里西亚的纺织工人》

注释

★ "这首诗与这个口号针锋相对，具有高度的思想性战斗性，它所表达的不是普通的愤怒感情，而是阶级觉醒的战斗呼喊，充满了彻底埋葬整个旧社会的热望和决心。"

——德国哲学家、马克思主义创始人　恩格斯

① mock [mɔk] *vt.* 嘲笑
② hoax [həuks] *vt.* 欺骗
③ deride [dɪ'raid] *vt.* 嘲弄
④ disgrace [dɪs'greis] *n.* 耻辱

《乘着歌声的翅膀》大约写于1822年，表达了诗人对爱情的美好向往。目前国内较著名的译本是杨能武的版本和冯至的版本。

On Wings of Song
乘着歌声的翅膀

There we will lie down,
under the palm-tree,
and drink of love and peacefulness,
And dream our blessed dream.
我们会躺在那儿
在那棕榈树下，
分享着爱和宁静，
幻想着我们幸福的梦想。

——*On Wings of Song*《乘着歌声的翅膀》

名著导读

On Wings of Song is a German Romantic poem by Heinrich Heine, which was set to music by Felix Mendelssohn. The lyric speaks of flying with a lover to a peaceful paradise in "the fields of the Ganges".

《乘着歌声的翅膀》是海因里希·海涅创作的一首德语浪漫主义诗歌，由费利克斯·门德尔松谱曲。这首抒情诗讲述诗人愿与爱人一起飞向"恒河流域"那个平静的天堂。

名段选读

On wings of song,
my love, I'll carry you away
to the fields of the Ganges
Where I know the most beautiful place.

There lies a red-flowering garden,
in the serene moonlight,
the lotus-flowers await
Their beloved sister.

The violets **giggle**① and **cherish**②,
and look up at the stars,
The roses tell each other secretly
Their fragrant fairy-tales.

The gentle, bright **gazelles**③,
pass and listen;
and in the distance murmurs
The waves of the holy stream.

There we will lie down,
under the palm-tree,
and drink of love and peacefulness,
And dream our blessed dream.

乘着歌声的翅膀
我的爱人，我会带你翱翔
去那恒河流域
我知道那是最美丽的地方。

那里有一座开满红花的花园，

在宁静的月光下，
荷花们在翘首期待，
期盼着她们亲爱的姐妹。

紫罗兰发出咯咯的笑声，
仰头深情凝视着星辰，
玫瑰花在悄声私语，
诉说她们充满芬芳的童话。

温柔伶俐的羚羊，
悄然经过，静静地聆听着；
圣河的波浪，
在远处窃窃低语。

我们会躺在那儿
在那棕榈树下，
分享着爱和宁静，
幻想着我们幸福的梦想。

——《乘着歌声的翅膀》（《欢乐颂》1–2节）

注释

① giggle [ˈgɪgl] *vi.* 咯咯地笑
② cherish [ˈtʃerɪʃ] *vi.* 珍爱
③ gazelle [gəˈzel] *n.* 羚羊

8 西方现代主义文学的先驱——弗兰兹·卡夫卡

Franz Kafka (July 3, 1883—June 3, 1924) was one of the most influential German-language novelists of the 20th century, whose works are now regarded existential classics; and among the highest achievements of world literature. The term "Kafkaesque" has become part of the English vernacular. Much of Kafka's work was unfinished, or prepared for publication posthumously by Max Brod. The novels *The Castle* (which stopped mid-sentence and had ambiguity on content), *The Trial* (chapters were unnumbered and some were incomplete) and *Amerika* (Kafka's original title was *The Man who Disappeared*) were all prepared for publication by Brod. His best-known Novella is *The Metamorphosis*.

弗兰兹·卡夫卡（1883年7月3—1924年6月3），20世纪最具影响力的德语小说家之一，如今，他的作品被视为存在主义的经典之作，是世界文学史上最高的成就之一。"卡夫卡式的"这个术语已成为了英国方言。卡夫卡的大多数作品都没有完成，在他去世后，马克思·布罗德代替他整理发表了一些作品。他的小说《城堡》（只写了一半且文章内容有歧义）、《审判》（章节没有编号且有些章节不完整）、《美国》(原来的名字是《失踪的人》)都是由布罗德整理发表的。卡夫卡最著名的中篇小说是《变形记》。

《变形记》*创作于1912年，发表于1915年。小说分成3部分,是卡夫卡短篇代表作和艺术上的最高成就，被认为是20世纪最伟大的小说作品之一。目前国内较著名的译本是叶廷芳的版本和李文俊的版本。

The Metamorphosis
变形记

He remembered his family with deep feelings of love. In this business, his own thought that he had to disappear was, if possible, even more decisive than his sister's.

他怀着满腔的爱想念着家人，如果可能的话，他真想让自己消失，比他妹妹都想。

——*The Metamorphosis*《变形记》

名著导读

Gregor Samsa awakes one morning to find himself inexplicably transformed from a human into a monstrous insect. His appearance horrifies his family and supervisor. No longer able to rely on Gregor's income, the other family members are forced to take on jobs and Grete's caretaking deteriorates. Gregor retreats to his room and collapses, finally succumbing to his wounds and starvation. The point of view shifts as, upon discovery of the corpse, the family feels a slight burden has been lifted from them, and start planning for the future.

一天早上，格里高尔·萨姆沙醒来后发现自己莫名其妙地变成了一只大甲虫。他的样子吓坏了他的家人和上司。因为没有了格里高尔的收入，家里的其他成员都不得不开始工作，他们对格里高尔的照顾也越来越敷衍了。格里高尔每天躲在房间里，最后由于伤口恶化和饥饿而死去。这时小说的视角转向了他的家人，在发现他的尸体后，他们都感到如释重负，并开始计划的新生活。

名段选读

Only when he was already in the door did he turn his head, not completely, because he felt his neck growing **stiff**① . At any rate he still saw that behind him nothing had changed. Only the sister was standing up. His last glimpse **brushed**② over the mother who was now completely asleep. Hardly was he inside his room when the door was pushed shut very quickly, bolted fast, and barred. Gregor was startled by the sudden **commotion**③ behind him, so much so that his little limbs bent double under him. It was his sister who had been in such a hurry. She had stood up right away, had waited, and had then sprung forward **nimbly**④ . Gregor had not heard anything of her approach. She cried out "Finally!" to her parents, as she turned the key in the lock.

"What now?" Gregor asked himself and looked around him in the darkness. He soon made the discovery that he could no longer move at all. He was not surprised at that. On the contrary, it struck him as unnatural that up to this point he had really been able up to move around with these thin little legs. Besides he felt relatively content. True, he had pains throughout his entire body, but it seemed to him that they were gradually becoming weaker and weaker and would finally go away completely. The rotten apple in his back and the **inflamed**⑤ surrounding area, entirely covered with white dust, he hardly noticed. He remembered his family with deep feelings of love. In this business, his own thought that he had to disappear was, if possible, even more decisive than his sister's. He remained in this state of empty and peaceful reflection until the tower clock struck three o'clock in the morning. From the window he witnessed the beginning of the general dawning outside. Then without willing it, his head sank all the way down, and from his **nostrils**⑦ flowed out weakly his last breath.

一直到门口，他才把头转了过来，但并不是完全地转过来，因为他觉得自己的脖子变得僵硬了。但至少他仍然可以看见，在他的身后，人们一动也没动，只有妹妹站了起来。他最后迅速看了一眼他的母亲，她睡得很熟。他一爬进自己房间，门就被迅速地关上了，并很快地被闩上，还用东西抵住了。格里高尔被身后突如其来的骚动吓到了，他害怕得把他那小小的四肢蜷缩在身体下面。做出如此迅速动作的是他妹妹。看到格里高尔，她立即就了站起来，等着他爬进去，然后就敏捷地跳了起来。格里高尔甚至都没有听见她靠近的声音。她转动了一下门锁里的钥匙，然后对父母大声说道："终于锁上了！"

"现在该怎么办呢？"格里高尔自言自语着，在黑暗中环顾了一下四周。他很快就发现自己已经动不了了。对此，他并不感到吃惊。相反，让他备受打击且觉得反常的却是自己竟然能够用这些又细又小的脚爬行。除此之外，他还感到一丝满足。的确，他全身都疼，但对于他来说，这种疼痛似乎正变得越来越微弱，最后会完全消失。他几乎没注意到，自己背上腐烂的苹果以及周围红肿发炎的地方，都蒙上了白色的灰尘。他怀着满腔的爱想念着家人，如果可能的话，他真想让自己消失，比他妹妹都想。他一直陷入这种空虚而平静的思绪中，直到塔钟敲响了凌晨三点的钟声。透过窗户，他看到了又一个黎明的到来。然后，在无意识中，他的头无力地垂下了，鼻孔里微弱地呼出了最后一口气。

——选自《变形记》第3部分

注释

★ "卡夫卡的《变形记》把我们带往不熟悉的另一世界，而其实，那另一世界原本属于我们的人性之邦，只是卡夫卡试图用另一套叙述方式与技巧来展示我们人性内部的黑暗王国。因为我们平时不朝它看上一眼，初见之下，才会感到它是如此的陌生、怪异和难以理解。"

——青年作家　郝晓波

① stiff [stɪf] *adj.* 僵硬的

② brush [brʌʃ] *vi.* 掠过

③ commotion [kə'məuʃən] *n.* 骚动

④ nimbly ['nɪmblɪ] *adv.* 敏捷地

⑤ inflamed [ɪn'fleimd] *adj.* 发炎的

⑥ nostril ['nɔstrəl] *n.* 鼻孔

《城堡》出版于1926年，是卡夫卡三部未长篇之一，篇幅最长，也最富有卡夫卡特色，被公认为他最重要的一部作品。目前国内较著名的译本是汤永宽的版本和高年生的版本。

The Castle
城堡

Strictly speaking, one is desperate, and speaking even more strictly, quite happy.

严格来说，我们的处境很绝望，但从更加严格的意义上来说，我们又非常快乐。

——*The Castle*《城堡》

名著导读

It involves a man named K who is commissioned as a 'Land Surveyor' at a Castle who must make his way without friends or allies. As he proceeds, he is thrust into an irrational universe of arbitrary rules and punishments, where there is both a callous indifference to the needs of man and a pious respect of absurdity and authority.

故事讲述的是一个叫K的人被任命为一座城堡的土地测量师，他必须在没有朋友或同盟的帮助下进入城堡。随着他一步步地靠近城堡，他被推进了一个充满专制和惩罚的荒谬世界，在这里，政府对人们的需求漠不关心，而同时人们对谬论和权力却有着一种虔诚的尊重。

名段选读

"...Strictly speaking, one is desperate, and speaking even more strictly, quite happy. Desperate, for the **vulnerability**① with which one sits there waiting for the party's plea, knowing that one must grant it as soon as it is uttered, even if it should, at any rate insofar as one can perceive this oneself, literally tear apart the official system—this vulnerability must surely be the worst thing that can befall one in the course of one's duty. Especially since—leaving everything else aside—especially since the **elevation**② in rank that one has forcefully claimed for oneself just then is beyond all comprehension. Our position is such that we are by no means authorized to grant requests of the kind at issue here, but through the proximity of the nocturnal visiting party our official powers increase, we promise to do things that are outside our own area and will actually fulfill them; at night, like a robber in the woods, the party forces from us sacrifices that we would never have been capable of otherwise—well, anyhow, that's the way it is right now while the party is still here, giving us strength and **coercing**③ us and spurring us on and everything is still half-unconsciously under way, but what will it be like afterward, when this is over, and the party, **replete**[4] and indifferent, leaves us, and we stand here alone, helpless in the face of our abuse of office—it is absolutely unthinkable. And yet we are happy. How suicidal happiness can be! We could naturally make an effort to hide the real situation from the party. After all, he barely notices anything on his own. To his mind, it was probably only for indifferent, accidental reasons—exhaustion, disappointment, inconsiderateness, and indifference—that he had out of exhaustion and disappointment penetrated into a room that was not the one he wanted, and sits there in complete ignorance, preoccupied with thoughts—if preoccupied with anything whatsoever—of his error or of his weariness. Cannot one simply let him be? One cannot. With the **loquaciousness**[5] of the fortunate one must explain everything to him. Without sparing oneself in the least, one must show him exactly what has happened and why it has happened, how extremely rare and singularly great an opportunity this is, one must show the party how, even though he has stumbled into this affair in an utter helplessness that no being other than a party is capable of, he can now, if he wants, Surveyor, take control of the entire situation, and to this end need only somehow present his request, for which the fulfillment is ready and even heading toward him—one must show all this to him; for the official it's the most difficult hour. But, Surveyor, once one has done this, then the most necessary things have been done, and one must simply content oneself and wait."

"……严格来说，我们的处境很绝望，但从更加严格的意义上来说，我们又非常快乐。我们之所以绝望，是因为我们只能无力地坐在这里等待政党提出要求，其他什么也做不了，而且我们都知道，一旦政党提出请求，我们就得答应，即使谁都知道这个请求肯定会把政府体制弄得四分五裂——这绝对是一个人任期内最糟糕的事。其他的先不说，尤其是在一个人对职位晋升的渴望到了不可理喻的地步之后。以我们现在的职位是没有权力答应这样的要求的，但是经过与夜间来访的政党的接触，我们的职权增加了，我们承诺会做职权以外的事情，并且保证完成。在深夜，政党就像绿林劫匪一样逼着我们做出我们从来都不可能做出的牺牲。然而，不管怎样，这就是现在政党在这里给我们施加压力、强迫我们、鞭策我们的方式。所有的事情都还只是在半隐蔽地进行着，然而当一切都结束了之后，又会怎样呢？政党会心满意足地、冷漠地抛弃我们，让我们孤立无援地面对滥用职权的惩罚——这一切真是想都不敢想。然而，我们又是快乐的，这是一种自我毁灭的快乐。我们自然会努力向政党隐瞒真实的情况。毕竟他很少留意自己，在他看来，只有在无关紧要的、偶然的情况下——疲劳、失望、考虑不周和漠不关心——他才会由于过度疲劳和失望走错房间，坐在那里，完全没有意识到自己走错了房间，脑子里装满了(如果他脑子里有东西的话)他犯下的错误和他的疲倦。我们能放任他这样子吗？不能。多嘴的人必须滔滔不绝地向他解释一切。这个人一点也不能偷懒，要仔细地告诉他发生了什么事、为什么会发生以及发生的事是多么罕见又是多么重要的一个机会；这个人还得告诉政党：虽然他是在完全无可奈何的状态下踌躇地参与到这件除了一个政党之外，没有什么人能够控制的事情

里来，但是，如果他愿意的话，测量师，他可以掌控全局并且只需要提出要求就行，因为一旦提出就会有人准备去满足它了，甚至早已经有人帮他办好了——我们必须得把这些都告诉他；对政府官员来说，这是最艰难的时刻。可是，测量员，一旦做了这些事，那么最需要做的事情就完成了，剩下的就只是满足地等待了。”

——选自《城堡》第23章

注释

① vulnerability [ˌvʌlnərəˈbɪlətɪ] *n.* 脆弱，无力

② elevation [ˌelɪˈveiʃən] *n.* 提高，晋级

③ coerce [kəʊˈɜːs] *vt.* 强制，强迫

④ replete [rɪˈpliːt] *adj.* 充分的，充足的

⑤ loquaciousness [ləˈkweɪʃəsnɪs] *n.* 多嘴，喋喋不休

《审判》是卡夫卡最为著名的长篇小说，1925年出版。小说揭示了西方现代国家机器的残酷和腐朽，以及普通人生存之中无处逃避的荒诞与恐惧。目前国内较著名的译本是曹庸的版本和钱满素的版本。

The Trial
审判

It is often better to be in chains than free.

带上镣铐常常比放任自由要好。

——*The Trial*《审判》

名著导读

A terrifying psychological trip into the life of one Joseph K., an ordinary man who wakes up one day to find himself accused of a crime he did not commit, a crime whose nature is never revealed to him. Once arrested, he is released, but must report to court on a regular basis—an event that proves **maddening**① , as nothing is ever resolved. As he grows more uncertain of his fate, his personal life—including work at a bank and his relations with his landlady and a young woman who lives next door—becomes increasingly unpredictable. As K. tries to gain control, he succeeds only in accelerating his own excruciating downward spiral. On the last day of K's thirty-first year, two men arrive to execute him.

故事讲述的是约瑟夫·K惊心动魄的心理经历。他是一个很平凡的人，一天早上醒来发现无辜的自己被控有罪，并且没有任何人向他透露那是一个怎样的罪行。被捕后，他又被释放了，但他必须定期地向法庭报告自己的情况——这让约瑟夫非常恼火，因为事情并未得到解决。他对自己的命运和个人生活——包括他在银行的工作以及与房东太太、住在隔壁的年轻女人的关系——感到越来越不确定了，一切都变得越来越无法预知了。K先生努力去掌控自己的一切，但这却加速了他在痛苦漩涡中的沉沦。在他31岁的最后一天，由两个人来对他实施了死刑。

名段选读

All this talk made K. impatient, rather than convincing him. He felt he could somehow tell from the lawyer's tone of voice what would await him if he were to give way: he would once more be fobbed off with **allusions**[②] to progress made with the submission, to the improved mood of the court officials but also to the great difficulties facing the task—in brief, everything he had already heard ad nauseam would be brought out again to **delude**[③] him with vague hopes and torment him with vague threats. An end had to be put to that, once and for all, so he said, "What do you propose to do in my case, should you continue to represent me?" The lawyer accepted even this insulting question and replied, "To continue with what I have already done for you." "I knew it," said K., "now further discussion is **futile**[④] ." "I will make one more attempt," said the lawyer, as if the things over which K. was getting agitated were not happening to K., but to him. "You see, I suspect that your false assessment of my legal advice, as well as your behaviour in general, are due to the fact that, even though you are a defendant, you have been treated too well, or, to be more precise, treated carelessly, as it would seem. This, too, has its reason; it is often better to be in chains than free. But I would like to show you how other defendants are treated, perhaps you will manage to learn from it. I'm going to call Block now, unlock the door and sit here by the bedside table." "With pleasure," said K., doing as the lawyer asked; he was always ready to learn. However, in order to secure himself against any **eventuality**[⑤] , he asked, "But you have taken note that you are no longer my legal representative?" "Yes," said the lawyer, "but you can still rescind your decision today." He got back into bed, pulled the eiderdown up to his chin, and turned to the wall. Then he rang.

这些话并没有说服K，反而让他更加不耐烦。他觉得自己多少可以从律师的口气中听出，如果他让步的话，等着他的将会是什么：他又会拿一些暗示来搪塞他——比如他的服从让案情有了进展，法官的情绪有所改善，但是这个案件还面临着巨大的困难，简单地说，他又会听到那些已经听到过无数遍的废话，律师会再一次地用模糊的希望来哄骗他，用含糊的威胁来折磨他。这一切必须彻底地结束，所以他说："如果你还想继续做我的律师

的话，下一步你打算怎么做？”虽然这个问题很无礼，但律师还是回答说：“我会继续做我已经为你做过的。”“我知道了，”K说道，“那么现在再讨论下去也没有必要了。”“我会再试一次，”律师说，就好像这件让K烦躁不安的事情，不是发生在K身上而是他自己身上。“事实上，我怀疑导致你对我的法律意见做出错误评价以及做出那些行为的原因是：作为被告，你受到的待遇太好了，或者，更确切地说，他们太放任你了。当然，这是事出有因的。带上镣铐常常比放任自由要好。可是我想让你看看其他被告受的是什么样的待遇，也许你会从中学到一些东西。我现在去叫布洛克，不要关门，就坐在桌子旁边等着。”“没问题，”K说道，他按律师说的做了；他一直很好学。然而，以防万一，他问了一句：“你是否注意到你已经不再是我的律师了？”“是的，”律师说，“但是你今天还有机会改变你的主意。”他回到床上躺下，将鸭绒被一直拉倒下巴那里，翻身对着墙。接着他按响了铃。

——选自《审判》第8章

注释

① maddening ['mædənɪŋ] *adj.* 令人发狂的，使人恼火的

② allusion [ə'lu:ʒən] *n.* 暗示，提及

③ delude [dɪ'lu:d] *vt.* 欺骗，哄骗

④ futile ['fju:tail] *adj.* 无用的，徒劳的

⑤ eventuality [ɪ'ventʃu'ælətɪ] *n.* 不测的事，可能出现的结果

⑥ rescind [rɪ'sɪnd] *vt.* 撤销，取消

9 名震四方的捷克作家——米兰·昆德拉

Milan Kundera (born April 1, 1929) is a writer of Czech origin who has lived in exile in France since 1975, where he became a naturalized citizen in 1981. He is best known for *The Unbearable Lightness of Being*, *The Book of Laughter and Forgetting, and The Joke*. Kundera has written in both Czech and French. He revises the French translations of all his books; these therefore are not considered translations but original works. In 1985, Kundera received the Jerusalem Prize. He has also been mentioned as a contender for the Nobel Prize for literature. In 2000, he was awarded the International Herder Prize. In 2007, he was awarded the Czech State Literature Prize.

米兰·昆德拉（出生于1929年4月1日）是一位捷克作家，自1975年起就流亡于法国，直到1981年才成为一名具有法国国籍的公民。他最为著名的作品是《生命中不能承受之轻》、《笑忘录》和《玩笑》。昆德拉用捷克语和法语两种语言进行创作。他校订了自己所有书的法语译文，因此，这些法译本被人们认为是原著而不是译本。1985年，昆德拉获得了耶路撒冷奖。他还被提名为诺贝尔文学奖的候选人。2000年，昆德拉荣获国际赫尔德奖。2007年，他被授予捷克国家文学奖。

《生命中不能承受之轻》发表于1984年，共7部，是一部哲学小说，同时也是米兰·昆德拉最负盛名的作品。这部作品目前国内有两个翻译版本，1985年版的译者是韩少功，译名是《生命中不能承受之轻》；新版本译者是许钧，译名为《不能承受的生命之轻》。

The Unbearable Lightness of Being
生命中不能承受之轻

We live everything as it comes, without warning, like an actor going on cold. And what can life be worth if the first rehearsal for life is life itself?

我们即将经历的每一件事都没有任何预兆，就像是一个演员不经过热身就开始了表演。而如果生活的第一场排练就是生活本身，那么人生的价值何在呢？

——*The Unbearable Lightness of Being*《生命中不能承受之轻》

名著导读

The Unbearable Lightness of Being follows the interconnected lives of four Czechs. Each struggles with the "lightness" and "heaviness" of life, and each must face the consequences of their chosen approach to dealing with that **dichotomy**① . The story orbits Tomáš, a doctor who masks his **frustrations**② with politics (heaviness) by engaging in sexual affairs (lightness). He is in love with one woman, Tereza, who cannot reconcile Tomáš' womanizing with the fidelity (heaviness) she needs. Tomáš best friend and mistress, Sabrina, attempts to embrace lightness through her self-defined war on **kitsch**③ , but struggles with her **puritanical**④ past. Finally, Sabrina's lover Franz wishes to escape the heaviness of his life of by participating in political protests and casting Sabrina.

《生命中不能承受之轻》讲述了四个捷克人相互联系的生活。他们每个人都在生命的"轻"与"重"之间纠葛，每个人都选择了处理"轻与重"的方式并必须承担这种选择带来的后果。故事围绕着托马斯展开，托马斯是一个医生，他用与人发生性关系(生命之轻)来掩饰自己在政治(生命之重)上的失意。他爱上了一个叫捷列扎的女人，但捷列扎不能容忍托马斯玩弄女人，无视她所需要的忠诚(生命之重)。托马斯的好朋友和情人萨拜娜，则试图通过她所谓的与粗俗艺术作品的"战争"拥抱生命之轻，但同时她也努力与自己禁欲的过去决裂。最后，萨拜娜的情人弗朗茨希望用参加政治抗议和抛弃萨拜娜来摆脱自己的生命之重。

名段选读

Now he was standing at the window trying to call that moment to account. What could it have been if not love declaring itself to him?

But was it love? The feeling of wanting to die beside her was clearly **exaggerated**⑤ : he had seen her only once before in his life! Was it simply the **hysteria**⑥ of a man who, aware deep down of his **inaptitude**⑦ for love, felt the **self-deluding**⑧ need to simulate it? His unconscious was so cowardly that the best partner it could choose for its little comedy was this miserable **provincial**⑨ waitress with practically no chance at all to enter his life!

Looking out over the courtyard at the dirty walls, he realized he had no idea whether it was hysteria or love.

And he was distressed that in a situation where a real man would instantly have known how to act, he was **vacillating**[10] and therefore depriving the most beautiful moments he had ever experienced (kneeling at her bed and thinking he would not survive her death) of their meaning.

He remained annoyed with himself until he realized that not knowing what he wanted was actually quite natural.

We can never know what to want, because, living only one life, we can neither compare it with our previous lives nor perfect it in our lives to come.

Was it better to be with Tereza or to remain alone?

There is no means of testing which decision is better, because there is no basis for comparison. We live everything as it comes, without warning, like an actor going on cold. And what can life be worth if the first **rehearsal**[11] for life is life itself? That is why life is always like a sketch. No, sketch is not quite the word, because a sketch is an outline of something, the groundwork for a picture, whereas the sketch that is our life is a sketch for nothing, an outline with no picture.

此时，他正站在窗前，试着去想明白那一刻。如果那不是爱的表现，又是什么呢？

但那是爱吗？那种想要在她身边死去的感觉显然是有些夸张了：他之前总共也才见过她一次！这难道只是一个男人内心无法控制的情绪冲动吗，只是因为他从心底意识到了自己的爱的拙劣，觉得有必要假装爱上某个人来哄骗一下自己？潜意识里的他是如此懦弱，以至于在这场小小的喜剧中，他能选择的最好搭档就是这个实际上没有任何机会进入他生活的可怜的乡下女服务员！

望着庭院里那堵脏兮兮的墙，他意识到，自己不知道这是冲动还是爱。

他感到很痛苦，因为在这样的情况下，一个真正的男人会立刻知道该怎样做，而他却优柔寡断，因此失去了他曾经历过的最美好的时刻(跪在她的床前，想着她死了，自己也无法独活)的意义。

他一直生着自己的气，直到他发现不知道自己想要什么实际上是非常正常的。

我们永远无法知道自己想要的是什么，因为人只有一次生命，我们既不能把它和我们先前的生活作比较，也不能在我们以后的生活中把它变得更完美。

和捷列扎一起更好，还是保持单身更好？

没有方法能够检验哪个决定更好，因为两者没有比较的基础。我们即将经历的每一件事都没有任何预兆，就像是一个演员不经过热身就开始了表演。而如果生活的第一场排练就是生活本身，那么人生的价值何在呢？这就是为什么生活总是像一幅草图。不，草图这个词并不是十分恰当，因为草图是事物的轮廓，是一幅画的基础，然而，那幅描绘我们生活的草图确实不是任何东西的基础，只有一片空白。

——选自《生命中不能承受之轻》第1部“轻与重”

注释

① dichotomy [daiˈkətəmɪ] *n.* 二分法

② frustration [frʌsˈtreiʃən] *n.* 挫折

③ kitsch [kɪtʃ] *n.* 粗劣作品

④ puritanical [ˌpjuərɪˈtænɪkl] *adj.* 清教徒的，极端拘谨的

⑤ exaggerated [ɪgˈzædʒəreitɪd] *adj.* 夸张的

⑥ hysteria [hɪsˈtɪəriə] *n.* 冲动，歇斯底里

⑦ inaptitude [ɪnˈæplɪtju:d] *n.* 拙劣

⑧ self-deluding [selfˌdɪˈlu:dɪŋ] *adj.* 自我欺骗的

⑨ provincial [prəˈvɪnʃl] *adj.* 都城以外的

⑩ vacillate [ˈvæsəleit] *vi.* 观点摇摆，动摇

⑪ rehearsal [rɪˈhɜ:sl] *n.* 排练

《可笑的爱》发表于1969年，是米兰·昆德拉最负盛名的作品之一，共计7篇短篇故事。这7篇故事各自独立，却又巧妙相连；由极单纯的人物、故事背景组成，串联出7个荒谬、可笑、自作自受的以“爱”为主轴的故事。目前国内比较著名的译本是余中先和郭昌京的合译本。

Laughable Loves
可笑的爱

If I obstinately told the truth to its face, it would mean that I was taking it seriously. And to take seriously something so unserious means to lose all one's own seriousness. I have to lie, if I don't want to take madmen seriously and become a madman myself.

如果我固执地当面说实话，这就意味着我把它当回事了。而把那些毫无严肃性可言的事情看得很严肃就意味着失去一个人自身所有的严肃性。如果我不想把疯子当回事，并且不想把自己也变成疯子的话，我就不得不说谎。

——*Laughable Loves*《可笑的爱》

名著导读

In one of these stories a young man and his girlfriend pretend that she is a stranger he picked up on the road—only to become strangers to each other in reality as their game proceeds. In another a teacher fakes piety in order to seduce a **devout**① girl, then jilts her and yearns for God. In yet another girl waits in bars, on beaches, and on station platforms for the same lover, a middle-aged Don Juan who has gone home to his wife. Games, fantasies, and schemes abound in all the stories while different characters react in varying ways to the sudden release of erotic impulses.

在其中一个故事里，一位年轻男子和他的女朋友假装她是他在旅途中遇到的一个陌生人——随着游戏的展开，不料，在现实生活中他们竟然真的成为了陌生人。另一个故事中，一位老师为了引诱一个虔诚的少女而假装虔诚，后来却抛弃了这位女子转而倾慕上帝。还有另外一个女孩在酒吧里、海滩上和站台上，等待同一个情人——一个中年的大众情人，而他却已经回家找他的妻子去了。所有故事都充满了游戏、幻想和阴谋，然而，在面对情色冲动的突然释放时，不同的人物的反应方式都不尽相同。

名段选读

"That woman, as a matter of fact, brought me some happiness too," said Eduard, lost in thought, and he told his brother that he had fallen in love with Alice, that he had **feigned**[②] a belief in God, that he had had to appear before a committee, that Cechackova had wanted to reeducate him, and that Alice had finally given herself to him, thinking he was a **martyr**[③] . The only thing he didn't tell was that he had forced the directress to recite the Lord's Prayer, because he saw disapproval in his brother's eyes. He stopped talking, and his brother said: "I may have a great many faults, but one I don't have: I've never **dissimulated**[④] , and I've said to everyone's face what I thought."

Eduard loved his brother, and his disapproval hurt, so he made an effort to justify himself, and they began to argue. In the end Eduard said: "I know you are a straightforward man and that you pride yourself on it. But put one question to yourself: Why in fact should one tell the truth? What obliges us to do it? And why do we consider telling the truth to be a virtue? Imagine that you meet a madman, who claims that he is a fish and that we are all fish. Are you going to argue with him? Are you going to undress in front of him and show him that you don't have **fins**[⑤] ? Are you going to say to his face what you think? Well, tell me!"

His brother was silent, and Eduard went on: "If you told him the whole truth and nothing but the truth, only what you really thought, you would enter into a serious conversation with a madman and you yourself would become mad. And it is the same way with the world that surrounds us. If I obstinately told the truth to its face, it would mean that I was taking it seriously. And to take seriously something so unserious means to lose all one's own seriousness. I have to lie, if I don't want to take madmen seriously and become a madman myself."

“事实上，那个女人也给我带来了一些快乐，”陷入深思的爱德华说。他告诉他的兄弟自己爱上了爱丽丝；告诉他自己假装信仰上帝；告诉他自己之前不得不在一个委员

会面前抛头露面，因为查尔科娃希望能够对他进行再教育；告诉他爱丽丝最终还是献身于自己，因为她认为自己是个殉道者。唯一一件他没有说的事就是，他强迫女主管背诵主祷文，因为他从他兄弟的眼神中看出了不满。他闭上了嘴巴，而他的兄弟说："我也许有很多缺点，但有一个我绝对没有：我从来不掩饰，我会当着每个人的面说出我所想的。"

爱德华爱他的兄弟，因此兄弟的反对伤害了他，所以他努力替自己辩护，于是他们开始争论起来。最后，爱德华说："我知道你是一个直率的人，而且为此感到自豪。但是问问你自己：一个人到底为什么要说实话呢？是什么迫使我们这样做？为什么我们认为说实话就是一种美德呢？试想如果你遇到一个疯子，他声称自己是一条鱼，而且说我们都是鱼。你要跟他争辩吗？你要在他面前脱掉衣服来向他证明你没有鳍吗？你要当着他的面说出你的想法吗？那么，告诉我！"

他的兄弟沉默了，爱德华接着说，"如果你告诉他全部的事实，只是事实，只是你真实的想法，那么你就会和一个疯子开始一场严肃的交谈，而你自己就会因此而发疯。对于我们周围的世界来说，也是同样的道理。如果我固执地当面说实话，这就意味着我把它当回事。而把那些毫无严肃性可言的事情看得很严肃就意味着失去一个人自身所有的严肃性。如果我不想把疯子当回事，并且不想把自己也变成疯子的话，我就不得不说谎。"

——选自《可笑的爱》：《爱德华与上帝》

注释

① devout [dɪ'vaut] *adj.* 虔诚的，衷心的

② feign [feɪn] *vt.* 假装，装作

③ martyr ['mɑːtə] *n.* 烈士，殉道者

④ dissimulate [dɪ'sɪmjuleit] *vi.* 掩饰，掩盖

⑤ fin [fɪn] *n.* 鳍

《不朽》出版于1990年，是米兰·昆德拉移居法国后所著的重要小说代表作之一，这也是他的第6部小说。与以往的作品相比，该书的政治意味减少了很多，取而代之的是更多的哲学思考。这部小说是作者最后一部用捷克语写的小说。目前作家出版社宁敏的译本比较流行。

Immortality
不朽

Death and immortality are an indissoluble pair of lovers, and the person whose face merges in our mind with the faces of the dead is already immortal while still alive.

死亡和不朽是一对难舍难分不可分割的情侣，当一个人的脸和死者的脸一起出现在我们脑海中时，尽

管他还活着，却已经是不朽的了。

——*Immortality*《不朽》

名著导读

While waiting for a friend, the image of the author, sees a woman in her sixties turn and wave girlishly to the lifeguard who has just given her a swimming lesson. From that gesture is born a word, Agnes, which in turn engenders a purely mental image of a young woman alone in a half-empty bed, and then of a husband, a daughter, a sister, a mother, and a father (dead five years this very day), whose secretary once used the same gesture made by the woman "actually" seen leaving the pool. It is this gesture, the secretary's, which Agnes will make her own, fashioning her very being, her immortal being as it were, from it until she sees her sister imitating her, taking not just her gesture but (Agnes believes) her very self.

作者的形象在等一位朋友的时候，看到一个60来岁的女人转过身向那个刚刚教过她游泳课的救生员少女般地挥手示意。那个手势让他想到了一个名字爱格妮思，并由此诞生了一个纯粹的年轻女人的形象，她独自躺在一张半空的床上，然后是丈夫、女儿、姐姐、母亲，和父亲(五年前去世了)的形象。父亲的秘书曾经做出与那位60岁的女人离开泳池时用过的同样的手势。正是秘书的这个手势，让爱格妮思成为了她自己，造就了自己不朽的生命，直到她看见妹妹在模仿她，不只是模仿她的手势，而且(爱格妮思认为)还模仿了爱格妮思自己。

名段选读

Naturally, when it comes to immortality people are not equal. We have to distinguish between so-called minor immortality, the memory of a person in the minds of those who knew him (the kind of immortality the village mayor longed for), and great immortality, which means the memory of a person in the minds of people who never knew him personally. There are certain paths in life that from the very beginning place a person face to face with such great immortality, uncertain, it is true, even improbable, yet undeniably possible: they are the paths of artists and statesmen.

Of all the European statesmen of our time, the one who has most occupied himself with the thought of immortality has probably been **Francois Mitterrand**[①]. I remember the unforgettable ceremony that followed his election as President in 1981. The square in front of the Pantheon was filled with an enthusiastic crowd, and he was **withdrawing**[②] from it: he was walking alone up the broad stairway (exactly as Shakespeare walked to the Temple of Fame on the curtain described

by Goethe), holding the stems of three roses. Then he disappeared from the people's sight and remained alone among the tombs of sixty-four illustrious corpses , followed in his thoughtful **solitude**④ only by the eyes of the camera, the film crew, and several million Frenchmen, watching their television screens from which thundered Beethoven's Ninth. He placed the roses one by one on three chosen tombs. He was like a surveyor planting the three roses like three markers into the immense building site of eternity, to stake out a triangle in the center of which was to be erected the palace of his immortality.

Valery Giscard d'Estaing, who was President before him, invited a **sanitation**⑤ worker to breakfast in the Elysee Palace. That was the gesture of a **sentimental**⑥ bourgeois who longed for the love of common people and wanted them to believe that he was one of them. Mitterrand was not so naive as to want to resemble sanitation workers (no president can fulfill such a dream!); he wanted to resemble the dead, which was much wiser, for death and immortality are an **indissoluble**⑦ pair of lovers, and the person whose face merges in our mind with the faces of the dead is already immortal while still alive.

自然，在不朽面前，人们并不是平等的。我们必须要把所谓的次要不朽和伟大的不朽区别开来，次要不朽就是相识的人在脑海中对某个人的记忆(这种不朽是村长们渴望的)，伟大的不朽则是那些素不相识的人在脑海中对某个人的记忆。在生活中，确实存在某些道路，在你踏上它的那一刻就会面对这种伟大的不朽，虽然不确定，但却是真实的，纵使看起来是不会发生的，但又不可否认存在这种可能性：那些就是艺术家和政治家所走的道路。

在我们这个时代的所有欧洲政治家中，脑海中充满了最多不朽思想的人可能就是弗朗索瓦·密特朗。我还记得1981年他当选总统后的那次难忘的典礼。先贤祠前的广场上满是热情的人群，他却从中抽身离开：手握着三只玫瑰，独自走在宽阔的阶梯上（就像歌德描述的莎士比亚走向名人堂那样）。然后他从人们的视线中消失了，在64个著名人物的坟墓中间独自一人伫立着，孤独地沉思，跟随他的只有摄像机镜头、影片摄制组和几百万双在贝多芬第九交响曲中看着电视屏幕的法国人的眼睛。他把玫瑰依次放在三个挑选出来的墓碑上。他像一名测量员一样种下三株玫瑰，就好像在巨大的不朽建筑中做了三个标志，立桩标出一个三角形，这个三角形的中心，将会竖立起他不朽的宫殿。

瓦莱里·吉斯卡尔·德斯坦——弗朗索瓦·密特朗的前任——邀请了一位环卫工人在爱丽舍宫共进早餐。这个姿态表明，一个感伤的资本家渴望得到普通人的爱戴，而且想让他们知道自己也是他们中的一员。密特朗没有如此天真地想要模仿环卫工人(没有哪个总统能实现这样的梦想！)；他想要模仿死者，这种做法更加明智，因为死亡和不朽是一对不可分割的情侣，当一个人的脸和死者的脸一起出现在我们脑海中时， 尽管他还活着，却已经是不朽的了。

——选自《不朽》第2部第2章

注释

① Francois Mitterrand，弗朗索瓦·密特朗(1916年10月26日—1996年1月8日)法国政治家，法国第21任总统。

② withdraw [wɪð'drː] *vi.* 撤退

③ corpse [kɔːps] *n.* 尸体

④ solitude [ˌsælɪtjuːd] *n.* 孤独

⑤ sanitation [ˌsænɪ'teiʃən] *n.* 公共卫生

⑥ sentimental [ˌsentɪ'mentl] *adj.* 感情脆弱的，伤感的

⑦ indissoluble [ˌɪndɪ'sɔljəbl] *adj.* 稳定持久的，牢不可破的

10 欧洲近代现实主义戏剧的杰出代表——亨利克·易卜生

Henrik Ibsen (March 20, 1828—May 23, 1906) was a major 19th-century Norwegian playwright, theatre director, and poet. He is often referred to as "the father" of modern theater and is one of the founders of Modernism in the theatre. Ibsen is often ranked as one of the truly great playwrights in the European tradition. Many consider him the greatest playwright since Shakespeare. The productive life of Ibsen is conveniently divided into three periods: the first ending in 1877 with the successful appearance of *The Pillars of Society*; the second covering the years in which he wrote most of the dramas of protest against social conditions, such as *Ghosts*; and the third marked by the symbolic plays, *The Master Builder and When We Dead Awaken*. The three historical plays, or dramatic poems, *Brand, Emperor and Galilean*, and Peer Gynt, written between 1866 and 1873, form a monumental epic.

亨利克·易卜生(1828年3月20日—1906年5月23日)是19世纪文坛举足轻重的挪威剧作家、戏剧导演和诗人。他常被称作是“现代剧院之父”和剧院现代主义的创始人之一。易卜生是欧洲历史上真正伟大的剧作家之一。很多人认为他是继自莎士比亚之后最伟大的剧作家。易卜生的创作生涯可以被划分为三个阶段：第一个阶段随着《社会支柱》这部作品的成功问世结束于1877年；第二个阶段中，他写了许多的抗议社会现状的戏剧，例如《群鬼》；第三个阶段则是以象征性的戏剧为代表的，例如《建筑大师》和《我们死人再生时》。创作完成于1866年到1873年间的三部历史剧(或称为戏剧诗歌)《布朗德》、《皇帝与加利利人》和《培尔·金特》组成了一部不朽的史诗。

《玩偶之家》共3幕，发表于1879年，形象生动地批判了资产阶级的市侩气和虚伪，揭露了男权社会对妇女的压迫,曾被比作“妇女解放运动的宣言书”。潘家洵的译本比较好。

A Doll's House
玩偶之家

I believe that before all else I am a reasonable human being, just as you are—or, at all events, that I must try and become one.

我认为我首先是个理性的人，就像你一样——或者，我无论如何也要试着成为那样的人。

——*A Doll's House*《玩偶之家》

名著导读

It is Nora's wish to maintain her happy household; its only shadow being the payment of her debt to Krogstad. When Krogstad, driven by the fear of losing his position (and therefore, any chance at respectability) at the bank, ups the ante and threatens to **blackmail**[①] Nora with exposure of the bond she forged, she frantically tries to satisfy his demand that she use her influence with her husband Torvald Helmer (the new bank manager) to keep his job. As Nora is unable to comply, Krogstad exposes her past actions to Torvald, who turns on Nora. Nora, expecting her husband to stand by her, is hurt and angered by his reaction. Once Krogstad, redeemed by the love of Mrs. Linde, returns the bond to Torvald, he forgives Nora and prepares to resume their marriage. In Nora's eyes, the marriage is irretrievably damaged, and she leaves.

诺拉的愿望是维持她幸福的家庭，而笼罩家庭的唯一阴影就是她要还债给柯洛克斯泰。柯洛克斯泰害怕会失去在银行的工作(和任何成为体面人的机会)，所以变本加厉，勒索诺拉，如果她不答应，就揭发她伪造票据的事情。诺拉疯狂地努力满足他的要求，她利用自己对丈夫托伐・赫尔默(新的银行经理)的影响来保住柯洛克斯泰的工作。后来因为诺拉没有遵从柯洛克斯泰的要求，所以他向托伐告发了她过去的行为，知道了那些事情之后托伐对诺拉很不满。诺拉本希望丈夫能够站在她这边，然而托伐的反应让诺拉感到心痛和愤怒。柯洛克斯泰被林德夫人的爱感动和救赎，把字据退还给了托伐，托伐原谅了诺拉并准备挽回他们的婚姻。然而在诺拉看来，这段婚姻已经破灭了，无法挽回，所以她离开了。

名段选读

Nora: I am going away from here now, at once. I am sure Christine will take me in for the night—

Helmer: You are out of your mind! I won't allow it! I forbid you!

Nora: It is no use forbidding me anything any longer. I will take with me what belongs to myself. I will take nothing from you, either now or later.

Helmer: What sort of madness is this!

Nora: Tomorrow I shall go home—I mean to my old home. It will be easiest for me to find something to do there.

Helmer: You blind, foolish woman!

Nora: I must try and get some sense, Torvald.

Helmer: To **desert**② your home, your husband and your children! And you don't consider what people will say!

Nora: I cannot consider that at all. I only know that it is necessary for me.

Helmer: It's **shocking**③. This is how you would neglect your most **sacred**④ duties.

Nora: What do you consider my most sacred duties?

Helmer: Do I need to tell you that? Are they not your duties to your husband and your children?

Nora: I have other duties just as sacred.

Helmer: That you have not. What duties could those be?

Nora: Duties to myself.

Helmer: Before all else, you are a wife and mother.

Nora: I don't believe that any longer. I believe that before all else I am a reasonable human being, just as you are—or, at all events, that I must try and become one. I know quite well, Torvald, that most people would think you right, and that views of that kind are to be found in books; but I can no longer content myself with what most people say, or with what is found in books. I must think over things for myself and get to understand them.

Helmer: Can you not understand your place in your own home? Have you not a **reliable**⑤ guide in such matters as that?—have you no religion?

Nora: I am afraid, Torvald, I do not exactly know what religion is.

Helmer: What are you saying?

Nora: I know nothing but what the **clergyman**⑥ said when I went to be confirmed. He told us that religion was this, and that, and the other. When I am away from all this, and am alone, I will look into that matter too. I will see if what the clergyman said is true, or at all events if it is true for me.

诺拉：我要离开这里，马上！我相信克里斯汀今晚会收留我的——

赫尔默：你疯了吗！我不允许你这样做！我禁止你这样做！

诺拉：禁止我做任何事情都没有用了。我将带走属于我的东西。我不会带走任何一样你的东西，不管是现在还是以后。

赫尔默：多么愚蠢的行为啊！

诺拉：明天我就会回家——我指的是我娘家。我在那里很容易找到事做。

赫尔默： 你这个失去了理智，愚蠢的女人！

诺拉： 我必须试一试，找到一些生活的意义，托伐。

赫尔默： 通过抛弃你的家、你的丈夫和孩子！而且你也不想想人家会怎么说！

诺拉： 我顾不得那些了。我只知道这是我必须做的。

赫尔默： 真是太耸人听闻了。你这么做是无视你最神圣的职责。

诺拉： 你认为我最神圣的职责是什么？

赫尔默： 这还用我说吗？难道不是你该对你的丈夫和孩子负责吗？

诺拉： 我还有其他同样神圣的职责。

赫尔默： 你没有。你还有能什么神圣的职责？

诺拉： 我对自己的责任。

赫尔默： 你首先是一个妻子和一个母亲，这是最重要的。

诺拉： 我已经不那么认为了。我认为我首先是个理性的人，就像你一样——或者，我无论如何也要试着成为那样的人。托伐，我很明白，大多数人都会认为你是正确的，你那样的观点在书里随处可见；但是我已经不能再为大多数人的想法或书中的观点而生活了。我必须思考一些我自己的事情，我想了解我自己。

赫尔默： 你难道不知道自己在家里的位置吗？你难道没有一个可靠的指引者引导你了解自己吗？——你难道没有宗教信仰吗？

诺拉： 恐怕，托伐，我根本不能确切地了解宗教信仰是什么。

赫尔默： 你在说什么？

诺拉： 当我行坚信礼时，除了牧师说的话，我什么也不知道。他告诉我们，宗教是这样，是那样。当我逃离这所有的一切，当我独自一人的时候，我也会想想这个问题的。我会看看那个牧师说的是不是真的，或者是不管怎样，它对我来说是不是真的。

——选自《玩偶之家》第3幕

注释

① blackmail ['blækmeil] *vt.* 勒索，敲诈

② desert [dɪ'zɜːt] *vt.* 遗弃

③ shocking ['ʃɔkɪŋ] *adj.* 使人震惊的

④ sacred ['seɪkrɪd] *adj.* 神圣的

⑤ reliable [rɪ'laɪəbl] *adj.* 可靠的

⑥ clergyman ['klɜːdʒɪmən] *n.* 牧师，教士

《培尔·金特》共5幕，发表于1867年，是易卜生剧作中最具文化内涵和哲学底蕴的一部。该剧反映的虽然是严肃的人生主题，但具有鲜明的讽刺喜剧特点及舞台闹剧因素，是国际戏剧舞台常演不衰的经典之作。国内比较著名的译本是夏平、萧乾的合译版本。

Peer Gynt
培尔·金特

Many a time has luck seemed dropping, and sprung up as high as ever!

很多次，当运气看起来要消失的时候，却又像往常一样迅速出现了！

——*Peer Gynt*《培尔·金特》

名著导读

Peer Gynt is the son of the once rich and highly regarded Jon Gynt. Peer wants to restore what his father had wrecked, but gets lost in boasting and day-dreams. He is involved in a fight and carries off the bride, Ingrid, on her wedding-day. He is outlaned and has to flee from the parish[①]. Solveig, whom Peer met at the wedding, and fell in love with, comes to his cabin in the forest to live with him, but he leaves her and goes on his travels. He is away for many years, takes part in various occupations and plays various roles. Then finally Peer, in ever greater despair, reaches Solveig, who has been waiting for him in the cabin ever since he left. She tells him that he has always been himself in her belief, hope and love.

培尔·金特是曾经十分富有且受人尊重的乔恩·金特的儿子。培尔想重整被他父亲败掉的家业和声誉，但是却在吹嘘和白日梦中惶惶度日。他卷入了一场争斗，从婚宴上抢走了新娘英格丽特。他脱离了正常的生活轨道，被追捕，不得不逃离了教区。培尔在英格丽特的婚礼上认识了索尔维格，并爱上了她。索尔维格来到培尔森林中的小屋，和他住在一起，但是他离开了她，继续浪迹天涯。他离开了很多年，从事各种行业，扮演各种角色。最终，培尔极度绝望地回到了索尔维格身边。自从他离开那天起，索尔维格就一直在小屋里等他回来。她告诉培尔，在她的信仰、希望和爱里，他始终是他。

名段选读

Peer: Come now, stop this old-wife's talk! Many a time has luck seemed dropping, and sprung up as high as ever!

Ase: Salt-strewn is the soil it grew from. Lord, but you're a rare one, you,—just as pert[②] and jaunty[③] still, just as bold as when the pastor, newly come from Copenhagen, bade you tell your Christian name, and declared that such a headpiece many a prince down there might envy; till the cob[④] your father gave him, with a sledge[⑤] to boot, in thanks for his pleasant, friendly talk.—Ah, but things went bravely then! Provost, captain, all the rest, dropped in daily, ate and drank, swilling, till they well-nigh burst. But 'tis need that tests one's neighbour. Still it grew and empty here from the day that "Gold-bag Jon" started with his pack, a **pedlar**[⑥] . *(Dries her eyes with her apron.)* Ah, you're big and strong enough, you should be a staff and pillar for your mother's frail old age, —you should keep the farm-work going, guard the **remnants**[⑦] of your gear; —*(Crying again.)* oh, God help me, small's the profit you have been to me, you **scamp**[⑧] ! Lounging by the hearth at home, grubbing in the charcoal embers; or, round all the country, frightening girls away from merry-makings—shaming me in all directions, fighting with the worst **rapscallions**[⑨] .

Peer: *(turning away from her)*. Let me be.

Ase: *(following him)*. Can you deny that you were the foremost **brawler**[⑩] in the mighty battle royal fought the other day at Lunde, when you raged like **mongrels**[⑪] mad? Who was it but you that broke Blacksmith Aslak's arm for him,—or at any rate that **wrenched**[⑫] one of his fingers out of joint?

Peer: Who has filled you with such prate?

Ase: *(hotly)*. Cottar Kari heard the yells!

培尔：拜托，别婆婆妈妈的了！很多次，当运气看起来要消失的时候，却又像往常一样迅速出现了！

艾斯：它可是要从撒了盐的土壤里生长出来啊。上帝啊，你这种人真是少见，你，——你还是那么鲁莽，那么快活，还记得那时候，从哥本哈根新来的牧师命令你说出你的教名，并宣称连那里的王子都会嫉妒这样的名字；直到你父亲为了感谢他愉快且友好的话语，送给了他一雪橇的玉米棒子。——哈，但从那时起，事情就变得棒透了！教务长、上校和所有其他的人，每天都来吃喝、痛饮，直到他们再也吃不进了为止。但是"日久见人心"啊。事情一直在这样继续，从"金袋乔恩"背着背包开始做小贩的那天开始，这里就空空如也了。(用围裙擦擦她的眼睛。)哈，你已经够高够壮了，你应该为你年迈的母亲干点活并且成为她的支柱了，你应该让农场继续经营下去，守住你仅有的家用(又开始哭。)噢，上帝帮帮我吧，你给带来我的好处太少了，你这淘气鬼！就知道在家里的灶台边闲逛，在木炭的余烬里翻掘；或者，在村子里走动，吓走那些正在欢庆的女孩子们——你想方设法让我感到羞愧，还跟最可恶的流氓打架。

培尔：(转过脸去不再看她)。你就让我这么过吧。

艾斯：(跟着他)。你能否认那天在伦德发生的激烈的混战中，你是最主要的参与者吗，你当时愤怒得像个疯狗？是不是你打断了铁匠阿斯拉克的胳膊，或者至少让他的一根手指脱臼了？

培尔：谁告诉你这些事情的？

艾斯：(激动愤怒地)。佃农卡利听到了叫喊声！

——选自《培尔·金特》第1幕第1场

注释

① parish [ˈpærɪʃ] *n.* 教区
② pert [pɜːt] *adj.* 无礼的，冒失的
③ jaunty [ˈdʒɔːntɪ] *adj.* 无忧无虑的
④ cob [kɔb] *n.* 玉米棒子
⑤ sledge [sledʒ] *n.* 雪橇
⑥ pedlar [ˈpedlə(r)] *n.* 小贩
⑦ remnant [ˈremnənt] *n.* 残余部分
⑧ scamp [skæmp] *n.* 淘气鬼，捣乱鬼
⑨ rapscallion [ræpˈskælɪən] *n.* 流氓，恶棍
⑩ brawler [ˈbrɔːlə] *n.* 争吵者，打架者
⑪ mongrel [ˈmʌŋgrəl] *n.* 混血儿；杂种，杂种动物
⑫ wrench [rentʃ] *vt.* 扭伤；折磨

《人民公敌》共5幕，发表于1882年，《人民公敌》以作为一本最早以开放式结局完结的小说而闻名。故事是关于一个勇敢的人在一个不容异见的社会中，依然为追求公义和真相而斗争。国内比较著名的译本是陶履恭的版本和潘家洵的版本。

An Enemy of the People
人民公敌

The majority has might on its side—unfortunately; but right it has not.

大多数人握有权力和力量；但不幸的是他们并没有掌握真理。

——*An Enemy of the People*《人民公敌》

名著导读

Dr. Thomas Stockmann is a popular citizen of a small coastal town in Norway. The town has recently invested a large amount of public and private money towards the development of baths, a project led by Dr. Stockmann and his brother, Peter Stockmann, the Mayor. However, just as the baths are proving successful, Dr. Stockmann discovers that waste products from the town's **tannery**① are **contaminating**② the waters, causing serious illness amongst the tourists. He expects this important discovery to be his greatest achievement, and promptly sends a detailed report to the Mayor, which includes a proposed solution which would come at a considerable cost to the town. To his surprise, Dr. Stockmann finds it difficult to get through to the authorities. The townspeople —eagerly anticipating the prosperity that the baths will bring—refuse to accept Dr. Stockmann's claims, and his friends and allies, who had explicitly given support for his campaign, turn against him en masse. He is taunted and denounced as a lunatic, an "Enemy of the People."

托马斯·斯多克芒是挪威一个沿海小镇上很受欢迎的医生。这个镇最近投资了一大笔公共和私人的资金来发展温泉汤浴，这是由斯多克芒医生和他担任市长的哥哥发起的一个项目。然而，就在这个温泉汤浴项目要成功的时候，斯多克芒医生却发现，镇上一家皮革厂的废弃物正在污染温泉水，致使游客患上了很严重的疾病。他认为这个重大发现会是他最大的成就，所以立即写了一份详细的报告给市长，并附上一份解决方案的建议书，但这个方案会令小镇付出相当大的代价。让他感到惊讶的是，让政府通过这个方案似乎很难。镇上的人们——都热切地期盼着温泉所能带来的经济效益——拒绝接受斯多克芒医生的建议，而那些以前明确支持他的朋友和同盟也全体反对他。他被人指责，并被称作是一个疯子，一个“人民公敌”。

名段选读

Dr. Stockmann: You may depend upon it—I shall name them! That is precisely the great discovery I made yesterday. *(Raises his voice.)* The most dangerous enemy of truth and freedom amongst us is the **compact**[3] majority—yes, the damned compact Liberal majority—that is it! Now you know! *(Tremendous* ***uproar***[4] *. Most of the crowd are shouting, stamping and* ***hissing***[5] *. Some of the older men among them exchange stolen glances and seem to be enjoying themselves. Mrs. Stockmann gets up, looking anxious. Ejlif and Morten advance threateningly upon some schoolboys who are playing* ***pranks***[6] *. Aslaksen rings his bell and begs for silence. Hovstad and Billing both talk at once, but are* ***inaudible***[7] *. At last quiet is restored.)*

Aslaksen: As Chairman, I call upon the speaker to withdraw the illconsidered expressions he has just used.

Dr. Stockmann: Never, Mr. Aslaksen! It is the majority in our community that denies me my freedom and seeks to prevent my speaking the truth.

Hovstad: The majority always has right on its side.

Billing: And truth too, by God!

Dr. Stockmann: The majority never has right on its side. Never, I say! That is one of these social lies against which an independent, intelligent men must wage war. Who is it that constitute the majority of the population in a country? Is it the clever folk, or the stupid? I don't imagine you will dispute the fact that at present the stupid people are in an absolutely overwhelming majority

all the world over. But, good Lord! —you can never pretend that it is right that the stupid folk should govern the clever ones I *(Uproar and cries.)* Oh, yes—you can shout me down, I know! But you cannot answer me. The majority has might on its side—unfortunately; but right it has not. I am in the right—I and a few other scattered individuals. The minority is always in the right. *(Renewed uproar.)*

斯多克芒医生：你们可能会指望它——但我要把它们(这些问题)提出来！！这确实是我昨天的重大发现。(提高了音量。)在我们之中，真理和自由最危险的敌人就是那些联合在一起的多数人——是的，那该死的自由主义群众——就是这回事！现在你们知道了！(强烈的骚动。人群中大多数人都在叫喊、跺脚并发出嘘声。一些老人偷偷交换着眼色，似乎兴致勃勃，陶醉其中。斯多克芒太太起床了，看起来很焦急。艾杰利夫和莫滕警告那些恶作剧的男孩子。阿斯拉克森摇响了铃，请求大家安静。霍夫斯泰德和比尔林立即开始讲话，但却听不见。最后，人群恢复了平静。)

阿斯拉克森：作为主席，我要求发言者收回他刚刚使用的不当言辞。

斯多克芒医生：阿斯拉克森先生，我决不会这样做！就是我们社会中的大多数人否定了我的自由，并试图阻止我说真话。

霍夫斯泰德：正义总是站在大多数人这一边的。

比尔林：真理也是一样，这是神授予的！

斯多克芒医生：真理从没有站在大多数人那一边。我说的是从来没有！那只是社会的一个谎言，一个独立的、睿智的人必须与这些谎言进行斗争。是哪种人组成了一个国家的大部分人口？是聪明的人还是愚蠢的人？我想你们会同意这个事实，那就是，现在全世界愚蠢的人占了绝大多数。但是，善良的主啊！你绝不能假装承认，让愚蠢的人来统治聪明的人是正确的(骚动和叫喊。)哦，是的，你们可以把我赶下来，我知道！但是你们却不能回答我的问题。大多数人握有权力和力量；但不幸的是他们并没有掌握真理。我和其他一些散布各地的个体一起，我们一起握有真理。真理总是掌握在少数人手中。(又一阵此起彼伏的骚动。)

注释

① tannery ['tænərɪ] *n.* 制革厂，硝皮厂

② contaminate [kən'tæmɪneit] *vt.* 污染，弄脏

③ compact [kəm'pækt] *adj.* 紧凑的，体积小的

④ uproar ['ʌprɔ:] *n.* 喧嚣，骚动

⑤ hiss [hɪs] *vi.* 发出嘶嘶声

⑥ prank [præŋk] *n.* 胡闹

⑦ inaudible [ɪn'ɔ:dəbl] *adj.* 听不见的

Chapter 5

其他名家名著榜

1 西班牙文学世界里最伟大的作家——塞万提斯

Miguel de Cervantes Saavedra (September 29, 1547—April 23, 1616) was a Spanish novelist, poet, and playwright. His magnum opus *Don Quixote*, often considered the first modern novel, is a classic of Western literature, and is regarded amongst the best works of fiction ever written. His work is often considered amongst the most important works in all of Western literature. His influence on the Spanish language has been so great that Spanish is often called "The language of Cervantes" (la lengua de Cervantes). He has been dubbed "The Prince of Wits" (El Príncipe de los Ingenios).

米格尔·德·塞万提斯·萨维德拉（1547年9月29日—1616年4月23日）是西班牙著名的小说家、诗人和剧作家。他的代表作《堂·吉诃德》被认为是第一部现代小说，是西方文学的经典之作，而且还被看作是所有小说中的典范。他的作品在整个西方文学中占有举足轻重的地位。他对西班牙语的发展影响巨大，以至于西班牙语常被称作“塞万提斯的语言”。而他本人则被称作“智慧之子”。

1605年《堂·吉诃德》*的第1部分出版，随即受到了公众的盛赞。1608年《堂·吉诃德》首次被翻译成英语，并于1612年出版。之后不久该书又被译成欧洲的其他语言，流传各地，被认为是全世界翻译版本最多的文学作品之一。本书分为上下2卷，上卷共52章，下卷共74章。目前，这部巨作国内最常见的翻译版本是北京燕山出版社刘京胜的译本和上海译文出版社张广森的译本。

Don Quixote
堂·吉诃德

To retire is not to flee, and there is no wisdom in waiting when danger outweighs hope, and it is the part of wise men to preserve themselves today for tomorrow, and not risk all in one day.

撤退并不意味着逃跑，当失败的可能大于胜利的可能时，在此等待并不是明智的做法，而且一个明智的人应该知道给自己留条后路而不是孤注一掷。

——*Don Quixote*《堂·吉诃德》

名著导读

Don Quixote is a middle-aged gentleman from the region of La Mancha in central Spain. Obsessed with the chivalrous ideals touted in books he has read, he decides to take up his lance and sword to defend the helpless and destroy the wicked. Together with his companion Sancho Panza, the self-styled Don Quixote sets out in search of adventures. In the end, the beaten and battered Don Quixote forswears all the chivalric truths he followed so fervently and dies from a fever.

堂·吉诃德是一位来自西班牙中部拉曼查地区的中年绅士。因痴迷于他曾读过的一本书中所推崇的骑士精神，他决定拿起手上的武器保护弱小，打击恶势力。于是，他自称是堂·吉诃德，与仆人桑科·潘萨一起开始了一场冒险之旅。最后，屡遭挫败、饱受折磨的堂·吉诃德发誓放弃自己一直以来所热切追寻的骑士精神，并最终死于发烧。

名段选读

"Thou art a coward by nature, Sancho," said Don Quixote, "but lest thou shouldst say I am obstinate, and that I never do as thou dost advise, this once I will take thy advice, and withdraw out of reach of that fury thou so dreadest; but it must be on one condition, that never, in life or in death, thou art to say to anyone that I retired or withdrew from this danger out of fear, but only in compliance with thy **entreaties**[①]; for if thou sayest otherwise thou wilt lie therein, and from this time to that, and from that to this, I give thee lie, and say thou liest and wilt lie every time thou thinkest or sayest it; and answer me not again; for at the mere thought that I am withdrawing or retiring from any danger, above all from this, which does seem to carry some little shadow of fear with it, I am ready to take my stand here and await alone, not only that Holy Brotherhood you talk of and dread, but the brothers of the twelve tribes of Israel, and the Seven Maccabees, and Castor and Pollux, and all the brothers and brotherhoods in the world."

"Senor," replied Sancho, "to retire is not to flee, and there is no wisdom in waiting when danger outweighs hope, and it is the part of wise men to preserve themselves today for tomorrow, and not risk all in one day; and let me tell you, though I am a clown and a **boor**[②], I have got some notion of what they call safe conduct; so repent not of having taken my advice, but mount Rocinante if you can, and if not I will help you; and follow me, for my mother-wit tells me we have more need of legs than hands just now."

“桑科，你天性懦弱，”堂·吉诃德说，“这次我听取你的建议，不去那令你如此惧怕的地方，免得你又说我固执己见，从不听你的意见；但是有一个条件，那就是不论我是死是活，当你与他人谈及此事时，永远不要说我因为害怕而在危机关头退缩或者撤退，而这只是因为你恳求我我才这样做的；除此以外的原因都是谎话，不管你什么时候那样说，我都会说你在撒谎，每当你有这种想法或者已经告诉别人的时候，我都不会承认；因为只要说到我在面对危险的时候离开，或者退缩，不管是怎么个说法吧，听起来都像含有害怕的意思，我是准备坚持我的立场留在这儿一个人等的，我不但要等你刚刚提到的令你害怕的至圣兄弟帮，还要等以色列十二部落的兄弟帮，还有马加比七兄弟帮，卡斯托尔和波卢克斯兄弟帮，以及全世界的兄弟帮派。

“主人，”桑科说，“撤退并不意味着逃跑，当失败的可能大于胜利的可能时，在此等待并不是明智的做法，而且一个明智的人应该知道给自己留条后路而不是孤注一掷；让我告诉你吧，我虽是一个粗人，但我知道什么叫稳妥；如果不听我的意见你会后悔的，如果你同意的话，就爬到罗西南地山上去，如果不同意，我就把你扛上去；听我的，我的直觉告诉我，我们现在并不怎么需要用手，而是需要用脚。

——选自《堂·吉诃德》上卷第23章

注释

★“在欧洲所有著名文学作品中，把严肃和滑稽、悲剧性和喜剧性、生活中的琐屑和庸俗与伟大和美丽如此水乳交融……这样的范例仅见于塞万提斯的《堂·吉诃德》。”

——俄国文学评论家　别林斯基

① entreaty [ɪn'triːtɪ] *n.* 恳求

② boor [buə(r)] *n.* 农民，粗野的人

2 现代意大利语的奠基者——阿利盖利·但丁

Dante Alighieri (May/June c.1265—September 14, 1321), commonly known as Dante, was an Italian poet of the Middle Ages. His *Divine Comedy*, originally called *Commedia* by the author and later nicknamed *Divina by* Boccaccio, is often considered the greatest literary work composed in the Italian language and a masterpiece of world literature. In Italy he is known as "the Supreme Poet". Dante, Petrarch, and Boccaccio are also known as "the three fountains" or "the three crowns". Dante is also called the "Father of the Italian language".

阿利盖利·但丁（大约1265年5月/6月—1321年9月14日），通常被人们称作但丁，是一位中世纪时期的意大利诗人。他的作品《神曲》原来被作者命名为《喜剧》，后来薄伽丘在原书名前加上了"神圣的"。《神曲》通常被认为是用意大利语写的最伟大的文学作品，是世界文坛的巨著。在意大利但丁被人们称为"至尊诗人"。但丁、彼特拉克、薄伽丘被称为"文坛三杰"，或"文坛三颗巨星"。但丁还被人称之为"意大利语之父"。

《神曲》写于1307年至1321年，全诗共分3部，《地狱》、《炼狱》、《天堂》各有33歌，加上长诗的序曲，共100歌，计14233行。在诗中，但丁坚决反对中世纪的蒙昧主义，表达了执著追求真理的思想，对欧洲后世的诗歌创作有着极其深远的影响。这部巨作目前国内最常见的版本是外语教学与研究出版社出版的黄国彬的译本。

Divine Comedy
神曲

Expect no more word or sign from me;
Free and upright and sound is thy free-will,
And error were it not to do its bidding;

Thee o'er thyself I therefore crown and mitre!"
不要期待再我说一个字或做一个手势；
你的意志是自由、正直而健全的
不按照它的命令行事你就会犯错；
我给你戴上了王冠，你是自己的国王！

——*Divine Comedy*《神曲》

名著导读

Divine Comedy is widely considered the preeminent work of Italian literature, and is seen as one of the greatest works of world literature. The poem's imaginative and allegorical vision of the afterlife is a culmination of the medieval world-view as it had developed in the Western Church. It is divided into three parts, the *Inferno, Purgatorio,* and *Paradiso*. On the surface the poem describes Dante's travels through Hell, Purgatory, and Heaven; but at a deeper level it represents allegorically the soul's journey towards God. At this deeper level, Dante draws on medieval Christian theology and philosophy, especially the writings of Thomas Aquinas.

人们普遍认为《神曲》是意大利文学领域的杰出著作，也是世界文学最伟大的作品之一。这部诗歌对于人死后生活的充满想象力且极具寓意的描述将中世纪世界观表达得淋漓尽致，因为中世纪的世界观正是在罗马教会中形成的。这部诗歌分为3部分：《地狱》、《炼狱》和《天堂》。表面上看，这部诗歌描述了但丁在地狱、炼狱和天堂的经历；但是从深层次上来看，它隐喻地描绘了人死后的灵魂朝上帝方向的旅途。在这一深入层次上，但丁引用了中世纪基督教神学和哲学理论，尤其是托马斯•阿奎那的著作。

名段选读

"That apple sweet, which through so many branches
The care of mortals goeth in pursuit of,
Today shall put in peace thy hungerings."
Speaking to me, Virgilius of such words
As these made use; and never were there **guerdons**①
That could in pleasantness compare with these.
Such longing upon longing came upon me
To be above, that at each step thereafter
For flight I felt in me the **pinions**② growing.
When underneath us was the stairway all

Run o'er, and we were on the highest step,
Virgilius fastened upon me his eyes,
And said: "The temporal fire and the eternal,
Son, thou hast seen, and to a place art come
Where of myself no farther I **discern**③.
By intellect and art I here have brought thee;
Take thine own pleasure for thy guide henceforth;
Beyond the steep ways and the narrow art thou.
Behold the sun, that shines upon thy forehead;
Behold the grass, the flowerets, and the shrubs
Which of itself alone this land produces.
Until rejoicing come the beauteous eyes
Which weeping caused me to come unto thee,
Thou canst sit down, and thou canst walk among them.
Expect no more word or sign from me;
Free and upright and sound is thy free-will,
And error were it not to do its bidding;
Thee o'er thyself I therefore crown and mitre!"

"穿过繁茂的枝叶，
人们费心地寻找着那颗香甜的苹果。
但是今天，你对苹果的渴望将会得到平息。"
维吉尔这样对我说道。
没有任何奖赏，
能比这些话更加让我欣喜。
我一直深深渴望着能够向上攀登，
那之后的每一步，
我都感觉自己长出了翅膀，能够飞翔。
脚下是刚攀爬完的所有台阶，
我们站在最高的一级台阶上，
维吉尔用坚定的眼神注视着我，
说道："我的儿啊，世俗的火焰和永恒的火焰，
你都已经看到了，你来到了
我所能辨认的最遥远的地方，
用智慧和技巧，我把你带到了这里；
你已经走完陡峭、狭窄的道路；

从今以后，就让快乐为你导航。
看看那太阳，它正照在你的额头上；
看看那草地、鲜花和矮树丛，
它们都是在这片大地土生土长。
在它们中间，你可以坐下休息，或是四处闲逛，
直到那双美丽的眼睛喜悦地来到这里
它们的哭泣让我来到你的身旁。
不要期待再我说一个字或做一个手势；
你的意志是自由、正直而健全的，
不按照它的命令行事你就会犯错；
我给你戴上了王冠，你是自己的国王！”

——选自《神曲》第二部“炼狱”第27歌

注释

① guerdon [ˈgɜːdən] *n.* 奖赏

② pinion [ˈpɪnjən] *n.* 鸟的翅膀

③ discern [dɪˈsɜːn] *vt.* 觉察

3 意大利文艺复兴运动的杰出代表——乔万尼·薄伽丘

Giovanni Boccaccio (1313—December 21, 1375) was an Italian author and poet, a friend, student, and correspondent of Petrarch, an important Renaissance humanist and the author of a number of notable works including *The Decameron*, *On Famous Women*, and his poetry in the Italian vernacular. Boccaccio is particularly notable for his dialogue, of which it has been said that it surpasses in verisimilitude that of virtually all of his contemporaries, since they were medieval writers and often followed formulaic models for character and plot.

乔万尼·薄伽丘(1313年—1375年12月21日)是意大利作家和诗人，是意大利诗人彼特拉克的朋友和学生，并与彼特拉克齐名。薄伽丘是文艺复兴时期重要的人文学者，他创作了大量的经典名作，包括《十日谈》、《西方名女》以及用意大利方言创作的诗歌。薄伽丘作品中的对白尤为著名，语言逼真度据说几乎超越了同时代的所有作家，因为中世纪的作家经常在人物和情节的设定上套用一定的模式。

《十日谈》创作于1313年至1375年，是意大利最著名的短篇小说集。当时，《十日谈》被称为“人曲”，与但丁的《神曲》齐名，被称为《神曲》的姊妹篇。目前国内最常见的译本是上海译文出版社方平、王科一的译本。

The Decameron
十日谈

And for that of all natural things love is that which least brooketh contrary counsel or opposition and whose nature is such that it may lightlier consume of itself than be done away by advisement.

在自然界所有事物中，爱情是最不受人约束和阻拦的，它会自己渐渐消逝但却不会因为他人的意见阻挠而消失。

——*The Decameron*《十日谈》

名著导读

The Decameron opens with a masterly description of the terrors of the pestis, and we are then introduced to a company of seven ladies and three young men who have come together at a villa outside Naples to escape the epidemic. Each in turn presides for a day over the company and on each of the ten days each of the company tells a story, so that at the end one hundred stories have been told.

《十日谈》开篇用熟练的手法描写人们对鼠疫的恐慌，接着向我们描述了七位女士和三位年轻的男士，为了躲避传染病而一起住进了那不勒斯郊外的一栋别墅。他们每人每天轮流当值统管所有人，并且在这十天中的每一天，每个人都要讲一个故事，这样，到最后他们一共讲了一百个故事。

名段选读

Emilia's story come to an end, Neifile, by the king's commandment, began thus: "There are some, noble ladies, who believe themselves to know more than other folk, **albeit** ①, to my thinking, they know less, and who, by reason thereof, presume to oppose their judgment not only to the counsels of men, but even to set it up against the very nature of things; of which **presumption** ② very grave ills have befallen aforetime, nor ever was any good known to come thereof. And for that of all natural things love is that which least brooketh contrary counsel or opposition and whose nature is such that it may lightlier consume of itself than be done away by advisement, it hath come to my mind to narrate to you a story of a lady, who, seeking to be wiser than **pertained** ③ unto her and than she was, nay, than the matter **comported** ④ in which she studied to show her wit, thought to tear out from an **enamoured** ⑤ heart a love which had belike been set there of the stars, and so doing, succeeded in expelling at once love and life from her son's body.

There was, then, in our city, according to that which the ancients relate, a very great and rich merchant, whose name was Lionardo Sighieri and who had by his wife a son called Girolamo, after whose birth, having duly set his affairs in order, he departed this life. The guardians of the boy, together with his mother, well and loyally ordered his affairs, and he, growing up with his neighbour's children, became familiar with a girl of his own age, the daughter of the tailor, more than with any other of the quarter. As he waxed in age, use turned to love so great and so ardent that he was never easy save what time he saw her, and certes she loved him no less than she was loved of him. The boy's mother, observing this, many a time chid and rebuked him therefor and after, Girolamo availing not to desist therefrom, complained thereof to his guardians, saying to them, as if she thought, thanks to her son's great wealth, to make an orange-tree of a bramble, 'This boy of ours, albeit he is yet scarce fourteen years old, is so enamoured of the daughter of a tailor our neighbour, by name Salvestra, that, except we remove her from his sight, he will peradventure one day take her to wife, without any one's knowledge, and I shall never after be glad; or else he will **pine away**[⑥] from her, if he see her married to another; wherefore meseemeth, to avoid this, you were best send him somewhither far from here, about the business of the warehouse; for that, he being removed from seeing her, she will pass out of his mind and we may after avail to give him some well-born **damsel**[⑦] to wife.' "

艾米利亚的故事结束了，于是妮菲尔遵照国王的命令，开始讲道："有这样一些高贵的女士，她们总是认为自己比别人知道的多——尽管在我看来，她们其实比其他人要无知得多——因此她们不但放肆地拒绝别人的意见，甚至还妄图违反自然规律；她们这样做只会让自己遭遇不幸，不会有好结果。在自然界所有事物中，爱情是最不受人约束和阻拦的，它会自己渐渐消逝但却不会因为他人的意见阻挠而消失。现在我就讲述一位女士的故事，她一直试图让自己超越天赋、打破常规的智慧表现方式，变得比常人更聪明。她妄想将一份如星辰一般闪闪发光的爱从一颗恋人的心中驱逐，结果却立刻夺走了她儿子的爱情和生命。

有个古老的传说，从前我们城里有一位很有钱的大商人，名字叫伦纳德・西纪厄利，他的妻子给他生了一个儿子，叫做纪洛拉莫。孩子刚出生不久，伦纳德把事情安排妥当后就去世了。孩子的监护人和母亲忠诚而妥善地替他打理一切，男孩和邻居家的孩子们一起长大，并与其中一位跟他年纪相仿的女孩关系格外好，她是一个裁缝的女儿。男孩渐渐长大，两人之间的关系转变成了美好而又热烈的爱情，若有一天见不着她，男孩都会坐立不安，女孩对男孩的爱意也丝毫不亚于男孩对她的爱。男孩的妈妈发现了，很不高兴，常常骂他，责备他，可男孩根本不听，于是她向男孩的监护人抱怨。因为她儿子很富有，她就认为自己能把灌木变成橘树。她说，'我们的这个孩子才十四岁，却深深爱上了邻居裁缝的女儿沙薇特，我们得趁早把他们俩分开，要不然某天在我们谁都不知情的情况下，这姑娘就成他妻子啦，那样的话我以后都不会开心的；又或者如果这孩子看见那女孩跟别人结了婚，他也会伤心欲绝的。所以，为了避免这样的事情发生，你们最好把他送到远远的，就跟他说去处理生意上的事，这样，俩人从此被分开，他就会忘了她，到时候我们可以给他介绍个出身好的姑娘做他的妻子。'"

注释

① albeit [ɔːl'biːɪt] *conj.* 尽管

② presumption [prɪ'zʌmpʃən] *n.* 推测，可能性

③ pertain [pə'tein] *vi.* 属于

④ comport [kəm'pɔːt] *vt.* 表现，举止

⑤ enamoured [ɪ'næməd] *adj.* 喜欢的，珍爱的

⑥ pine away【词组】消瘦，憔悴

⑦ damsel ['dæmzl] *n.* 少女

4 坚韧不屈的杰出女作家——埃塞尔·丽莲·伏尼契

Ethel Lilian Voynich (May 11, 1864—July 27, 1960) was an English novelist and musician, and a supporter of several revolutionary causes. Among his best-known works are *Stories from Garshin* (1893), *The Gadfly* (1897), *Jack Raymond* (1901), *Olive Latham* (1904). *The Gadfly* was very popular in the Soviet Union and was the top best seller and compulsory reading there; for similar reasons, the novel has been popular in the People's Republic of China as well.

埃塞尔·丽莲·伏尼契(1864年5月11日—1960年7月27日)是一位英国小说家和音乐家，还是一名革命事业的拥护者。她的著作包括《加尔申的故事》(1893)、《牛虻》(1897)、《杰克·雷蒙》(1901)、《奥利芙·瑟姆》(1904)。其中，《牛虻》在苏联影响巨大，它不仅是那里最畅销的书籍，还是苏联人民必读的书；同样，这部小说在中国也极受欢迎。

《牛虻》共26章，1897年出版。《牛虻》一书是作者伏尼契受到当时身边革命者的献身精神的激励写成的。它生动地反映了19世纪30年代意大利革命者反对奥地利统治者、争取国家独立统一的斗争，成功地塑造了革命党人牛虻的形象。最佳译本由李良民于1953翻译，由中国青年出版社出版。

The Gadfly
牛虻

They kill me because they are afraid of me; and what more can any man's heart desire?

他们之所以要杀我，是因为他们惧怕我；如果一个人拥有了这样的力量，还有什么值得遗憾的呢？

——*The Gadfly*《牛虻》

名著导读

The story centers on the life of the protagonist, Arthur Burton, as a member of the Youth movement, and his antagonist, Padre Montanelli. A thread of a tragic relationship between Arthur and his love Gemma simultaneously runs through the story. It is a story of faith, disillusionment, revolution, romance, and heroism.

故事围绕一位青年运动组织成员亚瑟•伯顿，以及他的敌手蒙泰尼里神父的生活展开叙述。其中还穿插着亚瑟和他的爱人琼玛充满悲情色彩的爱情故事。这是一个剖析信念、醒悟、革命、浪漫和英雄主义的故事。

名段选读

"Dear Jim."

The writing grew suddenly blurred and misty. And she had lost him again—had lost him again! At the sight of the familiar childish nickname all the hopelessness of her **bereavement**① came over her **afresh**②, and she put out her hands in blind desperation, as though the weight of the earth-clods that lay above him were pressing on her heart.

Presently she took up the paper again and went on reading:

"I am to be shot at sunrise tomorrow. So if I am to keep at all my promise to tell you everything, I must keep it now. But, after all, there is not much need of explanations between you and me. We always understood each other without many words, even when we were little things."

"And so, you see, my dear, you had no need to break your heart over that old story of the blow. It was a hard hit, of course; but I have had plenty of others as hard, and yet I have managed to get over them, even to pay back a few of them, and here I am still, like the **mackerel**③ in our nursery-book (I forget its name), 'Alive and kicking, oh!' This is my last kick, though; and then, to-morrow morning, and—'Finita la Commedia!' You and I will translate that: 'The variety show is over'; and will give thanks to the gods that they have had, at least, so much mercy on us. It is not much, but it is something; and for this and all other blessings may we be truly thankful!"

"About that same tomorrow morning, I want both you and Martini to understand clearly that I am quite happy and satisfied, and could ask no better thing of Fate. Tell that to Martini as a message from me; he is a good fellow and a good **comrade**④, and he will understand. You see, dear, I know that the stick-in-the-mud people are doing us a good turn and themselves a bad one by going back to secret trials and executions so soon, and I know that if you who are left stand together steadily and hit hard, you will see great things. As for me, I shall go out into the courtyard with as light a heart as any child starting home for the holidays. I have done my share of the work, and this death-sentence is the proof that I have done it thoroughly. They kill me because they are afraid of me; and what more can any man's heart desire?"

"It desires just one thing more, though. A man who is going to die has a right to a personal fancy, and mine is that you should see why I have always been such a sulky brute to you, and so slow to forget old scores. Of course, though, you understand why, and I tell you only for the pleasure of writing the words. I loved you, Gemma, when you were an ugly little girl in a gingham **frock**[⑤], with a scratchy tucker and your hair in a pig-tail down your back; and I love you still. Do you remember that day when I kissed your hand, and when you so **piteously**[⑥] begged me 'never to do that again'? It was a **scoundrelly**[⑦] trick to play, I know; but you must forgive that; and now I kiss the paper where I have written your name. So I have kissed you twice, and both times without your consent."

"That is all. Good-bye, my dear."

"亲爱的吉姆。"

信上的字突然变得模糊不清。她又一次失去了他——又一次失去了他！一看到这熟悉的小名，一股丧亲的绝望又涌上心头。她茫然无助地伸出双手，仿佛堆在他身上的土块重重地压在了她心上一样。

不一会儿，她又拿起信读了起来：

"明天日出的时候，我就要被枪决了。我曾向你承诺过会把一切都告诉你，而现在就是我该兑现诺言的时候了。但毕竟，你我之间不必过多解释。我们总能默契相通，不需要过多的言语，从小时候起，我们就是如此。"

"所以，你要明白，亲爱的，你不必为了往昔的痛苦而伤心。我当然知道那是很沉重的打击，但是，我经历过许多次同样的痛苦，而我已经跨过了那些坎儿，甚至让它们屈服在了我的脚下，现在的我，就如我们曾经读过的一本儿童图书中的那条鲭鱼一样(我忘了书名)，'欢快地游来游去！'尽管这是我的最后一次'戏水'。然后，明天早上我的'美好人生就此结束！'

你我会将其翻译成'演出结束'；然后感谢上苍，至少他们给予了我们深厚的关怀，虽然只是小恩小惠，但对我们而言却是有意义的；看在这些关怀以及其他众多恩惠的份上，我们要衷心地感谢！"

"明天早上，我希望你和马尔蒂尼能明白我是非常快乐和满足的，上苍已经赐予了我最好的一切。帮我把这话转达给马尔蒂尼；他是一个好人，是一位好同志。他会明白的。你瞧，亲爱的，那些顽固者替我们做了一件好事，而自己却吃了大亏，因为他们很快便进行了秘密审讯、私下处决。我知道如果像你一样活下来的人能够团结起来给他们以沉重的打击，你们就会看到胜利的曙光。至于我，我会像放假回家的小孩子一样，心情愉悦地步入庭院。我已经完成了我的使命，而死刑正是我光荣完成任务的最好证明。他们之所以要杀我，是因为他们惧怕我；如果一个人拥有了这样的力量，还有什么值得遗憾的呢？"

"可我还有一个愿望。一个即将死去的人也有幻想的权利，我希望你能明白为什么

我对你总是那么漠视、那么残忍、对往昔的不快总是不能释怀。当然，你肯定明白个中原因，我告诉你只是因为我写下这些话会让我很快乐。我爱你，琼玛，在你还是一个‘丑小鸭’时，我就深深被你吸引了。那时，你还穿着格子连衣裙，领布皱巴巴的，脑袋后面扎着一根麻花辫，即便那样，我还是爱你。还记得我吻你手背的那天吗，当时你求我‘再也不许这样了’。我知道那只是要流氓的行为，但你必须原谅我，现在我又在这张信纸上写有你名字的地方亲吻了一下。所以，我总共吻了你两次，两次都没得到你的同意。"

"就这样吧。再见，亲爱的。"

——选自《牛虻》第26章

注释

① bereavement [bɪ'riːvmənt] *n.* 丧失

② afresh [ə'freʃ] *adv.* 再度，重新

③ mackerel ['mækrəl] *n.* 鲭鱼

④ comrade ['kɔmreid] *n.* 同志

⑤ frock [frɔk] *n.* 连衣裙

⑥ piteously ['pɪtiəslɪ] *adv.* 可怜地

⑦ scoundrelly ['skaʊndrəlɪ] *adv.* 像无赖一般地

5 古典主义喜剧的创建者——莫里哀

Jean-Baptiste Poquelin(January 15, 1622—February 17, 1673), mostly known by his stage name Molière, was a French playwright and actor who is considered one of the greatest masters of comedy in Western literature. Among Molière's best-known dramas are *Le Misanthrope*(*The Misanthrope*), *L'École des femmes*(*The School for Wives*), *Tartuffe ou L'Imposteur*(*Tartuffe or The Hypocrite*), *L'Avare ou L'École du mensonge* (*The Miser*), *Le Malade imaginaire* (*The Imaginary Invalid*), and *Le Bourgeois gentilhomme* (*The Bourgeois Gentleman*).

让-巴蒂斯特·波克兰(1622年1月15日—1673年2月17日)，通常以艺名莫里哀为人们所熟知，他是法国剧作家和演员，被公认为是西方文学史上最伟大的喜剧创作大师之一。他的代表作有《愤世者》、《太太学堂》、《伪君子》、《守财奴》、《无病呻吟》以及《贵人迷》。

《伪君子》创作于于1664年至1669年间，前后写作5年，修改了3遍，是一部5幕喜剧。它从法国现实中提取题材，针对时弊，把攻击矛头对准教会，揭露它的虚伪性和危害性。剧作深刻揭露了教会的虚伪和丑恶，答尔丢夫也成为“伪君子”的代名词。目前国内较著名的译本是李健吾的版本。

Tartuffe or the Hypocrite
伪君子

Those whose own conduct's most ridiculous, are always quickest to speak ill of others.

那些自身行为荒诞的人总是在第一时间说别人的坏话。

——*Tartuffe or the Hypocrite*《伪君子》

名著导读

When the religious hypocrite Tartuffe ingratiates himself with Orgon and his mother Mme. Pernelle, he is taken into their home and promised Orgon's daughter's hand in marriage (even as he secretly attempts to seduce Orgon's wife, Elmire). Everyone else in the family sees through Tartuffe's pose, and his machinations and hypocrisies are eventually exposed. Finally, the police officer arrests Tartuffe. The drama ends well.

宗教伪君子答尔丢夫极力讨好奥尔贡以及他的母亲佩尔奈尔夫人，于是他得以进入他们家里并获得了与奥尔贡女儿的婚约(虽然他在私底下试图勾引奥尔贡的夫人艾耳密尔)。家中的其他人都看穿了答尔丢夫的装腔作势，而这个伪君子的阴谋和虚伪也最终得以大白于天下。最后，警察逮捕了答尔丢夫。戏剧圆满结束。

名段选读

Cleante: Eh! madam, can you hope to keep folk's tongues from wagging? It would be a grievous thing if, for the fear of idle talk about us, we had to sacrifice our friends. No, no; Even if we could bring ourselves to do it, think you that everyone would then be silenced? Against **backbiting**① there is no defence so let us try to live in innocence, to silly **tattle**② pay no heed at all, and leave the gossips free to vent their gall.

Dorine: Our neighbour Daphne, and her little husband, must be the ones who slander us, I'm thinking. Those whose own conduct's most ridiculous, are always quickest to speak ill of others; they never fail to seize at once upon the slightest hint of any love affair, and spread the news of it with glee, and give it the character they'd have the world believe in. By others' actions, painted in their colours, they hope to justify their own; they think, in the false hope of some resemblance, either to make their own **intrigues**③ seem innocent, or else to make their neighbours share the blame which they are loaded with by everybody.

Madame Pernelle: These arguments are nothing to the purpose. Orante, we all know, lives a perfect life; her thoughts are all of heaven; and I have heard that she **condemns**④ the company you keep.

Dorine: O admirable pattern! Virtuous dame! She lives the model of **austerity**⑤; but age has brought this piety upon her, and she's a prude, now she can't help herself. As long as she could capture men's attentions she made the most of her advantages; but, now she sees her beauty vanishing, she wants to leave the world, that's leaving her, and in the specious veil of haughty virtue she'd hide the weakness of her worn-out charms. That is the way with all your old coquettes; they find it hard to see their lovers leave 'em; and thus abandoned, their forlorn estate can find no occupation but a prude's. These pious dames, in their austerity, must carp at everything, and pardon nothing. They loudly blame their neighbours' way of living, not for religion's sake, but out of envy, because they can't endure to see another enjoy the pleasures age has weaned them from.

克雷央特：啊！夫人，难道您指望能够制止谣言吗？如果因为害怕谣言而牺牲我们的朋友，这该是多么令人伤心的事啊。不，不；即使我们那样去做了，您认为大家就会闭嘴了吗？我们无法抵御诽谤，那么就让我们活在清白中吧，不去理会别人无聊的谈论，随便那些八卦说些什么吧。

桃丽娜：我觉得我们的邻居达夫妮和她卑劣的丈夫肯定是造谣中伤我们的人。那些自身行为荒诞的人总是在第一时间说别人的坏话；他们总是可以立刻得知任何一件风流韵事，并欢天喜地到处散播，还不忘给故事添油加醋，好让全世界的人都相信他们。他们带着自己的想法看别人的行为，以此来为自己辩护；他们妄想有一些相似之处，这样就可以将自己的阴谋诡计伪装得很无辜，或者让四邻分担别人对他们的指责。

佩尔奈尔夫人：你们说的这些都是无稽之谈。我们都知道奥朗特的生活很完美，她的想法都很美好；而且我听说她对你交往的朋友圈子不满意。

桃丽娜：啊，她真是个令人称赞的楷模！德行高尚的女士！她就是一个典型的苦行者，但是岁月将这样的虔诚强加给她，使她现在成了一个过分正经的人，就连她自己也控制不了自己了。过去，只要是能够吸引男人的注意，她就会想尽一切办法利用自己的优势；但是，现在，眼看着自己的美貌逐渐消失，她突然想要离开这个世界，而这个世界也在渐渐远离她，在那层傲慢的面纱下隐藏的是她消失殆尽的美丽。这是所有卖弄风情的老女人选择的生活方式，她们很难接受爱人的离去；因此，一旦被抛弃了，她们就只能扮演一个假正经的角色。这些虔诚的夫人们，在她们的修行中，往往会挑剔所有东西，从不懂得宽恕。她们大声地斥责邻居的生活方式，不是因为她们的信仰，而是因为嫉妒，她们无法忍受别人享受着欢乐的时光，而自己却早已过了那个年纪。

——选自《伪君子》第1幕第1场

注释

① backbiting ['bækbaitɪŋ] *n.* 背后中伤

② tattle ['tætl] *n.* 闲话，饶舌

③ intrigue [ɪn'triːg] *n.* 阴谋

④ condemn [kən'dem] *vt.* 指责

⑤ austerity [ɔ'sterətɪ] *n.* 朴素，节俭

6 澳大利亚当代最有影响的作家之一——考琳·麦卡洛

Colleen McCullough-Robinson(June 1, 1937—), born in Wellington, is an internationally acclaimed Australian author. Colleen McCullough enjoys worldwide renown, and her novels are bestsellers in a multitude of languages. She is the author of *The Thorn Birds, Tim, A Creed for the Third Millennium, The Ladies of Missalonghi, The First Man in Rome, The Grass Crown, as well as Caesars Women.* She lives with her husband, Ric Robinson, on Norfolk Island in the South Pacific.

考琳·麦卡洛-罗宾逊（1973年7月1日出生至今），出生于惠灵顿，是一位国际知名的澳大利亚作家。考琳·麦卡洛享誉世界，她的小说被翻译为多种语言，几乎都是畅销书。她的代表作包括：《荆棘鸟》、《蒂姆》、《第三个千年的纲领》、《密萨隆基的淑女们》、《罗马主人》、《草冠》以及《凯撒的女人》。考琳现在和她的丈夫里克·罗宾逊生活在南太平洋的诺福克岛。

《荆棘鸟》共7部分，发表于1977年，一部澳大利亚的家世小说，以女主人公梅吉与神父拉尔夫的爱情纠葛为主线，描写了克利里一家三代人的故事，时间跨度长达半个多世纪之久。国内最普遍的是译本是译林出版社曾胡的译本。

The Thorn Birds
荆棘鸟

We create our own thorns, and never stop to count the cost. All we can do is suffer the pain, and tell ourselves it was well worth it.

我们为自己制造荆棘，且从不计较得失。我们所能做的就是忍受痛苦，并且告诉自己这是值得的。

——*The Thorn Birds*《荆棘鸟》

名著导读

The story begins in 1915 when Paddy Cleary moves his wife and seven children to an Australian sheep station owned by his autocratic and childless older sister. The young Cleary daughter, Meggie, falls in love with the local Catholic priest, Ralph de Briccasart, who is a good and ambitious man who certainly does nothing to encourage this love, but who certainly returns it as he regards Meggie as the daughter he can never have. As Meggie matures, he comes to regard her in a more romantic way. A great struggle arises between this love on the one hand and his ambition to become a Cardinal or perhaps more, on the other.

这个故事发生在1915年，那时帕迪·克利里带着他的妻子以及7个孩子来到了澳大利亚他姐姐的牧场。他姐姐个性专横，没有子女。克利里的小女儿梅吉爱上了当地的天主教神父拉尔夫·德·布瑞卡萨特，他是一个待人宽厚且有雄心壮志的人，他并不鼓励这份爱情，但是他把梅吉当做永远不可能拥有的女儿一样看待。随着梅吉渐渐成熟，拉夫尔也逐渐爱上了她。于是问题出现了，从一方面讲，他爱梅吉；但从另一方面讲，他又想成为主教，或者登上更高的位置，他陷入了两难的境地。

名段选读

"Ali, but you've changed, Ralph."

"In what way, my Meggie?"

"As if the **pedestal**① rocks with every passing breeze, and as if the view from up there is a disappointment."

"It is." He laughed soundlessly. "And to think I once had the **temerity**② to say you weren't anything out of the ordinary! I take it back. You're the one woman, Meggie. The one!"

"What happened?"

"I don't know. Did I discover even Church idols have feet of clay? Did I sell myself for a mess of pottage? Am I grasping at nothing?" His brows drew together, as if in pain. "And that's it, perhaps, in a nutshell. I'm a mass of clichés. It's an old, sour, **petrified**③ world, the Vatican world."

"I was more real, but you could never see it."

"There was nothing else I could do, truly! I knew where I should have gone, but I couldn't. With you I might have been a better man, if less august. But I just couldn't, Meggie. Oh, I wish I could make you see that!"

Her hand stole along his bare arm, tenderly. "Dear Ralph, I do see it. I know, I know...Each of us has something within us which won't be denied, even if it makes us scream aloud to die.

We are what we are, that's all. Like the old Celtic legend of the bird with the thorn in its breast, singing its heart out and dying. Because it has to, it's driven to. We can know what we do wrong even before we do it, but self-knowledge can't affect or change the outcome, can it? Everyone singing his own little song, convinced it's the most wonderful song the world has ever heard. Don't you see? We create our own thorns, and never stop to count the cost. All we can do is suffer the pain, and tell ourselves it was well worth it."

"That's what I don't understand. The pain." He glanced down at her hand, so gently on his arm, hurting him so unbearably. "Why the pain, Meggie?" "Ask God, Ralph," said Meggie. "He's the authority on pain, isn't He? He made us what we are, He made the whole world. Therefore He made the pain, too."

"可是你变了，拉夫尔。"

"哪里变了，梅吉？"

"你就像微风吹过的基石，就像从这里看到的风景，总有些不尽如人意。"

"是的，"他笑了，但没有笑出声。"我曾鲁莽地说过你并没有什么与众不同，现在我收回这句话，你是一个独一无二的女人，梅吉，你是独一无二的！"

"发生了什么事？"

"我不知道。是不是因为我发现了即使是教会的神也会有致命的弱点？还是我为了生活而出卖了自己？我是不是一无所有？"他眉头紧锁，似乎陷入了痛苦之中。"也许简单来说，我就是一个迂腐的人。这就是一个陈旧、腐朽、僵化的世界，罗马教廷的世界。"

"我更加真实，但是你永远不会看到。"

"我已经没有其他的办法了，真的！我知道我应该去哪，但是我不能去。和你在一起我可能会是一个更好的人，也许会不那么严肃。但是梅吉，我不能。哦，真希望能让你懂得这一切！"

她的手悄悄伸向了他那裸露的臂弯，动作很温柔。"亲爱的拉夫尔，我懂！我知道，我知道……我们彼此内心都有一些无法割舍的东西，即使它会令我们尖叫着死去。我们就是我们，仅此而已。就像古老的凯尔特传说里的荆棘鸟那样，将荆棘插进胸膛里，大声歌唱，然后死去。只是因为它必须这么做。也许我们在做一件事之前就知道这是错误的，但是我们的自知之明无法影响或改变结果，不是吗？我们每个人都在唱着属于自己的歌曲，并且相信这就是世界上最动人的歌曲。你难道不懂吗？我们为自己制造了荆棘，且从不计较得失。我们所能做的就是忍受痛苦，并且告诉自己这是值得的。"

"痛苦，这就是我无法理解的。"他低头看着她的手温柔地放在自己的手臂上，心里涌起一股无法忍受的痛苦。"为什么会有伤痛，梅吉？""问上帝吧，拉夫尔，"梅吉说道。"他是制造伤痛的神，不是吗？他创造了我们，创造了整个世界，因此他也创造了伤痛。"

——选自《荆棘鸟》第5部第17章

注释

① pedestal ['pedɪstl] *n.* 基座

② temerity [tə'merətɪ] *n.* 鲁莽

③ petrified ['petrɪfaid] *adj.* 僵化的

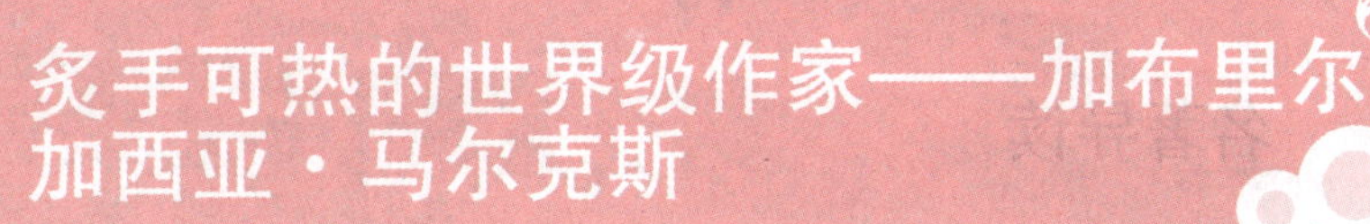

7 炙手可热的世界级作家——加布里尔 加西亚·马尔克斯

Concordia García Márquez (March 6, 1927—) is a Colombian novelist, short-story writer, screenwriter and journalist, known affectionately as Gabo throughout Latin America. He is considered one of the most significant authors of the 20th century. He was awarded the Nobel Prize in Literature in 1982, and is the earliest winner of this prize to be still alive. He is best-known for his novels, such as *One Hundred Years of* Solitude and *Love in the Time of Cholera* (1985). His works have achieved significant critical acclaim and widespread commercial success, most notably for popularizing a literary style labeled as magical realism, which uses magical elements and events in otherwise ordinary and realistic situations.

加布里尔·加西亚·马尔克斯(1927年3月6日出生至今)，哥伦比亚小说家、短篇小说家、编剧家、新闻记者。在拉丁美洲，人们亲切地称呼他为“加博”。他被认为是20世纪最杰出的作家之一。1982年，他荣获诺贝尔文学奖，是所有仍然在世的诺贝尔文学奖得主中，最早获得该奖项的人。他因《百年孤独》和《霍乱时期的爱情》(1985)而闻名。加西亚·马尔克斯的工作获得了评论界的认同并取得了广泛的商业成就，他将魔幻元素和普通的真实场景结合起来，使魔幻现实主义文风变得流行起来。

《百年孤独》共20章，发表于1967年，以魔幻现实主义的笔法描绘了加勒比海沿岸小城马贡多百余年的历史，被视为“20世纪最伟大小说之一”。目前国内最流行的译本是上海市译文出版社出版的黄锦炎先生的译本和北京10月文艺出版社高长荣先生的译本。

One Hundred Years of Solitude
百年孤独

Things have a life of their own. It's simply a matter of waking up their souls.

任何东西都有它的生命，我们只需唤醒它们的灵魂。

——*One Hundred Years of Solitude*《百年孤独》

名著导读

One Hundred Years of Solitude is the story of seven generations of the Buendía Family in the town of Macondo. José Arcadio Buendía, and Úrsula, his wife (and first cousin), leave Riohacha, Colombia, to find a better life and a new home. One night of their emigration journey, José Arcadio Buendía dreams of "Macondo", a city of mirrors that reflected the world in and about it. Upon awakening, he decides to found Macondo at the river side; after days of wandering the jungle, José Arcadio Buendía's founding of Macondo is utopia. Soon after its foundation, Macondo becomes a town frequented by unusual and extraordinary events that involve the generations of the Buendía family, who are unable or unwilling to escape their periodic self-inflicted misfortunes. Ultimately, a hurricane destroys Macondo.

《百年孤独》讲述了马孔多镇的布恩蒂亚家族七代人的故事。何塞•阿卡迪奥•布恩迪亚和他的妻子乌苏拉(第一个表妹)离开了哥伦比亚的里奥哈查，去寻找更好的生活和新家。在他们迁徙途中的一个晚上，何塞•阿卡迪奥•布恩迪亚梦见了“马孔多”，这是一个镜子的城市，它可以映射出这个世界。醒来后，他决定要找到这个坐落于河边的马孔多城。在丛林里徘徊数日后，何塞•阿卡迪奥•布恩迪亚建立的马孔多就是一个乌托邦。马孔多镇在建立后不久，布恩迪亚家族几代人便发生了一些奇异的事件，这个家族似乎永远无法摆脱也不愿意逃脱他们自己造成的周而复始的厄运。最后，一场飓风摧毁了马孔多。

名段选读

MANY YEARS LATER as he faced the firing squad, Colonel Aureliano Buendía was to remember that distant afternoon when his father took him to discover ice. At that time Macondo was a village of twenty adobe houses, built on the bank of a river of clear water that ran along a bed of polished stones, which were white and enormous, like prehistoric eggs. The world was so recent that many things lacked names, and in order to indicate them it was necessary to point. Every year during the month of March a family of ragged gypsies would set up their tents near the village, and with a great uproar of pipes and kettledrums they would display new inventions. First they brought the magnet. A heavy gypsy with an untamed beard and sparrow hands, who introduced himself as Melquíades, put on a bold public demonstration of what he himself called the eighth wonder of the learned alchemists of Macedonia. He went from house to house dragging two metal ingots and everybody was amazed to see pots, pans, tongs, and braziers tumble down from their places and beams creak from the desperation of nails and screws trying to emerge, and even objects that had been lost for a long time appeared from where they had been searched for most and went dragging along in turbulent confusion behind Melquíades' magical irons. "Things have a life of their own," the gypsy proclaimed with a harsh accent. "It's simply a matter of waking up their souls." José Arcadio Buendía, whose unbridled imagination always went beyond the genius of nature and even beyond miracles and magic, thought that it would be possible to make use of that useless invention to extract gold from the bowels of the earth. Melquíades, who was an honest man, warned him: "It won't work for that." But José Arcadio Buendía at that time did not believe in the honesty of gypsies, so he traded his mule and a pair of goats for the two magnetized ingots. Úrsula Iguarán, his wife, who relied on those animals to increase their poor domestic holdings, was unable to dissuade him. "Very soon well have gold enough and more to pave the floors of the house," her husband replied. For several months he worked hard to demonstrate the truth of his idea. He explored every inch of the region, even the riverbed, dragging the two iron ingots along and reciting Melquíades' incantation aloud. The only thing he succeeded in doing was to unearth a suit of fifteenth-century armor which had all of its pieces soldered together with rust and inside of which there was the hollow **resonance**① of an enormous stone-filled gourd. When José Arcadio Buendía and the four men of his expedition managed to take the armor apart, they found inside a **calcified**② skeleton with a copper locket containing a woman's hair around its neck.

许多年后，当他面对行刑队时，奥雷连诺·布恩蒂亚上校想起了父亲带他看冰的那个遥远的下午。那时，马孔多是一个由二十户土坯房组成的小村庄，房子建在河岸边，清澈的河水沿着布满石头的河床流过，河里的石头又白又大，就像史前的化石蛋。这个地方因为是新开发的，所以很多东西还没有名字，为了解释它们，就必须给它们命名。每年的三月份，一个衣衫褴褛的吉普赛家族就会在村边搭起帐篷，吹着笛子敲着鼓，来向我们展示一些新的发明。第一次，他们带来了磁铁。一个体型高大、满脸胡须、手指瘦得像麻雀一样的吉普赛人，自称是梅尔加德斯，他公开大胆地向观众展示了他所谓的马其顿炼金术士创造的世界第八大奇迹。他带着两块磁铁挨家挨户地拜访，大家惊讶地看着铁锅、铁盆、铁钳和铁炉从原处倒下，横梁因为钉子和螺丝的松动而咯吱作响，甚至是一些丢失很久的东西也从曾找过多次的地方突然冒了出来，人们纷至沓来，乱哄哄地跟在梅尔加德斯那块神奇的铁块后面。“任何东西都有它自己的生命，”这个吉普赛人用刺耳的声调说道，“我们只需唤醒它们的灵魂。”何塞·阿卡迪奥·布恩迪亚那无拘无束的想象力总是超越了大自然的创造力，甚至超越了奇迹和魔力，他认为这种无用的发明也许可以用来吸取地下的金矿。梅尔加德斯是一个诚实的人，他警告他说：“它没有这种功效。”但是何塞·阿卡迪奥·布恩迪亚当时认为吉普赛人不诚实，因此，他用一匹骡子和两只山羊换了两块磁铁。他的妻子乌苏拉还指望着用这些牲畜来赚钱养家，但她还是没能劝阻他。“很快我们就能拥有很多金子了，到时候，金子多得足以铺满我们家的地板。”她的丈夫回答说。他花了几个月的时间努力去证实自己的想法。他带着那两块磁铁，嘴里大声念着梅尔加德斯教他的咒语，勘察了整个地区的每一寸土地，甚至包括河床。但他唯一找到的东西，就是一件十五世纪的铠甲，它的各个焊接处都已经生满了锈，里面还有空洞的回音，就像是一个填满石头的葫芦所发出的声音。当何塞·阿卡迪奥·布恩迪亚和他的四名探险队员将铠甲掰开后，他们发现里面有一个已经腐朽的骷髅，骷髅脖子上挂着一个铜制的盒子，盒子里装着一个女人的头发。

——选自《百年孤独》第1章

注释

① resonance ['rezənəns] *n.* 回声

② calcified ['kælsɪfaid] *adj.* 钙化了的

8 法国现实主义戏剧的先驱者之一——亚历山大·小仲马

Alexandre Dumas, fils (July 27, 1824—November 27, 1895) was one of the leading French playwrights and novelists of the last quarter of the 19th Century. He was the illegitimate son of Alexandre Dumas, père, also a writer and playwright. Dumas fils gained fame with his novel The *Lady of the Camellias,* in which a fallen girl, the heroine, gives up her lover rather than see him become a social outcast. The story has been filmed several times.

亚历山大·小仲马（1824年7月27日—1895年11月27日），是19世纪最后25年里法国最主要的剧作家和小说家之一。他是亚历山大·大仲马的私生子，大仲马也是一位作家和剧作家。小仲马因为他的小说《茶花女》而出名，小说中的女主角——一个堕落的女子，放弃了自己的爱人，因为她不想亲眼目睹他被社会所抛弃。该故事曾被多次搬上银幕。

《茶花女》共27章，发表于1848年，是小仲马的代表作，故事讲述了一个青年人与巴黎上流社会的一位交际花的曲折凄婉的爱情故事。《茶花女》是第一本流传到我国的外国小说，当时由著名的翻译家林琴南先生用文言译就。现在也有很多翻译家译出的不错的译本，其中以王振孙的译本和郑克鲁的译本流传较广。

The Lady of the Camellias
茶花女

To take captive a heart which has had no experience of attack, is to enter an unfortified and ungarrisoned city.

俘获一颗未曾恋爱的心，就如同进入一座没有设防的城。

——*The Lady of the Camellias*《茶花女》

名著导读

Marguerite Gautier is a beautiful young courtesan suffering from tuberculosis. She is loved by Armand Duval, but their happiness ends abruptly, when M. Duval, Armand's father refuses to accept their relationship. He asserts that their romance will destroy his son's career and social position, also it prevents the marriage of his younger sister. Marguerite leaves her lover, pretending to be returning to a rich admirer. Armand follows her to Paris and wounds his rival in a duel and is forced to leave France. Marguerite's fortunes deteriorate rapidly, she is deserted by lovers and friends and moves to a shabby flat. Armand's father writes to his son of Marguerite's sacrifice and misfortunes. Armand returns to Marguerite's side and she dies in his arms.

玛格丽特·戈蒂埃是一个年轻貌美的交际花，她得了肺结核。阿曼德·杜瓦尔深爱着她，但他们的幸福突然间就结束了，因为阿曼德的父亲杜瓦尔先生拒绝接受他们之间的关系。他断言，他们的爱情将会毁了他儿子的事业和社会地位，同时，这还会妨碍到他妹妹的婚姻。玛格丽特离开了她的爱人，虚情假意地回到一个有钱的爱慕者身边。阿曼德追随她来到巴黎，在与他的竞争对手决斗时弄伤了对方，因此被迫离开了法国。玛格丽特的财富很快便耗尽了，她被她的情人和朋友们所抛弃，搬进了一个简陋的公寓。阿曼德的父亲写信给阿曼德，将玛格丽特所作的牺牲和遭遇的不幸都告诉了他儿子。阿曼德回到了玛格丽特的身边，而玛格丽特就这样死在了他的怀里。

名段选读

The streets were empty, the great city was still asleep, a sweet freshness circulated in the streets that a few hours later would be filled with the noise of men. It seemed to me as if this sleeping city belonged to me; I searched my memory for the names of those whose happiness I had once envied; and I could not recall one without finding myself the happier.

To be loved by a pure young girl, to be the first to reveal to her the strange mystery of love, is indeed a great happiness, but it is the simplest thing in the world. To take captive a heart which has had no experience of attack, is to enter an unfortified and ungarrisoned city. Education, family feeling, the sense of duty, the family, are strong **sentinels**①, but there are no sentinels so **vigilant**② as not to be deceived by a girl of sixteen to whom nature, by the voice of the man she loves, gives the first counsels of love, all the more ardent because they seem so pure.

The more a girl believes in goodness, the more easily will she give way, if not to her lover, at least to love, for being without mistrust she is without force, and to win her love is a triumph that can be gained by any young man of five-and-twenty. See how young girls are watched and guarded! The walls of convents are not high enough, mothers have no locks strong enough, religion has no duties constant enough, to shut these charming birds in their cages, cages not even strewn with flowers. Then how surely must they desire the world which is hidden from them, how surely must they find it tempting, how surely must they listen to the first voice which comes to tell its secrets through their bars, and bless the hand which is the first to raise a corner of the mysterious veil!

But to be really loved by a courtesan: that is a victory of infinitely greater difficulty. With them the body has worn out the soul, the senses have burned up the heart, **dissipation**[③] has blunted the feelings. They have long known the words that we say to them, the means we use; they have sold the love that they inspire. They love by profession, and not by instinct. They are guarded better by their calculations than a virgin by her mother and her convent; and they have invented the word caprice for that unbartered love which they allow themselves from time to time, for a rest, for an excuse, for a consolation, like usurers, who cheat a thousand, and think they have bought their own **redemption**[④] by once lending a sovereign to a poor devil who is dying of hunger without asking for interest or a receipt.

街道上空空荡荡，这座繁华的城市还在沉睡之中，再过几个小时，街上的清新舒畅就会被人们的吵闹声所充斥。对我而言，这座沉睡的城市似乎是完全属于我的；我在脑海中搜寻着一个个名字，我曾羡慕他们的快乐，而现在，我无法找到一个比我还快乐的人。

被一个纯洁的年轻女子爱着，成为第一个为她揭开爱情神秘面纱的人，这的确是一种巨大的幸福，但这也是世界上最简单的事情。俘获一颗未曾恋爱的心，就如同进入一座没有设防的城。教育背景、家庭观念、责任意识还有家人，这些都是最好的哨兵，但是，即使是再警觉的哨兵都免不了会被一个十六岁的少女所欺骗。通过她深爱的男人的声音，大自然给了她第一次爱情的忠告，因为这些忠告是如此纯洁，也就使得这一切都显得更加富有激情。

一个女孩越是相信善良，那么她就越容易屈服，即使不是向她的爱人屈服，但至少也会是向爱情屈服，因为没有了猜疑，她就没有了力量，赢得她的爱是任何一个25岁的年轻男子都能获得的胜利。看看这些女孩子受到了怎样严密的监视和看守！人们生恐修道院的围墙不够高，妈妈的锁不够结实，宗教戒律的约束力不够大，他们将这些美丽的小鸟关在笼子里，这些笼子里甚至都没有鲜花的点缀。她们该是多么渴望那个她们接触不到的世界啊，她们该会觉得这个世界多么诱人啊，当她们第一次隔着栅栏听到有人来向她们倾诉内心的秘密时该有多么高兴啊，对第一次揭开那神秘面纱一角的那只手，她们该是觉得如何庆幸啊！

但是，如果真正被一个交际花爱上：这是一种需要经历更大的困难才能获得的胜利。她们的身体脱离了灵魂，欲望在心中燃烧，放荡的生活让她们对感情变得麻木。她们已经听厌了我们说的甜言蜜语，看惯了我们使用的交际伎俩；她们已经出卖了内心曾渴望过的爱情。她们去爱只是出于职业需要，并非出于本能。她们精于计算，因而，她们比一个被母亲或者是修道院看守的处女的防范更加周全；她们把那些不在生意范围之内的爱情叫做逢场作戏，她们会时不时地有一些这样的爱情，她们把它当作一种休息，一个借口，一种安慰，就好像那些放高利贷的人，他们剥削了成百上千的人，却认为仅仅通过借一个金镑给一个快要饿死的穷人，不要利息和借据，自己的灵魂就能够得到救赎。

——选自《茶花女》第12章

注释

① sentinel ['sentɪnl] *n.* 哨兵

② vigilant ['vɪdʒɪlənt] *adj.* 警惕的

③ dissipation [ˌdɪsɪ'peiʃən] *n.* 放荡

④ redemption [rɪ'dempʃən] *n.* 拯救，赎罪

9 站在东西方文化桥梁上的巨人——罗宾德拉纳特·泰戈尔

Rabindranath Tagore (May 7, 1861—August 7, 1941), was a poet, novelist, musician, painter and playwright who reshaped Bengali literature and music. Tagore modernized Bengali art by spurning rigid classical forms. His novels, stories, songs, dance-dramas, and essays spoke to political and personal topics. *Gitanjali* （*Song Offerings*）, *Gora* （*Fair-Faced*）, and *Ghare-Baire* (*The Home and the World*) are his best-known works, and his verse, short stories, and novels were acclaimed for their lyricism, colloquialism, naturalism, and contemplation. Rabindranath Tagore was Asia's first Nobel Prize winner. He was awarded the Nobel Prize for literature in 1913 for his book *Gitanjali*.

罗宾德拉纳特·泰戈尔(1861年5月7日—1941年8月7日)是一位诗人、小说家、音乐家、画家和剧作家，他开创了孟加拉文学和音乐的新局面。泰戈尔摒弃了刻板的古典形式，使孟加拉艺术更加现代化。他的小说、故事、歌曲、舞蹈剧、散文都是关于政治和个人生活的。《吉檀迦利》、《戈拉》、《家与国》是他最著名的几部作品，他的诗、短篇故事和小说以其抒情风格、通俗性、自然主义和思想性被世人所称颂。罗宾德拉纳特·泰戈尔是亚洲第一位诺贝尔奖获得者。他在1913年凭借作品《吉檀迦利》获得诺贝尔文学奖。

《吉檀迦利》的孟加拉语诗作是韵律诗，共103首诗篇，翻译成英文之后变成了自由诗。泰戈尔亲自将它译成英语，1913年他因该英译诗集而获得了诺贝尔文学奖。国内最著名的是冰心女士的译本。

The Gitanjali
吉檀迦利

The shroud that covers me is a shroud of dust and death; I hate it, yet hug it in love.

我身上披着沾染了尘土与死亡的裹尸布；我恨它，但却又充满爱意地拥抱它。

——*The Gitanjali*《吉檀迦利》

名著导读

The Gitanjali is an illustrious work that echoes the true Indian Philosophy. It is a collection of religious poems. Tagore himself translated it into English and the book was first published in England in 1912. This English volume, although it shares the name of one of Tagore's earlier volume of Bengali verse, is actually comprised of poems from several of Tagore's previous volumes of poetry. In addition, Tagore heavily altered the structure and also the content of the poems when he translated them into English.

《吉檀迦利》是一部杰出的著作，它展现了真实的印度哲学。这是一部宗教诗歌集。泰戈尔自己将它翻译成了英文，1912年这本书在英格兰首次出版。尽管这部英文诗歌集与泰戈尔之前的一部孟加拉语诗集的名字相同，但它却是包含了泰戈尔多部诗集中的诗歌。除此之外，在翻译的过程中，泰戈尔还大大更改了这些诗歌的结构和内容。

名段选读

The song that I came to sing remains unsung to this day.

I have spent my days in stringing and in unstringing my instrument.

The time has not come true, the words have not been rightly set; only there is the agony of wishing in my heart.

The blossom has not opened; only the wind is sighing by.

I have not seen his face, nor have I listened to his voice; only I have heard his gentle footsteps from the road before my house.

The livelong day has passed in spreading his seat on the floor; but the lamp has not been lit and I cannot ask him into my house.

I live in the hope of meeting with him; but this meeting is not yet.

我一直想要唱的那首歌直至今也没机会唱。

我每天都在调试琴弦。

时间未到，词还未填，只有愿望之痛留在我心间。

花未开，只有风叹息着拂过。

仍未看见到他，亦未听见他的声音，只听到他的足音，轻轻从我家门前走过。

我终日为他在地上设座；但灯尚未亮起，我无法邀他进来。

我时刻盼望与他相见，只可惜相见之期还未来临。

——《吉檀迦利》第13篇

In the deep shadows of the rainy July, with secret steps, thou walkest, silent as night, eluding all watchers.

Today the morning has closed its eyes, heedless of the insistent calls of the loud east wind, and a thick veil has been drawn over the ever-wakeful blue sky.

The woodlands have hushed their songs, and doors are all shut at every house.

Thou art the solitary **wayfarer**① in this deserted street.

Oh my only friend, my best beloved, the gates are open in my house

—do not pass by like a dream.

七月的雨季，一片迷蒙，你避开所有看守者的目光，踏着静谧的步伐，如夜一般沉寂，来了。

今天，清晨闭上双眼，任凭东风不断呼啸，一层厚厚的面纱遮住了不眠的蓝天。

森林停止了歌唱，家家户户房门紧锁。

你独自走在冷清的街上。

哦，我唯一的朋友，我最爱的人，我的家门为你敞开

——请不要像梦一般经过。

——《吉檀迦利》第22篇

Obstinate are the **trammels**②, but my heart aches when I try to break them.

Freedom is all I want, but to hope for it I feel ashamed.

I am certain that priceless wealth is in thee, and that thou art my best friend, but I have not the heart to sweep away the **tinsel**③ that fills my room

The **shroud**④ that covers me is a shroud of dust and death; I hate it, yet hug it in love.

My debts are large, my failures great, my shame secret and heavy; yet when I come to ask for my good, I quake in fear lest my prayer be granted.

网至坚，但试图挣破这网时，我又心痛。

我只要自由，但这个希望却让我感到羞愧。

我深信无价的财富是你，因为你是我最好的朋友，但我却

不忍抛弃这满屋的俗丽饰物，

我身上披着沾染了尘土与死亡的裹尸布；我恨它，但却又充满爱意地拥抱它。

我债台高筑，我彻底失败，我的耻辱神秘而又沉重；而当我寻求庇佑的时候，我又害怕，怕我的祈求得到允诺。

——《吉檀迦利》第28篇

注释

① wayfarer ['weɪfeərə] *n.* 徒步旅行者

② trammel ['træml] *n.* 网

③ tinsel ['tɪnsl] *n.* 俗丽的东西

④ shroud [ʃraʊd] *n.* 裹尸布

10 与萧伯纳齐名的英国才子——奥斯卡·王尔德

Oscar Wilde (October 16, 1854—November 30, 1900) was an Irish writer, poet, and prominent aesthete who, after writing in different forms throughout the 1880s, became one of London's most popular playwrights in the early 1890s. Today he is remembered for his epigrams, plays and the tragedy of his imprisonment, followed by his early death. Oscar Wilde's reputation rests on his comic masterpieces *Lady Windermere's Fan* and *The Importance of Being Earnest*. Oscar Wilde's other best-known works include his only novel *The Picture of Dorian Gray* (1891), which deals very similar theme as Robert Louis Stevenson's *Dr. Jekyll and Mr. Hyde* (1886). Wilde's fairy tales are very popular—the motifs have been compared to those of Hans Christian Andersen.

奥斯卡·王尔德(1854年10月16日—1900年11月30日)是一位爱尔兰作家、诗人，同时也是卓越的美学家。在整个19世纪80年代，他撰写了多种形式的作品。19世纪90年代初期，他成为伦敦最著名的剧作家之一。如今，世人所铭记的除了他的警句和戏剧外，还有他因监禁而最终导致英年早逝的悲剧人生。喜剧杰作《温德米尔夫人的扇子》和《不可儿戏》令王尔德名声大振，除此之外，他最好的作品也包括他唯一的一本小说《道林·格雷的画像》(1891)，其主题同罗伯特·路易斯·史蒂文森的《化身博士》(1886)非常相似。王尔德的童话也非常有名，通常被人们拿来同汉斯·克里斯蒂·安徒生的作品相提并论。

《道林·格雷的画像》，共8章，1891年出版，是19世纪末唯美主义的代表作，堪称“为艺术而艺术”思潮在戏剧、小说及绘画方面的三绝。最佳译本是外国文学出版社荣如德的译本。

The Picture of Dorian Gray
道林·格雷的画像

Men marry because they are tired; women, because they are curious: both are disappointed.

男人结婚是因为厌倦，女人结婚是因为好奇，最终双方都会失望。

——*The Picture of Dorian Gray*《道林•格雷的画像》

名著导读

The novel tells of a young man named Dorian Gray, the subject of a painting by artist Basil Hallward. Basil is impressed by Dorian's beauty, believing his beauty is responsible for a new mode in his art. Dorian meets Lord Henry Wotton, a friend of Basil's, and becomes enthralled by Lord Henry's world view. Realizing that one day his beauty will fade, Dorian expresses a desire to sell his soul to ensure the portrait Basil has painted would age rather than himself. Dorian's wish is fulfilled, plunging him into debauched acts.

这篇小说讲述了一个名叫道林・格雷的年轻人的故事，他长得异常美丽，艺术家巴西尔・霍华德为他画了一副肖像。道林的美给巴西尔留下了深刻的印象，他认为他的美能为自己的艺术开创一种新的模式。道林认识了巴西尔的朋友亨利・华顿勋爵，并被他的世界观所吸引。当道林意识到终有一天自己的美貌会消逝时，他许下愿望，希望以灵魂为代价让巴西尔所画的画像替他衰老而自己青春永驻，他的愿望实现了，却同时把自己拉入了堕落的深渊。

名段选读

"Never marry a woman with straw-colored hair, Dorian," he said, after a few puffs.

"Why, Harry?"

"Because they are so sentimental."

"But I like sentimental people."

"Never marry at all, Dorian. Men marry because they are tired; women, because they are curious: both are disappointed."

"I don't think I am likely to marry, Harry. I am too much in love. That is one of your **aphorisms**①. I am putting it into practice, as I do everything you say."

"Whom are you in love with?" said Lord Henry, looking at him with a curious smile.

"With an actress," said Dorian Gray, blushing.

Lord Henry **shrugged**② his shoulders. "That is a rather common-place début," he murmured.

"You would not say so if you saw her, Harry."

"Who is she?"

"Her name is Sibyl Vane."

"Never heard of her."

"No one has. People will some day, however. She is a genius."

"My dear boy, no woman is a genius: women are a decorative sex. They never have anything to say, but they say it charmingly. They represent the triumph of matter over mind, just as we men represent the triumph of mind over morals. There are only two kinds of women, the plain and the colored. The plain women are very useful. If you want to gain a reputation for respectability, you have merely to take them down to supper. The other women are very charming. They commit one mistake, however. They paint in order to try to look young. Our grandmothers painted in order to try to talk brilliantly. **Rouge**[③] and esprit used to go together. That has all gone out now. As long as a woman can look ten years younger than her own daughter, she is perfectly satisfied. As for conversation, there are only five women in London worth talking to, and two of these can't be admitted into decent society. However, tell me about your genius. How long have you known her?"

"道林，千万不要和淡黄色头发的女人结婚，"他吸了几口烟后说道。

"为什么，亨利？"

"因为她们太多愁善感。"

"但是我喜欢多愁善感的人。"

"千万不要结婚，道林。男人结婚是因为厌倦，女人结婚是因为好奇，最终双方都会失望。"

"我认为我不会结婚，亨利，我爱得太深了。这是你的格言之一，我会将它付诸实践，就像我会听信你的每句话一样。"

"你在和谁谈恋爱？"亨利勋爵看着他，脸上挂着好奇的微笑。

"和一个女演员。"道林·格雷说道，羞涩得脸都红了。

亨利勋爵耸耸肩，含糊不清地咕哝着；"这是一个毫无新意的开端。"

"亨利，如果你看到她本人，你就不会这么说了。"

"她叫什么？"

"西比尔·范。"

"从没听说过。"

"是没有人听过，但是以后大家就会知道她了，她是个天才。"

"我亲爱的，没有女人会是天才：她们只是用来装饰的花瓶。她们说话的空洞无物，但是说话的方式却着实迷人。女人象征着物质对抗精神的胜利，就像我们男人象征着精神对抗道德的胜利。世上只有两种女人，一种是平凡的，一种是有姿色的。平凡的女人是个好帮手，如果你想赢得一个受尊敬的好名声，只要带她们去吃顿晚餐就可以了。另一类女人非常迷人，但是她们犯了一个错误，她们化妆是为了使自己显得年轻，而我们的祖母辈却是为了在与人家谈时显得精神奕奕。妆容和精神曾经是一致的，但是如今，这种观念却不复存在了。一个女人只要能看起来比她女儿年轻十岁，她就非常满意了。至于谈吐，全伦敦仅有五个女人值得与之交谈，其中的两个还不被上流社会所接纳。但是没关系，讲讲你的那位天才吧。你们认识多久了？”

——选自《道林·格雷的画像》第4章

注释

① aphorism [ˈæfərɪzəm] *n.* 格言，警句

② shrug [ʃrʌg] *vt.* 耸肩

③ rouge [ruːʒ] *n.* 胭脂，口红

11 爱尔兰文艺复兴运动的领袖——威廉·巴特勒·叶芝

William Butler Yeats (June 13, 1865—January 28, 1939) was an Irish poet and dramatist, and one of the foremost figures of 20th century literature. In 1923 he was awarded the Nobel Prize in Literature for what the Nobel Committee described as "inspired poetry, which in a highly artistic form gives expression to the spirit of a whole nation." He was the first Irishman so honored. Yeats is generally considered one of the few writers who completed their greatest works after being awarded the Nobel Prize, such works include *The Tower* (1928) *and The Winding Stair and Other Poems* (1929).

威廉·巴特勒·叶芝（1865年6月13日—1939年1月28日）是一位爱尔兰诗人和剧作家，他是二十世纪文学最重要的人物之一。他获得过1923年的诺贝尔文学奖，当时的诺贝尔奖委员会评论他"以其高度艺术化且鼓舞人心的诗作表达了整个民族的灵魂"。他是第一个获此殊荣的爱尔兰人。叶芝被广泛认为是少数几位在获得诺贝尔奖之后才创作出他们最伟大作品的作家之一，这些作品包括《塔楼》（1928）和《回梯与其他诗作》（1929）。

《当你老了》全诗12行，写于1893年，是叶芝献给女友毛特·冈妮热烈而真挚的爱情诗篇。最流行的译本是冰心女士的译本和袁可嘉的译本。

When You Are Old
当你老了

How many loved your moments of glad grace,
And loved your beauty with love false or true,
But one man loved the pilgrim soul in you,
And loved the sorrows of your changing face.
多少人曾为你的倩影倾倒，

爱恋你的容颜，或是真挚爱慕或是虚情假意，
唯有一人爱着你圣洁的灵魂，
和你饱经风霜的面庞上那丝丝忧伤。

——*When You Are Old*《当你老了》

名著导读

The poem, *When You Are Old*, appears to be a simple love poem on first reading. After careful analysis, however, one realizes that Yeats has created a small autobiography without ever using the first person singular. Through word choice and strategic punctuation and alliteration the poet has slowed down the tempo of the iambic pentameter to impart an aura of melancholy and desire to describe his love of a once beautiful woman for whom, despite her advancing age, he still yearns.

第一次读诗歌《当你老了》时，它看起来只是一首简单的爱情诗。然而，经过仔细的分析后，人们会发现叶芝是创作了一篇完全没有出现第一人称的短小自传。通过对词语的精挑细选、标点的巧妙运用和头韵的使用，诗人放慢了抑扬格五步格诗的节奏来渲染出一种忧郁的氛围，并以此表现出他想要对一个曾经美丽的女子表达爱意的愿望，尽管她逐渐老去，他依然对她充满渴望。

名段选读

When you are old and grey and full of sleep,
And nodding by the fire, take down this book,
And slowly read, and dream of the soft look
Your eyes had once, and of their shadows deep;

How many loved your moments of glad grace,
And loved your beauty with love false or true,
But one man loved the **pilgrim**① soul in you,
And loved the sorrows of your changing face;

And bending down beside the glowing bars,
Murmur, a little sadly, how love fled
And paced upon the mountains overhead
And hid his face amid a crowd of stars.

当你老了，白发苍苍，睡意朦胧，

在炉火旁打着盹，取下这本书，
慢慢品读，追忆你的眼神
当年是那样柔美，而又那样深幽；

多少人曾经为你的倩影倾倒，
爱恋你的容颜，或是真挚爱慕或是虚情假意，
唯独有一人爱着你圣洁的灵魂，
和你饱经风霜的面庞上那丝丝忧伤。

你在炉栏边俯下身来，
喃喃自语中透露着淡淡的感伤
爱情已经溜走，在头顶的山峦上踱着脚步，
还把脸藏在了璀璨的群星之中。

——《当你老了》

注释

① pilgrim ['pɪlgrɪm] *n.* 朝圣者

12 英国十九世纪初期伟大的浪漫主义诗人——乔治·戈登·拜伦

George Gordon Byron, 6th Baron Byron (January 22, 1788—April 19, 1824), commonly known simply as Lord Byron, was an English poet and a leading figure in Romanticism. Amongst Byron's best-known works are the brief poems She *Walks in Beauty, When We Two Parted*, and *So, We'll Go No More A Roving*, in addition to the narrative poems *Childe Harold's Pilgrimage* and *Don Juan*. He is regarded as one of the greatest British poets and remains widely read and influential.

乔治·戈登·拜伦（1788年1月22日—1824年4月19日）是拜伦家族第六代男爵，被人尊称为拜伦勋爵，他是一名英国诗人，也是浪漫主义的杰出代表。拜伦的作品中最著名的有短篇诗歌《她在美中行》、《昔日依依别》和《好吧，我们不在一起漫游》，另外还有叙事诗《哈罗德游记》和《唐璜》。拜伦被视为是英国最伟大的诗人之一，至今仍有广泛深远的影响。

《唐璜》★ 全诗共计16000余行，原计划写24章，诗人因赴希腊而辍笔，完成了前16章，第17章完成了开头14节，因而这是一部尚未完成的作品。但故事是完整的，人物形象仍然是丰满的。发表于1821年，以社会讽刺为基调的诗体小说，诗中描绘了西班牙贵族子弟唐璜的游历、恋爱及冒险等浪漫故事，揭露了社会中黑暗、丑恶、虚伪的一面，奏响了为自由、幸福和解放而斗争的战歌。国内最流行的译本是查良铮的译本。

Don Juan
唐璜

Man's love is of man's life a thing apart,
'Tis woman's whole existence.
爱情只是男人生命的一部分，
却是女人的全部。

——*Don Juan*《唐璜》

名著导读

Don Juan is considered Byron's foremost achievement and one of English literature's great long poems. Don Juan follows the travels and relationships of a youthful protagonist who, though he shares the same name, bears little resemblance to the heartless libertine of popular European legend. Juan's story, however, represents only a part of *Don Juan*. Through the series of adventures as overprotected teenager, castaway, lover, slave, soldier, kept man, and ornament in English society, Byron deliberates on a vast array of social, political, poetic, and metaphysical topics. Byron's use of a narrator with a distinct personality, as well as the presence of the poet's own voice in the work, allows him simultaneously to tell Juan's story and to comment on it from various perspectives.

《唐璜》被认为是拜伦最重要的作品以及英国文学上伟大的长诗之一。《唐璜》描述了年轻主人公的旅行经历和爱情纠葛，尽管主人公与广为流传的欧洲传说中的无情浪荡子同名，可是他们之间毫无相似之处。唐璜的故事仅仅是《唐璜》一书中的一个部分。通过描述唐璜从一个被保护过度的青少年到成为出海遇难者、深情的恋人、奴隶、士兵、宠臣和英国社会的花瓶人物所经历的一系列的冒险，拜伦广泛探讨了许多话题，话题涉及社会、政治、诗歌和哲学。拜伦使用了个性鲜明的叙述手法，并在诗歌中发表自己的意见，这样的做法让他在讲述唐璜的故事的同时得以从不同的角度对其做出评论。

名段选读

I loved, I love you, for this love have lost
State, station, heaven, mankind's, my own **esteem**①,
And yet can not regret what it hath cost,
So dear is still the memory of that dream;
Yet, if I name my guilt, 't is not to boast,
None can deem harshlier of me than I deem:
I trace this **scrawl**② because I cannot rest-
I've nothing to reproach, or to request.

Man's love is of man's life a thing apart,
'Tis woman's whole existence; man may range
The court, camp, church, the **vessel**③, and the mart;

Sword, gown, gain, glory, offer in exchange
Pride, fame, ambition, to fill up his heart,
And few there are whom these cannot estrange;
Men have all these resources, we but one,
To love again, and be again undone.

You will proceed in pleasure, and in pride,
Beloved and loving many; all is o'er
For me on earth, except some years to hide
My shame and sorrow deep in my heart's core;
These I could bear, but cannot cast aside
The passion which still rages as before
And so farewell—forgive me, love me—No,
That word is idle now—but let it go.

我过去爱你，现在仍爱着你，为了这份爱
我失去了国家、地位、天堂、人间和个人尊严；
但我并不为我付出的代价而懊悔，
这份如梦如幻的记忆依然是那么弥足珍贵。
然而，如果我列出自己的罪行，没有人会比我对自己更苛刻，
这并非夸大：
我写下这潦草的诗句，皆因为我无法成眠
我毫无怨言，也一无所求。

爱情只是男人生命的一部分，
却是女人的全部；男人可以
穿梭于宫廷、野外、教堂、船舰和市场，
用骄傲、名望和雄心壮志
来交换武力、权利、金钱、荣耀，以满足自己，
没有什么是他们不能舍弃。
男人拥有的是如此之多，而女人却只能
不断去爱，又不断看到爱情的幻灭。

你将继续愉悦地、骄傲地生活：
爱着许多人，也被许多人爱；而对我而言：
世间一切都已结束，徒留一些苟延残喘的岁月，

我将羞耻与悲痛深埋在心底。

这些我都可以忍受，

但我却依然无法抛弃肆虐如初的激情。

所以，永别了，请原谅我，爱我吧，

不，这个字已经没有意义了——就让它随风而逝吧。

——选自《唐璜》第1章

注释

★“《唐璜》是彻底的天才的作品——愤世到了不顾一切的辛辣程度，温柔到了优美感情的最纤细动人的地步……”

——德国诗人歌德

① esteem [ɪ'stiːm] *n.* 尊严

② scrawl [skrɔːl] *n.* 潦草书写

③ vessel ['vesl] *n.* 船舰

13 美国现代著名女作家、《飘》之母——玛格丽特·芒内尔林·米切尔

Margaret Munnerlyn Mitchell (November 8, 1900—August 16, 1949) was an American author, who won the Pulitzer Prize in 1937 for her epic novel *Gone with the Wind,* her only major publication. This novel is one of the most popular books of all time, selling more than 30 million copies. The film adaptation of it, released in 1939, became the highest-grossing film in the history of Hollywood, and it received a record-breaking ten Academy Awards.

玛格丽特·芒内尔林·米切尔（1900年11月8日—1949年8月16日）是一位美国作家，她在1937年凭借史诗小说《飘》获得普利策奖，而这部小说也是她发表的唯一一部巨作。《飘》在各个时代，一直位居最受欢迎的小说之列，从出版至今发行量高达三亿多本。而由小说改编而成的电影在1939年上映，成为好莱坞历史上票房最高的影片，并在当年破纪录地获得了十项奥斯卡奖。

《飘》共63章，发表于1936年，以美国南北战争时期南方社会为背景，以斯嘉丽为主线，描写了几对青年的爱情纠葛。国内最流行的译本是傅东华的译本。

Gone with the Wind
飘

Like must marry like or there'll be no happiness.

婚姻必定是志同道合者的结合，否则就没有幸福可言。

——*Gone with the Wind*《飘》

名著导读

Gone with the Wind takes place in the southern United States of America in the state of Georgia during the American Civil War (1861—1865) and the Reconstruction era (1865—1877) that followed the war. It depicts the experiences of Scarlett O'Hara, the spoiled daughter of a well-to-do plantation owner growing from a young woman into the responsibilities of adulthood. It traces the life of Scarlett O'Hara and her relationships with Rhett Butler, and Ashley and Melanie Wilkes.

《飘》所讲述的故事发生在美国南方的佐治亚州，时间是南北战争时期(1861—1865)和战后重建时期（1865年—1877年）。故事的主人公是一位富裕农场主的千金，名叫斯佳丽•奥哈拉，小说描写了斯佳丽从一位少女成长为一位富有责任感的成年人的人生历程。小说记叙了斯佳丽的人生历程以及她与白瑞德、阿什利和媚兰・威尔克斯三人之间的关系。

名段选读

Life and feeling and comprehension were beginning to flow back into her.

"But you just said you cared for me."

His warm hands hurt hers.

"My dear, must you make me say things that will hurt you?"

Her silence pressed him on. "How can I make you see these things, my dear. You who are so young and **unthinking**[①] that you do not know what marriage means."

"I know I love you."

"Love isn't enough to make a successful marriage when two people are as different as we are. You would want all of a man, Scarlett, his body, his heart, his soul, his thoughts. And if you did not have them, you would be miserable. And I couldn't give you all of me. I couldn't give all of me to anyone. And I would not want all of your mind and your soul. And you would be hurt, and then you would come to hate me—how bitterly! You would hate the books I read and the music I loved, because they took me away from you even for a moment. And I—perhaps I—"

"Do you love her?"

"She is like me, part of my blood, and we understand each other. Scarlett! Scarlett! Can't I make you see that a marriage can't go on in any sort of peace unless the two people are alike?"

Some one else had said that: "Like must marry like or there'll be no happiness." Who was it? It seemed a million years since she had heard that, but it still did not make sense.

她仿佛又找回了生命、情感和觉悟。

"但你刚才还说你喜欢我。"

他那双温暖的手把她握痛了。

"亲爱的，你为什么非要我说那些伤害你的话呢？"

她没有说话，他只好自己继续说下去："我怎样才能让你明白这些事呢，亲爱的。你还太年轻，考虑事情不太全面，你不知道婚姻意味着什么。”

“我只知道我爱你。”

“像我们这样截然不同的两个人，要想拥有幸福美满的婚姻，光有爱情是不够的。你要的是一个男人的全部，斯佳丽！他的身体，他的心灵，他的灵魂，他的思想。如果你不能拥有全部，你会痛苦不堪的。而我无法给你我的全部。我无法把我的全部给任何人。我也不想得到你全部的思想和灵魂。那样，你就会受到伤害的，你会恨我——恨透我的！你甚至会讨厌我喜欢读的书和喜欢听的音乐，因为那些东西会把我从你身边夺走，哪怕只是短暂的一会儿。而我——我也许——”

“你爱她吗？”

“她和我很像，已经融入了我的血液里，我们能相互理解对方。斯佳丽！斯佳丽！难道你还不懂吗？只有两个相像的人在一起才能使得婚姻生活稳定下来。”

有人曾经说过：“婚姻必定是志同道合者的结合，否则就没有幸福可言。”这话是谁说的？这话似乎已经流传了有一百万年，但对她来说，仍然是无法理解的。

——选自《飘》第6章

注释

① unthinking [ʌn'θɪŋkɪŋ] *adj.* 无思想的，无思虑的

14 美国传奇“遁世”作家——杰罗姆·大卫·塞林格

Jerome David Salinger (January 1, 1919—January 27, 2010) was an American author, best known for his 1951 novel *The Catcher in the Rye, as well* as his reclusive nature. The success of The Catcher in the Rye led to public attention and scrutiny: Salinger became reclusive, publishing new work less frequently. He followed Catcher with a short story collection, *Nine Stories* (1953), a volume containing a novella and a short story, *Franny and Zooey* (1961), and a volume containing two novellas, *Raise High the Roof Beam, Carpenters and Seymour: An Introduction* (1963). His last published work, a novella entitled *Hapworth* 16, 1924, appeared in *The New Yorker* on June 19, 1965.

杰罗姆·大卫·塞林格（1919年1月1日—2010年1月27日）是美国作家，其闻名于世的作品当属他1951年所写的小说《麦田里的守望者》，同样广为人知的还有他遁世的作风。《麦田里的守望者》的巨大成功引起了世人对他的频频关注和审视：塞林格因此行踪隐秘，也不再频繁发表新的作品了。在《麦田里的守望者》出版后，他还创作了一部短篇故事集《九个故事》（1953），以及《弗兰妮和佐伊》（1961），该书由一篇中篇小说和一篇短篇小说组成，以及一本由两篇中篇小说《高举顶梁，木匠们》和《西摩简介》(1963)组成的故事集。他出版的最后一部作品于1965年6月19日首次发表在《纽约时报》上，是一篇名叫《哈普沃思16，1924》的中篇小说。

《麦田里的守望者》发表于1951年，是塞林格唯一一部长篇小说。全书以出身美国中产阶级家庭的16岁中学生霍尔顿·考尔德的口吻叙述，塑造了美国当代文学中最早的反英雄形象之一。该书一经问世便风靡全球，在青少年中引起强烈共鸣，至今仍十分畅销。目前国内最著名的译本是施咸荣的版本。

The Catcher in the Rye
麦田里的守望者

It's funny. All you have to do is say something nobody understands and they'll do pract-ically anything you want them to.

多可笑啊。你只要说些谁也听不懂的话，他们就会一一照做。

——*The Catcher in the Ray*《麦田里的守望者》

名著导读

The majority of the novel takes place in December 1949. After being expelled from the school for poor grades, Holden takes a train to New York, but does not want to return to his family and instead checks into the **dilapidated**① Edmont Hotel. Holden spends a total of three days in the city, characterized largely by drunkenness and loneliness. Finally, He plans to go to a new school in the fall and is cautiously optimistic about his future.

小说所讲述的故事主要发生在1949年12月。故事的主人公霍尔顿因为成绩差而被学校开除。他搭了一辆火车回到纽约，但是他并不想回家，于是住进了破旧的埃德蒙宾馆。霍尔顿在纽约这座城市整整游荡了三天，终日饮酒度日，寂寞冷清。最后，他决定入秋就找一所新学校上学，对未来不敢再抱以盲目的乐观态度。

名段选读

The best break I had in years, when I got home the regular night elevator boy, Pete, wasn't on the car. Some new guy I'd never seen was on the car, so I figured that if I didn't **bump**② smack into my parents and all I'd be able to say hello to old Phoebe and then beat it and nobody'd even know I'd been around. It was really a terrific break. What made it even better, the new elevator boy was sort of on the stupid side. I told him, in this very casual voice, to take me up to the Dicksteins'. The Dicksteins were these people that had the other apartment on our floor. I'd already taken off my hunting hat, so as not to look suspicious or anything. I went in the elevator like I was in a terrific hurry.

He had the elevator doors all shut and all, and was all set to take me up, and then he turned around and said, "They ain't in. They're at a party on the fourteenth floor."

"That's all right," I said. "I'm supposed to wait for them. I'm their nephew."

He gave me this sort of stupid, suspicious look. "You better wait in the lobby, fella," he said.

"I'd like to—I really would," I said. "But I have a bad leg. I have to hold it in a certain position. I think I'd better sit down in the chair outside their door."

He didn't know what the hell I was talking about, so all he said was "Oh" and took me up. Not bad, boy. It's funny. All you have to do is say something nobody understands and they'll do practically anything you want them to.

I got off at our floor—**limping**③ like a bastard—and started walking over toward the Dicksteins' side. Then, when I heard the elevator doors shut, I turned around and went over to our side. I was doing all right. I didn't even feel drunk anymore. Then I took out my door key and opened our door, quiet as hell. Then, very, very carefully and all, I went inside and closed the door. I really should've been a **crook**④

那天是我几年以来度过的最好的放学时光，当时我像往常一样放学回家，通常在夜班电梯值班的男孩皮特正好不在。有个新来的男孩在电梯里，我估计，只要我不被我父母撞见，我或许可以跟老菲打个招呼，然后溜走，不会有人知道我就在附近的。真是太棒了。更幸运的是，新来的男孩还有些傻里傻气。我用一种漫不经心的语气跟他说，去迪克斯坦家。迪克斯坦家和我家住同一层楼。我早就摘下了我的猎帽，这样我看起来就不那么可疑了。我假装很匆忙的样子走进了电梯。

他把电梯门关上，按动了电梯，正准备带我上去，这时候，他转身对我说："他们不在家，他们在十四层楼办派对。"

"没关系，"我说。"那我就等会儿。我是他们的外甥。"

他傻里傻气，略带怀疑地看了看我。"你最好在大厅等他们，哥们，"他说。

"我也想啊——我真的很想，"我回答说。"但我腿有毛病，我得尽量保持同一个姿势。我想我还是坐在他家门口的椅子上等吧。"

他根本就不知道我在说什么，所以只能回答我说"哦"然后带我上楼，这小子不错。多可笑啊。你只要说些谁也听不懂的话，他们就会一一照做。

我在我们那一层下了电梯——假装一瘸一拐活像个瘸子——随即就朝着迪克斯坦家的方向走去。当听到电梯关门的声音后，我就掉头回自个儿家。我干得不错。甚至都不觉得有醉意了。然后我拿出房门钥匙悄悄地打开门，家里真是安静啊。随后，我非常，非常小心地走进屋里，关上门。我真应该去当小偷啊。

——选自《麦田里的守望者》第21章

注释

① dilapidated [dɪˈlæpɪdeitɪd] *adj.* 荒废的，要塌似的；破坏的

② bump [bʌmp] *vi.* 碰，撞

③ limp [lɪmp] *vi.* 跛行

④crook [krʊk] *n.* 小偷，骗子

15 美国伟大浪漫主义小说家——赫尔曼·梅尔维尔

Herman Melville (August 1, 1819—September 28, 1891) was an American novelist, short story writer, essayist, and poet. He is best known for his novel *Moby-Dick* and the posthumous novella *Billy Budd*. His first three books gained much contemporary attention, but after a fast-blooming literary success in the late 1840s, his popularity declined precipitously in the mid-1850s and never recovered during his lifetime. It was not until the "Melville Revival" in the early 20th century that his work won recognition, especially *Moby-Dick* which was hailed as one of the literary masterpieces of both American and world literature. He was the first writer to have his works collected and published by the Library of America.

赫尔曼·梅尔维尔(1819年8月1日—1891年9月28日)是美国著名小说家、短篇小说作家、散文家和诗人。他因小说《白鲸》和他去世后发表的中篇小说《比利·巴德》而闻名于世。他最初创作的三部作品让他在当时备受关注，但经历了十九世纪四十年代末在文学领域的迅速走红后，从十九世纪五十年代中期开始，他的身影突然从公众的视野里消失了，一直到去世。直到20世纪早期的“梅尔维尔复兴”，他的作品才赢得广泛认可，尤其是《白鲸》，这部作品一直被认为是美国和世界文学史上的杰作。他是第一位作品由美国图书馆整理并发表的作家。

《白鲸》★ 出版于1851年，共136章，已成为世界文坛公认的伟大杰作,被誉为“时代的镜子”和“美国想象力最辉煌的表达”。《白鲸》是一部融戏剧、冒险、哲理、研究于一体的鸿篇巨制。目前国内比较好的译本是曹庸的译本和成时的译本。

The Whale/Moby-Dick
白鲸

When beholding the tranquil beauty and brilliancy of the ocean's skin, one forgets the tiger heart that pants beneath it; and would not willingly remember, that this velvet pawbut conceals a remorseless fang.

看着眼前静谧的美景和壮丽的海面，大家都忘却了表象背后的野心；也不愿意记起，在这天鹅绒一般柔和的小爪子里藏着凶残的尖牙。

——*The Whale/Moby-Dick*《白鲸》

名著导读

Ahab is the captain of Pequod, a whaling ship. Ahab's purpose for this voyage is hunting down and killing Moby Dick, an old, very large sperm whale that crippled Ahab on his last whaling voyage. Finally Ahab harpoons the whale, but the unfolding harpoon-line catches him around his neck and he is dragged into the depths of the sea by the diving Moby Dick. The boat is caught up in the whirlpool of the sinking ship, which takes almost all the crew to their deaths. Only Ishmael survives, clinging to Queequeg's coffin-turned-life buoy for an entire day and night before the Rachel rescues him.

亚哈是"佩科特号"捕鲸船的船长。他们出航的目的是要捕获一头名叫莫比·迪克的成年白鲸并杀死它，莫比·迪克体型庞大，生性凶残，它让亚哈船长在上一次捕鲸时变成了残废。最后，亚哈船长将鱼叉刺到了白鲸身上，但系在鱼叉上的绳索缠住了他的脖子，他被下沉的白鲸拖入了海洋深处。捕鲸船陷入海洋漩涡中，最后船上大部分船员丧生，只有伊斯梅尔幸存下来。他靠魁魁格的棺材在海面上漂浮了整整一天，最后被瑞秋救起。

名段选读

Penetrating further and further into the heart of the Japanese cruising ground the Pequod was soon all **astir**① in the fishery. Often, in mild, pleasant weather, for twelve, fifteen, eighteen, and twenty hours on the stretch, they were engaged in the boats, steadily pulling, or sailing, or paddling after the whales, or for an **interlude**② of sixty or seventy minutes calmly awaiting their uprising; though with but small success for their pains.

At such times, under an **abated**③ sun; **afloat**④ all day upon smooth, slow heaving swells; seated in his boat, light as a birch canoe; and so sociably mixing with the soft waves themselves, that like hearth-stone cats they purr against the gunwale; these are the times of dreamy quietude, when beholding the tranquil beauty and brilliancy of the ocean's skin, one forgets the tiger heart that pants beneath it; and would not willingly remember, that this velvet paw but conceals a **remorseless**⑤ fang.

These are the times, when in his whale-boat the rover softly feels a certain **filial**⑥, confident, land-like feeling towards the sea; that he regards it as so much flowery earth; and the distant ship revealing only the tops of her **masts**⑦, seems struggling forward, not through high rolling waves, but through the tall grass of a rolling prairie: as when the western emigrants' horses only show their erected ears, while their hidden bodies widely wade through the amazing **verdure**.⑧

The long-drawn virgin vales; the mild blue hill-sides; as over these there steals the hush, the hum; you almost swear that play-wearied children lie sleeping in these solitudes, in some glad May-time, when the flowers of the woods are plucked. And all this mixes with your most mystic mood; so that fact and fancy, half-way meeting, **interpenetrate**⑨, and form one seamless whole.

Nor did such soothing scenes, however temporary, fail of at least as temporary an effect on Ahab. But if these secret golden keys did seem to open in him his own secret golden treasuries, yet did his breath upon them prove but **tarnishing**⑩.

"佩科特号"越来越深入到日本巡航海域的中心地带，这个消息不久就在捕鱼界引起了轰动。通常，在风和日丽的天气里，他们会划着小船，一连划上十二、十五、十八甚至二十个小时，不停地划着或者扬帆航行，寻找鲸鱼的踪迹，或者他们会中途静静地等上六七十分钟，等鲸鱼浮出水面；尽管他们常常徒劳无获。

这个时候，阳光不那么强烈，他们整日都坐在桦木舟般轻盈的小船上，漂浮在平静的、泛着微波的海面上；他们和这微波融为了一体，像炉边的小猫一样，他们愉悦地靠着船缘，看着眼前静谧的美景和壮丽的海面，感觉就像梦境般安宁，大家都忘却了表象背后的野心；也不愿意记起，在这天鹅绒一般柔和的小爪子里藏着凶残的尖牙。

在这样的时候，捕鲸船里的漂泊者们就会隐隐约约对大海产生一种依恋、孝顺的感觉，就像人们对陆地的感情一样，他们觉得大海是一片绚烂的土地；远处，一艘船的桅杆顶端露了出来，好像它不是在大海中劈波斩浪，而是在大草原上高高的杂草中挣扎着穿梭前行：就像西部牛仔骑的马，只露出它们竖起的双耳，身体掩映在草中，费力地穿过那片令人惊诧的翠绿。

绵延的原始山谷；缓缓的蓝色山坡；看到这样的情景，你会屏住呼吸，不由自主地发出心旷神怡的叹息；你会想象到，在灿烂的五月，一群天真活泼的孩子采摘把玩树林里的花，他们玩累了，正在这个静谧的地方熟睡。这种想象和你的心情交织在一起，现实和虚幻相互交融，形成了一个完美的整体。

这样的景象虽然短暂，但至少让船长亚哈能暂时放松了一下。但若这把金钥匙能开启他心中隐藏的宝藏，他只需对着它们吹一口气，它们就又失去了原有的光泽。

——选自《白鲸》第114章

注释

★"《白鲸》部分是戏剧，部分是历险故事，部分是哲学探讨，部分是科学研究，部分是史诗。它是一部神奇巨著。"

——英国学者伊恩·乌斯比

① astir [ə'stəː] *adj.* 活动的

② interlude ['ɪntəluːd] *n.* 幕间

③ abated [ə'beitɪd] *adj.* 减弱的

④ afloat [ə'fləut] *adj.* 漂浮的，在海上的

⑤ remorseless [rɪ'mɔ:sləs] *adj.* 冷酷无情的

⑥ filial ['fɪliəl] *adj.* 子女的，孝顺的

⑦ mast [mɑ:st] *n.* 桅杆

⑧ verdure ['vɜ:dʒə(r)] *n.* 碧绿

⑨ interpenetrate [ˌɪntə'penɪtreit] *vi.* 相互渗透

⑩ tarnish ['tɑ:nɪʃ] *vi.* 失去光泽

16 美国表现主义文学的代表作家——尤金·奥尼尔

Eugene Gladstone O'Neill (October 16, 1888—November 27, 1953) was an American playwright, and Nobel laureate in Literature. His plays were among the first to include speeches in American vernacular and involve characters on the fringes of society, engaging in depraved behavior, where they struggle to maintain their hopes and aspirations, but ultimately slide into disillusionment and despair. O'Neill wrote only one well-known comedy *Ah, Wilderness! Nearly* all of his other plays involve some degree of tragedy and personal pessimism.

尤金·奥尼尔（1888年10月16日—1953年11月27日）是美国剧作家和诺贝尔文学奖的获得者。他是首批在戏剧中加入了美国方言对白，并以处在社会边缘、行为堕落的人物为角色的作家，在他的小说中，虽然这些人都努力地维系自己的希望与抱负，但最终都滑入幻灭和绝望的深渊。《啊，荒野！》是奥尼尔唯一一部著名的喜剧，除此之外，他的所有作品都掺杂了一些悲剧成分和个人的厌世情怀。

《天边外》★是“美国戏剧之父”尤金·奥尼尔早期戏剧创作的典范，发表于1920年，分为3幕，每幕2场：一在室外，一眼看到天边；一在室内，看不到天边。这两种场景交替出现，表明理想与现实之间距离的遥远。它继承了古代的悲剧创作传统，为作者首次赢得普利策奖和1936年的诺贝尔文学奖。目前国内最流行的译本是王海若的译本。

Beyond the Horizon
天边外

Supposing I was to tell you that it's just Beauty that's calling me, the beauty of the faroff and unknown, the mystery and spell of the East, which lures me in the books I've read, the need of the freedom of great wide spaces, the joy of wandering on and on—in quest of the secret which is hidden just over there, beyond the horizon? Suppose I told you that was the one and only reason for my going?

假如我告诉你，是美在召唤着我，那遥远的、未知的绮丽，东方的魅力和神秘，它们在书中用对无尽的自由的希冀和环游世界所带来的愉悦诱惑着我——让我想要探寻那天边外的奥秘，假如我告诉你，这就是我出海的唯一的原因，你会怎么想？

——*Beyond the Horizon*《天边外》

名著导读

Two brothers, Robert and Andrew, are in love with the same woman, Andrew's girl Ruth. Robert resolves to go to sea on his uncle's ship. Just before he is to leave, he confesses his love to Ruth. She is **captivated**[①] by Robert's poetic nature, and believes that she is in love with him. As a result Rob stays home and Andrew runs off to sea in his place. Robert and Ruth get married, and Robert tries to run the farm, but he is unsuccessful. After the death of his father the farm **deteriorates**[②]. Ruth begins to regret her mistake, but when Andrew comes back he seems to have completely gotten over her. In the end Robert dies of tuberculosis still dreaming of something beyond the horizon, while Ruth hopes vainly that she might still find happiness with Andrew.

罗伯特和安德罗两兄弟爱上了同一个女人露丝，而露丝是安德罗的女朋友。于是罗伯特决定乘舅舅的船去航海，启程之前，他向露丝表达了爱意，露丝被他的诗意情怀打动，并自以为爱上了罗伯特。于是罗伯特留在了家里，而安德罗代替他出海了。罗伯特和露丝结了婚，他尝试着经营农场，却失败了。两兄弟的父亲去世之后，农场更为萧条。露丝开始懊悔自己错误的选择，但是当安德罗回来时，他似乎已从感情挫败的阴影中走了出来。最后，罗伯特因肺结核死去，临死前，他仍在幻想着天边外的某个东西，而露丝则徒劳地希望自己能和安德罗幸福地在一起。

名段选读

Andrew: Oh, of course. I know you're going to learn **navigation**[③], and all about a ship, so you can be an officer. That's natural, too. There's fair pay in it, I expect, when you consider that you've always got a home and grub thrown in; and if you're set on travelling, you can go anywhere you're a mind to, without paying fare.

Robert: (*With a smile that is half-sad.*) It's more than that, Andy.

Andrew: Sure it is. There's always a chance of a good thing coming your way in some of those foreign ports or other. I've heard there are great opportunities for a young fellow with his eyes open in some of those new countries that are just being opened up. And with your education you ought to pick up the language quick. (**Jovially**[④]) I'll bet that's what you've been turning over in your mind under all your quietness! (*He slaps his brother on the back with a laugh.*) Well, if you get to be a millionaire all of a sudden, call 'round once in a while and I'll pass the plate to you. We could use a lot of money right here on the farm without hurting it any.

Robert: (*Forced to laugh.*) I've never considered that practical side of it for a minute, Andy.

(*As ANDREW looks* **incredulous**[5].) That's the truth.

Andrew: Well, you ought to.

Robert: No, I oughtn't. You're trying to wish an eye-for-business on me I don't possess. (*Pointing to the horizon—dreamily.*) Supposing I was to tell you that it's just Beauty that's calling me, the beauty of the far off and unknown, the mystery and spell of the East, which lures me in the books I've read, the need of the freedom of great wide spaces, the joy of wandering on and on—in quest of the secret which is hidden just over there, beyond the horizon? Suppose I told you that was the one and only reason for my going?

安德罗：噢，我当然知道你要去学习航海和船舶方面的知识，这样你就可以当一名海员，那再自然不过了。我认为薪水是很不错的，只要想一下，你总是有住的地方，还有充裕的食物。而且如果你要去旅游，你可以去任何想去的地方，一个子儿也不用花。

罗伯特：（*苦笑。*）不止那些的，安迪。

安德罗：当然。在一些外国港口或其他什么地方，总是会有好机遇等着你。我听说，那些刚刚开放的新国家会提供给那些眼界开阔的年轻人很多良机。凭你受教育的程度，你可以轻松地掌握一门外语。（*愉悦地。*）我敢打赌，尽管你表现得很沉默，但你心里一直是这么想的。（*他笑着拍拍他兄弟的背。*）好吧，如果你一夜之间成了一个大富豪，偶尔来探望一下我，我会要你捐款的。我们可以把大笔的钱花在在农场上，这样做不会有任何坏处。

罗伯特：（*勉强地笑。*）我从来没想过这么实际的事情，安迪。（*迎着安迪怀疑的眼神。*）我说真的。

安德罗：你应该想一想的。

罗伯特：不，没有这个必要。你希望我有经商的眼光，可我没有。1（*指着地平线——充满梦想。*）假如我告诉你，是美在召唤着我，那遥远的、未知的绮丽，东方的魅力和神秘，在我读过的书中，对无尽自由的希冀和环游世界的愉悦诱惑着我——让我想要探寻那天边外的奥秘，假如我告诉你，这就是我出海的唯一的原因，你会怎么想？

——选自《天边外》第1幕第1场

注释

★“《天边外》的两大主题：第一是梦想对鼓舞人心的必要性，第二是人们对发掘蕴藏着人生真谛秘密的那股生命背后的神秘力量的探求。”

——美国作家弗吉尼亚·费洛伊德

① captivate [ˈkæptɪveit] *vi* 迷住，迷惑
② deteriorate [dɪˈtɪəriəreit] *vt.&vi.* 恶化
③ navigation [ˌnævɪˈgeiʃ ən] *n.* 航行，航海
④ jovially [ˈdʒəuviəlɪ] *adv.* 高兴地，快活地
⑤ incredulous [ɪnˈkredjələs] *adj.* 表示怀疑的

17 法国十九世纪著名的现实主义小说家——阿尔丰斯·都德

Alphonse Daudet (May 13, 1840—December 16, 1897) was a French novelist. He was the father of Leon Daudet and Lucien Daudet. The year 1872 brought the famous Aventures prodigieuses *Tartarin of Tarascon*, and the three-act play *The Girl From Arles*. But *Fromont Junior and Risler Senior* (1874) at once took the world by storm. It struck a note, not new certainly in English literature, but comparatively new in French. His creativeness resulted in characters that were real and also typical.

阿尔丰斯·都德(1840年5月13日—1897年12月16日)是一位法国小说家，也是利昂·都德和吕西安·都德的父亲。1872年，他撰写了著名的剧本《达拉斯贡的戴达伦》和三幕剧《阿莱城的姑娘》。但是，他在1874年撰写的《小弗罗孟和老利斯勒》一出版就席卷了世界。该书表现出来的格调在英国文学中不一定算新颖，但在法国文学中却相对前沿。他的才思使他创造出了既有真实感又具代表性的人物。

《最后一课》创作于普法战争刚结束的第二年(1873)，由于具有深刻的爱国主义内容和精湛的艺术技巧而享有极高的声誉，成为世界短篇小说中的杰作。这部小说的中文译本最早是由胡适翻译的，现在有人教版的全文译本。

The Last Class
最后一课

Ah! It has been the great misfortune of our Alsace always to postpone its lessons until tomorrow.

啊！我们阿尔萨斯人总是把事情推到明天，这是我们最大的悲哀。

——*The Last Class*《最后一课》

名著导读

The Last Class is the tender story of a young Alsatian boy and his last French lesson. The setting is an unnamed town in Alsace, and the story takes place near the beginning of the Prussian occupation of Alsace and Lorraine, about 1873. Little Franz is the narrator of the story. Having gotten a late start on this beautiful warm morning, Franz rushes to school. He is fearful that Monsieur Hamel will scold him because he is late and has not prepared his French lesson on participles. However, it turns out to be his last French class.

《最后一课》讲述了一个阿尔萨斯小男孩上他最后一堂法语课的悲痛故事。故事背景是在阿尔萨斯的一个无名小镇，发生在大约1873年普鲁士攻占法国阿尔萨斯和洛林之际。小弗朗茨是整个故事的叙述者。在一个温暖美丽的早晨，小弗朗茨起床晚了，匆匆忙忙往学校赶去。小弗朗茨很害怕韩麦尔先生会责骂他，因为自己迟到了，而且没有复习法语分词。然而，那堂课竟是他的最后一堂法语课了。

名段选读

"I will not scold you, my little Frantz; you must be punished enough; that is the way it goes; every day we say to ourselves: 'Pshaw! I have time enough. I will learn tomorrow.' And then you see what happens. Ah! It has been the great misfortune of our Alsace always to postpone its lessons until tomorrow. Now those people are entitled to say to us: 'What! You claim to be French, and you can neither speak nor write your language!' In all this, my poor Frantz, you are not the guiltiest one. We all have our fair share of reproaches to address to ourselves."

"Your parents have not been careful enough to see that you were educated. They preferred to send you to work in the fields or in the factories, in order to have a few more sous. And have I nothing to **reproach**① myself for? Have I not often made you water my garden instead of studying? And when I wanted to go fishing for **trout**②, have I ever hesitated to dismiss you?"

Then, passing from one thing to another, Monsieur Hamel began to talk to us about the French language, saying that it was the most beautiful language in the world, the most clear, the most substantial; that we must always retain it among ourselves, and never forget it, because when a people falls into **servitude**③, "so long as it clings to its language, it is as if it held the key to its prison." Then he took the grammar and read us our lesson. I was amazed to see how readily I understood. Everything that he said seemed so easy to me, so easy. I believed, too, that I had never listened so closely, and that he, for his part, had never been so patient with his explanations. One would have said that, before going away, the poor man desired to give us all his

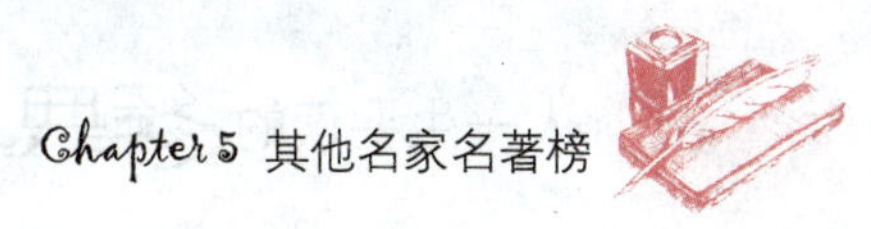

knowledge, to force it all into our heads at a single blow.

“我不会责怪你的，小弗朗茨，你已经受到惩罚了，就是这样的。每天我们都对自己说：‘哎呀，我有的是时间，我明天再学。’这就是我们对待生活的方式，现在你们看看发生了什么，啊！我们阿尔萨斯人总是把事情推到明天，这是我们最大的悲哀。现在，那些人有资格对我们说：‘什么！你们既不会说又不会写法语，还有脸说自己是法国人！’可怜的小弗朗茨，你不是最内疚的那个，我们每个人都该责备自己。”

“你们的父母没有对你们的教育给予足够的关心。他们更愿意把你们送到田里或是工厂去干活，这样可以多挣几个钱。难道我自己就没有该谴责的地方吗？难道我就没有让你们丢下功课来帮我浇花园吗？当我因为想去钓鲑鱼而让你们放学的时候，我不是也没有犹豫过吗？”

韩麦尔先生历数着一件件往事，最后他说到了法语，他说法语是世界上最美丽的语言，也是最明了、最丰富的语言。我们必须牢牢地记住自己的语言，永远都不要忘记，因为，当我们被奴役时，只要紧紧握住自己的语言不放，就好像拿着一把打开监狱之门的钥匙。”然后他拿出语法书，开始领着我们读课文。我惊讶万分地发现，我很容易就理解了课文，韩麦尔先生讲的每句话都是这么明白易懂。我也相信，我过去从来都没有如此聚精会神地听讲，而韩麦尔先生也从没有像现在这样耐心地讲解。你可能会说，这个可怜的人希望在他走之前把所有的知识都传输给我们，希望把知识一下子都塞进我们的脑子里。

——选自《最后一课》

注释

① reproach [rɪ'prəutʃ] *vt.* 谴责，责备

② trout [traʊt] *n.* 鲑鱼

③ servitude ['sɔːvɪtjuːd] *n.* 奴役状况

18 英国二十世纪最具影响力的诗人——托马斯·斯特尔那斯·艾略特

Thomas Stearns Eliot (September 26, 1888—January 4, 1965) was an American-born English poet, playwright, and literary critic, arguably the most important English-language poet of the 20th century. The poem that made his name, *The Love Song of J. Alfred Prufrock*—started in 1910 and published in Chicago in 1915—is regarded as a masterpiece of the modernist movement, and was followed by some of the best-known poems in the English language, including *Gerontion* (1920), *The Waste Land* (1922), *The Hollow Men* (1925), *Ash Wednesday* (1930), and *Four Quartets* (1945). He is also known for his seven plays, particularly *Murder in the Cathedral* (1935). He was awarded the Nobel Prize in Literature in 1948.

托马斯·斯特尔那斯·艾略特（1888年9月26日—1965年1月4日），是一位在美国出生的英国诗人、剧作家和文学评论家，他可以说是20世纪最重要的英语诗人。诗歌《J.阿尔弗雷德·普鲁弗洛克的情歌》是他的成名作，这部诗歌从1910年开始创作，于1915年在芝加哥发表，它被认为是现代主义运动的杰作，之后，他又发表了一些有名的英语诗歌，包括：《小老头》（1920)、《荒原》（1945）、《虚伪的人》（1925）、《圣灰星期三》（1930）、《四重奏》（1945）。他的七部剧本也十分出名，尤其是《大教堂中的谋杀》（1935）。艾略特在1948年获得了诺贝尔文学奖。

《荒原》共5章，是1922年出版的诗歌。它是现代英美诗歌的里程碑，是象征主义文学中最有代表性的作品，也是托马斯·艾略特的成名作和影响最深远的作品，表达了西方国家一代人在精神上的幻灭，被认为是西方现代文学中具有划时代意义的作品。最佳译本由赵萝蕤1980年翻译，上海文艺出版社出版。

The Waste Land
荒原

April is the cruellest month, breeding

Lilacs out of the dead land, mixing
Memory and desire, stirring
Dull roots with spring rain.
四月是最残忍的一个月，
它在荒原上孕育着丁香花，
将记忆和欲望交织在一起，
又用绵绵春雨唤醒了迟钝的根茎。

——*The Waste Land*《荒原》

名著导读

The first section, as the section title indicates, is about death. The section begins with the words "April is the cruellest month," which is perhaps one of the most remarked upon and most important references in the poem. Those familiar with Chaucer's poem *The Canterbury Tales* will recognize that Eliot is taking Chaucer's introductory line from the prologue—which is optimistic about the month of April and the regenerative, life-giving season of spring—and turning it on its head. Just as Chaucer's line sets the tone for The *Canterbury Tales*, Eliot's dark words inform the reader that this is going to be a dark poem.

如诗歌第一节的标题所示，它是关于死亡的。这一节开头写道："四月是最残忍的一个月，"这也许是这首诗中人们评论最多的、最经常引用的诗句之一。熟悉乔叟的诗集《坎特伯雷故事集》的人会发现艾略特借用了序诗中乔叟的介绍性诗句——它表达了对四月和生机盎然的春天的乐观向上的态度——并将它改成了完全相反的基调。正如乔叟的那句诗为《坎特伯雷故事集》设定下了语调一样，艾略特用阴暗的词语告诉读者这会是一首灰暗的诗歌。

名段选读

April is the cruellest month, breeding
Lilacs out of the dead land, mixing
Memory and desire, stirring
Dull roots with spring rain.
Winter kept us warm, covering
Earth in forgetful snow, feeding
A little life with dried **tubers**①.

Summer surprised us, coming over the Starnbergersee
With a shower of rain; we stopped in the **colonnade**[②],
And went on in sunlight, into the Hofgarten,
And drank coffee, and talked for an hour.
Bin gar keine Russin, stamm' aus Litauen, echt deutsch.
And when we were children, staying at the archduke's,
My cousin's, he took me out on a sled,
And I was frightened. He said, Marie,
Marie, hold on tight. And down we went.
In the mountains, there you feel free.
I read, much of the night, and go south in the winter.

What are the roots that clutch, what branches grow
Out of this stony rubbish? Son of man,
You cannot say, or guess, for you know only
A heap of broken images, where the sun beats,
And the dead tree gives no shelter, the **cricket**[③] no relief,
And the dry stone no sound of water. Only
There is shadow under this red rock,
(Come in under the shadow of this red rock),
And I will show you something different from either
Your shadow at morning striding behind you
Or your shadow at evening rising to meet you;
I will show you fear in a **handful**[④] of dust.

四月是最残忍的一个月，
它在荒原上孕育着丁香花，
将记忆和欲望交织在一起，
又用绵绵春雨唤醒了迟钝的根茎。
冬天让我们感觉温暖，
助人健忘的大雪覆盖着大地，
给那干枯的根茎提供了些许生的养分。
夏天总是带给人惊喜，伴随着阵雨
我们来到了斯坦伯吉斯；我们停留在廊柱下，
太阳出来后，继续前行，走进了霍夫加登花园，
我们喝着咖啡，聊了一个小时。

我根本就不是俄国人，我来自立陶宛，是一个真正的德国人。
小时候，我们住在在大公家里，
在我表哥家，他用雪橇拖着我，
当时我很害怕，他说，玛丽，
玛丽，抓紧了，我们要下坡了。
在山上，你会感觉自由自在。
晚上的大部分时间里，我都会看书，冬天就去南方。

什么树根在牢牢抓紧，
什么树枝从这堆乱石缝里长出来？是人子啊，
你们说不出也猜不到，因为你只知道
一大堆破碎的影像，太阳在炙烤着大地，
枯树下没有丝毫的阴凉，蟋蟀也不让人省心，
干涸的石头上没有流水的声音，
只有这块红石头下面有着一点点的阴凉，
(来吧，来到这红石头下乘凉吧)
我会给你看些不同的东西
既不同于早晨你身后大步走着的影子
也不同于晚上站起来与你相见的影子；
我将让你从一把尘土里看到恐惧。

——选自《荒原》第1章

注释

① tuber ['tju:bə(r)] 块茎，结节
② colonnade [ˌkɔlə'neid] *n.* 柱廊
③ cricket ['krɪkɪt] *n.* 蟋蟀
④ handful ['hændful] *n.* 一把

19 讽刺文学大师——乔纳森·斯威夫特

Jonathan Swift (November 30, 1667—October 19, 1745) was an Anglo-Irish satirist, essayist, poet. He is remembered for works such as *Gulliver's Travels, A Modest Proposal, A Journal to Stella, Drapier's Letters, The Battle of the Books, An Argument Against Abolishing Christianity, and A Tale of a Tub*. Swift is probably the foremost prose satirist in the English language, and is less well known for his poetry. He is also known for being a master of two styles of satire: the Horatian and Juvenalian styles.

乔纳森·斯威夫特（1667年11月30日—1745年10月19日），英裔爱尔兰讽刺作家、散文家和诗人。他以著作《格列佛游记》、《一个小小的建议》、《斯特拉日记》、《德雷皮尔的来信》、《书的战争》、《关于废除基督教的讨论》以及《桶的故事》闻名于世。斯威夫特可以称作是英语语言中最重要的散文讽刺作家，但他的诗歌却不是那么有名。他同时还是两种讽刺风格的代表人物：贺瑞斯式讽刺和朱维诺尔式讽刺。

《格列佛游记》★共4部分，1726年出版的一部杰出的游记体讽刺小说，作者用丰富的讽刺手法和虚构幻想的离奇情节，深刻的剖析了当时的英国社会现实。最佳译本由张健1962年翻译，人民文学出版社出版。

Gulliver's Travels
格列佛游记

Blindness is an addition to courage, by concealing dangers from us.

失明会使人更有勇气，因为它让我们看不到危险。

——*Gulliver's Travels*《格列佛游记》

名著导读

Gulliver's Travels recounts the story of Lemuel Gulliver, a practical-minded Englishman trained as a surgeon who takes to the seas when his business fails. When Lemuel Gulliver sets off from London on a sea voyage, little does he know the many incredible and unbelievable **misadventures**[①] awaiting him. Shipwrecked at sea and nearly drowned, he washes ashore upon an exotic island called Lilliput—where the people are only six inches tall! Next he visits a land of incredible giants called Brobdingnagians. They are more than sixty feet tall! He travels to Laputa, a city that floats in the sky, and to Glubbdubdrib, the Island of Sorcerers. His final voyage brings him into contact with the Yahoos—a brutish race of subhumans—and an intelligent and virtuous race of horse, the Houyhnhnms.

《格列佛游记》讲述了莱缪尔·格列佛的故事，他是一个崇尚现实主义的英国外科医生。在生意失败后，他便开始了海上航行。当莱缪尔·格列佛从伦敦起航时，他并不知道等待他的是一连串不可思议的不幸遭遇。船在海上遇难，他几乎淹死，最后死里逃生，漂到了一个叫利立浦特的小人国，这里的人都只有6英寸高。接着，他又来到了一个名为布罗卜丁奈格的巨人国，那里的人足有6英尺高。后来，他又来到了拉普塔浮岛，一个漂浮在天空中的岛国，然后来到了巫人岛。他最后来到了慧骃国——一个人形兽的部落——智慧且善良的马族部落，这使得他有机会认识人形兽。

名段选读

There are some other articles; but these are the most important, of which I have read you an abstract.

In the several debates upon this **impeachment**[②], it must be confessed that his **majesty**[③] gave many marks of his great **lenity**[④]; often urging the services you had done him, and endeavouring to **extenuate**[⑤] your crimes. The treasurer and admiral insisted that you should be put to the most painful and ignominious death, by setting fire to your house at night, and the general was to attend with twenty thousand men, armed with poisoned arrows, to shoot you on the face and hands. Some of your servants were to have private orders to strew a poisonous juice on your shirts and sheets, which would soon make you tear your own flesh, and die in the **utmost**[⑥] torture. The general came into the same opinion; so that for a long time there was a majority against you; but his majesty resolving, if possible, to spare your life, at last brought off the chamberlain.

Upon this incident, Reldresal, principal secretary for private affairs, who always approved himself your true friend, was commanded by the emperor to deliver his opinion, which he accordingly did; and therein justified the good thoughts you have of him. He allowed your crimes to be great, but that still there was room for mercy, the most commendable virtue in a prince, and for which his majesty was so justly celebrated. He said, the friendship between you and him was so well known to the world, that perhaps the most honourable board might think him **partial**⑦; however, in obedience to the command he had received, he would freely offer his sentiments. That if his majesty, in consideration of your services, and **pursuant**⑧ to his own merciful disposition, would please to spare your life, and only give orders to put out both your eyes, he humbly conceived, that by this expedient justice might in some measure be satisfied, and all the world would applaud the lenity of the emperor, as well as the fair and generous proceedings of those who have the honour to be his counsellors. That the loss of your eyes would be no **impediment**⑨ to your bodily strength, by which you might still be useful to his majesty; that blindness is an addition to courage, by concealing dangers from us; that the fear you had for your eyes, was the greatest difficulty in bringing over the enemy's fleet, and it would be sufficient for you to see by the eyes of the ministers, since the greatest princes do no more.

这里还有一些其他条款，但是，这些是最重要的，我已经给你读了摘要。

在对这次弹劾的数次讨论中，毫无疑问，陛下显示了他的宽宏大量，要知道，他经常强调你为他做过很多事情，并努力减轻你的罪行。但财务司长和海军司令坚持让你痛苦并屈辱地死去，他们要半夜去烧你的房子，并让将军带领两万名配备毒箭的士兵，朝着你的脸和手射箭。你的佣人将会接到密令，在你的衬衣和床单上撒上有毒的果汁，这会很快让你抓烂自己的肉，并在极度折磨中死去。将军也有同样的想法；因此，在很长一段时间里，大部分人都敌视你；但是，陛下下定决心，如果可能的话，一定要饶了你的性命，并最终营救出侍从。

内务大臣瑞德萨总自称为你真正的朋友，在这件事上，陛下派他来传达旨意，而瑞德萨确实这么做了，证明你对他有好印象是对的。他承认你的罪行重大，但还是有值得宽恕的地方，仁慈是一个国君身上最值得称赞的美德，而陛下也正是以此著称。他说，全世界都知道你和他的友谊，最尊敬的枢密院成员们也许会认为他很偏心；但是，陛下有权利自由地表达他的观点。如果陛下酌情考虑你的贡献，并遵从他自己仁慈的性格，那么，他就不会要你的命，只会挖去你的双眼，他相信，在这样的权宜之计下，全世界都会为陛下的仁慈而鼓掌，也会为那些有幸为陛下效力者受到的公正和宽容而鼓掌。失去双眼并不会对你的身体造成多大的障碍，对陛下来说，你可能仍旧是有用的；失明会使人更有勇气，因为它让我们看不到危险；你曾因为你的眼睛，而害怕带回敌人舰队，它们成为了你最大的阻碍，你通过大臣们的眼睛去看就足够了，因为，最伟大的国君也是这样做的。

——选自《格列佛游记》第1部分第7章

注释

★“《格列佛游记》有机智和讽刺，有巧妙的构思，洒脱的幽默，泼辣的讥嘲，痛快淋漓。它的文体精彩绝伦。至今没有人用我们这艰难的文字写得比斯威夫特更简洁、更明快、更自然的。”

——英国当代著名小说家及创作家　毛姆

① misadventure [ˌmɪsəd'ventʃə] *n.* 灾难，不幸遭遇

② impeachment [ɪm'piːtʃmənt] *n.* 弹劾，指控

③ majesty ['mædʒəstɪ] *n.* 陛下，王权

④ lenity ['lenɪti] *n.* 慈悲，宽大处理

⑤ extenuate [ɪk'stenjueit] *vi* 减轻，低估

⑥ utmost ['ʌtməust] *adj.* 极度的，最大的

⑦ partial ['pɑːʃl] *adj.* 偏爱的，偏袒的

⑧ pursuant [pə'sjuːənt] *adj.* 依据的

⑨ impediment [ɪm'pedɪmənt] *n.* 妨碍

20 与狄更斯齐名的维多利亚时代代表小说家——威廉·梅克比斯·萨克雷

William Makepeace Thackeray (July 18, 1811—December 24, 1863) was an English novelist of the 19th century. He was famous for his satirical works, particularly *Vanity Fair*, a tale of two middle-class London families, a **panoramic**① portrait of English society. Most of Thackeray's major novels were published as monthly serials. Thackeray studied in a satirical and moralistic light upper- and middle-class English life. He was once seen as the equal of his contemporary Dickens, or even as his superior.

威廉·梅克比斯·萨克雷（1811年7月18日—1863年11月24日），19世纪英国小说家。他以讽刺小说闻名，其中最著名的是《名利场》，它讲述了伦敦两个中产阶级家庭的故事，是对整个英国社会的写照。萨克雷大部分的小说都是以月刊杂志的形式刊登发表的。萨克雷一贯从讽刺和说教的角度来研究英国高层和中层阶级的生活。他曾一度被认为与狄更斯齐名，甚至比狄更斯还要略胜一筹。

《名利场》共67章，1848年出版，是萨克雷的成名作品，也是他生平著作里最经得起时间考验的杰作。最佳译本由杨必1994年翻译，人民文学出版社出版。

Vanity Fair
名利场

The world is a looking-glass, and gives back to every man the reflection of his own face. Frown at it, and it will in turn look sourly upon you; laugh at it and with it, and it is a jolly kind companion.

世界就像一面镜子，能映照出我们每个人的脸。如果你对它皱眉，它也会愤怒地看着你；如果你对它微笑，它也会成为一个很好的伙伴。

——*Vanity Fair*《名利场》

名著导读

In Miss Pinkerton's academy for young ladies, the advantaged Amelia Sedley is in stark contrast to the poor, but sharp-witted Rebecca Sharp. Rebecca Sharp is a relentless social climber, and her first effort to rise "above her station" is by trying to get Amelia's brother to marry her—an effort thwarted by George, Amelia's fiancé. So instead she gets married to another family's second son, Rawdon Crawley. Unfortunately, both young couples quickly get disinherited and George is killed. But Rebecca is determined to live the good life she has worked and married for—she obtains jewels and money from admiring gentlemen, disrupting her marriage.

在平克顿小姐的女子私立学校里，与得天独厚的阿米莉亚•塞德利形成鲜明对比的，是贫穷但聪明灵巧的丽贝卡•夏普。丽贝卡•夏普冷酷无情，只想挤入上流社会，而她第一个企图提高地位的努力就是让阿米莉亚的哥哥娶她，但她的这一行为却受到了阿米莉亚的未婚夫乔治的阻挠。因此，她嫁给了另一个家庭的第二个儿子——罗顿•克劳利。不幸的是，这两对年轻的夫妇都很快地失去了财产继承权，而乔治也被杀害了。但是，丽贝卡决意要过自己苦心经营并用婚姻作代价换取的优越生活——她从仰慕她的男士那里获得了珠宝和金钱，却亲手毁掉了自己的婚姻。

名段选读

For it may be remarked in the course of this little conversation (which took place as the coach rolled along lazily by the river side) that though Miss Rebecca Sharp has twice had occasion to thank Heaven, it has been, in the first place, for ridding her of some person whom she hated, and secondly, for enabling her to bring her enemies to some sort of perplexity or confusion; neither of which are very **amiable**[②] motives for religious gratitude, or such as would be put forward by persons of a kind and **placable**[③] disposition. Miss Rebecca was not, then, in the least kind or placable. All the world used her ill, said this young **misanthropist**[④], and we may be pretty certain that persons whom all the world treats ill, deserve entirely the treatment they get. The world is a looking-glass, and gives back to every man the reflection of his own face. Frown at it, and it will in turn look sourly upon you; laugh at it and with it, and it is a **jolly**[⑤] kind companion; and so let all young persons take their choice. This is certain, that if the world neglected Miss Sharp, she never was known to have done a good action in behalf of anybody; nor can it be expected that twenty-four young ladies should all be as amiable as the heroine of this work, Miss Sedley (whom we have selected for the very reason that she was the best-natured of all, otherwise what on earth was to have prevented us from putting up Miss Swartz, or Miss Crump, or Miss Hopkins, as heroine in her place!) it could not be expected that every one should be of the humble and gentle temper of Miss Amelia Sedley; should take every opportunity to vanquish Rebecca's hard-heartedness and ill-humour; and, by a thousand kind words and offices, overcome, for once at least, her hostility to her kind.

也许值得一提的是，在这次简短的谈话期间(当马车慵懒地沿着河岸行进时)，丽贝卡·夏普小姐曾两次感谢上帝：第一次是让她摆脱了她讨厌的人，第二次是让她的对手陷入了某种困境和麻烦之中。这两次感谢上帝的动机都是不友善的，或者说，一个善良而温和的人是不会这样的。丽贝卡小姐不是这样的人，她一点都不善良和宽容。这个涉世不深的愤世嫉俗者说，整个世界都虐待她，而我们可以非常确定的是，那些全世界都不会善待的人，肯定是罪有应得的。世界就像一面镜子，能映照出我们每个人的脸。如果你对它皱眉，它也会愤怒地看着你；如果你对它微笑，它也会成为一个很好的伙伴；所以，就让所有的年轻人自己选择吧。无疑的是，如果世界忽视了夏普小姐，那么，她永远都不会做有益于他人的事；不要期望所有24岁的年轻女子们都能像这本书中的女主角——塞德利小姐一样和善(我们之所以选她是因为她的本性最善良，否则，是什么原因阻止我们去推选斯沃茨小姐、克伦普小姐或者霍普金斯小姐代替她成为我们的女主角呢！)你不能指望所有人都拥有阿米莉亚·塞德利小姐的谦逊和温柔；她利用一切机会去打败丽贝卡的铁石心肠和坏脾气；同时，还对她说了很多善意的话语，至少有一次，她的努力让丽贝卡的敌意向善良妥协了。

——选自《名利场》第2章

注释

① panoramic [ˌpænəˈræmɪk] *adj.* 全景

② amiable [ˈeɪmiəbl] *adj.* 亲切的，友善的

③ placable [ˈplækəbl] *adj.* 温和的

④ misanthropist [mɪˈsænθrəpɪst] *n.* 厌世者

21 英国一位天才的女作家——艾米莉·简·勃朗特

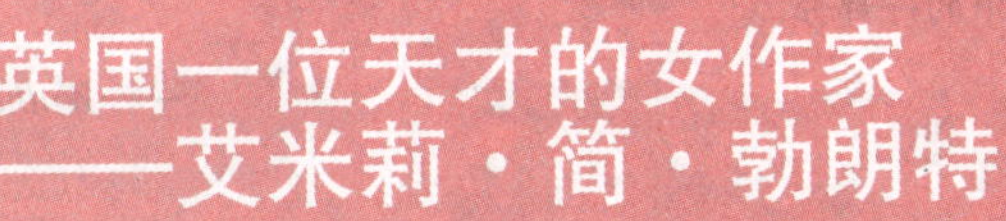

Emily Jane Brontë (July 30, 1818—December 19, 1848) was an English novelist and poet, pseudonym Ellis Bell, now best remembered for her novel *Wuthering Heights*, a classic of English literature. Emily was the second eldest of the three Brontë sisters, between Charlotte and Anne. Though Charlotte Brontë's *Jane Eyre* was generally considered the best of the Brontë sisters' works during most of the nineteenth century, many subsequent critics of *Wuthering Heights* argued that its originality and achievement made it superior. *Wuthering Heights* has also given rise to many adaptations and inspired works, including films, radio, television dramatisations, a musical by Bernard J. Taylor, ballet, opera, role-playing game, and song.

艾米莉·简·勃朗特（1818年7月30日—1848年12月19日）是英国小说家、诗人，笔名埃利斯·贝尔，以英国文学经典《呼啸山庄》而闻名于世。艾米莉在“勃朗特三姐妹”中排行老二，是安妮·勃朗特之姐，夏洛蒂·勃朗特之妹。夏洛蒂·勃朗特的著作《简爱》被公认为是十九世纪“勃朗特三姐妹”中最杰出的作品，然而，随后的评论家们认为，《呼啸山庄》在创意和文学造诣方面较《简爱》略胜一筹。《呼啸山庄》后经历多次改编，还被搬上了多种形式的艺术舞台，其中包括电影、广播、电视剧，由伯纳德·泰勒编排的音乐剧、芭蕾舞、歌剧、角色扮演游戏和歌曲。

《呼啸山庄》★共34章，发表于1847年，讲述了一个爱情和复仇交织的故事。艾米莉·勃朗特通过这个爱情悲剧，向人们展示了一幅畸形社会的生活画面，勾勒了被这个畸形社会扭曲了的人性及其造成的种种恐怖的事件。国内最著名的译本沈东子的译本和方平的译本。

Wuthering Heights
呼啸山庄

If all else perished, and he remained, I should still continue to be; and if all else remained, and he were annihilated, the universe would turn to a mighty stranger: I should not seem a part of it. 如果世界上所有的事物都消失了，但是他还在，那么我就能活下来；如果世界上所有的事物都在，而他却消失了，那么世界对我而言就是完全陌生的：我不该是其中的一部分。

——*Wuthering Heights*《呼啸山庄》

名著导读

Heathcliff is brought to Heights from the streets of Liverpool by Mr Earnshaw. Heathcliff is treated as Earnshaw's own children, Catherine and Hindley. After Mr Earnshaw's death Heathcliff is reduced to the status of a servant, running away when the young woman, Catherine he loves, decides to marry another. He returns later, rich and educated and sets about gaining his revenge on the two families that he believed ruined his life.

希斯克利夫被老庄主厄恩肖从利物浦的街上带回了山庄，老庄主像对待自己的亲生骨肉凯瑟琳和辛得雷一样对待他。厄恩肖死后，希斯克利夫沦为仆人，当他所爱的凯瑟琳要嫁给别人的时候，他从庄上逃走了。后来，变得家财万贯而且受过良好教育的希斯克利夫回到了山庄，他对他认为毁了自己人生的两家人展开了报复。

名段选读

"With your husband's money, Miss Catherine?" I asked. "You'll find him not so **pliable**① as you calculate upon; and, though I'm hardly a judge, I think that's the worst motive you've given yet for being the wife of young Linton." "It is not," retorted she, "it is the best! The others were the satisfaction of my **whims**②; and for Edgar's sake, too, to satisfy him. This is for the sake of one who comprehends in his person my feelings to Edgar and myself. I cannot express it, but surely you and everybody have a notion that there is or should be an existence of yours beyond you. What were the use of my creation, if I were entirely contained here? My great miseries in this world have been Heathcliff's miseries, and I watched and felt each from the beginning: my great thought in living is himself. If all else perished, and he remained, I should still continue to be; and if all else remained, and he were annihilated, the universe would turn to a mighty stranger: I should not seem a part of it. My love for Linton is like the foliage in the woods: time will change it, I'm well aware, as winter changes the trees. My love for Heathcliff resembles the eternal rocks beneath: a source of little visible delight, but necessary. Nelly, I AM Heathcliff! He's always, always in my mind: not as a pleasure, any more than I am always a pleasure to myself, but as my own being. So don't talk of our separation again: it is impracticable; and—"

She paused, and hid her face in the folds of my gown; but I **jerked**③ it forcibly away. I was out of patience with her folly!

"If I can make any sense of your nonsense, Miss," I said, "it only goes to convince me that you are ignorant of the duties you undertake in marrying; or else that you are a wicked, unprincipled girl. But trouble me with no more secrets: I'll not promise to keep them."

"You'll keep that?" she asked, eagerly.

"No, I'll not promise," I repeated.

"用你丈夫的钱吗，凯瑟琳小姐？"我问道。"你会发现他不像你想象的那样软弱。尽管我不是法官，但我认为你为了钱而嫁给小林顿的动机真是糟透了。"不是这样的，"她反驳道，"这个动机是最好的！其他的都只是为了满足我自己的愿望；我也是为了埃德加的缘故，为了使他高兴。因为他能理解我对埃德加的感情和我自己的感情。我无法用言语来表达；你和其他任何人一定都会有这样一种想法：每个人除了自己本身外还有，或者说应该有另外一个存在。如果我完全被困在这里，我的存在还有什么意义呢？如果希斯克利夫活得很痛苦，我也会承受世界上最大的痛苦，从一开始我就看到和感觉到了：我活着的信念只有他。如果世界上所有的事物都消失了，但是他还在，那么我就能活下来；如果世界上所有的事物都在，而他却消失了，那么世界对我而言就是完全陌生的，我不该是其中的一部分。我对林顿的爱就像林中的叶子，会随着时间的流逝而改变，我很清楚这一点，正如冬天会改变树木一样。而我对希斯克利夫的爱就像埋在地下永恒不变的岩石：虽然没有带给我清晰可见的快乐，但他对我来说是不可或缺的。内莉，我就是希斯克利夫！他永远都在我的心里：他给我带来的欢乐并不比我自己经历的欢乐多，但他是我的全部。所以，不要再说我们会分开了，那是办不到的，还有——"

她停了下来，将她的脸埋在我的长袍子里；但是我用力扯开了衣服。我对于她的愚蠢已经失去了耐心！

"就我对你这些胡言乱语的理解，小姐，"我说道，"我更加肯定你对婚姻要承担的责任完全一无所知；不然的话，你就是一个邪恶的，毫无原则的女孩子。请不要用你的秘密来烦我了：我可没承诺我会保守秘密。"

"你会替我保守秘密吗？"她迫切地问道。

"不，我不会的，"我重复道。

——选自《呼啸山庄》第9章

注释

★"我不知道还有哪一部小说其中爱情的痛苦、迷恋、残酷、执著，曾经如此令人吃惊地描述出来。"

——英国当代著名小说家及创作家　毛姆

① pliable ['plaɪəbl] *adj.* 柔软的，容易摆布的

② whim [wɪm] *n.* 一时的兴致

③ jerk [dʒɔːk] *vt.* 把……猛地一拉

22 第一位同时获得普利策奖和诺贝尔奖的女作家——赛珍珠

Pearl S. Buck (June 26, 1892—March 6, 1973) also known by her Chinese name Sai Zhenzhu, was an award-winning American writer who spent most of her time until 1934 in China. Her novel The *Good Earth was* the best-selling fiction book in the U.S. in 1931 and 1932, and won the Pulitzer Prize in 1932. In 1938, she became the first American woman to be awarded the Nobel Prize in Literature.

珀尔·巴克（1892年6月26日—1973年3月6日），中文名赛珍珠，是一位备受称赞的美国作家，1934年之前她一直居住在中国。其小说《大地》成为1931年和1932年美国最畅销的小说，并在1932年荣获了“普利策小说奖”。1938年，她成为首位获得诺贝尔文学奖的美国女性。

《大地》发表于1931年，是一个3部曲，第1部叫《大地》共34章，第2部叫《儿子》共29章，第3部叫《分家》共4章。《大地》是美国作家赛珍珠的诺贝尔文学奖获奖著作。小说叙述的是旧中国的农民王龙从一无所有而成的为一个富户的故事。目前国内最流行的是王逢振、马传禧的译本。

The Good Earth
大地

Out of the land we came and into it we must go—and if you will hold your land you can live—no one can rob you of land.

我们从土里来，也终要入土离世——只要有了土地，你就能生存下去——没人能抢走你们的土地。

——*The Good Earth*《大地》

名著导读

It begins with the story of an illiterate[①], poor peasant, Wang Lung, who ventures from the rural countryside and goes to town to the great house of Hwang to obtain a bride from those among the rank of slave. There, he is given the slave O-lan as his bride. Selfless, hardworking, the plain-faced O-lan supports Wang Lung's veneration of the land and his desire to acquire more land. She stays with him through thick and thin, through famine and very lean times, working alongside him on the land, making great sacrifices, and raising his children. Wang Lung's sons only make life difficult for him, and till the end of his days he is seeking peace in his house, remembering the old days as a pleasant. What land meant to Wang Lung and what it gave him and snatched away from him, can never be understood by his three sons who were brought up in luxury and thought it an insult to be considered a farmer's sons.

小说以一个目不识丁、穷困潦倒的农民的故事为开端。他叫王龙，从农村来到镇上一家姓黄的大户人家家里，想讨他们家的一个女仆做媳妇。这户人家把女仆阿兰嫁给了王龙。长相平凡的阿兰无私奉献，任劳任怨，她理解王龙对土地的尊崇，也支持他希望得到更多土地的夙愿。她不畏艰难险阻，忍受饥饿和拮据，始终和丈夫一起在土地上共同劳作，养育孩子，做出伟大牺牲。王龙的儿子们让王龙的生活变得艰难，直到生命的最后一刻，王龙都在家中试图回忆以往做农民时的情景，并从中寻求内心的平静。土地对于王龙的意义，它给予王龙的和它从王龙那里夺走的，这一切王龙的三个儿子永远也不会明白，他们在奢侈的环境中长大，认为被看做是农民的儿子是一种侮辱。

名段选读

But one day he saw clearly for a little while. It was a day on which his two sons had come and after they had greeted him courteously[②] they went out and they walked about the house on to the land. Now Wang Lung followed them silently, and they stood, and he came up to them slowly, and they did not hear the sound of his footsteps nor the sound of his staff on the soft earth, and Wang Lung heard his second son say in his mincing[③] voice,

"This field we will sell and this one, and we will divide the money between us evenly. Your share I will borrow at good interest, for now with the railroad straight through I can ship rice to the sea and I..."

But the old man heard only these words, "sell the land," and he cried out and he could not keep his voice from breaking and trembling with his anger,

"Now, evil, idle sons—sell the land!" He choked and would have fallen, and they caught him and held him up, and he began to weep.

Then they **soothed**[④] him and they said, soothing him,

"No—no—we will never sell the land—"

"It is the end of a family—when they begin to sell the land," he said brokenly. "Out of the land we came and into it we must go—and if you will hold your land you can live—no one can rob you of land—"

And the old man let his **scanty**[⑤] tears dry upon his cheeks and they made salty stains there. And he **stooped**[⑥] and took up a handful of the soil and he held it and he muttered,

"If you sell the land, it is the end."

And his two sons held him, one on either side, each holding his arm, and he held tight in his hand the warm loose earth. And they soothed him and they said over and over, the elder son and the second son,

"Rest assured, our father, rest assured. The land is not to be sold."

But over the old man's head they looked at each other and smiled.

但是一天，他很仔细地看了一会儿。那天，他的两个儿子回来了，一阵寒暄之后，他们就出去了，一路从屋子走到了田地。王龙静静地跟在后面，等到儿子们停了脚步，他也就慢慢地走上前去。儿子们没有听到王龙的脚步声，也没有听到他的拐杖跺在柔软的泥土中的声音，这时，王龙听见他的二儿子装腔作势地说道：

"我们要卖掉这块地，得到的钱我们平分。我会花高利息把你的那笔钱借过来，因为现在铁路交通通畅，我能将稻谷用船运输过海，而且我……"

但是老人家只听到了这几个字眼儿，"卖掉土地，"他歇斯底里地大吼着，因为太过愤怒，他的话语很不连贯，而且声音在颤抖。

"如今，你们这些游手好闲的不肖子孙——竟敢卖掉土地！"他气得说不出话了，整个人快要瘫倒，儿子赶紧扶住了他。之后，王龙开始流泪。

这时，他们开始安慰父亲：

"不——不——我们永远不会卖掉土地的——"

"你们卖掉田地之时，就是我们家族没落之日，"他断断续续地说着。"我们从土里来，也终将入土离世——只要有了土地，你就能生存下去——没人能够抢走你们的土地——"

老人家脸颊上稀疏的眼泪已经干了，留下了咸咸的泪痕。他俯身弯下腰，捧起一把泥土，喃喃自语道：

"如果卖掉了土地，那就完了。"

他的两个儿子扶起他，一人一边挽着他的胳膊，王龙的手里仍紧紧握着温暖而蓬松的泥土。两个儿子安慰着他，一遍又一遍地重复：

“父亲，请放心，请放心，我们不会卖地的。”

但是，他们两人却在老人的背后相视而笑。

——选自《大地》第1部第34章

注释

① illiterate [ɪ'lɪtərət] *adj.* 不识字的，文盲的

② courteously ['kɜːtiəslɪ] *adv.* 有礼貌地

③ mincing ['mɪnsɪŋ] *adj.* 装腔作势的

④ soothe [suːð] *vt.* 安慰

⑤ scanty ['skæntɪ] *adj.* 不足的，太少的

⑥ stoop [stuːp] *vi.* 弯腰，俯身

23 清教徒文学的重要代表人——约翰·弥尔顿

John Milton (December 9, 1608—November 8, 1674) was an English poet, polemicist, and civil servant for the Commonwealth of England. He is best known for his epic poem *Paradise Lost*. He was a scholarly man of letters, a **polemical**① writer, and an official serving under Oliver Cromwell. He wrote at a time of religious flux and political upheaval in England, and his poetry and prose reflect deep convictions and deal with contemporary issues. As well as English, he wrote in Latin and Italian, and had an international reputation during his lifetime. William Hayley's 1796 biography called him the "greatest English author". He remains generally regarded "as one of the preeminent writers in the English language and as a thinker of world importance."

约翰·弥尔顿（1608年12月9日—1674年11月8日）是一名英国诗人、辩论家和英联邦政府的行政官员。他以史诗《失乐园》而闻名于世。弥尔顿不仅是一位博学的文人，善辩的作家，还是奥利弗·克伦威尔统治时期的一名政府官员。在他创作期间，英格兰正处于宗教变迁和政治动荡中，所以他的诗歌和散文反映了他坚定的信念并涉及同时代的重大事件。弥尔顿不仅用英文写作，还使用拉丁文和意大利文。他终其一生都享有国际声望。威廉·海里在1796年的自传中称弥尔顿为“最伟大的英国作家”。他迄今为止仍然被普遍认为是“英语语言中最杰出的作家之一以及一位世界级的思想家”。

《失乐园》★ 共12卷，1667年出版。《失乐园》以史诗一般的磅礴气势揭示了人的原罪与堕落，体现了诗人追求自由的崇高精神，是世界文学史、思想史上的一部极重要的作品。最佳译本由朱维之1933年翻译，人民文学出版社出版。

Paradise Lost
失乐园

Better to reign in Hell than serve in Heaven.

地狱里的统治者好过天堂里的奴仆。

——*Paradise Lost*《失乐园》

名著导读

Paradise Lost is an epic poem in blank verse, considered by many scholars to be one of the greatest poems of the English language. Paradise Lost tells the biblical story of the fall from grace of Adam and Eve (and, by extension, all humanity) in language that is a supreme achievement of rhythm and sound. The main characters in the poem are God, Satan, Adam, and Eve. For centuries critics have both praised and derided Paradise Lost, as much has been written about Milton's powerful and sympathetic characterization of Satan. The Romantic poets William Blake and Percy Bysshe Shelley saw Satan as the real hero of the poem and applauded his rebellion against the tyranny of Heaven.

《失乐园》是一部无韵史诗，很多学者认为它是最伟大的英语诗歌之一。《失乐园》用韵律和语音绝佳的语言讲述了亚当和夏娃（乃至全人类）堕落的圣经故事。诗中的主要人物有上帝、撒旦、亚当和夏娃。几个世纪以来，因为弥尔顿对撒旦浓墨重彩和充满同情的刻画，批评家们对《失乐园》的评论褒贬不一。浪漫主义诗人威廉•布莱克和珀西•比希•雪莱认为诗中撒旦是真正的英雄，并为他反抗天堂的暴政而喝彩。

名段选读

"Is this the region, this the soil, the **clime**①,"
Said then the lost Archangel, "this the seat.
That we must change for Heaven?—this mournful gloom
For that celestial light? Be it so, since he
Who now is sovereign can **dispose**② and bid
What shall be right: farthest from him is best
Whom reason hath equalled, force hath made supreme
Above his equals. Farewell, happy fields,
Where joy for ever dwells! Hail, horrors! hail,
Infernal③ world! and thou, profoundest Hell,
Receive thy new possessor—one who brings
A mind not to be changed by place or time.
The mind is its own place, and in itself

Can make a Heaven of Hell, a Hell of Heaven.
What matter where, if I be still the same,
And what I should be, all but less than he
Whom thunder hath made greater? Here at least
We shall be free; th' Almighty hath not built
Here for his envy, will not drive us hence:
Here we may reigh secure; and, in my choice,
To reign is worth ambition, though in Hell:
Better to reign in Hell than serve in Heaven.
But wherefore let we then our faithful friends,
Th' associates and co-partners of our loss,
Lie thus astonished on th' **oblivious**[④] pool,
And call them not to share with us their part
In this unhappy mansion, or once more
With rallied arms to try what may be yet
Regained in Heaven, or what more lost in Hell?"

"这片领域，这块土地，这个地方，"
失落的大天使说道，
"就是代替我们的天堂的地方吗?
——这阴郁的黑暗要代替那天国的光明吗？就这样吧，
现在的最高统治者能随意处置，发号施令
明智的选择是：离他越远越好
他就是理，强权使他的决议至高无上。
再见了，那充满欢乐的土地，欢乐永驻的土地！万岁，恐惧！
万岁，可怕的地狱！哦，那深不见底的地狱啊
欢迎你新的主人吧——他有着坚定的信念，
不会因空间和时间而改变。
他的思想牢固不移，
能让地狱变成天堂，天堂变成地狱。
如果我不曾改变，我身在何处又有什么关系?
我将成为什么样的人，无论如何都无法战胜他
雷电使他更强大。
在这里，至少我们是自由的；
上帝不是因为嫉妒建造了这里，
因此，他也不会赶我们走：

在这里，我们能安稳地生活，在我看来，
尽管是在地狱，统治也是值得追求的：
地狱里的统治者好过天堂里的奴仆。
但是，为何让我们和我们衷心的朋友
承受我们的失落，
让我们为被遗忘的友谊感到惊讶，
不要让他们和我们一起分享他们的生活
在这个不快乐的地方，
或者我们可以再次团结起来尝试去天堂收复失地，
在地狱里还有什么可失去的?

——选自《失乐园》第1卷

注释

★ “《失乐园》贯穿着宏伟精神，吸引着虔诚君子，吓跑了渎神小人；你把神明处理得如此恰当，既不渎神，也不玷污自己。”

——英国玄学派诗人 马韦尔

① clime [klaɪm] *n.* 地区，气候带

② dispose [dɪ'spəuz] *vi.* 处置

③ infernal [ɪn'fɜːnl] *adj.* 阴间的，地狱的

④ oblivious [ə'blɪviəs] *adj.* 遗忘的，未注意的

24 英国现代小说的三大奠基人之一——亨利·菲尔丁

Henry Fielding (April 22, 1707—October 8, 1754) was an English novelist and dramatist known for his rich earthy humor and satirical prowess, and as the author of the novel *Tom Jones.* Aside from his literary achievements, he has a significant place in the history of law-enforcement, having founded (with his half-brother John) what some have called London's first police force, the Bow Street Runners, using his authority as a magistrate. His younger sister, Sarah, also became a successful writer.

亨利·菲尔丁（1707年4月22日—1754年10月8日）是英国小说家，戏剧家。他因丰富朴实的幽默和讽刺手法以及小说《弃儿汤姆·琼斯史》闻名于世。除了文学上的成就，亨利·菲尔丁还在执法方面发挥了重要的作用，他在担任地方治安法官时，他(和同父异母的兄弟约翰一起)利用自己的权力建立了伦敦第一支警察部队——鲍街侦缉队。他的妹妹莎拉也是一名出色的作家。

《弃儿汤姆·琼斯史》出版于1749年，是菲尔丁第3部小说且是他艺术上最成熟的代表作，全书共18卷，是一部包罗英国18世纪生活一切方面的社会生活小说。小说虽然情节复杂，人物众多，但作者布局精巧，层次井然，有条不紊。目前国内较著名的译本是黄乔生的版本和张谷若的版本。

The History of Tom Jones, a Foundling
弃儿汤姆·琼斯史

When children are doing nothing, they are doing mischief.

当孩子们无所事事时，他们就会恶作剧。

——*The History of Tom Jones, a Foundling*《弃儿汤姆·琼斯史》

名著导读

Tom Jones is a **foundling**[①] discovered on the property of a very kind, wealthy landowner, Squire Allworthy, in Somerset in England's West Country. Tom grows into a vigorous and lusty, yet honest and kind-hearted youth. He develops affection for his neighbour's daughter, Sophia Western. However, Tom's status as a **bastard**[②] causes Sophia's father and Allworthy to oppose their love.

汤姆·琼斯是一个弃儿，他被英国西南部索美塞的一位善良富有的乡绅斯夸尔·奥尔沃西收养。当汤姆长大后，成为了一个精力充沛但又十分忠厚善良的年轻人。他渐渐爱上了邻居的女儿——索菲亚·维斯顿，但因为汤姆是私生子，索菲亚的父亲和奥尔沃西强烈反对他们相爱。

名段选读

I remember a wise old gentleman who used to say, "When children are doing nothing, they are doing mischief." I will not enlarge this **quaint**[③] saying to the most beautiful part of the creation in general; but so far I may be allowed, that when the effects of female jealousy do not appear openly in their proper colours of rage and fury, we may suspect that **mischievous**[④] passion to be at work privately, and attempting to undermine, what it doth not attack above-ground.

This was exemplified in the conduct of Lady Bellaston, who, under all the smiles which she wore in her **countenance**[⑤], concealed much **indignation**[⑥] against Sophia; and as she plainly saw that this young lady stood between her and the full indulgence of her desires, she resolved to get rid of her by some means or other; nor was it long before a very favourable opportunity of accomplishing this presented itself to her.

The reader may be pleased to remember, that when Sophia was thrown into that consternation at the playhouse, by the wit and humour of a set of young gentlemen who call themselves the town, we informed him, that she had put herself under the protection of a young nobleman, who had very safely conducted her to her chair.

This nobleman, who frequently visited Lady Bellaston, had more than once seen Sophia there, since her arrival in town, and had conceived a very great liking to her; which liking, as beauty never looks more amiable than in distress, Sophia had in this fright so encreased, that he might now, without any great impropriety, be said to be actually in love with her.

It may easily be believed, that he would not suffer so handsome an occasion of improving his acquaintance with the beloved object as now offered itself to elapse, when even good breeding alone might have prompted him to pay her a visit.

我记得一位智叟曾说过：“当孩子们无所事事时，他们就会恶作剧。”一般来说，我不会将这种有趣的说法延伸到人类最美好的那部分天性上去；但是迄今为止我可以这样说，当女人的嫉妒没有以合理的愤怒和激动坦率地表现出来时，我们完全可以怀疑恶意的情绪正在私下酝酿着，并试图暗中破坏那些无法在表面上攻击的东西。

贝拉斯顿女士的行为就是一个典范，她那伪装的镇定自若的笑容下隐藏的是对索菲亚无比的愤怒；当她清楚地看到这名年轻的女子身处于她和她充满放纵的欲望之间时，她就下定决心要想方设法来摆脱她；不久她就遇到一个能够达到目的的大好机会了。

读者应该可以愉快地回想起来，当索菲亚在戏院，被一群自称为当地市民的年轻男子的风趣和幽默弄得惊慌失措时，我们提到过他。索菲亚就是在这位年轻贵族的保护下，安全地来到了自己的座位。

自从索菲亚来到了小镇后，这位频繁拜访贝拉斯顿女士的贵族青年不止一次地见到了索菲亚，并对她产生了极大的好感；对于这种好感，就像美好的事物在危难中会越发显得亲切一样，索菲亚越来越恐慌，现在甚至可以很恰当地说他实际上已经爱上她了。

容易令人相信的是，他不会再有像现在这样的大好机会来与自己挚爱的人相识了，此时哪怕只是出于良好的教养，他都应该去拜访她。

——选自《弃儿汤姆·琼斯史》第15卷第2章

注释

① foundling ['faundlɪŋ] *n.* 弃儿

② bastard ['bɑːstəd] *n.* 私生子

③ quaint [kweint] *adj.* 古雅的

④ mischievous ['mɪstʃɪvəs] *adj.* 有害的

⑤ countenance ['kauntənəns] *n.* 面容

⑥ indignation [ˌɪndɪg'neiʃən] *n.* 愤怒

25 "美国梦"的破灭者——约翰·恩斯特·斯坦贝克

John Ernst Steinbeck, Jr. (February 27, 1902—December 20, 1968) was an American writer. He wrote the Pulitzer Prize-winning novel *The Grapes of Wrath* (1939) and *East of Eden* (1952) and the novella *Of Mice and Men* (1937). He wrote a total of twenty-seven books, including sixteen novels, six non-fiction books and five collections of short stories. In 1962, Steinbeck received the Nobel Prize for Literature. His later work reflected his wide range of interests, including marine biology, politics, religion, history, and mythology. One of his last published works was *Travels with Charley,* a travelogue of a road trip he took in 1960 to rediscover America.

小约翰·恩斯特·斯坦贝克（1920年2月27日—1968年12月20日）是一位美国作家。他的作品包括荣获普利策文学奖的小说《愤怒的葡萄》（1939）以及《伊甸园以东》（1952）和中篇小说《人与鼠》（1937）。他一生总共写了27本书，其中包括16部小说，6部非小说类的书籍，5部短篇故事集。1962年，斯坦贝克荣获诺贝尔文学奖。他的后期作品表现出他广泛的兴趣爱好，涉及海洋生物学、政治、宗教、历史和神话等多个主题。《同查利旅行》是他出版的最后一批作品之一，是本游记，书中讲的是他在1960年重游美国的旅行见闻。

《愤怒的葡萄》出版于1939年，共30章，是美国30年代大萧条时期的一部史诗，反映了广大人民群众对现存社会的日益不满和叛逆精神，具有鲜明的时代特征。目前国内较著名的译本是胡仲持的版本。

The Grapes of Wrath
愤怒的葡萄

The bank is something more than men, I tell you. It's the monster. Men made it, but they can't control it.

银行可是超越于人之上的，我可告诉你了。它是个怪物。人们开办了银行，但是他们控制不了银行。

——*The Grapes of Wrath*《愤怒的葡萄》

名著导读

Set during the Great Depression, the novel focuses on the Joads, a poor family of **sharecroppers**[①] driven from their Oklahoma home by drought, economic hardship, and changes in financial and agricultural industries. Due to their nearly hopeless situation and in part because they were trapped in the Dust Bowl, the Joads set out for California. Along with thousands of other "Okies", they sought jobs, land, dignity and a future.

小说的背景是美国大萧条时期，作者集中笔墨讲述了贫穷的佃户乔兹一家，他们被干旱、经济萧条以及经济和农业运行方式的改变所驱使，被迫离开家乡俄克拉荷马州。由于濒临绝境，同时也因为沙尘暴的困扰，乔兹一家动身去了加州。和其他数千背井离乡的人一样，他们寻找工作，争取土地，追求尊严，憧憬未来。

名段选读

We know that—all that. It's not us, it's the bank. A bank isn't like a man. Or an owner with fifty thousand acres, he isn't like a man either. That's the **monster**[②].

Sure, cried the **tenant**[③] men, but it's our land. We measured it and broke it up. We were born on it, and we got killed on it, died on it. Even if it's no good, it's still ours. That's what makes it ours—being born on it, working it, dying on it. That makes ownership, not a paper with numbers on it.

We're sorry. It's not us. It's the monster. The bank isn't like a man.

Yes, but the bank is only made of men.

No, you're wrong there—quite wrong there. The bank is something else than men. It happens that every man in a bank hates what the bank does, and yet the bank does it. The bank is something more than men, I tell you. It's the monster. Men made it, but they can't control it.

The tenants cried, Grampa killed Indians, Pa killed snakes for the land. Maybe we can kill banks—they're worse than Indians and snakes. Maybe we got to fight to keep our land, like Pa and Grampa did.

And now the owner men grew angry. You'll have to go.

But it's ours, the tenant men cried. We—

No. The bank, the monster owns it. You'll have to go.

We'll get our guns, like Grampa when the Indians came. What then?

Well—first the **sheriff**[④], and then the troops. You'll be stealing if you try to stay, you'll be murderers if you kill to stay. The monster isn't men, but it can make men do what it wants.

But if we go, where'll we go? How'll we go? We got no money.

我们都知道——知道一切。土地不再归我们所有，而是属于银行了。银行可不像人那样。一个拥有五万亩土地的人，也不再像人了，而是怪物。

是啊，佃户们哭了，但是那是我们的土地啊。是我们丈量，我们开垦的。我们出生在这片土地上，在上面拼死拼活地劳作，死后还要安葬在这里。就算它毫无用处，它也是我们的。它之所以归我们所有，是因为我们在这片土地上出生，在这片土地上劳作，在这片土地上死去。那才是真正的所有权，绝不是一张写着一串数字的地契。

很遗憾的是，土地不是我们的了，它属于怪物的了。银行可不像人那样。

是的，但是银行还是由人来操纵的。

不，如果你这样认为，那你就错了——大错特错。银行可不是仅仅是人，它意味着更多。每个在银行工作的人都痛恨银行所做的事，但银行还是会去做。银行可是超越于人之上的，我可告诉你了。它是个怪物。人们开办了银行，但是他们控制不了银行。

佃户们都哭了：我们的祖父们为了土地，杀了印度人；我们的父辈为了土地，杀死了毒蛇；也许我们也能杀死银行——它们比印度人和毒蛇更加可恶。也许我们应该像我们的父辈和祖父辈那样，站起来抗争，捍卫我们的土地。

现在土地的主人们生气了。你们必须马上离开。

但是，土地是我们的，佃户们哭喊起来。我们——

不，是银行，是这个怪物拥有它。你们必须马上离开。

我们拿起枪来，就像我们的祖父们面对印第安人那样，。可之后呢？

到那时，首先到来的是州长，然后是军队。如果你坚持要留在土地上，那你犯的就是盗窃罪；如果为了留下杀人，你犯的就是谋杀罪。怪物不是人类，但是它能唆使人去办它想办到的事。

但是如果我们离开，我们能去哪儿？我们又怎样去？我们身无分文啊。

1——选自《愤怒的葡萄》第5章

注释

① sharecropper['ʃeəˌkrɔpə] *n.* 收益非常的佃农

② monster ['mɔnstə(r)] *n.* 怪物

③ tenant ['tenənt] *n.* 佃户

④ sheriff ['ʃerɪf] *n.* 州长

26 现代小说之父——司汤达

Henri Beyle (January 23, 1783—March 23, 1842), better known by his pen name Stendhal, was a 19th-century French writer. Known for his acute analysis of his characters' psychology, he is considered one of the earliest and foremost practitioners of realism in his two novels The Red and the Black (1830) and The Charterhouse of Parma (1839).

亨利·贝尔（1783年1月23日—1842年3月23日）是十九世纪法国作家，其笔名司汤达更为世人所知。他以准确敏锐的人物心理分析而闻名。小说《红与黑》(1830)和《巴马修道院》（1839）的成功使他被认为是最重要和最早的现实主义的实践者之一。

《红与黑》★ 分2卷，第1卷30章，第2卷45章，发表于1830年，是欧洲批判现实主义文学的奠基作。小说紧紧围绕主人公于连个人奋斗与最终失败的经历这一主线，广泛展现了“19世纪最初30年间压在法国人民头上的历届政府所带来的社会风气”，反映了19世纪早期法国的政治和社会生活中的一些本质问题。国内比较著名的译本是罗新璋的版本和郝运的版本。

The Red and the Black
红与黑

In our calling, we have to choose; we must make our fortune either in this world or in the next, there is no middle way.

但是对于我们信徒来说，我们不得不作出选择；我们要么在现世中积累财富，要么就在来世得到救赎，别无他选。

——*The Red and the Black*《红与黑》

名著导读

Handsome, ambitious Julien Sorel is determined to rise above his humble provincial origins. Soon realizing that success can only be achieved by adopting the subtle code of hypocrisy by which society operates, he begins to achieve advancement through deceit and self-interest. His triumphant career takes him into the heart of glamorous Parisian society, along the way conquering the gentle, married Madame de Renal, and the haughty Mathilde. But then Julien commits an unexpected, devastating crime and brings about his own downfall.

长相英俊、野心勃勃的于连·索黑尔一心想摆脱卑微的乡下农民身份，爬向上层社会。他很快就意识到只有微妙地运用社会上的伪善法则才能获得成功，于是他开始通过欺诈和利己主义的手段来获取向上攀爬的机会。成功的事业带他走进了富有魅力的巴黎上流社会的圈子。在这个过程中，他征服了温柔已婚的德•雷纳尔夫人，以及傲慢的玛蒂尔德小姐。但是，最终于连出人意料地犯下一桩毁灭性的罪行，导致了他的落败。

名段选读

The angelic sweetness which Madame de Renal derived from her own character as well as from her present happiness was interrupted only when she happened to think of her maid Elisa. This young woman received a legacy, went to make her confession to the cure Chelan, and revealed to him her intention to marry Julien. The cure was genuinely delighted at his friend's good fortune; but his surprise was great when Julien informed him with a resolute air that Miss Elisa's offer could not be accepted.

"Pay good **heed**[①], my son, to what is taking place in your heart," said the cure, frowning; "I congratulate you on your vocation, if it is to it alone that must be ascribed your scorn of a more than adequate provision. For fifty-six years and more have I been cure at Verrieres, and yet, so far as one can see, I am going to be deprived. This distresses me, albeit I have an income of eight hundred livres. I tell you of this detail in order that you may not be under any illusion as to what is in store for you in the priestly calling. If you think of paying court to the men in power, your eternal ruin is assured. You may make your fortune, but you will have to injure the poor and needy, flatter the Sub-Prefect, the Mayor, the important person, and minister to his passions: such conduct, which in the world is called the art of life, may, in a layman, be not wholly incompatible with salvation; but in our calling, we have to choose; we must make our fortune either in this world or in the next, there is no middle way. Go, my dear friend, reflect, and come back in three days' time with a definite answer. I am sorry to see underlying your character, a smouldering ardour which does not suggest to my mind the moderation and complete **renunciation**[②] of earthly advantages necessary in a priest; I augur well from your intelligence; but, allow me to tell you," the good cure went on, with tears in his eyes, "in the calling of a priest, I shall tremble for your salvation."

德·雷纳尔夫人先天的美好性情，再加上眼下幸福的生活使她像天使一般甜蜜，只是一想起她的女仆爱丽莎，这种甜蜜就荡然无存了。年轻的爱丽莎得到了一笔遗产，于是她向西郎神父袒露心扉，表露她想要嫁给于连的想法。神父为自己朋友的好运气由衷地高兴，但是于连很果断地向他表示不能接受爱丽莎小姐的求爱，这让神父惊诧不已。

"孩子，好好想想在你心里什么最重要，"神父皱着眉头说道；"如果你对这笔相当可观的财富不屑一顾，仅仅是因为对自己事业的考虑，那么我祝贺你。我在维里埃当神父已经56年了，但大家都看的出来，我还是会被剥夺职位。这着实让我感到痛苦不堪，尽管我有八百利佛(古时法国货币)的收入。我之所以跟你讲这些，是不想让你对神父一职抱有太大的幻想。如果你想对大权在握的人献殷勤，你就彻底毁了。你可以积攒财富，但是你就不可避免地会去伤害那些贫穷受苦的人。奉承州佐，市长，那些大人物还有大臣们，使他们高兴。这样的行为被世人称作处世之道，对于世俗的人来说，这种处世之道和救赎并不是完全不相容的。但是对于我们信徒来说，我们必须作出选择；要么在现世积累财富，要么在来世得到救赎，别无他选。回去吧，我亲爱的朋友，回去好好反思下，三天后再来给我一个明确的答复。很遗憾，我发觉了潜藏在你性格背后隐隐燃烧着的热情，我认为这与作教父所必备的节制和彻底摆脱世俗利益的原则是相违背的。以你的聪明才智，肯定会有一个美好的未来，但是，请容我告诉你，"神父眼睛里噙着泪水，继续说道，"作为一名神父，我对你的救赎感到担忧。"

——选自《红与黑》第1卷第8章

注释

★"司汤达的《红与黑》中的于连是19世纪欧洲文学中一系列反叛资本社会主义的英雄人物的'始祖'。"

——前苏联无产阶级作家　高尔基

① heed [hi:d] *n.* 留心，注意

② renunciation [rɪˌnʌnsi'eiʃən] *n.* 摆脱，抛弃

27 大英帝国女爵士——达夫妮·杜穆里埃

Daphne du Maurier (May 13, 1907—April 19, 1989) was an English author and playwright who published romantic suspense novels, mostly set on the coast of Cornwall. Many of her works have been adapted into films, including the novels *Rebecca*, which won the Best Picture Oscar in 1941, *Jamaica Inn,* and her short stories *The Birds* and *Don't Look Now.* The first three were directed by Alfred Hitchcock.

达夫妮·杜穆里埃(1907年5月13日—1989年4月19日)是一名英国作家和剧作家，她发表了很多浪漫悬疑小说，其中大部分故事发生在康沃尔郡海岸。她有多部作品都被搬上银幕，其中包括在1941年荣获奥斯卡最佳影片奖的小说《蝴蝶梦》，以及《牙买加客栈》和她的短篇小说《群鸟》与《现在别看》，前三部作品由阿尔弗莱德·希区柯克执导。

《蝴蝶梦》(另译《丽贝卡》)发表于1938年，共27章，作者通过刻画丽贝卡那种放浪形骸之外的腐化生活，以及她与德温特的畸形婚姻，对英国上层社会中的享乐至上、尔虞我诈、穷奢极侈、势利伪善等现象作了生动的揭露。最佳译本是译林出版社孙致礼的译本。

Rebecca
蝴蝶梦

Happiness is not a possession to be prized, it is a quality of thought, a state of mind.

幸福不是一笔用来珍藏的财富，而是一种思想状态，一种心境。

——*Rebecca*《蝴蝶梦》

名著导读

The story concerns a woman who marries an English nobleman and returns with him to Manderley, his country estate. There, she finds herself haunted by reminders of his first wife, Rebecca, who died in a boating accident less than a year earlier. In this case, the haunting is psychological, not physical: Rebecca does not appear as a ghost, but her spirit affects nearly everything that takes place at Manderley. The narrator, whose name is never divulged, is left with a growing sense of distrust toward those who loved Rebecca, wondering just how much they resent her for taking Rebecca's place. In the final chapters, the book turns into a detective story, as the principal characters try to reveal or conceal what really happened on the night Rebecca died.

故事讲述的是一个女人嫁给了一位英国贵族，并随丈夫回到他的曼陀丽庄园生活。她发现在庄园里，处处有丈夫的第一任妻子丽贝卡的影子，丽贝卡在不到一年前死于沉船意外，这让她烦扰不堪。在这个故事中，闹鬼只是心理上的作用，并不是真实存在的：丽贝卡不是以鬼魂的形式出现，但是她的灵魂几乎影响着曼陀丽庄园所有的一切。故事的叙述者的名字并未透露，她对庄园里那些深爱着丽贝卡的人们逐渐失去了信任，最终离开，她想知道那些人心中是多么憎恨她取代了丽贝卡的位置。在故事的最后几个章节，这本书变成了一个侦探故事，小说的主要人物开始揭露或者隐瞒在丽贝卡死去的那晚所发生的一切。

名段选读

We can never go back again, that much is certain. The past is still too close to us. The things we have tried to forget and put behind us would stir again, and that sense of fear, of **furtive**[①] unrest, struggling at length to blind unreasoning panic—now mercifully stilled, thank God—might in some manner unforeseen become a living companion, as it had been before.

He is wonderfully patient and never complains, not even when he remembers…which happens, I think, rather more often than he would have me know.

I can tell by the way he will look lost and puzzled suddenly, all expression dying away from his dear face as though swept clean by an unseen hand, and in its place a mask will form, a sculptured thing, formal and cold, beautiful still but lifeless. He will fall to smoking cigarette after cigarette, not bothering to extinguish them, and the glowing stubs will lie around on the ground like **petals**[②]. He will talk quickly and eagerly about nothing at all, snatching at any subject as a **panacea**[③] to pain. I believe there is a theory that men and women emerge finer and stronger after suffering, and that to advance in this or any world we must endure **ordeal**[④] by fire. This we have done in full measure, ironic though it seems. We have both known fear, and loneliness, and very

great distress. I suppose sooner or later in the life of everyone comes a moment of trial. We all of us have our particular devil who rides us and torments us, and we must give battle in the end. We have conquered ours, or so we believe.

The devil does not ride us any more. We have come through our crisis, not **unscathed**⑤ of course. His premonition of disaster was correct from the beginning; and like a ranting actress in an indifferent play, I might say that we have paid for freedom. But I have had enough melodrama in this life, and would willingly give my five senses if they could ensure us our present peace and security. Happiness is not a possession to be prized, it is a quality of thought, a state of mind. Of course we have our moments of depression; but there are other moments too, when time, unmeasured by the clock, runs on into eternity and, catching his smile, I know we are together, we march in unison, no clash of thought or of opinion makes a barrier between us.

毋庸置疑，我们再也回不到从前了。往事仍然历历在目。那些我们试图忘掉，抛之脑后的回忆会再次搅乱心扉；那种恐惧，那些隐隐的不安，最终变成了盲目的不受理性控制的恐慌——如今，谢天谢地，幸运地已经平静下来了——这些可能以某种无法预见的方式伴随我们一生，就像从前那样。

他相当有耐性，从不抱怨什么，甚至当他记起……所发生的事情的时候，他也不抱怨，我认为他一定常常回忆起，只是没让我知道罢了。

我能从他脸上突然浮现的迷茫和失落的表情看出来。这些表情会很快从他那可爱的脸上消退，就像是被一只无形的手擦拭掉了一样，取而代之的是一张戴了面具的脸，像是雕刻一般，拘谨而冷峻，仍然英俊但是毫无生气。接着，他会一根接着一根地抽烟，烟蒂也不熄灭，冒着火星的烟蒂就像花瓣一样散在地上。他会急切迅速地说些空洞无物的话语，随便抓住什么话题不放，仿佛它们是可以治愈伤痛的灵丹妙药一样。我相信这样的理论：伤痛使人变得更好、更坚强，人生在世，我们必须在苦难中浴火重生。尽管这话听起来充满讽刺，但我们曾经以各种方式经历过，我们都曾经品尝过恐惧、孤独，以及巨大的伤痛。我相信，我们每个人迟早都要经受考验。在我们每个人内心深处都有一个魔鬼，它驾驭我们，折磨我们，最终我们要和它展开搏斗。我们已经战胜了心中的魔鬼，或者说我们相信自己已经战胜了它。

这个魔鬼再也不能驾驭我们了。我们已经安然地度过危机，当然伤痕仍在。他对灾难的预感从一开始就是对的；就像是在一出无关紧要的戏剧中说着豪言壮语的女演员，我得说：我们的自由是付出了代价的。我的生命中已经经历了够多的戏剧性事件了，我宁愿放弃我的感知能力来换取现在的平静和安稳。幸福不是一笔用来珍藏的财富，而是一种思想状态，一种心境。当然，我们每个人都会有沮丧的时候；但是也有一些美好的瞬间：那时，时间无法用钟表来度量，它进入了永恒。看见他的微笑，我就知道我们在一起，我们携手共进，彼此之间，毫无阻碍，心灵相通。

——选自《蝴蝶梦》第2章

注释

① furtive [ˈfɜːtɪv] *adj.* 秘密的，隐蔽的

② petal [ˈpetl] *n.* 花瓣

③ panacea [ˌpænəˈsɪə] *n.* 万能药

④ ordeal [ɔːˈdiːl] *n.* 严酷的考验，痛苦的经验

⑤ unscathed [ʌnˈskeiðd] *adj.* 未受伤的

28 积极的废奴主义者——哈里特·比彻·斯托

Harriet Beecher Stowe (June 14, 1811—July 1, 1896) was an American abolitionist and author. Her novel *Uncle Tom's Cabin* (1852) depicted life for African-Americans under slavery; it reached millions as a novel and play, and became influential in the United States and United Kingdom. It energized anti-slavery forces in the American North, while provoking widespread anger in the South. She wrote more than 20 books, including novels; three travel memoirs, and collections of articles and letters. She was influential both for her writings and her public stands on social issues of the day.

哈里特·比彻·斯托（1811年7月14日—1896年7月1日）是一位美国废奴主义者和作家。她的小说《汤姆叔叔的小屋》（1852）描述了奴隶制下的美国黑人生活，数百万人通过小说和戏剧等形式了解到这部作品，该小说在美国和英国产生了巨大的影响。这本书激发了美国北部反奴隶制的力量，同时也使南方人的愤怒情绪高涨。斯托夫人写有20多本书，包括小说，3本旅游回忆录和一些文章与书信的集册。她不仅因为她的作品，还因为她在当时社会问题上的公众立场而颇具影响力。

《汤姆叔叔的小屋》发表于1852年，共45章。这部感伤小说深刻地描绘出了奴隶制度残酷的本质，并在某种程度上激化了导致美国内战的地区局部冲突。这部作品在国内有很多优秀的翻译版本，目前最常见的是人民文学出版社王家湘的译本，译林出版社林玉鹏的译本和北京燕山出版社李彭恩的译本。

Uncle Tom's Cabin
汤姆叔叔的小屋

We don't own your laws; we don't own your country; we stand here as free, under God's sky, as you are; and, by the great God that made us, we'll fight for our liberty till we die.

我们不受你们所谓的法律和国家的支配，我们站在上帝的天空之下，和你们一样自由；伟大的上帝创造了我们，我们将为自由而战，直到死去。

——*Uncle Tom's Cabin*《汤姆叔叔的小屋》

名著导读

Uncle Tom's Cabin opens with a description of Arthur Shelby's Kentucky plantation during the **antebellum**① period. Shelby has incurred serious debts—prompting him to sell some slaves to avoid financial ruin. Mr. Haley, the slave trader, purchases Uncle Tom, Shelby's loyal servant since childhood, and five-year-old Harry, a beautiful and talented child. His mother is Eliza and she decides to flee the plantation with her son. She also tries to convince Uncle Tom to save himself and come with her. Uncle Tom, however, must remain loyal to his master and does not accompany Eliza.

《汤姆叔叔的小屋》以美国南北战争为背景展开，亚瑟·谢尔比是肯塔基州一个种植园的主人。谢尔比因遭遇严重债务问题，不得不卖掉几个奴隶以避免经济损失。奴隶贩子哈利选中了自谢尔比童年时代就对他忠心耿耿的仆人汤姆叔叔，以及五岁的哈里，一个漂亮又聪明的孩子。哈里的妈妈伊丽莎决心带着儿子逃离种植园，走之前，她也试图劝说汤姆和他们一起逃走。然而，汤姆叔叔仍然保持着对主人的忠心，不愿意和伊丽莎一起逃走。

名段选读

At this moment, George appeared on the top of a rock above them, and, speaking in a calm, clear voice, said,

"Gentlemen, who are you, down there, and what do you want?"

"We want a party of runaway niggers," said Tom Loker. "One George Harris, and Eliza Harris, and their son, and Jim Selden, and an old woman. We've got the officers, here, and a warrant to take 'em; and we're going to have 'em, too. D'ye hear? An't you George Harris, that belongs to Mr. Harris, of Shelby county, Kentucky?"

"I am George Harris. A Mr. Harris, of Kentucky, did call me his property. But now I'm a free man, standing on God's free soil; and my wife and my child I claim as mine. Jim and his mother are here. We have arms to defend ourselves, and we mean to do it. You can come up, if you like; but the first one of you that comes within the range of our bullets is a dead man, and the next, and the next; and so on till the last."

"O, come! come!" said a short, **puffy**② man, stepping forward, and blowing his nose as he did so. "Young man, this an't no kind of talk at all for you. You see, we're officers of justice. We've got the law on our side, and the power, and so forth; so you'd better give up peaceably, you see; for you'll certainly have to give up, at last."

"I know very well that you've got the law on your side, and the power," said George, bitterly. "You mean to take my wife to sell in New Orleans, and put my boy like a calf in a trader's pen, and send Jim's old mother to the **brute**③ that whipped and abused her before, because he couldn't abuse her son. You want to send Jim and me back to be whipped and tortured, and ground down under the heels of them that you call masters; and your laws will bear you out in it,—more shame for you and them! But you haven't got us. We don't own your laws; we don't own your country; we stand here as free, under God's sky, as you are; and, by the great God that made us, we'll fight for our liberty till we die."

George stood out in fair sight, on the top of the rock, as he made his declaration of independence; the glow of dawn gave a flush to his **swarthy**④ cheek, and bitter indignation and despair gave fire to his dark eye; and, as if appealing from man to the justice of God, he raised his hand to heaven as he spoke.

就在这时，乔治从岩石的顶端露出脸来，用沉着而清晰的嗓音说道：

"先生们，你们是谁，你们想干什么？"

"我们在找一伙逃走的黑奴，"汤姆·洛克说道，"乔治·哈里斯、伊丽莎·哈里斯、他们的儿子，还有吉姆·赛尔登和一个老女人。我们把警察带来了，这儿还有捉拿他们的逮捕证，我们会抓到他们的。你听清了吗？你不就是肯塔基州谢尔比庄园哈里斯先生的奴隶乔治·哈里斯吗？"

"我是乔治·哈里斯。不错，过去，我的确是肯塔基州哈里斯先生的奴隶，但现在，我是一个自由的人了，我站在上帝赐予我们的自由的大地上，我的妻子和孩子是属于我的，吉姆和他的妈妈现在也在这儿。我们手上有武器可以保护自己，而且我们打算这么做。你们想抓我们就过来抓吧，不过第一个过来抓我们的人会死在我的枪口下，然后是第二个、第三个，直到最后一个。

"噢，上！大家都上！"一个矮小、肥胖的男人说道。他一边喘着气，一边走上前，"年轻人，你没资格说这些话。你看看，我们是司法人员，法律和权力等都站在我们这一边，你最好是乖乖就范，因为你最终肯定会这样做的。"

"我非常清楚法律和权力都站在你们那边，"乔治怨恨地说道，"你们打算把我的妻子卖到新奥尔良，让我的孩子像牲畜一样被关在奴隶贩子的围栏里，让吉姆的老妈妈回到那个一直鞭打她、虐待她的畜生那里去，因为这样他就没法对吉姆施虐。你们会把吉姆和我送回去，遭受鞭打和虐待，让我们被你们所说的主人践踏。当然，你们的法律会支持你们——我真为你们和其他那些人感到羞耻！但是，你们逮不到我们。我们不受你们所谓的法律和国家的支配，我们站在上帝的天空之下，和你们一样自由；伟大的上帝创造了我们，我们将为自由而战，直到死去。"

乔治在讲这番独立宣言时，站在岩石顶上，整个人清晰地凸现出来，黎明的曙光给他黝黑的脸颊抹上了一层激动的绯红，充满仇恨的愤怒和绝望在他黝黑的眼睛里燃烧；在说这番话时，他朝天空举起一只手臂，仿佛在请求上帝公正的审判。

——选自《汤姆叔叔的小屋》第17章

注释

①antebellum [ˌæntɪˈbeləm] *n.*（美国南北）战争前

② puffy [ˈpʌfɪ] *adj.* 肥胖的，肿胀的

③ brute [bruːt] *n.* 畜生，残酷的人

④ swarthy [ˈswɔːðɪ] *adj.* 黑黝黝的

29 黑色幽默文学的代表人物——约瑟夫·海勒

Joseph Heller (May 1, 1923—December 12, 1999) was an American satirical novelist, short story writer and playwright. He wrote the influential novel *Catch-22* about American servicemen during World War II. The title of this work entered the English lexicon to refer to absurd, no-win choices, particularly in situations in which the desired outcome of the choice is impossibility, and regardless of choice, the same negative outcome is a certainty. Heller is widely regarded as one of the best post-World War II satirists. Although he is remembered primarily for *Catch-22*, his other works center on the lives of various members of the middle class and remain exemplars of modern satire.

约瑟夫·海勒（1923年5月1日—1999年12月12日）是美国讽刺小说家、短篇小说家和剧作家。他撰写的极具影响力的《第二十二条军规》讲述了二战期间美国军人的故事，这部作品的标题已被收入英语辞典，特指那些荒谬的、必败的选择，尤其是在渴望的结果完全不可能实现的情况下，而且无论你的选择是怎样的，也必定不会得到好结果。海勒被广泛认为是二战后世界上最优秀的讽刺作家之一。虽然他最为著名的作品是《第二十二条军规》，但他的其他作品都以描述各种各样的中产阶级成员的生活为主，它们仍然是现代讽刺文学中的范本。

《第二十二条军规》发表于1961年，共分42章。美国“黑色幽默”文学的代表作。该小说被誉为60年代以来享誉最盛的小说，被译成几十种文字，发行量高达1000万册。这部作品目前国内比较好的翻译版本是上海译文出版社南文、赵守垠、王德明的译本的译本。

Catch-22
第二十二条军规

And you can't let crazy people decide whether you're crazy or not, can you?

可你不能让一群疯子来判断你是不是疯了，对吧？

——*Catch-22*《第二十二条军规》

名段选读

American army pilot John Yossarian is an antihero, that is, a protagonist lacking some traditionally heroic qualities. He is obsessed with being rotated out of active flight duty. His commander, Colonel Cathcart, keeps raising the number of missions the men in the squadron must fly before they can be rotated out. Consequently, Yossarian is desperate to find another way out of his dilemma. He asks the squadron's doctor, Doc Daneeka, to declare him unfit for duty by reason of insanity. Doc refuses, citing the mysterious Catch-22: if Yossarian asks to be let out of his duties, he must be sane. Only a crazy man would want to continue to fly missions, but the only way Daneeka can ground him, according to Catch-22, is if he asks to be grounded—which would indicate his sanity.

美国陆军飞行员约翰·尤萨林是作品中的非英雄主角，也就是说，他身上缺乏一些传统意义上的英雄品质。他整天想的都是结束频繁的飞行任务，他的指挥官卡思卡特上校不停地增加空军中队飞行员退役回家之前需要达到的飞行任务次数。结果，尤萨林不顾一切地寻找其他摆脱困境的办法。他请求中队的丹尼卡医生宣布他因为精神错乱不适合再去执行任务，医生拒绝了，并引用了不可思议的第二十二条军规：如果尤萨林希望免除任务，那他肯定是神智健全的。只有一个疯子才会想继续执行飞行任务，但是根据第二十二条军规，尤萨林可以停飞的唯一途径就是自己主动要求被停飞——但是这又表明他精神没有问题。

名段选读

"You're wasting your time," Doc Daneeka was forced to tell him.

"Can't you ground someone who's crazy?"

"Oh, sure. I have to. There's a rule saying I have to ground anyone who's crazy."

"Then why don't you ground me? I'm crazy. Ask Clevinger."

"Clevinger? Where is Clevinger? You find Clevinger and I'll ask him."

"Then ask any of the others. They'll tell you how crazy I am."

"They're crazy."

"Then why don't you ground them?"

"Why don't they ask me to ground them?"

"Because they're crazy, that's why."

"Of course they're crazy," Doc Daneeka replied. "I just told you they're crazy, didn't I? And you can't let crazy people decide whether you're crazy or not, can you?" Yossarian looked at him soberly[①] and tried another approach. "Is Orr crazy?"

"He sure is," Doc Daneeka said.

"Can you ground him?"

"I sure can. But first he has to ask me to. That's part of the rule."

"Then why doesn't he ask you to?"

"Because he's crazy," Doc Daneeka said. "He has to be crazy to keep flying combat missions after all the close calls he's had. Sure, I can ground Orr. But first he has to ask me to."

"That's all he has to do to be grounded?"

"That's all. Let him ask me."

"And then you can ground him?" Yossarian asked.

"No. Then I can't ground him."

"You mean there's a catch?"

"Sure there's a catch," Doc Daneeka replied. "Catch-22. Anyone who wants to get out of combat duty isn't really crazy." There was only one catch and that was Catch-22, which specified[②] that a concern for one's own safety in the face of dangers that were real and immediate was the process of a rational mind. Orr was crazy and could be grounded. All he had to do was ask; and as soon as he did, he would no longer be crazy and would have to fly more missions. Orr would be crazy to fly more missions and sane if he didn't, but if he was sane he had to fly them. If he flew them he was crazy and didn't have to; but if he didn't want to he was sane and had to. Yossarian was moved very deeply by the absolute simplicity of this clause of Catch-22 and let out a respectful whistle[③].

"你纯粹是在浪费时间，" 丹尼卡医生无奈地告诉他。

"你难道不能让精神错乱者停飞？"

"当然可以，我必须这样。有一条规定说我必须让疯了的人停飞。"

"那你为什么不肯让我停飞？我是个疯子，不信你去问克莱文杰。"

"克莱文杰？他在哪儿？你把他找来，我会问他的。"

"你可以去问任何一个人，他们都会告诉你我是多么的不正常。"

"他们都疯了。"

"那你为什么不让他们都停飞呢？"

"为什么他们没要求我让他们停飞？"

"因为他们都是疯子啊，这就是原因。"

"他们的确是疯了，" 丹尼卡医生答道。"我刚才告诉你说他们都疯了，不是吗？可你不能让一群疯子来判断你是不是疯了，对吧？" 尤萨林冷静地看着他，试图换种方式。"奥尔是疯子吗？"

"他当然是，" 丹尼卡医生说。

“那你能让他停飞吗？”

“我当然可以。但是首先，这必须是他自己的要求，这是规则的一部分。”

“那他为什么没有向你提申请呢？”

“因为他是个疯子，”丹尼卡医生说道。“在经历那么多次死里逃生后，他还在继续战斗飞行任务，这足以证明他疯了。当然，我可以让奥尔停飞，但首先他必须自己向我提出来。”

“如果他要停飞，只要自己提出来就可以了吗？”

“是的，让他跟我提出来。”

“这样你就可以让他停飞了吗？”尤萨林问道。

“不，如果他那样做，我就不能让他停飞。”

“你的意思是有陷阱？”

“当然是有陷阱了，”丹尼卡医生答道。“就是第二十二条军规。那些想免除作战任务的人不是真的疯了。”如果存在一个陷阱，那它只能是第二十二条军规。它明确指出，一个人在面对真实的和即将发生的危险时对自身安危的担忧是一种理性思维的表现。奥尔精神错乱了，他可以停飞，他要做的只是自己主动提出请求，但是，一旦他真的这么做了，就表明他是个正常人，他就要继续去完成更多的飞行任务。如果他去飞行那么他就是个疯子，如果他不去那他就神智健全，若是神智健全，他就必须完成任务。尤萨林深深折服于第二十二条军规无懈可击的简单明了性，并发出了一声尊敬的哨音。

——选自《第二十二条军规》第5章

注释

① soberly ['səubə(r)lɪ] *adv.* 严肃地，冷静地

② specify ['spesɪfai] *vt.* 明确规定

③ whistle ['wɪsl] *n.* 口哨声

30 黎巴嫩文坛骄子——卡里·纪伯伦

Khalil Gibran (January 3, 1883—April 10, 1931) was a Lebanese American artist, poet, and writer. Gibran's first works were written in Arabic and are considered central to the development of modern Arabic literature. Gibran also wrote for journals published by the Lebanese and Arab communities in the U.S. From 1918 he wrote mostly in English and managed to revolutionize the language of poetry in the 1920s and 1930s. His first book for the publishing company Alfred Knopf was *THE MADMAN* (1918), a slim volume of aphorisms and parables written in biblical cadence somewhere between poetry and prose. He is chiefly known in the English speaking world for his 1923 book *The Prophet,* a series of philosophical essays written in English prose. Gibran is the third best-selling poet of all time, behind Shakespeare and Lao-Tzu.

卡里·纪伯伦（1883年1月3日—1931年4月10日）是一名黎巴嫩美籍艺术家、诗人和作家。纪伯伦早期的作品是用阿拉伯语写就的，这些作品被认为对现代阿拉伯文学的发展至关重要。他也为在美国的黎巴嫩人和阿拉伯团体出版的杂志撰稿。1918年起，纪伯伦的大多数作品都是用英语写作，20世纪20年代到30年代间，他开始设法改革诗歌语言。阿尔弗雷德·瑙弗出版社出版的纪伯伦的第一本书名叫《疯人》（1918），是一本薄薄的按圣经韵律创作的格言和寓言集，体裁介于诗歌和散文之间。纪伯伦发表于1923年的哲学随笔散文集《先知》在英语国家中最为著名。纪伯伦是有史以来第三大最畅销的诗人，名列莎士比亚和老子之后。

《先知》出版于1919年，包括24首散文诗。作者用反复比喻的手法，讲述了许多平易近人而又合情合理的道理，耐人寻味。《先知》是纪伯伦步入世界文坛的巅峰之作，曾被译成20多种文字在世界各地出版。目前国内较著名的译本是冰心的版本和东岐明的版本。

The Prophet
先知

It is well to give when asked, but it is better to give unasked, through understanding.

在别人要求时给予是好的，但是，出于理解，在别人没有要求时给予会更好。

——*The Prophet*《先知》

名段选读

The Prophet is not a novel or a story book, instead it is a series of philosophical prose, with a back story about a prophet, Al-Mustafa who has lived in the foreign city of Orphalese for 12 years is about to board a ship which will carry him home. He is stopped by a group of people, with whom he discusses many issues of life and the human condition. The book is divided into chapters dealing with love, marriage, children, giving, eating and drinking, work, joy and sorrow, houses, clothes, buying and selling, crime and punishment, laws, freedom, reason and passion, pain, self-knowledge, teaching, friendship, talking, time, good and evil, prayer, pleasure, beauty, religion, and death. Each part is a farewell gift to people.

《先知》不是一本小说或是一本故事书，它是一系列的哲理散文，全书的背景是这样一个故事：先知阿尔-穆斯塔法在一个外国城市奥菲里斯城居住了12年后即将乘船返回家乡，却被一群人拦了下来，于是他和他们一起讨论人生和人类处境。本书分不同的章节讨论了爱情、婚姻、孩子、给予、吃喝、工作、喜悲、房屋、衣服、买卖、罪惩、法律、自由、理智与激情、痛苦、自知、教导、友谊、谈话、时间、好恶、祈祷、愉悦、美丽、宗教和死亡。每个部分都是他给人们的辞行礼物。

名段选读

Then said a rich man, "Speak to us of Giving."

And he answered:

You give but little when you give of your possessions.

It is when you give of yourself that you truly give.

For what are your possessions but things you keep and guard for fear you may need them tomorrow?

And tomorrow, what shall tomorrow bring to the **overprudent**[①] dog burying bones in the trackless sand as he follows the pilgrims to the holy city?

And what is fear of need but need itself?

Is not dread of thirst when your well is full, thirst that is unquenchable?

There are those who give little of the much which they have—and they give it for recognition and their hidden desire makes their gifts **unwholesome**[②].

And there are those who have little and give it all.

These are the believers in life and the bounty of life, and their coffer is never empty.

There are those who give with joy, and that joy is their reward.

And there are those who give with pain, and that pain is their baptism.

And there are those who give and know not pain in giving, nor do they seek joy, nor give with mindfulness of virtue;

They give as in yonder valley the myrtle breathes its fragrance into space.

Through the hands of such as these God speaks, and from behind their eyes He smiles upon the earth.

It is well to give when asked, but it is better to give unasked, through understanding;

And to the open-handed the search for one who shall receive is joy greater than giving

And is there aught you would withhold?

All you have shall some day be given;

Therefore give now, that the season of giving may be yours and not your inheritors'.

You often say, "I would give, but only to the deserving."

The trees in your orchard say not so, nor the flocks in your pasture.

They give that they may live, for to withhold is to perish.

Surely he who is worthy to receive his days and his nights is worthy of all else from you.

And he who has deserved to drink from the ocean of life deserves to fill his cup from your little stream.

And what deserve greater shall there be than that which lies in the courage and the confidence, nay the charity, of receiving?

And who are you that men should rend their bosom and unveil their pride, that you may see their worth naked and their pride unabashed?

See first that you yourself deserve to be a giver, and an instrument of giving.

For in truth it is life that gives unto life—while you, who deem yourself a giver, are but a witness.

And you receivers—and you are all receivers—assume no weight of gratitude, lest you lay a **yoke**[③] upon yourself and upon him who gives.

Rather rise together with the giver on his gifts as on wings;

For to be overmindful of your debt, is to doubt his generosity who has the free-hearted earth for mother, and God for father.

尔后，一个富人说，“请向我们讲讲给予吧。”

于是他答道：

给予你的财产不过是微渺的给予。

只有奉献你自己才是真正的给予。

什么是财产呢，无非是担心明天或许会需要它们于是就保存和保护起来的东西！

跟着清教徒去朝拜圣地的狗谨慎地把骨头埋在荒无人迹的沙漠里，可是，明天，明天又会给予它什么呢？

为需要而忧虑还是忧虑需要本身呢？

当你的井蓄满清泉时仍然担心会口渴，这种口渴又怎是我们所能抑制住的呢？

有些人拿出自己财产的很小一部分用于施舍，而他们的目的却是为了获得赞誉，隐藏其中的欲望让他们的礼物变得肮脏。

也有一些人，虽然拥有的不多，却愿意奉献出所有。

这些人相信生活，相信生活的慷慨，他们的箱柜永远不会空。

有些人快乐地给予，那快乐就是对他们的奖赏；

还有些人心痛地给予，那心痛就是对他们的洗礼；

还有些人在给予时既没有感到痛苦也不是为了获得欢愉，更不是为了美德，

他们的给予就像远处峡谷里的桃金娘把芳香带给人间，

上帝通过他们的手说话，透过他们善良的眼眸在云端微笑。

在别人要求时给予是好的，但是，出于理解，在别人没有要求时给予会更好。

对于那些慷慨的人，寻找一个愿意接受的人，这种快乐甚至要比给予本身还要多。

难道还需要有所保留吗？

你所拥有的在某一天都会被给予出去；

因此，现在就给予吧，给予的季节应该属于你，而不属于你的后代。

你常说，“我愿意给予，但只限于那些值得给予的对象。”

你果园里的树不会这样说，你牧场上的羊群也不会这样说。

他们活着就会给予，因为他们知道，保留就会灭亡。

有权享有白天和黑夜的人就有资格接受你所有的馈赠，

有权从生命的海洋取水的人就有资格用你的溪流斟满杯子，

有什么比自信而勇敢地接受你馈赠的人更有资格获得馈赠呢？

而你又有什么资格让他人敞开心胸，让他人揭去自己骄傲的面纱，让你看到他们赤裸的价值和不畏的尊严呢？

首先审视一下你自己有没有资格当一个给予者，一件给予的工具。

这不过是一个生命对另一个生命的馈赠，而你自己，虽自视为给予者，实际上，却不

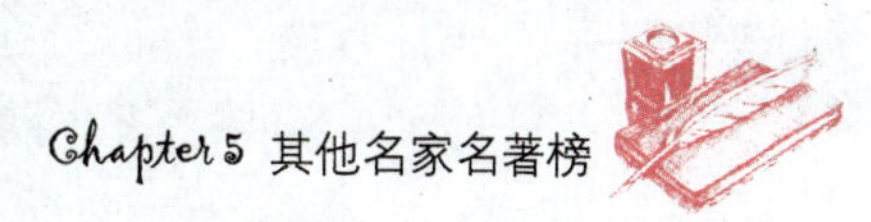

过是个见证者。

你是被给予者——你们每一个人都是被给予的对象——不要抱有任何感激，这会令你自己和给予的人套上枷锁。

还不如和给予者一起，把这份馈赠当作飞翔的翅膀，

因为，过于担忧你所领受的恩惠，就是对给予者慷慨的质疑，而他，有一颗博大的心，把大地视为母亲，把上帝视为父亲。

——选自《先知》“论施予”

注释

① overprudent [ˌəuvəˈpruːdnt] *adj.* 过于谨慎的

② unwholesome [ʌnˈhəulsəm] *adj.* 不适合健康的，无道德的

③ yoke [jəuk] *n.* 束缚，枷锁

读石油版书，获亲情馈赠

《人一生要读的经典英文名著大全集》意见反馈卡

亲爱的读者朋友，首先感谢您阅读我社图书，请您在阅读完本书后填写以下信息。我社将长期开展“读石油版书，获亲情馈赠”活动，凡是关注我社图书并认真填写读者信息反馈卡的朋友都有机会获得亲情馈赠，我们将定期从信息反馈卡中评选出有价值的意见和建议，并为填写这些信息的朋友免费赠送一本好书。

1.您购买本书的动因：书名、封面吸引人☐ 内容吸引人☐ 版式设计吸引人☐

2.您认为本书的内容：很好☐ 较好☐ 一般☐ 较差☐

3.您认为本书在哪些方面存在缺陷：内容☐ 封面☐ 装帧设计☐

4.您认为本书的定价：较高☐ 适中☐ 偏低☐

5.您认为本书最好应附送：MP3☐ CD☐ 磁带☐ 其他__________

6.您还读过哪些英语课外书？__________

7.您对本书有哪些不满意之处？

8.您还需要哪些英语课外读物？

9.您在何处购买的本书？

10.您对本书的综合评价：

您的联系方式：

姓名 __________

单位 __________ 邮政编码 __________

地址 __________ 电 话 __________

手机 __________ E—mail __________

回信请寄：北京安定门外安华西里3区18号楼 石油工业出版社
社会图书出版中心 王敏娴(收)

邮政编码：100011

电子信箱：newscoming@126.com （复印有效）